Ius Gentium: Comparative Perspectives on Law and Justice

Volume 125

Ius Gentium is a book series which discusses the central questions of law and justice from a comparative perspective. The books in this series collect the contrasting and overlapping perspectives of lawyers, judges, philosophers and scholars of law from the world's many different jurisdictions for the purposes of comparison, harmonisation, and the progressive development of law and legal institutions. Each volume makes a new comparative study of an important area of law. This book series continues the work of the well-known journal of the same name and provides the basis for a better understanding of all areas of legal science.

The *Ius Gentium* series provides a valuable resource for lawyers, judges, legislators, scholars, and both graduate students and researchers in globalisation, comparative law, legal theory and legal practice. The series has a special focus on the development of international legal standards and transnational legal cooperation.

Ayush Dimri

Non-Performing Loans

A Cross Country Comparison of Regulatory and Policy Responses

Springer

Ayush Dimri
School of Law
University of Leeds
Leeds, UK

ISSN 1534-6781 ISSN 2214-9902 (electronic)
Ius Gentium: Comparative Perspectives on Law and Justice
ISBN 978-3-031-92951-9 ISBN 978-3-031-92952-6 (eBook)
https://doi.org/10.1007/978-3-031-92952-6

This Springer imprint is published by the registered company Springer Nature Switzerland AG
The registered company address is: Gewerbestrasse 11, 6330 Cham, Switzerland

Preface

The financial and banking system witnessed one of the greatest periods of stress due to the Global Financial Crisis (GFC) and the COVID-19 pandemic. Many banks across the globe failed due to a bubble in the real estate sector, which was triggered in the USA and percolated around the world in no time, resulting in a liquidity crunch. As a result, the non-performing loans (NPLs) increased in developed and emerging nations. The financial sector takes excessive risks to generate more profits and grossly ignores the due diligence process required to grant loans, including evaluation of collateral, assessment of re-payment capacity, etc., thus leading to long-term cascading effects on financial stability, resulting in the failure of banks across the globe.

The book examines the regulatory, supervisory, and policy-related measures adopted by the UK, India, and Ireland at the macro and micro levels. It concludes that these measures alone will remain ineffective in curtailing the level of NPLs due to the ever-evolving financial sector, with the excessive use of new technology that has led to the evolution of new payment methods in the banking business.

The book also examined how proactive sovereign support during the GFC and COVID-19 pandemic through liquidity injection and effective policy and regulatory measures has rescued the banks from possible insolvency. It also looked into the risk management system at the micro level by conducting three case studies involving the Lloyd Banking Group, Punjab National Bank, and Bank of Ireland Group.

The book further examined the initiatives these jurisdictions had taken to mitigate the issues that emerged due to the COVID-19 pandemic. Lastly, it has identified some suggestive interventions that mainly focus on new policy and regulatory interventions and structural changes in the institutional framework to address the problem of NPLs more effectively and avoid a downturn.

The book consists of eight chapters. The first chapter, the **'Introduction',** focuses on reviewing the existing literature in-depth on delineated issues, covering a wide range of contributions to discover the gaps in the existing literature. It also discusses the research methodology adopted to conduct the present research. This chapter aims to answer the research questions that the present study seeks to address. It critically analyses and compares the definition of NPLs suggested by Basel, the OECD, and the Reserve Bank of India (RBI). The chapter also briefly discusses the role of economic and non-economic determinants, which influence the level of NPLs, and the trend of NPLs in select developed and developing countries from the GFC to COVID-19. It further delineates the possible impact of NPLs in the post-COVID-19 scenario. It also briefly assesses the impact of supervisory, policy, and regulatory responses across jurisdictions to present a snapshot of issues the research intends to examine in its coherent framework.

The second chapter, **'Analysis of the Impact of Macroeconomic Determinants on NPLs',** critically examines the relationship between macroeconomic determinants and NPLs. The important macroeconomic determinants covered in the chapters include GDP, inflation, unemployment, wages, and exchange rates. The relationship between NPLs and macroeconomic determinants has been established using simple statistical tools. Similarly, the third chapter, **'Analysis of the Impact of Macroeconomic Determinants on NPLs'**, examines the relationship between NPLs and microeconomic determinants such as asset quality, liquidity ratio, return on assets (ROA), return on equity ROE), net-interest margin (NIM), bank size, inefficient bank management and cost efficiency, etc. This chapter also compares the progress of the UK, India, and Ireland through a composite index.

The fourth chapter, **'Non-Performing Loans and Regulatory and Supervisory Responses',** examines the effectiveness of the regulations and directives in addressing the problem of NPLs, besides presenting the global scenario of regulatory and supervisory responses. This chapter presents a detailed comparative analysis of the legal and supervisory architecture of the UK, India, and Ireland to deal with the issues arising due to increasing NPL ratios. It also discusses the role of regulators in regulating the banking sector, along with a critical examination of legislation. The fifth chapter, **'Resolution of Non-Performing Loans: Policy Response',** probes into the role and effectiveness of various bank-specific and country-specific policy measures such as on-balance sheet guarantees, internal structuring unit, off-balance sheet SPE, debt restructuring-out-of-court workouts (OCWs), write-offs, direct sales, securitisation, Asset Protection Scheme (APS), AMCs, Mergers and Acquisitions (M&A), and Purchase Assumption and Transaction (PAT) to deal with asset resolution and restructuring.

The sixth chapter, **'Empirical Analysis of NPLs Through Case Studies of Commercial Banks from the UK, India, and Ireland',** elaborates on the progress of these institutions on their financial performance, assets quality, risk management system, and regulatory and supervisory response for managing the financial crisis that emerged due to GFC, Brexit, and COVID-19 pandemic so that NPLs remain within their control. This chapter presents a comparative picture of these FIs and realises various similarities and dissimilarities concerning risk management.

The seventh chapter, **'Non-Performing Loans in Post-COVID-19 Scenario: Impact on Survival, Repair, and Reconstruct',** compares the impact of the COVID-19 pandemic on the GFC and analyses their similarities and dissimilarities. The chapter also discusses the impact of COVID-19 on the NPLs in the jurisdictions under the purview of our study, besides briefly touching upon the global scenario of COVID-19 and how the pandemic affected the global economy. This chapter also examines how survival, repair, and reconstruction remained the top agenda during the pandemic and post-pandemic periods to avoid long-term impact. Lastly, this chapter draws attention to these jurisdictions' initiatives to ensure financial stability and avert a future financial crisis. The last chapter, **'Conclusion and Suggestions',** summarises the research findings and sketches out specific indicative interventions for implementation.

Leeds, UK Ayush Dimri

Acknowledgements

I wish to express my deepest gratitude to Prof. Andrew Campbell and Dr. Steven Montagu Cairns for their unwavering support, motivation, and guidance throughout this project. Their encouragement kept me focused and determined, even when faced with challenges, such as the difficult environment brought on by the pandemic when I began this work four years ago. I still fondly recall our first meeting, where their warm and supportive approach immediately put me at ease and set a positive tone for the progression of this research. Their invaluable feedback and constructive comments were instrumental in shaping the outcome of this work, and I am profoundly grateful for their mentorship throughout the entire process.

I extend my sincere thanks to Professor Louise Ellison, Head of the School of Law at the University of Leeds, for providing me with the opportunity to undertake teaching assignments as a postgraduate researcher (PGR). This experience greatly enriched my academic journey and professional development.

My heartfelt appreciation also goes to Dr. Alison Lui of Liverpool John Moores University and Dr. Virag Blazsek of the University of Leeds for their thorough and thoughtful feedback. Their suggestions greatly strengthened my arguments and contributed significantly to improve the quality of this work.

I am grateful to the university library staff for their dedication and assistance in providing a wealth of resources that were readily accessible. Their efforts saved researchers valuable time and energy and facilitated an in-depth exploration of relevant materials.

This book is dedicated to my grandmother, Uma, whose belief in the importance of academic excellence and constant celebration of our achievements inspired me to strive for success.

I am deeply thankful to my parents, Dr. Anil, and Rekha, for their boundless love, motivation, and unwavering support throughout this journey. Their hard work, sacrifices, and encouragement have been the bedrock of my endeavours, making this experience both fulfilling and comfortable. I hope to continue making them proud in every step I take. I would also like to thank my sister Ayushi and brother-in-law Abhijit for their continuous support, love, and motivation, which provided me with strength throughout this process.

Finally, I extend my appreciation to my friends and fellow research scholars for being constant sources of encouragement and sounding boards during the most challenging stages of this journey. Their companionship and shared understanding made the tough times easier to navigate.

Competing Interests The author has no competing interests to declare that are relevant to the content of this manuscript.

About the Book

Non-performing loans (NPLs) continue to pose a major challenge for developing and emerging markets, with the issue becoming significantly worse after the 2008 global financial crisis (GFC). The collapse of major financial institutions like JP Morgan Chase, Goldman Sachs, Bank of America, Morgan Stanley, Lehman Brothers, and Bear Stearns intensified this problem, leading to debates at both national and global levels. This escalating concern drew attention at both national and international levels, where solutions were urgently sought. International regulatory bodies and governments responded by crafting robust policy, regulatory, and supervisory frameworks to curb the rise of NPLs and improve financial oversight.

This book delves into the NPLs issue, exploring how macroeconomic and microeconomic factors impact NPLs, along with the regulatory, policy, and supervisory measures undertaken by the UK, India, and Ireland from GFC through the post-COVID-19 period (2008 to 2022). It also presents three detailed case studies—Lloyds Banking Group (UK), Punjab National Bank (India), and Bank of Ireland Group (Ireland)—it highlights remedial measures taken to mitigate the problem, offering valuable insights for researchers, academics, banking, and financial sector professionals and practitioners. The book also evaluates the measures taken by these jurisdictions to counter the impact of COVID-19 on the economy in general and financial sector business in particular.

Contents

About the Author

Ayush Dimri holds a PhD in International Banking Law from the University of Leeds, UK, and a Master's Degree in International Commercial Law from the University of Strathclyde, Glasgow. He specialises in teaching and researching international banking law and corporate law, with a primary focus on restructuring and resolving non-performing loans (NPLs), insolvency and bankruptcy law, and corporate finance.

Dr. Dimri has substantial experience in teaching, assessment, moderation, and pastoral support for undergraduate and postgraduate students, including dissertation supervision. He has served as a Sessional Lecturer at the School of Justice Studies, Liverpool John Moores University, and currently holds a position as a Tutor/Lecturer at the School of Law, University of Leeds.

In addition to his teaching, Dr. Dimri is an active researcher. His recent publication include '*Resolution of Non-Performing Assets: Regulatory, Supervisory and Policy Response in India in pre-and Post-Covid-19 Scenario*' published online (11 April 2025) in Journal of Banking Regulation and '*Restructuring Non-Performing Loans through Asset Management Companies: A Global Scenario'*, appeared in the *International Company and Commercial Law Review (ICCLR).*

Earlier in his career, Dr. Dimri worked as a Junior Legal Associate at a law firm, where he managed contract drafting and vetting legal documents for an international IT company.

Abbreviations

AA	Adjudicating Authority
AE	Aggregate Exposure
AIB	Allied Irish Bank
ALA	Alternative Liquidity Approach
AMCs	Asset Management Companies
AOC	Air Operator Certificate
APF	Asset Purchase Facility
APS	Asset Protection Scheme
AQR	Asset Quality Review
ARC	Asset Restructuring Company
ARCIL	Asset Reconstruction Companies India Limited
B&B	Bradford & Bingley
BBLS	Bounce Back Loan Scheme
BCBS	Basel Committee on Banking Supervision
BIFR	Board for Industrial and Financial Reconstruction
BIG	Bank of Ireland Group
BLRC	Bankruptcy Law Reforms Committee
BoE	Bank of England
BRRD	Bank Recovery and Revolution Directive
CAP	Corrective Action Plan
CAR	Capital Adequacy Ratio
CBI	Central Bank of Ireland
CBILS	Coronavirus Business Interruption Loan Scheme
CBRE	Coldwell Banker Richard Ellis
CC	Cash Credit
CCB	Capital Conservation Buffer
CCMA	Code of Conduct on Mortgage Arrears
CCyB	Countercyclical Capital Buffer
CD	Corporate Debtor
CDR	Corporate Debt Restructuring
CEE	Central and Eastern Europe

CET	Common Equity Tier
CFT	Countering the Financing of Terrorism
CIRP	Corporate Insolvency Resolution Process
CLBILS	Coronavirus Large Business Interruption Loan Scheme
CLOC	Collateralised Loan Obligations Category
CMA	Competition and Markets Authority
CoR	Certificate of Registration
CPC	Consumer Protection Code
CRAR	Capital to Risk-weighted Assets Ratio
CRD	Capital Requirement Directive
CRE	Commercial Real Estate
CRILC	Central Repository of Information on Large Credits
CRR	Capital Requirement Regulation
CRR	Cash Reserve Ratio
CSPP	Corporate Sector Purchase Programme
DCCO	Date of Commencement of Commercial Operation
DCOR	Distressed Credit Operations Review
DFRs	Deposit Facility Rates
DRT	Debts Recovery Tribunal
EBA	European Banking Authority
EC	European Council
ECB	European Central Bank
ECJ	European Court of Justice
ED	Enforcement Directorate
EEA	European Economic Area
EEC	European Economic Community
EIOPA	European Insurance and Occupational Pensions Authority
ELG	Eligible Liabilities Guarantee
ERMF	Enterprise Risk Management Framework
ESG	Environmental, Social and Governance
ESMA	European Securities and Market Authority
ESRB	European Systemic Risk Board
EU	European Union
FCA	Financial Conduct Authority
FCs	Financial Creditors
FDI	Foreign Direct Investment
FDIC	Federal Deposit Insurance Corporation
FIs	Financial Institutions
FITL	Funded Interest Term Loan
FMC	Forward Market Commission
FMP	Financial Measures Programme
FPC	Financial Policy Committee
FRS	Federal Reserve System
FSA	Financial Services Authority
FSAP	Financial Sector Assessment Programme

FSMA	Financial Service and Market Act
FTSE	Financial Times Stock Exchange
GAAP	General Accepted Accounting Principles
GACS	Guarantee on Securitisation of Non-Performing Loans
GDP	Gross Domestic Product
GFC	Global Financial Crisis
GIA	Group Internal Audit
GMM	Generalised Methods of Moments
GNPA	Gross Non-Performing Asset
GRPCs	Group Risk Policy Committees
G-SAP	G-sec Acquisition Programme
HAQ	High Assets Quality
HBOS	Halifax Bank of Scotland
HC	High Court
HMT	Her Majesty Treasury
HQLA	High-Quality Liquidity Assets
IBA	Indian Banking Association
IBBI	Insolvency and Bankruptcy Board of India
IBC	Insolvency and Bankruptcy Code
IBRC	Irish Bank Resolution Corporation
ICA	Inter Creditor Agreement
ICAAP	Internal Capital Adequacy Assessment Process
ICG	Individual Capital Guidance
ICICI	Industrial Credit and Investment Corporation of India
ICO	Initial Coin Offering
ID	Income Diversification
IDBI	Industrial Development Bank of India
IEO	Initial Exchange Offering
IFRS	International Financial Reporting Standard
IFSA	Integrated Financial Services Authority
IMF	International Monetary Fund
IRDA	Insurance Regulatory and Development Authority of India
IRMS	Integrated Risk Management System
ISI	Insolvency Service of Ireland
ISM	International Safety Management
JLF	Joint Lender's Forum
KAMCO	Korean Asset Management Corporation
LAQ	Low Assets Quality
LBG	Lloyds Banking Group
LCR	Liquidity Coverage Ratio
LLP	Loan Loss Provisions
LoU	Letter of Understanding
LSE	London Stock Exchange
LTROs	Long-Term Repo Operations
M&A	Mergers and Acquisitions

MART	Mortgage Arrears Resolution Targets
MBS	Mortgage-Backed Securities
MiFID	Markets in Financial Instruments Directive
MiFIR	Markets in Financial Instruments Regulation
MPC	Monetary Policy Committee
MREL	Minimum Requirement for Own Funds and Eligible Liabilities
MRO	Marginal Refinancing Operations
NAMA	National Asset Management Agency
NARM	Northern Rock Asset Management
NBFCs	Non-Banking Financial Companies
NCLAT	National Company Law Appellate Tribunal
NCLT	National Company Law Tribunal
NII	Net Interest Income
NIM	Net-Interest Margin
NNPA	Net Non-Performing Asset
NPEs	Non-Performing Exposures
NPLs	Non-Performing Loans
NSFR	Net Stable Funding Ratio
NTMA	National Treasury Management Agency
NVA	Net Value Added
NYSE	New York Stock Exchange
OCAP	Out-Court Agreement on Payments
OCC	Office of the Comptroller of Currency
OECD	Organisation for Economic Cooperation and Development
OMS	Open Market Operations
OT	Operation Twist
OTS	Office of Thrift Supervision
PAT	Purchase Assumption and Transaction
PB	Payment Break
PBT	Profit Before Tax
PCA	Prompt Corrective Action
PCAR	Prudential Capital Assessment Review
PFRDA	Pension Fund Regulatory and Development Authority
PIA	Personal Insolvency Agreement
PIRD	Pan India Recovery Drive
PLAR	Prudential Liquidity Assessment Review
PNB	Punjab National Bank
PPF	Public Provident Fund
PRA	Prudential Regulatory Authority
PRISM	Probability on Banks' Risk Impact System
PSBs	Public Sector Banks
PSD	Payment Service Directive
RAO	Regulated Activities Order
RBI	Reserve Bank of India
RBS	Royal Bank of Scotland

RCs	Reconstruction Companies
RDBFI	Recovery of Debts Dues to Bank and Financial Institutions
RMBS	Residential Mortgage-Backed Securities
ROA	Return on Assets
ROE	Return on Equity
RTC	Resolution Trust Corporation
RWA	Risk-Weighted Assets
S4A	Scheme of Sustainable Structuring of Stressed Asset
SAR	Substantial Acquisition Rules
SARFAESI	Securitisation and Reconstruction of Financial Assets and Enforcement of Security Interest
SASTRA	Stressed Assets Targeted Resolution Action
SBI	State Bank of India
SC	Supreme Court
SCBs	Scheduled Commercial Banks
SD	Standard Deviation
SDR	Strategic Debt Restructuring
SEBI	Security and Exchange Board of India
SICA	Sick Industrial Companies Act
SLR	Statutory Liquidity Ratio
SMA	Special Mention Account
SMEs	Small and Medium Enterprises
SPV	Special Purpose Vehicle
SR	Security Receipt
SREP	Supervisory Review and Evaluation Process
SRM	Single Resolution Mechanism
SRMR	Single Resolution Mechanism Regulation
SSM	Single Supervisory Mechanism
SSMR	Single Supervisory Mechanism Regulation
SST	Solvency Stress Test
STS	Simple Transparent and Standardised
SWIFT	Society for Worldwide Interbank Financial Telecommunications
TCR	Total Capital Ratio
TISM	Total Interpretive Structural Modelling
TLTROs	Targeted Long-Term Repo Operations
TTP	Temporary Transitional Powers
UKAR	United Kingdom Asset Resolution
UKFI	UK Financial Investments Limited
VaR	Value at Risk
VOA	Value of Assets

Abbreviations of Legal Terms

art/arts	article/articles
ch/chs	chapter/chapters
cl	clause
CUP	Cambridge University Press
Edn	edition
OUP	Oxford University Press
para/paras	paragraph/paragraphs
pt/pts	part/parts
r/rr	rule/rules
s/ss	section/sections
sch/schs	schedule/schedules
sub-s/sub-ss	subsection/subsections

List of Figures

List of Tables

Chapter 1
Introduction

1.1 Background

The banks play an important role in facilitating institutional and individual banking requirements with respect to commitment to loans, letters of credit, and guarantees for investment-related obligations. In certain cases, they also provide access to alternative sources of external finance.[1] The banking industry deals with credit facilities, retail investment, and other financial transactions.[2] The banks also facilitate collecting money in current, savings, and fixed deposit accounts through cheques and other instruments. They also deal with the receipts and payments of funds from the depositors' accounts using several instruments[3] for individual and institutional requirements. The Banking and Financial Institutions (FIs) consist of central banks, retail banks, commercial banks, shadow banking, investment banks, corporate banks, credit unions, savings and loan associations, private banks, online banks and other platforms. These entities advise entrepreneurs, industries, and individual investors on the banking business.[4]

However, the banking functions have evolved and diversified, necessitating radical changes in banking activities. It has transformed into a multiproduct financial service conglomerate. In addition to performing traditional operations, it deals with retail banking, asset management, brokerage, insurance, investment banking, and wealth management.[5] Post diversification of the banking business, various types of risks have cropped up, including risks related to liquidity, asset quality, interest rate, banks' profitability, market speculation, foreign exchange fluctuation, and political

[1] Berger et al. (2012).

[2] Amadeo (2020), para 2 3.

[3] Manish et al. (2017), pp. 55–56.

[4] Maveric (2020), para 2.

[5] Berger et al. (2012).

A. Dimri, *Non-Performing Loans*, Ius Gentium: Comparative Perspectives on Law and Justice 125, https://doi.org/10.1007/978-3-031-92952-6_1

interferences[6] resulting in a growing number of cases of banking defaults, systemic fraud and non-performing loans (NPLs) in jurisdictions and banks.

The banks take several precautionary measures while granting credit facilities and loans to an individual or institution, such as reviewing the borrower's information and assessing the application concerning the credit rating, borrowers' creditworthiness, financial condition, collateral strength, and capability to repay the loan. However, a loan becomes a default when a borrower cannot pay back the loan according to the period mentioned in the agreement containing terms and conditions for the said loan.[7] Usually, the creditors give extra time before imposing any penalty on the borrowers for missing the first deadline. The period between missing the loan re-payment deadline and when the loan is classified as NPLs is known as delinquency.[7] This period allows the debtors to make a scheduled payment to avoid liquidation and bankruptcy.

Non-performing assets (NPAs) or bad loans refer to non-payment of a loan and its interest in a scheduled 90 days or more without realisation of collateral. It has an impact on creditors and debtors. The debtors' credit score would reduce substantially, apart from the chances of seizure of the collateral. Therefore, if an individual or an institution takes a loan, it should be paid on time to avoid such complications, further inviting legal proceedings. It also significantly impacts the creditors, who are generally the banks. Due to the effect of NPLs, there would not be a smooth flow of credit, resulting in a liquidity shortage in the market. As a result, the banking business would reduce substantially, adversely impacting the banks' income and lending capabilities. The non-availability of a smooth flow of credit and the liquidity problem will adversely impact the banking business in general and the country's economic condition in particular. The NPLs adversely affect macroeconomic factors such as GDP,[8] unemployment rate, real wages, saving and investment, exchange rate, cash flow and credit risk.[8]. The risk of increasing NPLs is higher in banks with poor asset management, low creditworthiness, inadequate collateral assessment, lack of monitoring, underwriting, and postponing costs for the future, as well as insufficient capitalisation.[9] The government's economic and social commitments, mainly in developing countries, influence banks' lending decisions.[10] Since the banking business worldwide is closely interlinked, the problems that arise in a bank will rapidly percolate across the banks and jurisdictions and may lead to a Global Financial Crisis (GFC).

The GFC, 2007–2009, extensively impacted the global economy. Many countries, including advanced economies, were severely affected during the crisis, often called the 'Great Recession'.[11] The GFC was a period of extreme stress in the global

---

[6] Heffernan (2005).

[7] Kucukkacaoglu and Ayhan (2016), p. 52.

[8] Dietrich and Wanzenried (2011), p. 307.

[9] Berger and Young (2017), p. 849.

[10] Bonin and Huang (1999).

[11] IslamIyanatu (2010).

financial markets and the banking system, resulting in millions of job losses. With the recession in the US by the end of 2007 and mid-2008, the housing market mutated and thoroughly blew. The financial crisis severely affected the world, resulting in a slowdown in all sectors of the economy, including multilateral agencies and investors. In addition, many banks around the globe suffered significant losses and relied on the government to avoid bankruptcy.[11] The fundamental causes of the GFC were excessive risk-taking in a favourable economic environment, increased borrowing by banks and investors and deficiencies in regulations and policies mainly related to mortgage-backed securities (MBS).

There was a considerable increase in the supply of houses due to a persistent trend of investment in the housing sector, which peaked in 2007. However, when housing prices started falling, the borrowers' repayment capacity also started declining, which increased NPLs, causing instability in the banking sector, and more than 160 jurisdictions experienced a financial crisis.[12] In 2008, significant banks across the globe, including JP Morgan Chase, Goldman Sachs, Bank of America and Morgan Stanley,[13] and investment banks such as Lehman Brothers and Bear Stearns miserably failed. An estimate revealed that more than 500 banks failed from 2008–2015 globally. Consequently, most jurisdictions witnessed a severe impact on their economies, resulting in a significant increase in NPL ratios.[14] The immediate policy response by the central banks was to lend a large amount of money to banks at significantly low-interest rates and increase government spending.

Under such circumstances, several effective policy and regulatory responses have been taken across jurisdictions to control the level of NPLs. Early detection of problematic banks, bailout plans as temporary relief, off-balance sheet and on-balance sheet strategies, injection of liquidity, and management of impaired loans through Asset Management Companies (AMCs) were important policy measures. In addition, some policy prescriptions also included identifying distressed debt markets, mergers and acquisitions, purchase assumption and transaction (PAT) of default banks, and finally, removing such entities from the system to minimise the effect.

Similarly, jurisdictions across the globe have made several efforts on the regulatory front to address the problem of NPLs. For instance, the EU developed several regulations and directives, including a 'framework for the recovery and resolution of credit institutions and investment firms'.[15] The regulations on 'uniform rules and a uniform procedure for resolving credit institutions and certain investment firms' also play a significant role. Cyprus, Ireland, Italy, Portugal, France, etc., have recently strengthened their judicial system. India enacted the Insolvency and Bankruptcy Code (IBC) 2016 with time-to-time amendments. Similarly, the UK's PRA and FCA played a vital role in regulating the financial sector. Therefore, this

---

[12] Ariccia et al. (2005).

[13] Hanson and Essenburg (2014), p. 18.

[14] Hanson and Essenburg (2014), p. 18.

[15] Miglionico (2017).

book presents a comparative analysis of policy and supervisory and regulatory treatments adopted by the UK, India, and Ireland to control and regulate the level of NPLs.

1.2 Literature Review

Several studies have investigated the phenomenon of NPLs, including a research study on the credit policies of the NPLs ratio in the European Union (EU) banking sector, which has a high level of impaired loans. It analysed the level of NPLs in the select EU Member States from 2008 to 2017[16] using static panel models. It concluded that macroeconomic and microeconomic factors were responsible for high NPLs. The authors have further emphasised that high interest rates in newly granted loans also increase the level of NPLs. Most of the determinants were similar in all types of banks. The study concludes that the surveyed countries' supervisory authorities should ensure that banks critically assess the borrowers' capacity before approving new loans.

In a research study on a group of 855 banks from Italy, Greece, and Spain, the authors pointed out that the borrowers' financial situation improved as the macroeconomic situation improved.[17] The possibility of timely repayment of debts increased significantly. Similarly, in a study of 26 advanced countries from 1998–2009, the authors argued that NPLs significantly weaken macroeconomic performance. On the other hand, the GDP and NPLs ratio has a strong correlation, and real GDP growth is the primary driver of NPLs.[18] With the improvement in GDP, the NPLs' share in banks' loan portfolios declines sharply, and the other research studies also substantiate this argument. These studies focus on identifying the factors responsible for the rise in NPLs. It argued that no comprehensive solutions address the problem, which may be considered a significant research gap in NPLs.

Another essential factor that determines the bank loan portfolio is the unemployment rate. An increase in the unemployment rate deteriorates the quality of the loan portfolio. With the loss of employment, the borrower's ability to repay reduces, and the loan profile also deteriorates significantly. The authors established such a relationship using the Generalised Methods of Moments (GMM). The model used in the Euro area banks from 1990 to 2015 concluded that the employment rate significantly impacted the deterioration in the loan portfolio quality.[19] A study covering seven countries from Central and Eastern Europe (CEE) from 2007 to 2012 drew a similar conclusion. The research on the relationship between inflation and the

[16] Ciukaj and Kil (2020), p. 22.

[17] Jakubík and Thomas (2013), p. 48.

[18] Beck et al. (2015), p. 525.

[19] Anastasiou et al. (2016), p. 116.

quality of bank loan portfolios[20] from the largest banks in CEE revealed that the level of unpaid loans and inflation rate are positively correlated. With the increase in inflation, the NPLs also increase. Another research study[21] concluded that with the rise in the inflation, debt becomes cheaper and improves the quality of bank loan portfolios.

Several studies examined the influence of sovereign debts on loans[22] and revealed that sovereign debts that curb investments impact loan portfolios.[23] Thus, increasing public debt also increases fiscal burdens imposed on the citizens and substantially influences their capacity to repay. The authors concluded that large banks excessively increase their lending activities, compromising credit standards, thus exposing themselves to the risk of credit loss on the granted loans.

The findings on banks' related factors from 1996 to 1999[24] concluded that banks' size and the value of their assets are negatively correlated. As a result, the credit risk was witnessed more in large banks than in smaller ones. The researchers have also examined the relationship between bank loan quality, cost efficiency and capital. It concludes that banks allocating lesser resources to credit and monitoring may be cost-effective in the short run but likely to witness significant NPLs in the long run. Thus, this empirical study establishes a positive relationship between the bank's capital and credit quality.[25]

On the other hand, some studies[26] emphasised that the effectiveness of bank management regarding ROA, ROE, and NIM needed serious attention. Effective bank management reduces the share of NPLs to total loans. Thus, effectively managed banks have better asset quality and generate higher profits. Another study substantiates[27] findings on NPLs and NIM, where the authors have concluded that adverse changes in NIM can cause changes in lending policy by making it riskier. In this situation, the loan portfolio will be affected adversely. Cost-effectiveness and NPLs are also closely associated. Banks that spend relatively fewer funds to investigate and monitor the creditworthiness of borrowers are at risk in the short run, but such banks fetch more profit in the long run. A study examining the instability of the Argentine banking system from 1993 to 1996[28] concludes that excessive lending leads to increased NPLs. Therefore, the Total Capital Ratio (TCR) and Capital Adequacy Ratio (CAR) are crucial[29] for analysing NPLs. The larger banks have a

---

[20] Klein (2013).

[21] Teresa et al. (2008), p. 60.

[22] Cifter (2015), p. 117.

[23] Ghosh (2015), p. 128.

[24] Hu and Chiu (2004), p. 405.

[25] Gambacorta and Mistrulli (2003).

[26] Klein (2013) and Cifter (2015).

[27] Espinoza and Prasad (2010), p.3.

[28] IMF working paper 97/27, Catao (1997).

[29] Rime (2001), p. 789.

greater selective capacity to grant loans and rely on potential public financial support.[30]

Supervisors should ensure adequate policies are available to minimise risk in prevention and control.[31] The author further suggests that the focus should be on effective management of the impaired assets that would create greater value, and poor management would have the opposite consequences. The paper also discussed the pros and cons of AMCs while dealing with NPLs, besides discussing possible treatment options for insolvent banks. Finally, it concluded that M&A and PAT are the possible solutions to overcome bank insolvency, besides pointing out the international best practices for regulating and supervising banks provided by the Basel Committee on Banking Supervision (BCBS).

An IMF[32] staff discussion note examined the problem of NPLs in European banks and concluded that comprehensive strategies address the issue of NPLs. It further suggested three important pillars: enhanced supervision, insolvency reforms, and developing a distressed debt market to address high NPLs. Since European banks tend to operate in multiple jurisdictions within and outside the eurozone, a successful NPLs resolution strategy would require close coordination between the EU and competent national authorities. The authors argued[33] that different approaches are available to address the NPLs problem, and strategies vary between 'on and off-balance sheet approaches'. The former involves the internal workout of NPLs supported by regulatory guidance on provisioning, loan restructuring, and the protection of borrowers. The latter involves outright sales to private investors or AMCs. The study further emphasised that the legal and judicial framework must be conducive to the swift and efficient resolution of NPLs.

A comprehensive study[34] on regulatory and accounting treatment of asset quality concerning the International Financial Reporting Standard (IFRS-9), an accounting standard for loan loss provisions (LLP) in G20 countries, discusses efforts towards harmonising the NPLs definition, but it continues to vary between jurisdictions. It analysed the variations in the treatment of NPLs across countries and pointed out that NPLs identification and measurement practices vary considerably across jurisdictions due to the application and design of different accounting procedures.[16] It has identified significant differences across key jurisdictions and provided various prudential policy options to identify NPLs and provide suitable treatment. Benchmarks exist in these countries for defining NPLs, including 90 days to declare non-payment of loans as NPLs.

Another study classified the assets into five categorises[35] viz-a viz. standard, watch, substandard, doubtful, and loss. It argued that the treatment of collateral in

---

[30] Stern and Feldman (2004).

[31] Campbell (2007), pp. 25–26.

[32] IMF Discussion paper, Aiyar et al. (2015), pp. 1–2.

[33] Grodzicki et al. (2015), p. 146.

[34] Bholat et al. (2018), pp. 1–3.

[35] Katia et al. (2014).

regulatory provisioning requirements varies widely across the EU Member States. Although the European Banking Authority (EBA) has provided the benchmark for harmonising the regulatory treatment for forbearance exposures to regional supervisors, divergence practices adopted in loan forbearance further complicate the problem. The study also noted that a well-thought out macro-prudential policy stance in loan classification and provisioning is essential. Many prudential supervisors of developed countries have done away with asset classification systems and now rely on IFRS to identify and provide impaired loans.

Several studies investigated the problems of NPLs in India and concluded that the banking sector is in a crisis with the increased burden of bad loans and the decline in profitability.[36] These research studies also capped the government's regulatory and policy measures to address the problem of NPLs. The essential regulatory treatments included enacting the SARFAESI ACT 2002, debt settlement through *Lok Adalats*, Debt Recovery Tribunal (DRT) and Corporate Debt Recovery (DRT),[37] and enacting IBC 2016 and its amendments. The RBI Report, 2018 and the Standing Committee on Finance (2018) presented a detailed analysis of the problem of NPLs. It envisaged that Basel norms and IFRS are essential guidelines to deal with the Capital Risk-weighted Assets Ratio (CRAR). The RBI recommended that commercial banks keep a one per cent higher CRAR than the global Basel norms. The report also emphasised that the RBI revised Prompt Corrective Action (PCA) criteria and classified banks based on three risk parameters: capital adequacy, net non-performing assets (NPAs), and ROA and leverage.

While assessing the factors related to NPL in the British and Brazilian banking systems and the behaviours expected during the COVID-19 pandemic, a study revealed that these jurisdictions took several measures to subside the negative impact of COVID-19 on the economy.[38] It concluded that there was a positive influence on the real interest rate and a negative one between GDP and NPLs. It also highlighted the impact of the current geopolitical risk, the global rise in inflation and the current political environment on NPLs. NPL ratios of Chinese banks increase when COVID cases rise, and the banks with high equity ratios and high Tier 1 capital ratios have significantly lower NPL ratios during the COVID crisis.[39] The NPL ratios were considerably lower in the Big Five as compared to non-Big Five domestic banks. The banks and their regulatory authorities are looking to disseminate the negative impacts on the NPL ratios.

A study with a sample consisting of 2073 listed and unlisted banks in 106 countries from 2016 to 2021 concluded that the outbreak of COVID-19 has significantly decreased bank performance and stability.[40] The impact was due to specific factors of the banks and the country, and the financial condition during the pandemic was

---

[36] Sharadha and Jain (2016).

[37] D'Souza (2017), p. 42.

[38] Diniz and Costa (2022), p. 15.

[39] Kryzanowsk et al. (2023).

[40] Shabir et al. (2023).

an important factor for its survival. Banks' performance and stability were most negatively affected by COVID-19 in smaller, undercapitalised, less diversified, foreign, and government-owned banks. However, a better regulatory environment, superior institutional quality, and higher financial development minimise the adverse impacts of COVID-19 on banks' performance and stability.

Thus, plenty of literature is available on studying NPLs and their determinants and regulatory, supervisory and policy responses to address the problem. Some studies focused on macroeconomic factors such as GDP, unemployment rates, inflation, etc. In contrast, others focused on bank-related factors such as asset quality, liquidity ratio, interest rates, bank size, management, etc. A fragmented literature on supervisory and policy measures and regulatory treatment of NPLs is also available. There are considerable research gaps in the existing literature, particularly comparing supervisory, regulatory, and policy efforts in extreme situations. More importantly, the literature on the impact of COVID-19 on NPLs is also insufficient.

This book deals with the determinants of NPLs, their impact on NPLs, and vice versa. It also examines the UK, India, and Ireland's regulatory, supervisory, and policy measures to control the level of NPLs through a comparative study. In addition, the study also undertakes an in-depth analysis of three case studies involving LBG, PNB and BIG, representing these jurisdictions to understand the micro-level management of NPLs, besides touching on the initiatives taken during the COVID-19 pandemic.

1.3 Research Questions

International standards set for the banking system through the Basel guidelines for the disbursement of loans are broadly accepted by most jurisdictions. Banks must critically assess borrowers' financial health before sanctioning and disbursing a loan. Despite preventive measures, individual debtors, Small and Medium Enterprises (SMEs), and Commercial Real Estate (CRE) such as Hovnanian Enterprises, Inc., Lennar Corporation, Land Source, CBRE, and large corporations such as Lehman Brothers become defaulters. Individual loan defaults were due to reduced household income and unemployment. Negative cash flow, poor liquidity and profitability ratio, the speculative factors in CRE, and the collapse of property prices resulted in non-payment of loan instalments in the stipulated time, shooting up NPLs, thus causing a rise in the number of defaults in SMEs, large corporations and even at individual borrowings.

Efforts have been made at the regulatory and policy levels to develop a suitable mechanism to control the high level of NPLs. Nevertheless, the desired results have not been achieved in many countries worldwide due to varying NPL treatment strategies. For example, in India, such measures could not achieve the desired result due to the dual control of banks by the RBI and the government in power, which pressures the banking business to fulfil its social and political agenda. On the contrary, the level of interference in the United Kingdom is minimal, resulting in a significant reduction in NPLs. These NPLs stood at 4% after the GFC from 2008 to 2012 and consequently dropped and have consistently remained at less than 1% after 2012. NPLs in Ireland remained consistently higher despite several efforts at the policy and regulatory level. Considering this, the present book shall seek to evaluate existing regulatory, supervisory, and policy measures and their effectiveness in controlling NPLs, as well as assess the impact of COVID-19 on the existing situation of NPLs. It will also suggest harmonised treatment and prudential policy measures. Thus, the book will address the following research questions:

- Do existing regulatory regimes have strong provisions to regulate NPLs?
- Have the central banks made effective policy mechanisms to address the problem of NPLs?
- What is the level of effectiveness between regulatory and policy measures, and how does dual vs. single control on banks influence performance?
- Is there a requirement for a new policy, supervisory and regulatory measures to bridge the gap?
- What will be the impact of COVID-19 on NPLs?

1.4 Research Methodology

To address the issues that emerged in the research questions, an in-depth analysis of regulatory, supervisory, and policy measures to level down NPLs needs significant attention. Studying the relationship between macroeconomic and microeconomic determinants with NPLs helps determine the real cause of the rising NPLs. The present research examines various issues influencing NPLs using doctrinal, quantitative and comparative research methodologies while analysing the legal and policy documents related to NPLs and their determinants.

The doctrinal research methodology involves assembling relevant facts, identifying legal issues, analysing the problems related to the law, locating, and reading background information and synthesising the content of the law. This method critically examines the essential features of the legislation, and all the relevant elements are combined to establish an arguably correct and complete statement of the law on the related topic under examination.[41]

The research method also has several challenges, including its pervasive influence on determining the research questions. In addition, doctrinal research takes an insider's view of the law, which is studied in isolation from its context and is intrinsic to the common law.[41] The doctrinal research method has challenges regarding the complexity of the legal text, the volume of legal material, legal interpretation, and applications. In the present book, the doctrinal research method facilitated the investigation of legal documents, such as legislation and case law, which directly or indirectly impact NPLs.

[41] Hutchinson (2017).

A quantitative research method deals with quantifying and analysing variables to get results. It involves utilising and analysing numerical data using specific statistical techniques to answer questions.[42] Quantitative research is a method used to scientifically investigate phenomena by collecting, collating, and analysing numerical data. Quantitative methods are often applied in legal research to study issues related to law and economics, such as the impact of legal rules on economic behaviour and vice versa, the efficiency of legal regulations, or the economic effects of legal disputes.

Extensive statistical analysis, which is difficult for researchers with non-statistical backgrounds, poses serious challenges for law students. Due to inconsistency, there may be ambiguity in the result, which will lead to ambiguous results. Moreover, legal researchers are hesitant to use quantitative techniques because legal researchers are more comfortable with investigating legal resources than quantifying them due to limited exposure to quantitative research methods, despite it has several advantages as it usefully supplements doctrinal research.[43] Using the quantitative research method in the present research helped to establish a relationship between NPLs and macroeconomic and microeconomic determinants.

A comparative research method in law 'presents a new perspective, allowing one critically to illuminate a legal system—another or one's own as much in the same way'.[44] A comparative analysis combines several objects or elements of one or more objects to examine the degrees of similarity and conclude that each analysis alone would not necessarily have allowed one to draw inferences. Nevertheless, new knowledge will likely emerge from comparing the legislations in comparative research. It also provides an enhanced and broader perspective, besides cross-cultural insight. Despite its advantages, it also has challenges, which include over-simplification of complex phenomena, ignorance of the multifaceted nature of the subjects, looking for data comparability across different contexts and setting the availability and quality of data narrows the research's applicability. Therefore, preconception and subjectivity in selecting and interpreting data can significantly influence comparative research outcomes.[44]

Thus, the present research uses doctrinal research methodology to analyse the suitability of legislation and case law, quantitative methods to analyse and establish the relationship between NPLs and microeconomic and macroeconomic determinants and the comparative research method to compare legislation and the impact of microeconomic and macroeconomic determinants on NPLs and vice versa.

---

[42] Williams (2011).

[43] Klerman (2018), p. 343.

[44] Samuel (2017).

1.4.1 Selection of Jurisdictions

The present research study analysed the NPLs ratio of 31 jurisdictions for 14 years, from the GFC to COVID-19 (2008 to 2021). World Development Indicator, a World Bank database, is a comprehensive database that collects and maintains country-wise data on many indicators, including NPLs. The main criterion for selecting 31 jurisdictions was the availability of consistent NPLs data for 14 years. In addition, these jurisdictions also represent both developed and emerging nations. After computing average NPLs of 14 years for each jurisdiction, these jurisdictions were placed in ascending order based on their average NPLs to prepare a hierarchy of jurisdictions. Depending on the intensity and impact of NPLs, the author placed them in different strata. Accordingly, the jurisdictions with less than 1% average NPLs were categorised as no impact jurisdictions, 1% to 5% moderate impact jurisdictions, 5% to 10% high impact jurisdictions and more than 10% average NPLs as very high impact jurisdictions. The selection of the average NPLs limit for each category and their classification into specific categories was random and based on the visible natural break in the data series.

A stratified random sampling technique was used to select the UK, India, and Ireland. However, their NPLs level, regulatory and policy measures adopted by them and the failure and success of these measures remained the main criteria while reviewing existing literature. For instance, in the UK, there was a substantial increase in NPLs after the GFC, with average NPLs of 2.10%. However, a proactive response by regulatory authorities brought it down to the original level in a relatively short period. Despite several regulatory and policy measures, India's NPLs problem is perpetual, with average NPLs of 5.72%. The impact of the GFC was severe and long-lasting in Ireland, with many individuals, SMEs, and corporate insolvencies. The average NPLs of Ireland was 11.45%, which was as high as 22.23% in 2012 (Table 1.1). Thus, the author selected three jurisdictions with distinct characteristics representing a developed nation- the UK, an emerging nation- India, and a jurisdiction with a relatively higher NPLs ratio with the long-lasting impact of the GFC-Ireland.

The author collected information on major operational banks from these jurisdictions and analysed their customer base, business volume, fluctuation in NPLs ratios, asset quality, etc., as well as bail-out support received from the government. For instance, LBG is the second largest bank in the UK, and its NPLs ratio reached 10.6% in 2010, the highest among the commercial banks operational in the UK, and the average NPL ratio of the UK was 3.96% in 2010. Similarly, PNB is India's third-largest bank; its GNPA was 18.38% in 2018, against the average GNPA in 9.96% of India. On the other hand, BIG is also the second largest bank in Ireland; its NPLs were 9.4% in Ireland in 2010, which was relatively higher (see Table 6.2, Chap. 6). The selection of these banks for the micro-level study was random. However, the intensity of the NPLs problem, bail-out support during crisis and transaction volume remained important criteria for selecting them for a micro-level study.

1.4.2 Data/Information

To derive better results, the study conducted an analysis of the primary and secondary sources of information. The primary sources included existing regulations, directives, resolutions, guidelines, decrees, case laws, acts, and statutes. These legal instruments are available on the websites of respective governments and organisations, such as Eur-Lex, the Official Home of UK Legislation, the National Portal of India, and the Electronic Irish Book Statute (eLSB).

The secondary sources included published books, reports, banking law journals, online journals, newspaper articles, columns, blogs, websites, and press releases. International agencies such as the IMF, World Bank, EBA, European Court of Justice (ECJ), OECD, Asian Development Bank, and European Union also upload relevant reports on their official website, which are authentic sources and accessible to the public. Similarly, the study referred to the reports of central banks of individual countries, such as the Bank of England (BoE), the RBI, and the Central Bank of Ireland (CBI) and annual reports of LBG, PNB and BIG being available on their website.

The book used 14 years of NPL data (2008–2021) to prepare a hierarchy of jurisdictions to select three jurisdictions for the present study. In addition, it also used 13 years of data (2008–2020) in Chaps. 2 and 3 to establish a relationship between NPLs and economic determinants such as GDP, inflation, unemployment, exchange rates, asset quality, bank size, ROA, ROE, etc., based on the availability of consistent data on these variables. The World Bank compiles the World Development Indicators (WDI) from internationally recognised sources. It presents the most current, accurate, consistent, authentic, precise, and reliable global development data, including national, regional, and global estimates.[45] Such data is easily accessible from the World Bank's Official website under the database section for the public.

1.4.3 Online Data Resource

The data and information were also accessed from websites and online library catalogues of the University of Leeds, besides ProQuest, Westlaw, Lexis-Nexis tool, and Hein Online library, using the credentials available for the staff and students to access such resources. In addition, where necessary, information is also accessed using the Google search engine. The information available on the websites of national and international agencies/organisations/institutions is also authentic, reliable, and consistent, and accessibility depends on the availability of user credentials.

---

[45] Information is available on the website of the World Bank under Data Bank.

1.4.4 Analysis of Information and Data

The data was thus collected, collated, and tabulated with the help of an Excel sheet. User-friendly statistical methods, such as mean, standard deviation, correlation, etc., were applied to establish a relationship between NPLs and macroeconomic and microeconomic determinants. The purpose of using such tools was to make comparative analysis more meaningful. Mean was used to obtain the average NPLs of 13 years so that the jurisdictions could be placed in ascending order of average NPLs. Standard Deviation (SD) represents the deviation of the data from the mean. If the SD values are within a range of ±2, the data is consistent and significant, having less variability in the data trend. Consistent SD data also fetches better results when correlation coefficients are applied.

On the other hand, the correlation coefficient value represents a positive and negative relationship between two variables (for instance, NPLs and GDP). The correlation coefficient value ranges from −1 to +1. The correlation values +0.01 to +0.99 are positive, with +0.01 to +0.49 being a weak positive and +0.50 to +0.99 being a strong positive. Similarly, correlation values −0.01 to −0.99 are negative, with −0.01 to −0.49 weak negative, and with −0.50 to −0.99 strong negative.

In this book, we also prepared a composite priority index using the average performance of 13 years on each determinant. We ranked the jurisdictions 1, 2, and 3 based on their thirteen-year average performance. Then, we multiplied the average score of 13 years by the individual rank to obtain the final score. After totalling all individual scores, the researcher calculated a composite score and ranked jurisdictions accordingly. The composite score helped to analyse the performance of individual jurisdictions, comparing them with each other.

1.5 Defining Non-Performing Loans

The jurisdictions have adopted many approaches to classify loans as non-performing and have used different terminologies. It is also known as NPAs, stressed assets (SA), bad loans, stressed loans, and non-performing exposure. Generally, NPLs occur when a debtor cannot repay the loan and its interest thereon in a scheduled time frame of 90 days or more, depending on the term of the loan agreement, without the realisation of collateral for the loan.

Accordingly, the OECD[46] has prepared a scoreboard of twenty-third countries that used different terms for NPLs, such as loan delinquency, impaired loans, and insolvent loans. The period for declaring loans as NPLs varies significantly across jurisdictions from, 30 days to 90 days and beyond. For instance, Chile, Finland, Portugal, and the USA have considered 30 days. Estonia and Sweden took 60 days, and Colombia, Czech Republic, Canada, Greece, Hungary, Spain, Turkey, Korea,

[46] OECD Scoreboard (2015).

France, etc., took 90 days and beyond. There are ‘no explicit agreements about NPLs’ as different countries have used different methods to define NPLs.[31]

The latest guidelines of the Basel Committee (2015, 2017) on banking supervision analysed the range of practices adopted concerning the definition of credit risk management. It concludes that different jurisdictions’ key terms include weakened, forbearance, non-performing loans, loss, and write-offs for credit categorisation schemes. The wide variation across jurisdictions was due to the absence of a ‘consistent international framework guiding the banks and the supervisors. Thus, Basel developed guidelines for two important terms, ‘non-performing exposures’ (NPEs) and ‘forbearance’, on the commonalities in existing definitions with credit categorisation issues on qualitative and quantitative criteria. Nevertheless, the ‘weakened’, ‘loss’ and ‘write off’ had a lower degree of commonalities and conflicts that also prevailed within jurisdictions; therefore, Basel did not attempt to harmonise them.

Thus, Basel (2017) emphasises explaining the attributes related to the definition of NPEs, such as the scope of NPLs, harmonised re-organisation criteria, the role of collateralisation, the level of application and upgrading non-performing to performing loans. As a result, the Basel guidelines considered the following exposures as non-performing:

- The bank considers that the obligator is unlikely to pay its credit obligations to the banking group in full, without recourse by the bank to actions such as realising security.
- The obligator is over 90 days past due on any material credit obligation to the banking group.
- In the case of retail and public sector entities’ obligations, for the 90-day figure, a supervisor may substitute up to 180 days for different products as considered appropriate to local conditions.
- All exposures that are not defaulted or impaired but nevertheless:
  - Are material exposures that are more than 90 days past dues?
  - There is evidence that full re-payment based on the contractual terms, original or modified the re-payment of principal and interest is unlikely without the bank’s realisation of collateral.

The Basel definition also emphasises explaining forbearance because timely identification of forbearance may reduce the chances of NPEs. Forbearance occurs when a debtor is experiencing financial difficulty meeting the financial commitments, and a bank grants a concession otherwise not considered. The categorisation of NPLs depends on the loan’s reliability. Thus, assets are grouped into four categories viz-a-viz, standard, sub-standard, doubtful, and loss. This classification does not provide a minimum threshold. If a ‘borrower starts repaying the loan classified as a non-performing loan, these loans are considered’ re-performing loans’.[47]

On the other hand, the RBI[48] defines an asset (including a leased asset) as non-performing when it stops generating income for the bank. Thus, an NPA is a loan or an advance where:

- Interest and/or instalment of principal remain overdue for a specified period of more than 90 days in respect of the term loan.
- The account remains out of order regarding an overdraft/ cash credit (OD/CD).

[47] Bank of International Settlement (2017a), pp. 1–3.

[48] Reserve Bank of India (2020).

- The bills remain overdue for more than 90 days in case of bills purchased and discounted.
- A loan granted for short-duration crops will be treated as NPA if the instalment of principal or interest thereon remains overdue for two crop seasons (one crop season for a long-duration crop).
- The liquidity facility remains outstanding for more than 90 days regarding a securitisation transaction undertaken in terms of the guidelines on securitisation.
- Regarding derivative transactions, the overdue receivables represent positive mark-to-market value of a derivative contract if these remain unpaid for 90 days from the specified due date for payment.

Despite several efforts defining NPLs, the '90-day approach is a valuable tool'.[31] Still, a prompt approach is needed to monitor the problems continuously. The preceding paragraphs compared the definitions of OECD, Basel, and RBI. The OECD has presented a consolidated framework of the prevailing practices across a limited number of jurisdictions, but has not suggested a harmonised approach for implementation across jurisdictions.

The Basel guidelines evaluated the different approaches before harmonising the definition of NPLs. Besides placing loans into different categories, it distinguished between NPEs and forbearance.[47] It further envisaged that early detection of the problem with constant monitoring would reduce the chances of debts becoming NPLs. On the other hand, the RBI definition contextualised the same to the prevailing local conditions. The period extends up to two crop seasons, roughly 180 days. However, later on RBI, classified the distressed loan accounts as special mentioned accounts with loan default of 0-30 days SMA, 31-60 days SMA01 and 61-90 days SMA02. In the present study, a harmonised approach suggested by Basel, which seems complete in all respects, will be considered a reference point in our discussion.

1.6 Cross-Country Analysis of the Current Level of NPLs

After critically analysing the definition of NPLs, this section examines the current level of NPLs across some advanced and emerging jurisdictions, including the UK, India, and Ireland, by categorising jurisdictions into different strata. The analysis of NPLs trend from the World Bank data revealed that the NPL ratios were higher in advanced countries in the post-financial crisis than in the pre-crisis period. In 2019, NPL ratios in Greece (36.6%), Italy (18%), Ireland (15.9%) and Portugal (11.9%) were significantly higher. There was a significant improvement in the NPLs of these jurisdictions, and in 2021, it stood at 9.16% for Greece, 3.35% in Italy, 2.84% in Ireland and 3.68% in Portugal (Figs. 1.1 and 1.2).[49]

A study on NPLs ratios in 57 emerging and advanced countries envisaged that the average NPLs ratios of advanced countries dropped from 3.9% to 1.5% and emerging countries from 13.3% to 4.4% in the early part of the first decade of the

---

[49] Detailed information is available on the website of the World Bank under Data Bank.

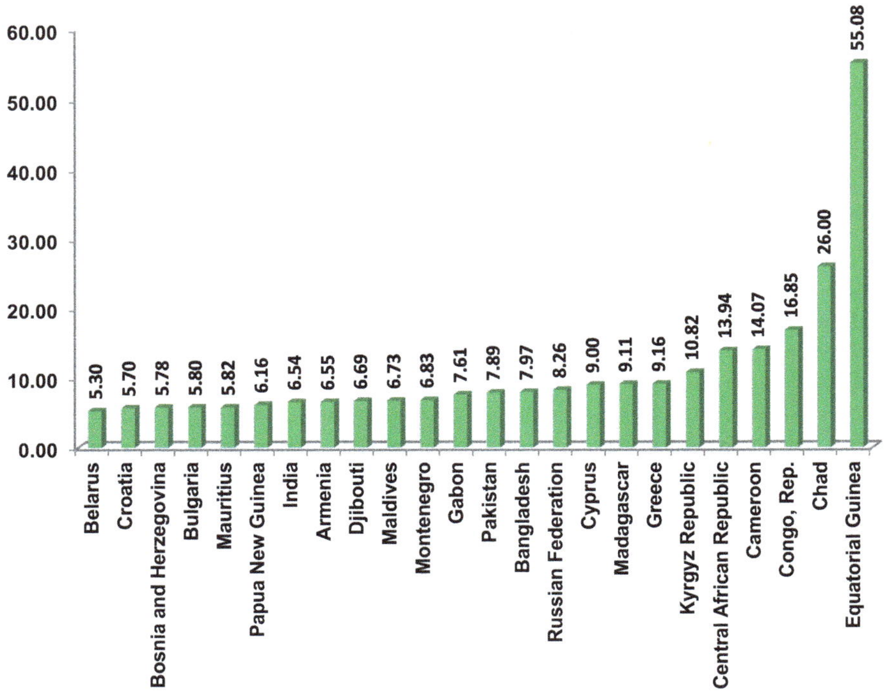

Fig. 1.1 Jurisdictions with more than 5% NPLs to Gross Loan Ratio (2021). Source: Developed by the researcher based on the data from World Development Indicators, World Bank

twenty-first century during the pre-crisis period (Fig. 1.2).[50] A similar trend persisted in advanced and emerging countries in the post-crisis period up to 2015. However, the quality of loans further deteriorated quickly in these countries, but the recovery process was relatively higher in the advanced countries.

There is a possibility that in such a closely related financial system, the problems of NPLs will adversely affect the credit supply and economic growth [16] The continued stress of NPLs poses significant risks to economic growth and financial stability worldwide. There is an urgent need to identify ways to enhance the quality of the loan profiles of the banks by constantly monitoring their effectiveness in achieving the targets.[51] It is also crucial for the banks to assess their internal capabilities to manage and reduce NPLs. Therefore, macroeconomic conditions, market expectations and regulatory framework, supervisory and policy initiatives, and capital planning are important considerations that need critical analysis.

[50] Kuzucuand and Kuzucu (2019), p. 1694.

[51] European Central Bank (2017).

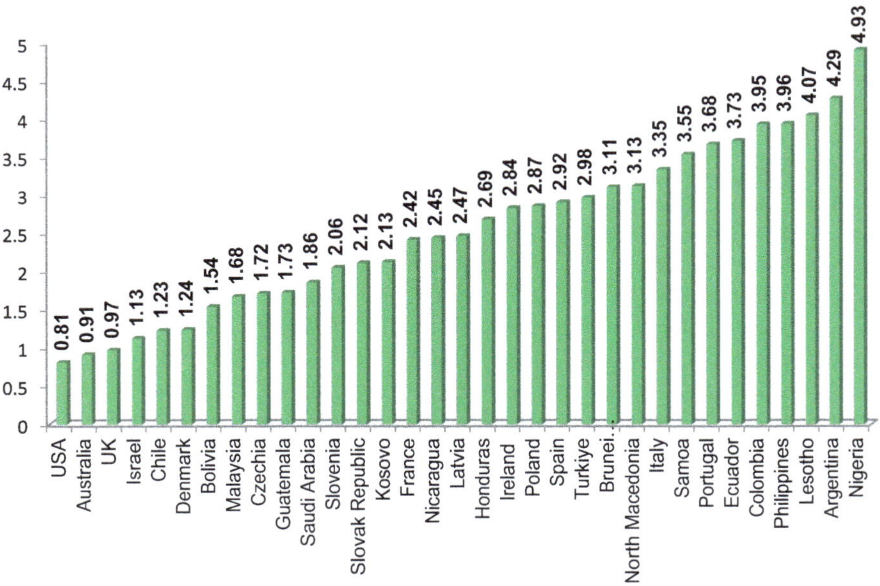

Fig. 1.2 Jurisdictions with Less than 5% NPLs to Gross Loan Ratio (2021). Source: Developed by the researcher based on the data from World Development Indicators

1.7 NPLs Trends from GFC to COVID-19

In the following section, the author prepared a hierarchy of 31 jurisdictions using average NPLs data for 14 years, covering the period from the GFC to the post-COVID-19. After calculating the average NPLs ratio, jurisdictions were placed in ascending order and grouped into four categories. The jurisdictions with less than 1% NPLs are placed under the no impact category, 1% to 5%, moderate impact, 5–10% high impact, and more than 10% very high impact category. These jurisdictions were categorised into different strata randomly and based on existing natural breaks.

1.7.1 No Impact

It is evident that GFC has a low impact on the NPLs in three countries, including Luxembourg, Sweden, and Finland, and their average NPLs ratio was less than 1% during the last 14 years (Table 1.1). In Luxembourg, the NPLs remained around 1%, with the highest at 1.03% in 2020. There was a marginal fluctuation in the NPLs in Sweden and Finland. In Finland, the highest NPLs were 1.24% in 2014, and in Sweden, the highest was 1.51% in 2019.

Both Sweden and Finland suffered from the Nordic crisis during 1991–93,[52] and taking lessons from the situation, Sweden took several initiatives to overcome the problem of loan default, including an initiative to set up a recapitalisation fund in 1992, which has contributed significantly to bringing down NPLs at a manageable ratio.[53] The government provided a blanket guarantee for the financial obligations in the banking system.

Furthermore, it focused on acting early rather than working correctly and enforcing adequate legal and institutional framework for the resolution procedures with open-ended public funding, full disclosure of information by the banks, differentiated resolution policy, government financial intervention and design of sound macroeconomic policies to end up the crisis both in the real economy and financial sector. Therefore, the Swedish model of the 1990s was very effective in dealing with NPLs, resulting in a minimal impact. Several countries suffering from financial turmoil after the GFC also took a clue from this effort and were able to minimise the impact of the crisis.

1.7.2 Moderate Impact

Moreover, 13 jurisdictions, including the USA and the UK, experienced a moderate impact of the crisis on NPLs, with average NPL ratios of 1% to 5%. While analysing the trend over 14 years, the NPLs were low during the GFC, peaked in the post-GFC, started receding from 2013 onwards and remained stable during the COVID-19 pandemic (Fig. 1.3 and Table 1.1). For instance, in Czech, NPLs were 2.82% in 2008, peaked at 5.64% in 2014 and down to 1.69% in 2019. In Spain, it was 2.81% in 2008, peaked at 7.12% in 2013, and dropped to 2.85% in 2020. The NPLs of this group peaked from 2010 to 2014, and the variation in NPLs was relatively less except in Estonia at 4.29%, with the highest at 5.28% and the lowest at 1.09%. In the USA, it was 3.11% in 2008, 4.96% in 2009, and 1.07% in 2020, showing a marginal increase. Similarly, in the UK, it was highest in 20,11(3.96%) and lowest in 2021 with 9.96%. The NPLs of the UK were 1.56% at the start of the GFC in 2008.

These jurisdictions took several initiatives to reform their existing insolvency regimes to control the rising level of NPLs. For instance, France amended its insolvency regime in 2012[54] and used protective measures in the context of insolvency proceedings. The commingling of assets, controlling mismanagement and disposal, amending insolvency law to ease debt restructuring, smoothing bankruptcy proceedings, and enabling subordination agreements [34] were some significant initia-

[52] Jonung (2009).

[53] Fromlet, 2012), p. 1.

[54] Petiet (2012).

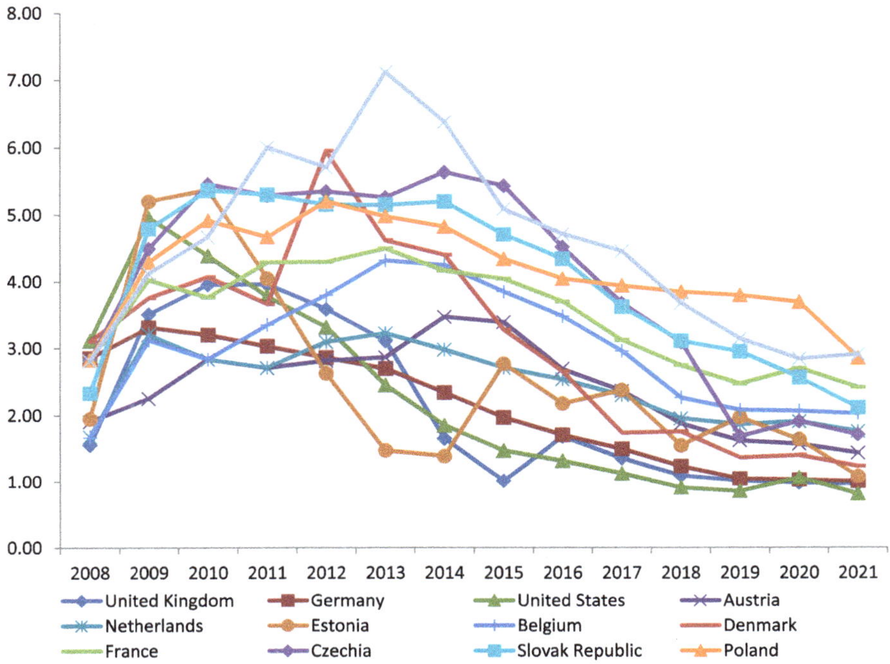

Fig. 1.3 Trend of NPLs in the Jurisdictions with Moderate NPLs (2008–2021). Source: Developed by the researcher using data from World Development Indicators, World Bank

tives to improve and address the problems of NPLs. Through the amendment in the insolvency regime in 2014, France introduced new insolvency proceedings, which promoted the enhanced obligation to inform the statutory auditor about pre-insolvency proceedings, pre-packed sale of the business, amendment in a grace period and increase in debtor's obligations. Under accelerated safeguards proceedings, the debtor's plan is approved by most creditors and subsequently by courts within 3 months. [20]

In ordinary safeguard proceedings, the creditors were allowed to submit an alternative plan, and the courts direct the shareholders to pay their unpaid capital. The safeguard proceedings were converted into re-organisation if the creditor's committee did not adopt the safeguard plan.[54] Moreover, a judicial representative is appointed to restore shareholders' equity under re-organisation procedures. Without a plan, the administrator requests the court to transfer either partial or total business. [32] France has adopted strong legal and policy measures to address the insolvency issues and unresolved insolvent cases. However, the problem of NPLs persists in France, and constant monitoring is essential to bring NPLs under control.

Table 1.1 Trend of NPLs in Select Jurisdictions from GFC to COVID-19

Country	2008	2009	2010	2011	2012	2013	2014	2015	2016	2017	2018	2019	2020	2021	Total	Average	Ranking	Hierarchy
Luxembourg	0.65	0.67	0.25	0.38	0.15	0.21	0.31	0.34	0.90	0.79	0.90	0.74	1.03	0.79	8.11	0.58	1	No Impact
Sweden	0.46	0.83	0.78	0.65	0.70	0.61	1.24	1.17	1.06	1.12	0.49	0.58	0.51	0.42	10.64	0.76	2	
Finland	0.41	0.57	0.51	0.46	0.45	0.44	0.85	0.93	1.05	0.73	0.95	1.51	1.45	1.47	11.76	0.84	3	
UK	1.56	3.51	3.95	3.96	3.59	3.11	1.65	1.01	1.69	1.36	1.10	1.02	0.98	0.97	29.46	2.10	4	Moderate Impact
Germany	2.85	3.31	3.20	3.03	2.86	2.70	2.34	1.97	1.71	1.50	1.24	1.05	1.03	1.01	29.80	2.13	5	
USA	3.11	4.96	4.39	3.78	3.32	2.45	1.85	1.47	1.32	1.13	0.91	0.86	1.07	0.81	31.43	2.24	6	
Austria	1.90	2.25	2.83	2.71	2.81	2.87	3.47	3.39	2.70	2.37	1.88	1.63	1.58	1.44	33.83	2.42	7	
Netherlands	1.68	3.20	2.83	2.71	3.10	3.23	2.98	2.71	2.54	2.31	1.96	1.87	1.91	1.76	34.80	2.49	8	
Estonia	1.94	5.20	5.38	4.05	2.62	1.47	1.39	2.77	2.18	2.38	1.55	1.97	1.64	1.09	35.63	2.55	9	
Belgium	1.67	3.11	2.83	3.35	3.80	4.32	4.25	3.85	3.48	2.96	2.27	2.09	2.07	2.03	42.08	3.01	10	
Denmark	3.10	3.75	4.07	3.66	5.95	4.62	4.40	3.28	2.66	1.74	1.76	1.37	1.41	1.24	43.00	3.07	11	
France	2.82	4.02	3.76	4.29	4.29	4.50	4.16	4.05	3.70	3.12	2.75	2.47	2.71	2.42	49.06	3.50	12	
Czech	2.82	4.49	5.46	5.29	5.35	5.26	5.64	5.44	4.52	3.68	3.10	1.69	1.91	1.72	56.38	4.03	13	
Slovakia	2.33	4.79	5.37	5.31	5.16	5.16	5.20	4.71	4.35	3.63	3.12	2.96	2.57	2.12	56.75	4.05	14	
Poland	2.82	4.29	4.91	4.66	5.20	4.98	4.82	4.34	4.05	3.94	3.85	3.80	3.70	2.87	58.24	4.16	15	
Spain	2.81	4.12	4.67	6.01	5.71	7.12	6.38	5.09	4.72	4.46	3.69	3.15	2.85	2.92	63.70	4.55	16	
India	2.45	2.48	2.55	2.67	3.37	4.03	4.35	5.88	9.19	9.98	9.46	9.23	7.94	6.54	80.12	5.72	17	High Impact
Malta	5.01	5.78	7.02	7.09	7.75	8.95	9.05	7.10	5.29	4.07	3.36	3.21	3.66	3.44	80.78	5.77	18	
Slovenia	4.22	5.79	8.21	11.81	15.18	13.31	11.73	9.96	5.07	3.20	6.01	3.36	3.02	2.06	102.94	7.35	19	
Russia	3.81	9.58	8.31	6.63	6.06	6.02	6.81	8.38	9.24	9.66	9.75	8.83	8.26	8.11	109.44	7.82	20	
Latvia	3.04	20.27	22.29	14.05	8.72	6.41	4.60	4.64	6.26	5.51	5.29	5.00	3.09	2.47	111.65	7.98	21	
Portugal	3.11	4.33	4.69	6.38	8.19	9.21	10.45	16.74	16.57	13.19	9.43	6.18	4.89	3.68	117.03	8.36	22	
Lithuania	5.99	22.14	21.31	17.64	14.11	11.59	8.19	4.95	3.66	3.18	2.27	1.04	0.97	0.51	117.56	8.40	23	
Hungary	3.23	8.13	10.04	13.68	16.04	16.83	15.62	11.66	7.42	4.17	2.47	1.51	3.95	3.66	118.41	8.46	24	
Romania	2.75	7.89	11.85	14.33	18.24	21.87	13.94	13.51	9.62	6.41	4.96	4.09	3.83	3.35	136.63	9.76	25	

Bulgaria	2.40	6.42	11.92	14.97	16.63	16.88	16.75	14.61	13.17	10.43	7.80	6.62	5.80	5.64	150.05	10.72	26	Very High Impact
Italy	6.28	9.45	10.03	11.74	13.75	16.54	18.03	18.06	17.12	14.38	8.39	6.75	4.36	3.35	158.23	11.30	27	
Croatia	10.11	10.90	11.00	12.30	13.8	15.4	16.70	16.3	13.60	11.20	9.70	7.00	6.50	5.70	160.22	11.44	28	
Ireland	1.92	9.80	12.47	16.12	21.31	22.37	20.65	16.91	12.63	11.46	5.46	3.36	3.36	2.48	160.30	11.45	29	
Cyprus	3.59	4.51	5.82	9.99	18.37	38.56	44.97	47.75	36.70	31.39	19.52	17.09	15.02	9.00	302.28	21.59	30	
Greece	2.47	3.77	5.62	9.20	15.72	27.81	29.99	35.71	37.36	45.57	41.99	36.45	26.98	9.16	327.81	23.41	31	

Source: Compiled from World Development Indicators, World Bank

Similarly, Poland's reforms came in 2015 with four restructuring procedures for insolvent debtors, including arrangements for approval of proceedings, accelerated arrangement proceedings, and remedial proceedings. However, the Polish court has faced many challenges concerning recent bankruptcy cases, mainly in selling company assets in bankruptcy proceedings. For instance, while restructuring 'Small Planet Airlines', the company tried to sell its investments using the pre-pack procedure. The company sought an investor to take over the Air Operator Certificate (AOC). The Civil Aviation Office did not allow this, arguing that the AOC could not be transferred to a third party and suggested that the potential buyer should obtain such a licence separately. This example pointed out the cavity in Article 317 of Poland's bankruptcy law,[55] Thus, proposing amendments to augment the proceedings and make them more practical and implementable. It certainly draws the attention of lawmakers, who must be more pragmatic while drafting the law.

General Accepted Accounting Principles (GAAP) in the USA limit the bank manager's discretion.[56] The USA has imposed two vital regulatory requirements on banks: suspending and reserving interest income on NPLs once the loan is 90 days past due, and promptly writing down the loan balance on the bank's accounting statement to recoverable collateral value. The loan balance that exceeds the recoverable value is charged against the collateral value. The banks' ability to collect default loans through loan sales judges the banks' strength and ability to deal with the situation. [34] Additionally, a non-accrual loan is returned to accrual status after the borrowers' conditions improve. However, the creditors' losses were recognised early, avoiding a mismatch in the loan portfolio.

On the other hand, the Insolvency Code 2012 by Germany, namely 'protective shield proceedings' available for debtors in imminent insolvency, not in actual illiquidity, provides scope for the debtors to prepare pre-packed restructuring plans during the opening stage, and the court evaluates its feasibility. Before the formal commencement of insolvency proceedings, the debtor's plan is ready for evaluation.[57] The judge may allow the debtors to make administrative claims for a subsequent formal insolvency proceeding. However, the German insolvency code controlled the NPLs in the country to a considerable level.

1.7.3 High Impact

The third hierarchy of jurisdictions represents nine countries, six from the EU Member States, India, and Russia. The NPL trends in these countries fluctuated highly. For instance, in Portugal, it varies from 3.11% to 16.74% and in India, from 2.45% to 9.98%. The highest fluctuation recorded in Lithuania ranged from 0.51%

[55] Krolik et al. (2022).

[56] Federal Reserve Bank of New York (2013).

[57] Halladay and Jark (2012).

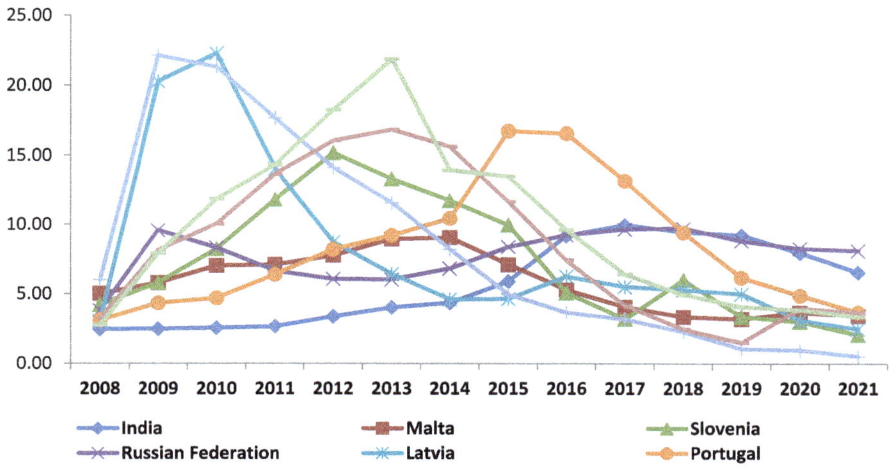

Fig. 1.4 Trend of NPLs in the Jurisdictions with High NPLs (2008–2021). Source: Developed by the researcher using data from World Development Indicators, World Bank

to 23.3%, having an undulating trend. Similarly, it fluctuated from 2.06% to 15.3% in Slovenia, and in Hungary, it ranged from 1.5% to 16.8%. Lithuania was the only country with a consistently decreasing trend over the last 14 years, except in 2012 (Fig. 1.4).

In Spain, the Out of Court Agreement on Payments (OCAP) was enacted in 2012 to resolve the financial crisis of small businesses with the help of professional mediators. In 2014, a decree later codified as the law allowed the companies to reach a pre-insolvency agreement with the creditors without clawback provisions.[58] There was a provision for collective refinancing arrangements with judicial approval for strengthening and protecting debt with write-offs and debt-to-equity swaps.

The decree introduced several arrangements in 2014 and 2015, which changed the legal framework. These amendments facilitated the business restricting both in and out of court settlements. New provisions included no limits to writing down loans, rescheduling loan recovery up to 10 years, dividing creditors into four classes based on socio-economic criteria, and the majority (50% or 65%) of creditors required to approve the restructuring plan.[58] Similarly, OCAP's write-off and write-down limits extended beyond 25% with 3 years of a moratorium and the commercial registry requirement.

In Lithuania, a law on restructuring companies in financial difficulty was enacted in 2012, dealing with liabilities and the discharge of liabilities. It also has a provision for restructuring administrators for the management of the company and its assets termination, which leads to the closure of its plan.[59] On the other hand, Latvia provided out-of-court restructuring guidelines with global principles of multi-credit

[58] Perera (2015), p. 649.

[59] Kirsiene and Miseviciute (2016), p. 171.

workouts. The legal protection proceedings enacted in 2010 enable the rehabilitation of viable firms. It has two essential clauses, including expedited court approval procedures and court procedures for developing a rehabilitation plan after filing a petition. The rehabilitation plan lasts 2 years, with a further extension of another 2 years. It also requires approval from two-thirds of the secured and most unsecured creditors. There was an amendment in the insolvency law in 2015 that has a provision for the management board of a company to file for insolvency if the company has not settled its debt for over 2 months.

Despite issuing guidelines for extrajudicial recovery on consensus aligned with INSOL[60] principles, Portugal's improvement plan was not encouraging. Therefore, it uses a debt restructuring tool with special recovery procedures and a fast-track court introduced in 2012 to achieve a restructuring plan. It provided relaxation of the mandatory creditors' meeting to facilitate the debtors and to meet the objective of the debt restructuring plan. In 2015, it lowered the creditors' majority required for approval of the restructuring plan. It also enhanced the priority of providing new money to the debtors and enforcement actions for the debtor's guarantors without much success. The out-of-court settlement was introduced for SMEs through mediation by developing a System for the Recovery of Undertakings. It was further amended in 2015 to improve the validity of the diagnosis; nevertheless, NPLs remained very high.

Romania introduced corporate debt restructuring (CDR) guidelines in 2010 and insolvency law in 2014,[61] but the NPLs increased to 21.87% in 2013, came down to 3.35% in 2021, and the average remained at 9.76%. The impact of reform was visible, but the pace was relatively low and slow. The insolvency law limited the observation period and introduced coordinating procedures for group companies and, more importantly, interim measures to safeguard debtors' assets and private sector tests and strengthen the protection of post-commencement financing.

1.7.4 Very High Impact

On the other hand, in six jurisdictions, GFC had a very high impact on NPLs, with the average NPLs during the last 14 years ranging from 11.44% (Croatia) to 23.44%(Greece) (Table 1.1 and Fig. 1.5). The average NPLs in Italy was 11.30%, with the highest at 18.1% in 2015. A consistently high NPLs ratio prompted Italy to initiate reforms from 2009 to 2015 with a new Corporate Crisis Code (Legislative Decree) in 2019. The court approves the restructuring agreement provided it has an expert opinion on its feasibility and receives 60% of the creditors' claims.[62] It also

[60] INSOL International is a worldwide federation of national associations of accountants and lawyers who specialise in insolvency, and it presently has over 44 member associations.

[61] Voica (2019), pp. 191–192.

[62] Bertone (2019), p. 108.

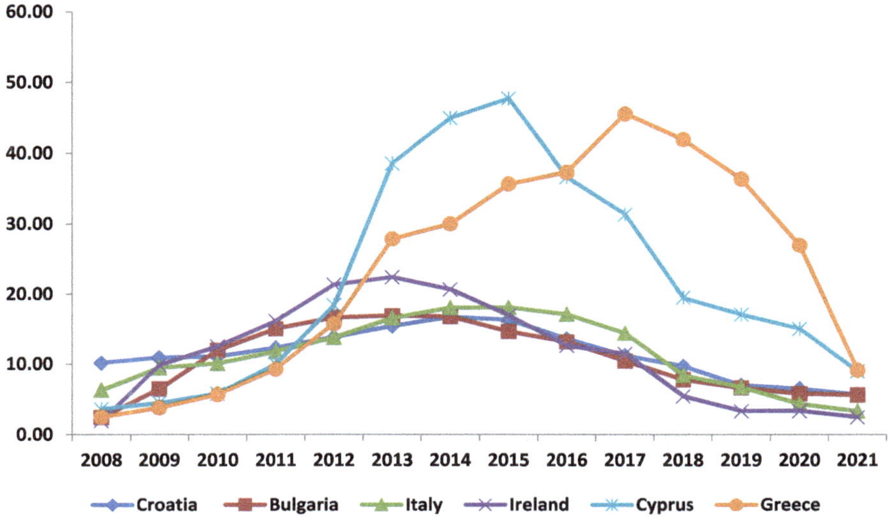

Fig. 1.5 Trend of NPLs in the Jurisdictions with very High NPLs (2008–2021). Source: Developed by the researcher using data from World Development Indicators, World Bank

has a provision for a rescue plan in case the company has temporary illiquidity. It is possible to reach an agreement with financial creditors(FCs) if the company has more than 50% of its outstanding. Italy has introduced many restructuring and reorganisation mechanisms, which have improved the NPLs ratio.[63]

In Ireland, the average NPLs for the last 14 years was 11.45%, ranging from 2.48% to 25.7%, and started receding from 2016 onwards. As a result, Ireland enacted the new Personal Insolvency Act 2012, providing debt settlement and personal insolvency arrangements.[64] As per the provision, the creditors' enforcement actions could be 70 days with the extendable condition of relieving the debtors. Cyprus and Greece are the most vulnerable jurisdictions, with relatively more fluctuation in the NPL ratios. It fluctuated from 3.59% to 47.8% in Cyprus and Greece from 2.47% to 45.6%, with average NPLs of 21.59% and 23.47%, respectively, for the last 14 years.

Cyprus amended its bankruptcy law in 2015, introducing new procedures with personal payment schemes for secured and unsecured debt[65] where a stable source of income is possible. The required majority of creditors approved the re-payment schemes, and it became binding upon confirmation by the court. However, a 90-day stay is provided to the debtors to prepare a re-payment scheme with the assistance of the insolvency practitioners. Despite all these provisions, the NPL scenario has

[63] Barkbu et al. (2013), pp. 22–26.

[64] Higgins (2016), pp. 22–23.

[65] Stamatiou (2016), p. 16.

not improved in the country, and it remains very high and warrants suitable regulatory and policy interventions.

Greece introduced a law on insolvency in 2010 with an amendment in 2012 and 2015 with three provisions: a voluntary mediation process, a re-payment plan, and judicial settlement with the provision for a stay petition for the enforcement of action.[66] The conflicts on the interpretation of law have realised that both courts and practitioners need to improve their know-how and expertise. The insolvency system must be conducive for the institutions responsible for its implementation; however, the situation remained highly alarming. The jurisdiction should reassess its policy and regulatory responses to make them more robust in controlling the problem so that NPLs are manageable. In Croatia and Bulgaria, NPLs increased from 7% and 6.6% to 16.7%; the average also remained around 13%. The slow impact of reforms delayed the downward trend from 2014 onwards. These jurisdictions need to look at their policy and regulatory options more critically to ensure that the NPLs ratio remains within manageable limits.

The analysis of non-performing loans (NPLs) across these jurisdictions highlights the trends and the effectiveness of their responses in addressing the issue. However, the outcomes were mixed—while some jurisdictions successfully managed NPL levels, others experienced prolonged challenges, underscoring the need to further examine policy, regulatory, and supervisory measures. A more detailed discussion of the UK, India, and Ireland in the following chapters will provide deeper insights into the diverse approaches taken by these jurisdictions.

1.8 Determinants of Non-Performing Loans

The preceding section analysed the trend of NPLs across various jurisdictions covering the EU Member States, the UK, India, Russia, etc., and their insolvency and bankruptcy regimes. This section aims to identify macroeconomic and microeconomic determinants, referred to as economic and non-economic factors and their impact on NPLs.[67] The economic determinants discussed include GDP, inflation, unemployment, exchange rate, etc.; non-economic determinants refer to bank size, bank efficiency, income diversification, bank management, etc.

These determinants may have a positive and a negative impact on NPLs and vice versa. For instance, an increase in the GDP may decrease the NPLs level, whereas, with an increase in the unemployment rate, NPLs will also increase.[68] The borrowers' cash flow is also closely associated with the demand for the products, and due to a decrease in cash flow, the demand for the products remains weak. [68] Less

[66] Paulus et al. (2015), p. 27.

[67] Boldeanu and Constantinescu (2015), p. 329.

[68] Bayar (2018), p. 95.

production in the corporate sector reduces employment; hence, individual borrowers' repayment capacity substantially declines.

The reduction in GDP adversely influences real estate, resulting in decreased housing sector prices. Another equally important factor in determining the NPLs ratios is the bank failure and financial crisis in developed and developing countries regarding their solvency.[69] The banks have given substantial importance to regulatory authorities to be more concerned about financial stability.

Several studies covering jurisdictions and banks worldwide have assessed the impact of economic and non-economic determinants on NPLs. It is imperative to analyse the findings of such studies to point out essential determinants relevant to our analysis and act as a framework for policymakers and bankers. The jurisdictions with high NPLs may deal with such determinants effectively to control NPLs. The main reason for loan loss in 2470 commercial banks in the USA during 1979–85[70] was the deteriorating economic condition and poor performance in certain sectors of the economy. Additionally, microeconomic and macroeconomic factors such as high interest rates, excessive lending and volatile funds, and depressed regional economic conditions contributed to the high loan losses in the large commercial banks in the USA from 1984 to 1987.[71]

The credit growth and loan delinquencies significantly contributed to loan losses. The rapid credit growth, which was associated with lower credit standards, contributed to higher loan losses.[72] Thus, there is evidence of a strong relationship between credit growth and impaired assets. Similarly, the lending policy[73] and credit terms[74] are important determinants of NPLs. The bank lending policy without adequately assessing the debtors' strengths before giving a loan is also responsible for the loan losses. [74] Therefore, appropriate policy interventions are required to deal with the problem of NPLs effectively.

The risks of banks increase with poor bank management, low creditworthiness, inadequate collateral assessment, and lack of monitoring. Moreover, underwriting and postponing costs for the future, inadequately capitalised banks,[10] and government economic and social commitments,[10] particularly in developing countries, influence banks' decisions to grant loans in the projects/schemes, and such biased lending also becomes a default.[75] Thus, banks' lending policies and credit terms provided by banks have been important determinants of NPA.[75] Similarly, real GDP growth, rapid credit expansion, bank size, capital ratio, market power, terms of credit, induced risk preferences, macroeconomic shocks,[76] and inflation impact

[69] Marco (2004), p. 165.

[70] Keeton and Morris (1987), p. 3.

[71] Sinkey and Greenawalt (1991), p. 43.

[72] Keeton (1999), p. 3–4.

[73] McGovern (1993), p. 44.

[74] Meacci (1996), pp. 69–70.

[75] Lu et al. (2001).

[76] Ahmed (2006).

NPLs significantly. In addition, the Treasury bill[77] is also an important determinant for explaining the variation in NPLs.

Higher government ownership structure[78] in commercial banks, recorded lower NPLs, and stricter supervision[79] appears to reduce impaired loans. On the other hand, quality management[80] also plays a crucial role in determining the level of NPLs. Also, the bank-specific variables, such as growth in total loans and relative market share, seem to have explanatory power over NPLs. In addition, other equally important factors strongly correlated with NPLs comprise the loans-to-deposits ratio, ROA, ROE, and CAR.

A hierarchical model of the determinants of NPLs applying ISM and TISM was used in the Indian context to identify the drivers and dependents of NPLs. Ten major determinants and drivers influencing NPLs are political factors, environmental conditions, ownership patterns, economic factors, socio- cultural factors related to respective banks, technological factors, factors confronting borrowers, legal aspects, and adherence to the regulatory framework.[81] These factors are further divided into autonomous, linkages, dependent and independent drivers and determinants to construct a relationship with the broader economic and political environment.

The analysis of bank-related and macroeconomic factors in the pre-crisis and post-crisis situations was constructed using a model[50] to establish a relationship. It was concluded that macroeconomic variables significantly impact NPLs more than banking sector-specific variables. Thus, GDP, growth and inflation for emerging nations, GDP growth, and employment for advanced jurisdictions were statistically significant in the pre-crisis period. In the post-crisis period, GDP, growth, current account, exchange rate, and FDI impacted NPLs in emerging countries and GDP, growth, and inflation in advanced countries.

Loans are generally the most sizeable item in a bank's assets and carry the potential threat to its capital account. The loan quality determines the credit risk, ultimately influencing the bank's profitability.[82] The banks decide to lend to a qualified borrower after due consideration. Loan recovery is not within a bank's control as it depends on the debtor's capacity to repay. If the repaying capacity is weak, it reflects on the asset quality, and poor asset quality is a major contributing factor to the rise in NPL ratios. There are several examples where banks suffer losses due to poor asset quality.[83] For instance, the collapse of Ireland's real estate, labour, and mortgage markets from 2007 onwards was among the most callous international experiences concerning the recent crisis of high NPLs. The Hypo-Alpe-Adria-bank in

[77] Greenidge and Grosvenor (2010), p. 80.

[78] Hu and Chiu (2004).

[79] Boudriga et al. (2009), p. 28.

[80] Louzis et al. (2012), p.1012.

[81] Rizvi et al. (2019), p. 3834.

[82] Athanasoglou, et al. (2006), p. 121.

[83] Financial Times (July 12 2004).

Italy struggled to recover from a long history of poor asset quality and widespread fraudulent lending.

On the other hand, African banks recorded some of the world's highest NPLs ratios, which were in line with a business model based around unsecured retail lending at high interest rates, and the bank gained 48% growth.[84] Although this strategy appeared to hit the buffers in 2003, the returns on capital subsequently collapsed and recorded a loss of more than 55%. Petro-commerce banks lost over half of their capital in Russia due to relatively highly concentrated corporate loan portfolios. Postal Savings Bank in China, Shanking Central Bank in Japan, and WGZ in Germany tend to hold government bonds or other state-guaranteed assets, reducing risk-based capital and inviting risk for them. Canadian Commercial Bank in Canada, Banco and Espanol de Credito in Spain and Credit Lyonnais in France are some examples of bad asset quality. Poor asset quality reduces credit growth and worsens loan quality,[85] which could stem from lower economic growth, poor exchange rate, depreciation, weaker terms of trade and a fall in debt-creating capital inflows. Poor asset quality negatively impacts profitability when measured as LLP over total loans as a proxy for credit risk.

Capital adequacy, the ratio of equity to an asset, is also an important factor impacting NPLs[86] and the chances of insolvency are less if the ratio of liquidity over assets is higher. A study concerning 55 American bank holding companies and 10 Canadian banks from 1997 to 2009 concluded that liquidity is closely associated with profitability. The authors have argued that liquid assets within certain limits would likely improve the bank's profitability. However, beyond a threshold point, the performance and profitability of the bank will reduce significantly. Therefore, the impact of liquidity on a bank's profitability could also be vague. The high cost of holding liquidity may result in bank failures since liquidity increases operating costs and erodes profits.[87]

In contrast, a study on bank-related determinants in the Indian banking sector concludes that there are chances of generating higher returns by lending.[88] The authors argued that liquidity and bank size have a statistically significant impact on the profitability of Indian banks. On the other hand, in Portuguese, banks with a higher share of operational costs to total income are less profitable. They tend to suffer more during crisis periods than more diversified banks.[89] Thus, liquidity plays a crucial role in deciding the level of NPLs, and highly liquid banks tend to have low NPLs ratios.

Another vital activity contributing to the banks' income includes lending, income from interest and non-interest activities, such as trading and derivative transactions. Interest share is also an important determinant that influences the performance of

---

[84] Bock and Demyanets (2012).

[85] Garcia and Guerreiro (2016), p. 80.

[86] Kosmidou (2008), p. 146.

[87] Allen and Carletti (2010), p 1.

[88] Sufian et al. (2012) pp. 1–3.

[89] Garcia and Guerreiro (2016).

banks. A study conducted on the banking sectors in Switzerland[8] reveals that the share of interest income significantly impacts banks' profitability, and banks that are dependent on interest income are not profitable. Further, research suggested[90] that income diversification (ID) is essential, and there was a significantly positive relationship between NIM and non-interest income. The risk-adjusted returns on assets and non-interest income also establish the same connection to reduce NPLs.

Banking management has also been considered an important factor for bank failure and the rise in NPLs, such as the banks' operating inefficiency. The reduction in costs of non-productive components can result in higher profits. Efficient banks are more profitable than non-efficient ones.[8] The impact of GFC 2007–2009 on the profitability of commercial banks in Switzerland concludes that the main determinants of a bank's profitability were operational efficiency, the growth of total loans, funding costs, interest income share and the LLP. There was a significant increase in NPLs during the GFC, which also affected banks' profitability. Similar findings[9] concerning commercial banks in the United Kingdom, concluded that decreased cost efficiency would impact loan defaults. Those managers who could not control operating expenses and their loan portfolio management suffered the most. The relationship between operating efficiency, capitalisation and NPLs in commercial banks indicates that operating efficiency increases NPLs.[91]

Thus, the analysis of macroeconomic and bank-related determinants through various empirical investigations envisaged that these determinants play a significant role in determining the level of NPLs across jurisdictions. Therefore, jurisdictions with high NPLs ratios should also consider these factors while initiating supervisory and policy measures to control NPLs. Moreover, in-depth analysis and critical evaluation of these factors are essential to suitably design interventions at the regulatory and policy front for dealing with the problem of NPLs and bringing it down to a manageable level.

1.9 Basel Committee on Banking Supervision

This section examines the guidelines of the Basel Committee on Banking Supervision and Regulation.[92] Basel has issued a series of international standards on banking regulation since its establishment in 1975. The most landmark publications on capital adequacy are Basel I, Basel II, and, most recently, Basel III. The BCBS provided core principles for adequate banking supervision in 1997 to set a minimum standard. These principles were considered international best practices and described

---

[90] Nguyen (2012), p. 2429.

[91] Benthem (2017).

[92] G10 countries comprise of representatives of central bank and banking regulators from Belgium, Canada, France, Germany, Italy, Japan, Luxembourg, the Netherlands, Spain, Sweden, the United Kingdom, and the United States of America.

as 'soft law par excellence'.[93] The essential pre-conditions for effective banking supervision include operational independence, adequate resources, a suitable legal framework, powers to address compliance with laws, legal protection for supervisors, sharing information with supervisors, protecting the confidentiality of such information and international banking operations.[94]

It has strong provisions and guidelines for licensing, which envisages that the permissible activities of licensed institutions are subject to supervision. The licensing authority must have the right to set criteria and reject applications that do not meet the required standard. The supervisor can review and reject proposals to transfer ownership, control, and authority. It also establishes criteria for reviewing acquisitions or investments, ensuring corporate affiliations do not expose the banks to undue risks.[94]

Under prudential regulations and requirements, banking supervisors must set prudent, appropriate minimum capital adequacy requirements. Such provisions should reflect the risks that the banks are likely to undertake. It must define the capital components, considering their ability to absorb losses. Supervisors must ensure banks have adequate policies and procedures for identifying, monitoring, and controlling risk.[94] The supervisor should also ensure that the banks have a comprehensive risk management process with internal control, including strict 'know-your-customer' (KYC) rules. It promotes high ethical and professional standards in the financial sector and prevents the bank from intentionally or unintentionally using criminal elements.

There should be provision for on-site and off-site supervision and regular contact with bank management to understand how the institution operates. Such a move will facilitate collecting information, reviewing, and analysing the banks' prudential reports and statistical returns. These efforts need the independent validation of supervisory information and the ability of the supervisors to supervise the banking group on a consolidated basis. Moreover, the supervisors must be satisfied that each bank maintains adequate records drawn up by consistent accounting policies and practices that enable the supervisor to obtain an accurate and fair view of the financial condition. Its business profitability, which is regularly published, reflects fine financial conditions.[94]

The supervisors must have adequate supervisory measures to take timely corrective action when banks fail to meet prudential requirements. Such requirements include a minimum CAR when there are regulatory violations. Lastly, the banks must practise consolidated global supervision over their internationally active banking organisations in cross-border banking. The adequate monitoring and application of appropriate prudential norms to all aspects of the business conducted by these banking organisations worldwide, primarily at their foreign branches, joint ventures, and subsidiaries, is also essential. A supervisor should also establish contact and exchange information with the other supervisors to avoid possible financial crises.[94]

---

[93] Cransto (2020), p. 64.

[94] Bank of International Settlement (1997).

Despite developing comprehensive guidelines for banking supervision, the Basel guidelines failed to achieve consensus on the definition. It has placed an overemphasis on individual institutions that were reluctant to deal with crisis resolution schemes and policies on sanctions, and lacks empirical evidence. It also failed to develop an early-warning system for distressed banks[95] so the countries could use their standard as per their circumstances.[96] The lack of a strong regulatory and supervisory ecosystem may harm the entire banking system, raise systemic risk, and increase moral hazard.[97] However, despite the criticism, the World Bank recognised the Basel core banking principles, and the IMF made its acceptability across the member jurisdictions for the Financial Sector Assessment Programme (FSAP) to strengthen the assessment and monitoring of the financial system.[98]

The Basel guidelines emphasised that the supervisors should be satisfied with the credit risk management process and identify measures to monitor and control credit risk with prudent policies and procedures. It further envisaged that a proper evaluation of loans and investment portfolios is necessary before granting a loan and making an investment.[99] The core principles also guide several matters related to lending and risk reduction policies. The original framework established many parameters, including management oversight, control culture, risk recognition and assessment, control activities, segregation of duties, information and communication, monitoring activities and correcting deficiencies.[99] Similarly, guidelines provided in 2006 have ten principles that fall into two broad categories, including supervisory expectations concerning sound credit risk assessment for loans and supervisory evaluation of credit risk assessment for loan control and capital adequacy.[96]

Basel III further strengthened Basel II guidelines on banking supervision and regulation. The poor management of liquidity, poor governance and credit risk management, and inappropriate incentives resulted in liquidity risk and unprecedented credit growth due to mispricing. Basel II responded to these risk factors and suggested sound liquidity risk management and supervision principles. It also offered a capital framework for treating certain complex securitisation positions, off-balance-sheet vehicles, and trading book exposures to strengthen them. The main motive of the Basel Committee was to improve the regulation and supervision of internationally active banks. The higher minimum capital standards for commercial banks were announced in 2010, followed by capital liquidity reform known as Basel III.[100]

Two crucial Basel guidelines focused on the international framework for liquidity risk management, standards and monitoring, and a global regulatory framework for more resilient banks and banking systems in a phased manner. The purpose was to focus on more essential requirements, such as the quality and quantity of

[95] Wendschlag (2013), p. 203.

[96] Campbell and Cartwright (2002).

[97] Hupkes (2000), p.89.

[98] Gianviti (2005), p. 217.

[99] Bank of International Settlement (2006), pp. 3–6.

[100] Bank of International Settlement (2017b).

regulatory capital and the capital conservation buffer (CCB), to meet the minimum common equity requirement and reduce banks' losses in credit busts. A leverage ratio—a minimum amount of loss-absorbing capital, a minimum liquidity ratio, the Liquidity Coverage Ratio (LCR), and the Net Stable Funding Ratio (NSFR) to address maturity mismatches over the entire balance sheet is considered vital for cross-border supervision and resolution.[100]

The main objective of the revised reforms was to reduce the excessive variability of risk-weighted assets.[101] The empirical analysis revealed a worrying degree of variability in calculating the RWA across jurisdictions at the peak of the GFC. As a result, many stakeholders lost faith in banks' reported risk-weighted capital ratios. The flaws noticed in the RWA modalities suggested revising the regulatory framework to restore credibility in RWA calculation by enhancing the robustness and risk sensitivity. The standardised credit and operational risk approaches constrain internally prescribed processes and complement the risk-based framework with a revised leverage ratio.[100]

To follow the supervisor's guidelines, banks keep some percentage of their assets in cash as a Cash Reserve Ratio (CRR), and the proportion of such ratio varies considerably across jurisdictions. However, the recent Basel guidelines suggest it should not exceed 4.5% of banks' total assets. Moreover, it is the depositors' entitlement to receive the repayments of their deposit; such deposits are a liability on the bank's balance sheet as they are liquid and can be claimed at any time. On the other hand, most commercial and savings banks' asset quality depends on loan portfolios, depending on terms and conditions. Depending on the portfolios' nature and size, the deposits spread from less than 5 years to more than 25 years, and all such portfolios are illiquid and restrict the bank's business.[32]

If the bank problem is related to liquidity, regulatory compliance usually restores it in the short run. However, if the banks' portfolios are doubtful, the supervisor decides on immediate corrective measures to improve the portfolio. In insolvency, the supervisor or the Central Bank should help the banks improve the situation by selling the portfolios to minimise the impact of insolvency and quickly closing the bank to minimise its effect on the financial system.[102]

The Basel guidelines have covered many supervisory issues a country needs to implement to strengthen its banking system and counter the banks' systemic failure. However, the jurisdictions' divergent approaches dilute the international best practices for dealing with the NPLs. The guidelines issued in 2017 suggest constantly monitoring the banking system to identify risk at the forbearance level and accordingly make suitable treatments for NPLs to avoid insolvency. Thus, implementing Basel guidelines for supervisory and regulatory treatment is essential to address the problem of NPLs.

[101] RWA is the minimum amount of capital that must be held by the banks and other financial institutions to reduce the risk of insolvency.

[102] Adrian and Song (2010), p. 418.

1.10 Non-Performing Loans and Policy Response

Jurisdictions worldwide encounter many impediments that play a detrimental role in resolving the problem of NPLs. Recent studies conducted by the IMF grouped these obstacles into five categories: 'supervisory framework, the legal framework, distressed debt markets, informational shortcomings and the tax regime'.[32] Among the five barriers identified by the IMF, the legal framework and the underdeveloped distressed debt markets have low scores. They are the most challenging obstacles because they are interlinked, and difficulties in one area compound in other areas. Thus, the countries with relatively high obstacle scores in one area also tend to have relatively high scores in another.[100]

European Central Bank[51] recommended that the banks assess their internal capabilities, such as 'strength, gap and area of improvement' and external factors like macroeconomic conditions, market exceptions, investors' demand, and regulatory framework to deal with high NPLs ratios. Furthermore, banks with high NPLs must arrange buffer capital to clean up existing NPLs. In this context, the ECB came out with harmonised strategies dealing with impaired assets, such as creating an 'assessment and operating environment, developing the NPLs strategy, implementing the operational plan, embedding the NPLs strategy and supervisory reporting'. All these steps are closely interlinked, and these distinct aspects are essential to bringing NPLs to a manageable level, but more efforts are required to treat insolvent banks.

Early detection of banks having NPLs is essential because the liquidity problem does not appear at this stage. The banks and the depositors can also not foresee such a situation where NPLs are likely to crop up because such a situation lacks confidence in the banking system.[31] Once the banks start accruing interest on the NPLs, the portfolios of the bad [31] loans deteriorate significantly, and the problem magnifies,[103] which is a warning sign. There are instances where the Central Bank in Ireland, Spain, India, etc., comes up with a bailout plan as a temporary treatment. It is an 'off-balance-sheet strategy' that removed the NPLs portfolio from the balance sheet by transferring the loans' legal ownership to the external entities, which was a quick relief.[104] On the other hand, the on-balance sheet strategies pursue the gradual recovery process over the medium and long term through 'restructuring, forbearance, liquidation and foreclosure' activities.[104]

Effectively managing impaired assets is essential and would achieve greater value in the long run than the immediate sale. Different valuation methods adopted by potential investors and banks lead to 'uncertainty associated with information asymmetries about the quality of credits for sale'. Therefore, the balance sheet approach is better for dealing with impaired loans. Suppose there is no realistic chance of recovering the loan; under such circumstances, the cost and time for recovery are very high. Therefore, in such a case, the banks should also dispose of

[103] Banks for International Settlements (1999).

[104] Fell et al. (2017), p. 71.

the loan immediately. However, it would not be easy for the banks to sell it off on priority due to the non-availability of potential buyers for impaired assets and the lack of an appropriate methodology to assess the actual value.

There are two types of NPLs policy measures, including country-specific and bank-specific. Important bank-specific measures are on-balance sheet guarantee, internal structuring unit, off-balance sheet special purpose exposure (SPE) and bad bank spinoff. Similarly, country-specific policy measures are debt restructuring-out-of-court workouts (OCWs), write-offs, direct sales, securitisation, APS and AMCs, M&A and PAT. The following paragraphs briefly examine these policy options and their effectiveness in controlling NPLs.

AMCs, as an assets management tool, were widely used during the banking crisis to control NPLs; therefore, after the saving and Loan (S&L) crisis, the USA established Resolution Trust Corporation (RTC) in the early 1990s to deal with NPLs. Sweden established Securum, and again, during the Asian crisis, Danaharta in Malaysia and KAMCO in the Republic of Korea came into existence.[105] The GFC 2008 marked the renewal of the use of this tool to support the resolution of the financial crisis. As a result, NAMA in Ireland, UKAR in the UK, and SAREB in Spain were established and intended to either resolve insolvent FIs and their assets or purchase assets from open banks. Most successful AMCs had a narrow mandate of focusing on asset management, restructuring, and disposition. However, there are examples such as Danaharta, which managed the assets of failed banks. The government, banks and private investors established AMCs to acquire loans, other assets, and their subsequent management. Thus, the important role of AMCs is to purchase assets, manage them effectively and finally, dispose of the impaired loans of one or more banks.[106]

AMCs are like vehicles sponsored by the government to pool distressed assets for sale acquired from the banks to maximise profits and provide clean banks to potential buyers.[107] The AMC may benefit from economies of scale due to enhanced synergies and coordination in handling the troubled loans with a multi-origin[108] and developing its expertise in this field. It is also essential that the disposal of assets can be spread over time to affect sales negatively.[109] The use of this tool to buy impaired loans has become popular because many countries used this tool effectively to resolve impaired loans despite lacking expertise and efficacy to maximise the value of the impaired loan.

Thus, AMCs have mixed track records of success as they have resource problems and government control. In addition, they are overly bureaucratic and lack the legal power to control impaired loans effectively. The borrowers take advantage of the absence of legal power and avoid repayment, knowing that no legal action is against

[105] Bank for International Settlement (2002), pp. 1–3.

[106] Cerruti and Cerruti (2016), pp. 1–2.

[107] Klingebiel (2002).

[108] Woo (2000).

[109] Cas and Peresa (2016), p. 148.

them. Similarly, political interference in the case of state-owned enterprises is another problem which AMCs usually face. Nevertheless, despite being costly, AMCs are effective tools for dealing with distressed assets.[110] In addition, private AMCs have played a significant role in purchasing assets from public AMCs and introducing proper workout practices into the local market. AMCs will be successful if they promptly repay all their liabilities and some initial equity.

Different approaches applied by AMCs to deal with impaired assets, such as RTC, KAMCO, and NAMA, focus on political consensus. Securum and Danaharta have developed comprehensive and coordinated reform programmes to strengthen financial sector regulation, supervision, risk management, workout practices within the banks, corporate restructuring, and legal and regulatory reforms to remove restructuring impediments. On the other hand, SAREB created a solid diagnostic and a critical mass of impaired assets. Similarly, Danaharta determined the threshold of eligible loans to remove a significant portion of NPLs in the banking system. Sweden has a history of responsible ownership of state-owned enterprises. KAMCO also broadened its mandate on acquiring and resolving NPLs as granted by a dedicated law. On the other hand, Securum and Danaharta have a narrow mandate with the necessary powers to accomplish tasks.

Along with strong regulation, extraordinary power will be required for AMCs to resolve the NPLs problem if it is not in the existing legal framework. It is also essential that AMCs are resolution authorities and need certainty while purchasing impaired assets. Moreover, the court should not mediate and decide the matters of AMCs. Thus, managing distressed assets with the intervention of AMCs may fetch a positive result, and countries with high NPLs should consider this option and other options.

On the other hand, there is debate on "leaning" versus "cleaning", that is, whether it is less costly for a Central Bank to take measures that prevent a financial crisis or, instead, to respond by cleaning up after a crisis has materialised.[111] There are two approaches to dealing with impaired loans: firstly, the supervisor should liquidate and restructure the bank if the problem is manageable, and secondly, the insolvent bank should be closed to minimise its impact.[31]

If a bank falls into insolvency, it is inevitable for the supervisor to take the necessary action as quickly as possible to minimise its impact. However, the supervisors must assess the bank's systemic importance and impact on depositors and deposit issuance funds and appoint a conservator to control the bank. Moreover, in some countries, the judicial process is different and is done under administrative action, while in others, judicial decisions are required, irrespective of the action. Thus, the response should be immediate so that the problem does not percolate to the rest of the financial system.[112]

---

[110] Bacon (2009).

[111] White (2009), p. 14.

[112] Bean et al. (2010).

If the insolvent bank is ineffective, another equally important restructuring plan that the supervisor may consider is mergers and acquisitions. If no alternative to liquidation is available, the supervisor will close the bank until the bank returns to public fund injection compliance. However, in place of public fund injection, the option of mergers and acquisitions would be better, and this will require a change in the mindset of many countries to promote private sector solutions. The apprehension regarding mergers and acquisitions, particularly in a developing country, is due to the non-availability of domestic banks due to a lack of funds for acquiring insolvent banks. In addition, regulatory and policy issues will arise if a foreign bank acquires a domestic one. However, the major advantage of this process is that the insolvent bank's legal entity will cease, and it will minimise market disruption.

Another equally important policy response is a purchase and assumption transaction, provided the same provision exists in the jurisdictions' law. Since finding a willing party for mergers and acquisitions is difficult, the Federal Deposit Insurance Corporation (FDIC) of the United States has designed a purchase and assumption[113] transaction. A financially healthy bank will buy the insolvent bank's assets partially or entirely, provided the assets of the insolvent are excluded from the sale. Assets and liabilities are mostly transferred in purchase and assumption transactions, whereas corporate bodies and licences are acquired in mergers and acquisitions, and the former is considered a better tool for dealing with insolvent banks.

The measures covered in this section are significant in dealing with the problem of NPLs, and the supervisor's role also becomes important in providing guidelines to the banks to control the level of NPLs. In addition, some jurisdictions had also used APS, where the Government pumped in funds to salvage the banks whose financial conditions deteriorated during the financial crisis. Similarly, jurisdictions also used the securitisation process by converting bad debts into security and selling them into the open market to maximise the recovery of distressed assets besides out-of-court workouts, where the court's involvement is minimal. Hence, in the respective chapter, the present book will analyse all policy prescriptions used by the UK, India and Ireland to control NPLs.

1.11 Regulatory Treatment

This section briefly outlines the regulatory responses undertaken by the UK, India, and Ireland to deal with the problem of NPLs. As a part of the EU, the UK and Ireland transposed the EU regulations and directives into their domestic law. After Brexit, such bindings do not apply to the UK. The EU has made several efforts to provide legal grounds for NPLs. The EU Directive 2014/59/EU establishes a

[113] Federal Deposits Insurance Corporation (1984).

framework for recovering and resolving credit institutions and investment firms.[114] EU Regulation (EU) 806/2014 establishes uniform rules and procedures for resolving the issues of credit institutions, besides enacting legislation dealing with loan restructuring and resolution to make the law more practical. The effectiveness of such regulations, directives, and domestic law requires critical examination.

The Irish banking system experienced a systemic crisis; as a result, NPLs reached the highest level (32%) in 2013 in the Euro area, despite Central Bank efforts to ensure financial stability and prudential and consumer protection responsibilities. The Code of Conduct on Mortgage Arrears (CCMA) was introduced in 2009 and subsequently strengthened and revised to control NPLs.[115] In Ireland, three major areas with high NPLs were the residential mortgage market, small and medium-sized enterprises (SME), and CRE projects. The excessive lending in these sectors increased NPLs, collapsing the real estate, labour, and mortgage markets. Consequently, the unemployment rate reached 15.1% in 2013, deteriorating the macroeconomic situation. The Government established NAMA, an AMC, in 2009 and transferred NPLs to NAMA from Irish Banks' balance sheets, but the problem of NPLs remained alarming.

The Irish government established the Insolvency Service of Ireland (ISI) and the Personal Insolvency Agreement (PIA) to control NPLs, besides the Mortgage Arrears Resolution Targets (MART). All these efforts improved NPLs and helped to address the problem of NPLs from late 2013 onwards. Central Bank also took several other measures to control NPLs, including the launch of the Financial Measures Programme (FMP), Assessment of Independent Loan Loss Forecast, Prudential Liquidity Assessment (PLA), Prudential Capital Assessment Review (PCAR) and Distressed Credit Operations Review (DCOR).[116] Despite all these efforts, the situation in Ireland remained grim for an extended period and started improving from 2018 onwards.

On the other hand, the UK has a robust regulatory system that regulates the banking market through the HM Treasury, the PRA, and the FCA. The Financial Policy Committee (FPC) is vigilant in identifying, monitoring, and taking decisive action to reduce systemic banking risk and protect and enhance the UK financial system's resilience. In addition, PRA and FCA enjoy power through the Financial Services and Markets Act 2000 (FSMA). The UK has prepared a list of regulated activities and regularly updates it to ensure that firms undertake financial activities within the boundaries of existing law. It is a criminal offence in the UK to engage in "regulated activities" through a business unless authorised or exempted.[117] Besides protecting consumers' interests and promoting effective competition among FIs in a regulated

---

[114] Council Regulation (EC) No 806/2014/EU of 15 July 2014 establishing uniform rules and a uniform procedure for the resolution of credit institutions and certain investment firms in the framework of a single resolution mechanism and a single resolution fund and amending regulation (EU) No 1093/2010 [2014] OJ L 225/1.

[115] Donnery et al. (2018), p. 54.

[116] Robert and Malley (2016), pp. 22–23.

[117] Lovegrove and Bainbridge (2019).

market, the PRA and FCA protect and secure the UK financial system and its integrity.

The Markets in Financial Instruments Directive (MiFID II) and Markets in Financial Instruments Regulation (MiFIR) are fundamental legal instruments for financial sector issues. In addition, certain other directives to regulate currency, binary, contracts, and emissions are the Payment Service Directive (PSD), Fifth Anti-Money Laundering Directive (5AMLD), Capital Requirement Directive (CRD)[118] and Capital Requirement Regulation (CRR). The UK Financial Services Act 2021 guides various banking and financial sector issues that emerged due to Brexit. The Financial Services and Markets Act 2023 (FSMA 2023) makes major changes to the framework for financial services regulation to reflect the United Kingdom's (UK) position outside of the European Union (EU).[119] It reforms UK's financial regulations and introduces new system for resolving central counterparties(CCP) to protect and enhance financial stability, public confidence and public funds etc. The strong regulatory response with effective implementation reduces the NPLs ratio in the UK. Thus, the level of NPLs is significantly low in the UK despite touching 4% post-GFC in 2012. The impact of the post-Brexit, COVID-19, and geopolitical situations, such as the Russia-Ukraine war, is visible in the economy, particularly the rising prices.

On March 20, 2020, the UK government published its Corporate Insolvency and Governance Bill, which was enacted on June 25, 2020. The Corporate Insolvency and Governance Act 2020 include permanent and temporary measures to relieve companies facing a financial crisis due to the COVID-19 pandemic. The Governance Act has also introduced a provision for a moratorium to be provided to companies to shield them from claims by creditors. At the same time, they try to restructure and rescue their companies in a difficult time.[120] All such contingent measures need further investigation in the post-COVID-19 scenario.

The problem of NPA captured attention in India in 1990. As a result, Narasimham Committee I &II[121]and Andhyarujina Committee[36] came into existence. Their reports pointed out that poor credit decisions by bank management, the challenging recovery environment and the fulfilment of the government's social commitment were reasons for the rise in NPA. Both committees' recommendations suggested enacting legislation to empower banks and FIs. Thus, several regulatory measures came into force in India to address the problem of NPLs pre- and post-GFC. Pre-GFC efforts included the enactment of the Sick Industrial Companies (Special Provisions) Act that is Board of Industrial and Financial Reconstruction (BIFR) 1985), Recovery of Debts Dues to Bank and Financial Institutions Act (RDBFI, 1993), CDR Cell (CDR, 2001) and SARFAESI ACT 2002. The initiatives taken in

[118] Council Directive (EC) 2013/36/EU of 26 June 2013 on access to the activity of credit institutions and the prudential supervision of credit institutions and investment firms, amending Directive 2002/87/EC and repealing directives 2006/48/EC and 2006/49/EC [2013] OJ L 176. 27.

[119] Financial Services and Markets Act 2023.

[120] Sinha and Sood (2020), p. 219.

[121] Reserve Bank of India (2018).

the post-GFC included Announced Asset Classification Forbearance on Restructuring (2014), Revitalising Distressed Assets in the Economy (SMA and JLF, 2014), Flexible Structuring of Long-Term Loans (2014), Strategic Debt Restructuring (SDR, 2015) 2015, Scheme of Sustainable Structuring of Stressed Asset (2016), Guidelines on Sale of Stressed Assets by Bank (2016), IBC 2016), Prudential Framework (2018–2019) and RBI Notification of Resolution Framework 1.0 and 2.0 to provide banks and business relieve from the effect of covid 19.

Initially, the Securitisation and Reconstruction of Financial Assets and Enforcement of Security Interest (SARFAESI) Act, 2002, became a robust regulatory measure. It ensured the recovery of debts through four-tier *Lok Adalats* for an out-of-court settlement. The Legal Services Authority Act gave legal status to debt settlement through *Lok Adalats*. Debtors and creditors can approach the civil courts in disputes, but the process is time-consuming. Another legal body to resolve the NPA issue in India is the DRTs, but these DRTs could not meet the intended objective and have remained unsuccessful. The efforts made by the Assets Reconstruction Companies (ARCs), CDR and Credit Information Bureau established before 2016[122] were unsuccessful, considering the ever-rising level of NPA. Hence, the recovery through these channels was abysmal, with only a 26.4% recovery in government sector banks and 40% in private banks during 2017. The average amount recovered through existing legal recovery channels such as DRTs, *Lok Adalats,* and the SARFAESI Act was 10.8%. As a result, the Government of India enacted the IBC in 2016,[123] consolidating and amending various reorganisation and insolvency resolution laws.

As notified, the IBC covers individuals, companies, limited liability partnerships, partnership firms, and other legal entities. The regulation seeks insolvency resolution in a time-bound manner, i.e., within 180 days (extendable up to 270 days).[32] This code has been considered a very effective legal measure to address NPA's issue. It yielded the desired result; however, the settlement process took longer than the stipulated time. Therefore, several amendments have also been made to the IBC to make it further effective. However, in some instances, the intervention of courts protected the borrowers and pointed out the act's limitations. All these efforts at the regulatory front achieved mixed results; therefore, the book critically examines them in detail in the relevant chapter.

1.12 NPLs in Post COVID-19 Scenario

The COVID-19 pandemic severely impacted all sectors of the economy, including the banking sector. The economic growth that has witnessed a slowdown will experience negative growth, resulting in another financial crisis. Critics argued that 'this

[122] Lok Sabha Secretariat (2018).

[123] The Gazette of India (2016).

crisis will significantly transform the financial services industry worldwide'[124] COVID-19 provides a platform to assess the impact of reforms by most banks worldwide after the financial crisis in 2007–2009.[124] To build confidence in society,[125] the role of banks and credit societies is crucial for reinforcing trust, aligning with stakeholders' expectations, responding to material value drivers, and creating new opportunities.

Thus, the banks must respond to their customers' needs, assess their loan repayment capacity in the post-COVID-19 scenario, and design new strategies accordingly. The banks may have to worry about the situation because, due to the impact of COVID-19, large-scale insolvency among the borrowers, including individual borrowers, SMEs, and the corporate and retail sectors, may arise. The post-COVID-19 world for the banking sector is a different and challenging experience. It accelerates trends in the banking sector and influences the private and public players in the industry. It would be difficult for small banks to survive, and mergers and acquisitions would be a prevalent approach.

In India, the government introduced a three-month moratorium period for all types of loans to support the borrowers. This resulted in an exemption for the customers to pay a principal amount for 3 months. The government also waived interest on interest with a further extension of 3 months to ensure the availability of cash to enhance purchasing power and positively impact the economy. On the other hand, the RBI has infused liquidity to boost the economy. However, banks are reluctant to lend to mature customers with established businesses due to banking fraud and increased awareness.[126]

The UK and Ireland also introduced several measures to help the borrowers, besides announcing a three-month moratorium. The UK schemes of the Coronavirus Business Interruption Loan Scheme (CBILS), the Bounce Back Loan Scheme (BBLS), the Coronavirus Large Business Interruption Loan Scheme (CLBILS) and the Future Fund Schemes were very popular during COVID-19. The UK also used LLP among its leading banks during the early COVID-19 pandemic to smoothen their income. The schemes were so successful that 92.5% of loan applications backed by a UK government loan guarantee increased the UK contingent liability by £70 billion on its COVID-19 loan guarantee.

It is possible to 'ramp up lending to the business, particularly, extra demands for loans to survive, repair and reconstruct their COVID-19 battered business, but 'banks are not ready to take an extra risk.'[126] The fear psycho was more in a situation where NPLs norms of 90 days are relaxed with the moratorium period of six months. The banking sector needs to restructure deeply, accelerating the pre-COVID-19 trend, with 'medium-sized banks suffering the most as cost efficiencies will also play a vital role. The impact of COVID-19 raises many questions about the 'ability of some banks. It is imperative to see whether they will 'survive the crisis or

[124] Carletti et al. (2020).

[125] Robins et al. (2020).

[126] Rawat (2020), para 7.

generate and attract the capital' and what the future structure of the bank will be after the pandemic.[124]

The bankers and analysts expected a spike in the NPLs[127] and expressed apprehension about addressing the problem of increased NPLs. The current crisis significantly differs from the GFC of 2007–2009; the true ramifications remain concealed within the womb of the future. The COVID-19 waves were coming one after another, and the chances of further deteriorating the financial condition of certain jurisdictions and the efficiency of the banks worldwide are to be analysed. The impact of regulatory and policy reforms implemented after the 2007–2009 financial crisis needs in-depth analysis in the post-COVID-19 scenario. Therefore, assessing the existing system to control one more GFC is crucial, along with the new measures to mitigate the crisis and the destruction of the worldwide economy at an enormous pace.

There will be new challenges and opportunities that world must face after the pandemic. It is feasible that NPLs in most sectors are likely to exist and will increase further. The interest rates will remain low for extended periods, and the banking sector will struggle to cope with the losses. Suitable adjustment in the operating procedure remains inevitable. According to the situation, the banks must adjust as face-to-face interaction will be less than in the pre-COVID-19 scenario. Technology and online support services motivated defaulters to settle pending loans.

Thus, there will be a massive difference in the pre-and post-COVID-19 scenario for the banking sector. The banking industry will implement new regulations and policy measures. High NPLs will also be a reason for worry for the banks, as low interest rates will result in low profitability.[127] Therefore, whether the banks and the government will control the situation or the world should be ready for another GFC to arise. Thus, the relevance of the present book is significant in the context of prevailing circumstances. It also mainly examines and compares the UK, India, and Ireland's regulatory, supervisory and policy measures in a post-COVID-19 scenario. This book shall also analyse the effectiveness of the existing policy and regulations and the requirement of a new policy and legal regime in such circumstances.

1.13 Concluding Remarks

The present chapter conceptualised understanding the various facets of NPLs to comprehend the issues raised in the research questions by conducting an in-depth investigation. Analysing macroeconomic and microeconomic determinants of NPLs, such as GDP, unemployment, inflation, exchange rate, asset quality of banks, liquidity ratio, etc., sets the pace for developing and discussing the issues in the succeeding chapters. However, the existing literature review shows the absence of a harmonised policy and regulatory response to address the problem of NPLs.

[127] Shetty (2020).

Nevertheless, jurisdictions across the globe have adopted several approaches to measure NPLs. Hence, Basel guidelines were important landmarks for harmonising the definition of NPLs. However, the questions raised in this chapter remain unanswered and warrant an in-depth investigation with appropriate methodologies and statistical tools.

Moreover, the present research identifies the gaps and lapses in existing supervisory, regulatory and policy measures, the implementation process, and the interventions required to control NPLs. It also suggests corrective measures in the banking system for the UK, India, and Ireland. Thus, the present comparative study will identify the significance of a particular regulatory, policy and supervisory measure to control NPLs with the help of doctrinal quantitative and comparative research methods, measuring the results with the help of statistical tools such as calculating mean, standard deviation, correlation, etc. Accordingly, it also prepares a composite priority index, placing indicators in the cohesive frame of the study. A comparative analysis of the extreme economies with different legal systems will provide the theoretical framework. The findings will significantly contribute to existing literature and may provide direction for the banking sector to deal with the problem of NPLs.

Analysing policy and regulatory gaps in the banking system will also contribute to further improvement. In addition, the assessment of the impact of COVID-19 on NPLs ratios and the effectiveness of existing policy and regulatory responses and requirements of the new regime will also be important in the prevailing COVID-19 crisis. Lastly, the book will contribute new knowledge by critically analysing supervisory, regulatory, and policy measures, and it will present a cross-country framework by synthesising the findings. Therefore, this book purports to assess the success and failure of these measures so that the identified gaps will help the jurisdictions to strengthen their insolvency and bankruptcy laws and even amend the laws to make them more effective and significant.

References

Adrian T, Song H (2010) Liquidity and leverage. J Financ Intermed 19(3):418

Ahmed S Z (2006) An investigation of the relationship between non-performing loans, macroeconomic factors, and financial factors in the context of private commercial banks in Bangladesh (2006) School of Business, Independent University, Bangladesh. http://www.sb.iub.edu.bd/internship/spring2006/0120269.pdf. Accessed 12 Jan 2020

Aiyar S, Bergthaler W, Jose M et al. (2015) A strategy for resolving Europe's problem loans. IMF Staff Discussion Note. https://www.imf.org/en/Publications/Staff-Discussion-Notes/Issues/2016/12/31A-Strategy-for-Resolving-Europe-s-Problem-Loans-43286. Accessed 21 Dec 2020

Allen F, Carletti E (2010) An overview of the crisis: causes, consequences, and solutions. Int. Rev Finance 1

Amadeo K (2020) Banking and how it works: Can you imagine a world without banks? The Balance July 16, para 2, 3. https://www.thebalance.com/what-is-banking-3305812. Accessed 10 Dec 2020

Anastasiou D, Louri H, Tsionas M (2016) Determinants of non-performing loans: evidence from Euro area countries. Financ Res Lett 18:116

Ariccia G D, Detragiache E, Rajan R (2005) The real effect of banking crisis. Working Paper 05/63. https://ssrn.com/abstract=776745. Accessed 22 Dec 2020

Athanasoglou PP, Delis MD, Staikouras CK (2006) Bank-specific, industry-specific and macroeconomic determinants of bank profitability. J Int Financ Mark Inst Money 18(2):121

Bacon P (2009) Evaluation of options for resolving property loan impairments and associated capital adequacy of Irish credit institutions: proposal for a National Asset Management Agency (NAMA). National Treasury Management Agency. https://ptfs-oireachtas.s3.amazonaws.com/DriveF/Data/Library3/BaconEvaluationofOptionsfo rResolving124304.pdf. Accessed 12 Jan 2021

Bank for International Settlements (1997) Core principles for effective banking supervision. https://www.bis.org/publ/bcbs30a.pdf. Accessed 10 Mar 2021

Bank for International Settlements (1999) Strengthening the banking system in China: Issues and experiences. BSI Policy Paper No. 7. https://www.bis.org/publ/plcy07.pdf. Accessed 20 Dec 2020

Bank for International Settlements (2002) Basel Committee on banking supervision, supervisory guidance on dealing with weak banks report of the task force on dealing with weak. BIS 1. https://www.bis.org/publ/bcbs88.pdf. Accessed 31 Jan 2021

Bank for International Settlements (2006) Basel Committee on banking supervision core principles for effective banking supervision. BIS 1. https://www.bis.org/publ/bcbs129.pdf. Accessed 31 Jan 2021

Bank for International Settlements (2017a) Basel Committee on banking supervision, prudential treatment of problem assets- Definitions of non-performing exposures and forbearance. Bank of International Settlements. https://www.bis.org/bcbs/publ/d403.pdf. Accessed 30 Dec 2020

Bank for International Settlements (2017b) Basel III: Finalising post-crisis reforms. https://www.bis.org/bcbs/publ/d424.pdf. Accessed 31 Jan 2021

Barkbu B, Nadege J, Kenneth K (2013) Strategy for fostering a market for distressed debt in Italy. IMF Country Report 13/299 International Monetary Fund

Bayar Y (2018) Macroeconomic, institutional, and bank-specific determinants of non-performing loans in emerging market economies: a dynamic panel regression analysis. J Central Bank Theory Pract 3:95

Bean M C, Paustian M, Penalver A et al. (2010) Monetary policy after the fall. https://www.bis.org/review/r100901d.pdf. Accessed 29 Jan 2020

Beck R, Jakubík P, Piloiu A (2015) Key determinants of non-performing loans: new evidence from a global sample. Open Econ Rev 26(3):525

Benthem CV (2017) The relation among non-performing loans, operating efficiency, and capitalisation in commercial banking. University of Twente

Berger A, Young RD (2017) Problem loan and cost efficiency in banks. J Bank Financ 21(6):849

Berger AN, Molyneux P, Wilson JOS (2012) The Oxford handbook of banking. Oxford University Press

Bertone G (2019) Italy: Insolvency–new insolvency code. Int Comp Commer Law Rev 30(12):108

Bholat D, Lastra RM, Markose SM et al (2018) Non-performing loans at the dawn of IFRS 9: Regulatory and accounting treatment of asset quality. J Bank Regul 19(1):1

Bock RD, Demyanets A (2012) Bank asset quality in emerging markets: determinants and spillovers. IMF Working Paper No. 12/71. https://ssrn.com/abstract=2028247. Accessed 22 July 2023

Boldeanu FT, Constantinescu L (2015) The main determinants affecting economic growth. Bull Transilvania Univ Braşov 8(57):329

Bonin J, Huang Y (1999) Dealing with bad loan of the Chinese bank. https://ssrn.Com/abstract=197528. Accessed 21 Dec 2020

Boudriga AK, Taktak NB, Jellouli S (2009) Banking supervision and nonperforming loans: a cross-country analysis. J Financ Econ Policy 1(4):286

Campbell A (2007) Banking insolvency the problem of nonperforming loans. J Bank Regul 9(1):25
Campbell A, Cartwright P (2002) Banks in crisis: the legal response. Ashgate
Carletti E, Claessens S, Fatás A et al (2020) The bank business model in the post-COVID-19 world. Centre for Economic Policy Research. CEPR Press. https://www.iese.edu/media/research/pdfs/ST-0549-E.pdf. Accessed 28 Oct 2020
Cas SM, Peresa I (2016) What makes a good bad bank: The Irish, Spanish and German experience. European Union Discussion Paper No. 36 148. https://ec.europa.eu/info/sites/info/files/dp036_en.pdf. Accessed 11 Nov 2020
Catao L (1997) Banks, credit in Argentina in the aftermath of the Mexican crisis: supply and demand constrained. IMF Working Paper 97/32. https://ssrn.Com/abstract=882270. Accessed 21 Dec 2020
Cerruti C, Cerruti R N (2016) Public asset management companies. A toolkit. World Bank Group 1
Cifter A (2015) Bank concentration and non-performing loans in Central and Eastern European Country. J Bus Econ Manag 16(1):117
Ciukaj R, Kil K (2020) Determinants of the non-performing loan ratio in the European Union banking sector with a high level of impaired loans. Econ Bus Rev 6(20):22
Cransto R (2020) Principles of banking law. Oxford University Press, p 64
Dietrich W, Wanzenried G (2011) Determinants of bank profitability before and during the crisis: evidence from Switzerland. J Int Financ Mark Inst Money 21(3):307
Diniz FB, Costa JPV (2022) The Impact of central bank interventions on non-performing loans under the COVID-19 pandemic in the United Kingdom and Brazilian Study Case. Bank for International Settlements
Donnery S, Fitzpatrick T, Greaney D et al (2018) Resolving non-performing loans in Ireland: 2010–2018. Q Bull 2:54
D'Souza A (2017) Rising non-performing assets in scheduled commercial banks of India: is securitisation a solution? NITTE Manage Rev 11(1):42
ECB (2017) Guidance to banks on non-performing loans. https://www.managementsolutions.com/sites/default/files/publicaciones/eng/201705-ecb-guidance-on-non-performing-loans.pdf. Accessed 15 Nov 2020
Espinoza R, Prasad A K (2010) Nonperforming loans in the GCC banking systems and their macroeconomic effect. Working Paper 10/224. https://ssrn.com/abstract=1750712. Accessed 10 Jan 2020
Federal Deposit Insurance Corporation (1984) The first fifty years-a history of the FDIC) 1933–1983. FDIC. https://www.fdic.gov/resources/publications/first-fifty-years/index.html. Accessed 30 Jan 2020
Federal Reserve Bank of New York (2013) Quarterly Trends for Consolidated U S Banking Organisations First Quarter. https://www.newyorkfed.org/research/banking_research/quarterly_trends.html. Accessed 10 Mar 2021
Fell J, Grodzicki M, Martin R et al (2017) A role for systemic asset management companies in solving Europe's non-performing loan problems. Eur Econ 1:71
Financial Times (2004) Top 1000 world banks: Asset quality-Eurozone overcoming poor asset quality. The Financial Times London, July 12 2014. https://www.proquest.com/trade-journals/top-1000-world-banks-asset-quality-ozone/docnview/1542388290/2?accountd=14664. Accessed 1 Jan 2021
Fromlet H (2012) Predictability of financial crises: lessons from Sweden for other countries. Natl Assoc Bus Econ 47(4):1
Gambacorta L, Mistrulli P E (2003) Banks capital and lending behaviour: empirical evidence from Italy. Working Paper No. 486. https://econpapers.repec.org/RePEc:bdi:wpte mi:td_486 _03. Accessed 5 Jan 2021
Garcia MTM, Guerreiro JPSM (2016) Internal and external determinants of banks Profitability: the Portuguese Case. J Econ Stud 43(1):90
Ghosh A (2015) Impact of non-performing loans on US products and labour markets. J Financ Econ Policy 9(3):128

Gianviti F (2005) Legal aspects of the financial sector assessment programme, in current development in monetary and financial law. IMF 217

Greenidge K, Grosvenor T (2010) Forecasting non-performing loans in Barbados. J Bus Finance Econ Emerg Econ 5(1):80

Grodzicki M, Laliotis D, Leber M et al. (2015) Resolving the legacy of non-performing exposures in Euro area banks. Financ Stabil Rev 146. https://www.ecb.europa.eu/pub/pdf/fsr/art/ecb.fsrart201505 03.en.pdf?e4667bef71acfa5c77b3feb861>2113f0. Accessed 20 Dec 2020

Halladay S, Jark P (2012) Summary of German insolvency law. DLA Piper, 2012. https://www.dlapiper.com/en/asiapacific/. Accessed 10 Mar 2021

Hanson LK, Essenburg TJ (2014) The new faces of American poverty: a reference guide to the great recession. ABC-CLIO

Heffernan SA (2005) Modern banking in theory and practice. Wiley

Higgins I (2016) Personal insolvency: amendment to legislator. J Int Bank Law 31(2):22

Hu JL, Chiu YH (2004) Ownership and non-performing loans: evidence from Taiwan's banks. Dev Econ 42(3):405

Hupkes E (2000) The legal aspect of bank insolvency: a comparative analysis of Western Europe, The United States and Canada. KLI, London, p 89

Hutchinson T (2017) Doctrinal research: reaching the jury. In: Watkins D, Burton M (eds) Research methods in law, 2nd edn. Routledge, Oxford

IslamIyanatu VS (2010) The Great Recession of 2008–2009: Causes, consequences, and policy responses. Institute of Study of Labour (IZA). Discussion Paper 4934 5

Jakubík P, Thomas R (2013) Determinants of nonperforming loans in Central, Eastern and South-Eastern Europe, focus on European economic integration. Aust Central Bank 3:48

Jonung L (2009) The Swedish model for resolving the banking crisis of 1991–93: Seven reasons why it was successful. Economic Paper No. 360. European Commission

Katia H, Valeria S G, Raque L, (2014) Loan classification and provisioning: current practices in 26 ECA countries. Financial Sector Advisory Centre, Working Paper Series, World Bank. https://openknowledge.worldbank.org/handle/10986/21109License:CCBY3.0IGO. Accessed 20 Dec 2020

Keeton WR (1999) Does faster loan growth lead to higher loan losses differ? Econ Rev 72:3

Keeton WR, Morris C (1987) Why do banks loan losses differ? Federal Reserve Bank of Kansas city. Econ Rev 72(5):3

Kirsiene J, Miseviciute G (2016) Are auditors at fault for the collapse of financial institutions in Lithuania? Baltic J Law Polit 9(2):171

Klein N (2013) Non-performing loans in CESEE: Determinants and impact on macroeconomic performance. IMF Working Paper 13/7. https://www.imf.org/en/Publications/WP/Issues/2016/12/31/Non-Performing-Loans-in-CESEE-Determinants-and-Impact-on-MacroeconomicPerformance-40413. Accessed 5 Jan 2021

Klerman D (2018) Quantitative legal history. In: Dubber MD, Tomlin C (ed) Oxford handbook of legal history: p 343. https://doi.org/10.1093/oxfordhb/9780198794356.013.19. Accessed 3 Apr 2024

Klingebiel D (2002) The use of asset management companies in the resolution of banking crises. NBER Working Paper No. 7042

Kosmidou K (2008) The determinants of banks' profits in Greece during the period of EU financial integration. Manag Financ 43(1):146

Krolik A, Czarnota A, Tatara K et al. (2022) Spotlight: insolvency proceedings in Poland. Lexology 26 October 2022. https://www.lexology.com/library/detail.aspx?g=689aed0e-1675-4c9b-96dc-99bac27647cb. Accessed 30 Nov 2022

Kryzanowsk L, Lui J, Zhang J (2023) Effect of COVID-19 on non-performing loans in China. Financial Research Letters 22. https://www.sciencedirect.com/science/article/pii/S1544612322005499. Accessed 9 Oct 2024

Kucukkacaoglu G, Ayhan AM (2016) Using Non-performing loan ratios as default rates in the estimation of credit losses and macroeconomic credit risk stress testing: a case from Turkey. Risk Gov Contr Financ Mark Inst 6(1):52

Kuzucuand N, Kuzucu S (2019) What drives non-performing loans? Evidence from emerging and advanced economies during pre- and post-global financial crisis. Emerg Mark Financ Trade 55(8):1694

Lok Sabha Secretariat (2018) Standing committee on banking sector in India--Issues, challenges and the way forward including non-performing assets/stressed assets

Louzis D, Vouldis A, Metaxas VL (2012) Macroeconomic and bank-specific determinants of non-performing loans in Greece: a comparative study of mortgage, business and consumer loan portfolios. J Bank Financ 36(4):1012

Lovegrove S, Bainbridge A (2019) Banking regulation 2019. Global Legal Insights. https://www.globallegalinsights.com/practice-areas/banking-and-finance-laws-and-regulations/united-kingdom. Accessed 28 Jan 2020

Lu *D*, Thangavelu S, Hu Q (2001) The link between bank behaviour and non-performing loans in China. Working Paper of the National University of Singapore, Department of Economics

Manish PM, Kasale S, Simon AD (2017) Banking and BIG data analytics. J Bus Manag 6(10):55. https://www.iosrjournals.org/iosr-jbm/papers/Conf.17037-2017/Volume-6/10.%2055-58.pdf. Accessed 21 Dec 2020

Marco S (2004) Stress-testing financial systems: an overview of current mythologies. BIS Working Papers 165

Maveric JB (2020) Types of investment banks. Investopedia, 29 May 2020 para 2. https://www.Investopedia.com/articles/active-trading/121715/bulge-bracket-vs-mid-market-vs-boutique-investment-banks.asp. Accessed 14 Dec 2020

McGovern J (1993) Why bad loans happen to good banks. J Commer Lending 75(6):44

Meacci S (1996) Non-performing bank loans, cyclical patterns, and sectoral risk. Review of Economic Conditions in Italy 69

Miglionico A, (2017) Normative framework of nonperforming loans: regulatory and accounting issues. Open Review of Management and Finance, University of London

Nguyen J (2012) The relationship between net interest margin and non-interest income using a system estimation approach. J Bank Financ 36(19):2429

OECD (2015) Financing SMEs and entrepreneurs 2015: an OECD Scoreboard. OECD Publishing: para 6 70

Paulus CG, Potamitis S, Tirado I (2015) Insolvency law as a main pillar of the market economy—a critical assessment of the Greek insolvency law. Int Insolv Rev 125(1):27

Perera A C (2015) Security rights in Spanish insolvency law: an updated guide for foreign investors J Int Bank Law Regul 30(12): 649

Petiet B (2012) Rights of unsecured creditors in French insolvency law (International Insolvency Institute Twelfth Annual International Insolvency Conference, Paris, June 2012)

Rawat V (2020) NPA levels to increase post-COVID-19: will that impact lending by banks? Economic Times, New Delhi 20 April 2020 para 7. https://cfo.economictimes.indiatimes.com/news/npa-levels-to-increase-post-covid-19-will-that-impact-lending-by-banks/75368832. Accessed 18 Oct 2020

RBI (2020) Income recognition, asset classification, provisioning, and other related matters. https://www.rbi.org.in/Scripts/BS_ViewMasCirculardetails.aspx?id=9908. Accessed 15 Dec 2020

Reserve Bank of India (2018) Report on trend and progress of banking in India 2017–18. RBI https://rbidocs.rbi.org.in/rdocs/Publications/PDFs/0RTP2018FE9E97E7AF7024A4B94321734CD76DD4F.PDF. Accessed 10 Aug 2019

Rime B (2001) Capital requirements and bank behavior: empirical evidence from Switzerland. J Bank Financ 24(4):789

Rizvi NU, Kashiramka S, Singh S et al (2019) Hierarchical model of the determinants of non-performing assets in banks: an ISM and MICMAC approach. Appl Econ 3834

Robert K, Malley TO (2016) The good, the bad and the impaired: a credit risk model of the Irish mortgage market. J Financ Stab 22

Robins N, Tickell S, Irwin W (2020) Financial climate action with positive social impact: How banking can support a just social transition in the UK. LSE https://www.lse.ac.uk/granthaminstitute/publication/financing-climate-action-with-positive-social-impact-how-banking-can-support-a-just-transition-in-the-uk/. Accessed 28 Jan 2021

Samuel G (2017) Comparative law and its methodology. In: Watkins D, Burton M (eds) Research methods in law, 2nd edn. Routledge

Shabir MS, Jiang P, Wang, W, Işık O (2023) COVID-19 pandemic impact on banking sector: A cross-country analysis. J Multinatl Financ Manag https://www.ncbi.nlm.nih.gov/pmc/articles/PMC9896081/. Accessed 10 Oct 2024

Sharadha C, Jain A (2016) The impact of SARFAESI Act 2002 in recovering the non-performing assets in public sector banks: a study on recovery in SBI, CBI, CB, BOB and PNB 2008-2014. Int J Appl Eng Res 11(7):5218

Shetty RS (2020) Impact of COVID on stressed assets. https://www2.deloitte.com/content/dam/Deloitte/in/Documents/finance/in-fa-impact-of-covid-19-on-stressed-assets-noexp.pdf. Accessed 12 Nov 2020

Sinha UK, Sood S (2020) The IBC imbroglio challenges in light of COVID-19 and solutions. In IBBI (eds) Insolvency and bankruptcy regime in India: A narrative. Insolvency and Bankruptcy Board of India 219

Sinkey JF Jr, Greenawalt MB (1991) Loan-loss experience and risk-taking behaviour at large commercial banks. J Financ Serv Res 5:43

Stamatiou C (2016) Cyprus insolvency: Licensing of insolvency practitioners. Int Comp Commer Law Rev 27(2):16

Stern GH, Feldman RJ (2004) Too BIG to fail: the hazards of bank bailouts. Brookings Institution Press

Sufian F, Akbar M, Noor NM (2012) Determinants of bank performance in a developing economy: does bank origins matters? Glob Bus Rev 13(1):1

Teresa GM, Fernandez R, Dolores M (2008) Risk-taking behaviour and ownership in the banking industry: the Spanish evidence. J Econ Bus 60:332

The Gazette of India (2016) The insolvency and bankruptcy code 2016. Government of India Press

The World Bank. Data Bank. www.https://databank.worldbank.org/databases. Accessed 4 Apr 2024

Voica I (2019) Scope of the simplified procedure regulated by law No 151/2015 concerning the insolvency of natural persons in Romania. Juridical Tribune 9(1):191

Wendschlag M (2013) The Basel committee on banking supervision–a history of the early years 1974–1997. Scand Econ Hist Rev 61(2):203

White WR (2009) Should monetary policy lean or clean? Federal Reserve Bank of Dallas Working Paper No. 34 14. https://www.dallasfed.org/-/media/Documents/institute/wpapers/2009/0034.pdf. Accessed 29 Jan 2021

Williams C (2011) Research methods. J Bus Econ Res 5(3)

Woo D (2000) Two approaches to resolving nonperforming assets during financial crisis IMF Working Paper WP/33. https://www.imf.org/en/Publications/WP/Issues/2016/12/30/Two-Approaches-to-Resolving-Nonperforming-Assets-During-Financial-Crises-3460. Accessed 15 Oct 2022

Chapter 2
Analysis of the Impact of Macroeconomic Determinants on NPLs

2.1 Introduction

The previous chapter coherently examined various issues surrounding NPLs to understand the causes and effects of the problem. An in-depth analysis of the approaches adopted to define NPLs, the direction provided in Basel guidelines and regulatory and policy measures adopted by the jurisdictions to address the problem provided a greater understanding of the topic. The chapter also briefly touched upon the possible impact of the COVID-19 pandemic on NPLs, besides analysing the trend of NPLs from the GFC to the COVID-19 pandemic, covering the jurisdictions having relatively higher NPL ratios and representing global scenarios. The discussion on the macroeconomic and microeconomic determinants and their impact on NPLs and vice versa enhanced the understanding of the relationship between these variables. Therefore, the chapter provided a foundation for investigating the issues associated with NPLs and outlined the problems the research intends to cover in the subsequent chapters.

NPLs have increased significantly in many jurisdictions after the GFC, and due to its impact on macroeconomic and microeconomic determinants and vice versa, the economic growth of several jurisdictions has slowed down considerably. Consequently, many jurisdictions worldwide have encountered a severe crisis in the banking sector, and the problem was further aggravated and continued due to poor management and operating performance.[1] The deterioration of loan performance was uneven across the jurisdictions despite several interventions by the respective regulators and supervisors to bring down NPLs to a manageable level.[1]

Many research studies established a strong relationship between NPL ratios and macroeconomic determinants and argued that macroeconomic factors significantly

[1] Lee et al. (2020), p. 11.

A. Dimri, *Non-Performing Loans*, Ius Gentium: Comparative Perspectives on Law and Justice 125, https://doi.org/10.1007/978-3-031-92952-6_2

impact NPL ratios.[2] The credit markets are pro-cyclical, and due to information asymmetries between lenders and borrowers, the balance sheet effect intensifies and increases credit market shocks to the economy.[3] Essentially, determinants of NPLs and the individual bank's characteristics have co-integration. The shareholders' and managerial decisions and activities can also directly influence these characteristics. The joint dynamics of credit flows and macroeconomic activities of 40 large EU banks were significantly nonlinear.[4] Similarly, while assessing the economies of scale and estimating the cost-effectiveness of the banking sector, a balanced panel model was used on the mergers of 130 Norwegian banks [4] from 1987 to 1998.[5] It revealed that macroeconomic determinants adversely affected the banking sector's returns to scale, cost efficiency, and cost efficacy.[5]

Thus, macroeconomic determinants played a vital role in controlling the level of NPLs. For instance, an increase in the GDP may decrease the NPLs level, whereas, with an increase in the unemployment rate, the NPLs may also increase.[5] These are interrelated factors that influence the NPLs ratio and consequently affect economic growth and development to a large extent.[6] The important macroeconomic determinants covered in this chapter include GDP, unemployment, inflation, exchange rate, and interest rate. These determinants[7] have both positive and negative impacts on the NPL ratios. The chapter looks more systematically at all the possible determinants of asset quality[8] by analysing the relationship between NPLs and macroeconomic determinants with the help of statistical tools using data series of 13 years from 2008 to 2020 and calculating mean, standard deviation (SD) and correlation to make the comparative analysis more meaningful.

2.2 Macroeconomic Determinants

In recent decades, the NPLs have attracted more attention as several studies have examined bank failures and concluded that asset quality influences insolvency and a higher level of impaired loans results in a bank failure.[9] The financial performance indicators determine the number of micro-domestic factors affecting bad loans.[10] A study reveals that a bank's NPLs ratio, monetary policy, corporate governance, and overall economic variables have long-term co-integration relationships with NPLs.[1]

[2] Ranjan and Chandra (2003), p. 81.

[3] Bernanke et al. (1998), p. 6455.

[4] Graham et al. (2005), p. 3.

[5] Sapci and Miles (2019).

[6] Boldeanu and Constantinescu (2015), p. 329.

[7] Bayar (2018), p. 95.

[8] Beck et al. (2015), p. 525.

[9] Selma and Jou (2013), p. 852.

[10] Leka (2019), pp. 88–89.

Thus, the critical examination of these determinants would help to understand their impact on the performance of the banks and the extent to which these determinants were responsible for enhancing the NPL ratios.

NPLs are considered a compelling cause of economic stagnation, and a decrease in loan portfolio quality is the main reason for banks' liquidity problems, leading to the financial crisis in developed and developing economies. Many economists and policymakers have widely researched the effect of macroeconomic and bank-specific variables on loan quality[11] and argued that GDP growth is considered the most crucial factor affecting the NPLs and has an inverse relation with NPLs. Therefore, the following section critically analyses the impact of major macroeconomic determinants on NPLs and vice versa.

2.2.1 Gross Domestic Product

Gross Domestic Product (GDP) is one of the crucial factors that could considerably affect the NPLs, and it has a detrimental role in deciding the NPL ratios, particularly in emerging nations.[12] Neither GDP nor NPLs remain stable due to fluctuations in credit growth.[13] Therefore, due to unpredictable market behaviour, the Prompt Corrective Action (PCA) must subdue the impact of GDP on the banking sector's stability.[14] The total GDP ratio compares a country's debt to GDP, and gross fixed capital significantly determines economic growth. In contrast, its external debt has the opposite effect.[15] Therefore, GDP growth is an explanatory variable determining the influence of business cycles and NPLs.

The research conducted on the banking sector in Spain[16] shows a negative impact of GDP on NPLs. It signifies the immediate effect of economic growth on the loan-paying capability of individuals, SMEs, and corporations. When the growth rate improves, it will increase the borrowers' ability to repay the scheduled loan. The deteriorating economy will cause them difficulty repaying a bank loan on time. Another study conducted in Tunisia concluded that GDP has a negative and significant correlation with NPLs.[17] Therefore, the effect on working capital, investment credit, and consumer credit is also important in establishing a relationship with GDP and NPLs.[12]

A negative GDP growth leads to deterioration in loan quality after some time, leading to poor loan recovery and increasing external government debt, significantly

[11] Faith (2012), p. 33.

[12] Fajar and Umanto (2017), p. 67.

[13] Radivojevic and Jovovic (2017).

[14] Balgova et al. (2016), p.

[15] Arham et al. (2020), p. 707.

[16] Salas and Saurina (2002), p. 203.

[17] Abid et al. (2014), p. 58.

influencing the country's economic growth[18] It becomes challenging to break such a vicious circle. The relationship between external debt and economic growth examines its impact on the selected emerging economies from 2002 to 2016. The findings show an adverse effect of external debt on economic conditions.[19] Therefore, the results indicate a positive and a negative relationship between GDP and NPLs. Thus, the following paragraphs examined the relationship between NPLs and GDP for the UK, India, and Ireland from 2008 to 2020 based on the data presented in Annexure 1 and Fig. 2.1.

The trend of NPLs in the UK remained fluctuating, with the highest NPL ratios (3.96%) in 2011. The period from 2009 to 2013 has been a period of extreme distress. The situation improved marginally in 2015, and the NPLs ratio remained at 1% and 0.96% in 2016 and 2017, respectively. The NPLs marginally increased to 1.07% in 2018 and touched 1.22% in 2020. The impact of the COVID-19 pandemic was visible but remained extremely limited in the initial year. Thus, despite witnessing a surge in NPLs after the GFC, the UK could reduce it after 2013 due to effective policy and regulatory measures, as discussed in Chaps. 4 and 5.

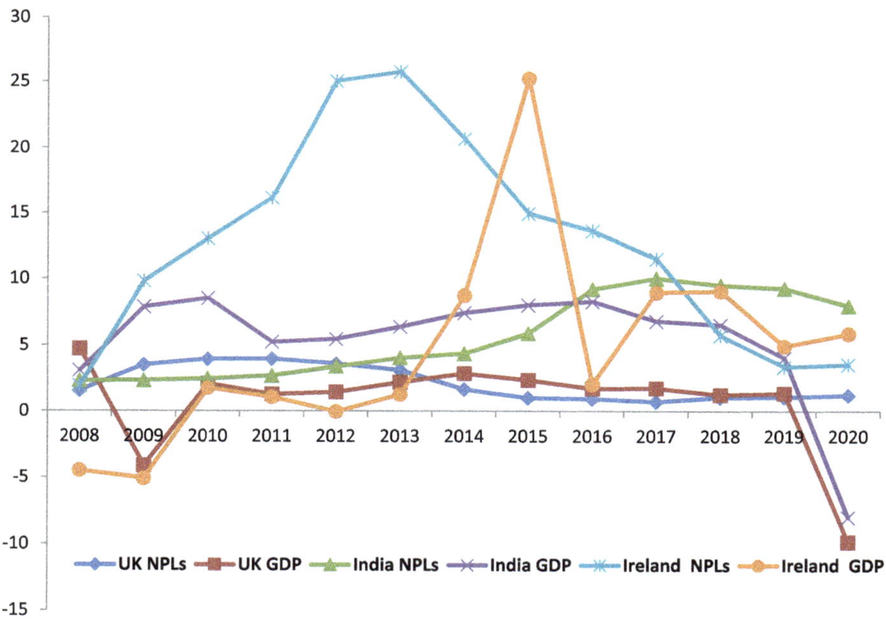

Fig. 2.1 Trend of NPLs and GDP (%). Source: Developed by the researcher using data from the World Development Indicators, World Bank. Data is placed in Annexure-1

[18] Endut et al. (2013), p. 57.

[19] Zaghdoudi (2020), p. 447.

Similarly, GDP of the UK has also shown a fluctuating trend, and it remained negative during two significant crises that the world has witnessed in recent times. Immediately after the GFC, GDP reduced from 4.73% in 2008 to −4.11% in 2009, registering a sharp decline. The impact of the COVID-19 pandemic was also visible, and GDP considerably dipped, registering a negative growth of −9.79% in 2020. Therefore, the impact of the pandemic was more severe than that of the GFC as far as GDP growth is concerned. It is evident that with the rise in NPLs, the GDP declined sharply. A significant decline in economic activities in the first half of the pandemic reflected how COVID-19 had reduced the demand for goods and services in the UK. The impact on the ability of businesses to supply products was visible, resulting in many companies ceasing their operations,[20] consequently decreasing employment opportunities and increasing instances of default loans. Despite the severe impact of the pandemic, its steady recovery continued in the post-COVID-19 arena. Nevertheless, the UK economy still must make up nearly half of the GDP[21] lost since the pandemic, reducing its impact on NPLs. Ukraine had a severe impact on energy prices, which were increased by 10%, resulting in a —1.03% decrease in the GDP in 2022–2023.

Statistical tools such as mean, SD, and correlation establish a relationship between macroeconomic determinants and NPLs. The SD value of NPLs for the UK was 1.29, indicating that the deviation was insignificant and the data clustered around the mean value. The SD value for GDP was 3.70, which was significantly higher. SD value with ±2 is not considered closer to the mean, and the data is more scattered and less reliable. The correlation results were also negative between NPLs and GDP, with −0.002. The negative correlation indicates that with the increase in the NPLs ratio, GDP decreases as it moves in the opposite direction. Several research studies,[16,19] substantiated our findings and indicated that GDP growth stands out as the most crucial driver of NPLs.[22]

India has witnessed a continuous increase in the NPLs/NPAs ratios from 2008 to 2017, with a sharp rise of 9.98% in 2017. However, there has been a marginal decline in NPLs after 2018. The immediate impact of the COVID-19 outbreak has not been seen on the NPL ratios in India, as it was 7.94% in 2020, which is relatively less than the NPLs of previous years (9.23%). The factors responsible for high NPLs in India include improper evaluation of loan applications, poor credit monitoring, ineffective DRTs, poor implementation of existing laws, the high lending rate in the priority sector, and government interference in lending activities.[23]

India's GDP growth remained unstable and fluctuated from 3.09% in 2008 to 8.26% in 2016 and reduced to 6.80% in 2017, showing deterioration in all the macroeconomic and financial indicators including industrial production and growth.[24]

[20] Chowdhury et al. (2020).

[21] Scruton (2020).

[22] Beck et al. (2013), p. 15.

[23] Poornima (2015), p. 655.

[24] Viswanathan (2010), p. 41.

However, there was steady growth from 2012 to 2016, but due to demonetisation, it marginally decreased. In addition, COVID-19 made it vulnerable as the GDP remained at −7.96% in 2020.

The mean value for NPLs (6.23) and GDP (5.36) was relatively higher, indicating that there has been wide variation in the data. The SD result was also higher than the normal value of ±2, which was 2.85 and 4.46, respectively, for NPLs and GDP. There was a negative correlation between NPLs and GDP, which indicates that the GDP tends to decrease with the increase in NPLs.

On the other hand, Ireland witnessed a significant increase in NPLs immediately after the GFC. It was probably one of the most badly hit jurisdictions with high NPL ratios due to large-scale loan defaults at corporate, SMEs, and individual borrowings.[25] The housing sector witnessed a boom before the GFC. The NPL ratios of Ireland were only 1.92% in 2008, which increased to 25.71% in 2013, mainly due to the collapse of the housing sector.[26] A large part of the domestic financial crisis emanated from a highly leveraged banking sector that was over-concentrated on property-related lending. The deterioration in the macroeconomic determinants that partially resulted from a reversal in credit-fuelled property prices led to a steep decline in economic growth and a pronounced rise in unemployment. The decline in asset quality resulted in a rapid increase in NPLs, which grew to such a level that compromised the solvency of the domestic Irish banking system.[27]

However, some improvements from 2013 onwards brought NPLs to less than 4% during 2019 and 2020, with NPL ratios of 3.36% and 3.54%, respectively. The reduction was possible due to several initiatives the Irish Government took on the supervisory and regulatory front. The recapitalisation of banks through the PCAR to provide a stable environment and, consequently, the transfer of a substantial amount of NPLs of CRE Markets to Assets Management Companies (AMCs) was an important strategy to control NPLs. Therefore, from 2009 to 2017, it remained highly vulnerable despite implementing all these policies and regulatory measures. Nevertheless, the progress remained slow due to the complex and slow-moving nature of many NPLs cases, particularly the profound nature of the systemic solvency crisis.[28]

On the other hand, the GDP was 4.49% in 2008 and 1.76% in 2010, and it also demonstrated a fluctuating trend over the reference period. It was recorded as positive in 2010, registering a growth of 1.76%. The results of our statistical analysis for Ireland are interesting, as there has been a significantly higher mean value of 12.58% for the NPLs ratio and 4.55% for GDP. The SD value computed was 7.58 for NPLs and 7.56 for GDP, which is considerably higher than the ±2, confirming our results. However, a positive correlation between NPLs and GDP confirms that both moved in the same direction.

---

[25] Byrne and Kelly (2017).

[26] Robert and Malley (2016).

[27] McCann (2017).

[28] Donnery et al. (2018).

GDP is one of the important indicators to assess economic strength, and strong growth in real GDP usually translates into more income, which improves the debt servicing capacity of the borrowers, which in turn contributes to lower NPLs. A research investigation concluded that the effect of GDP growth on the level of NPLs presents a negative and insignificant relationship between the two variables;[29] an increase in GDP growth results in a decrease in the levels of NPLs and vice versa. These findings align with the work done by other researchers[30] in different settings, who concluded that GDP growth has an insignificant negative relationship with NPLs and, this coincides with our results.

The authors[31] behind this conclusion argued that, in theory, an improvement in the real economy should see an immediate reduction in the NPLs. Generally, a growing economy increases borrowers' income and ability to repay debts and contributes to financial stability. Thus, when getting higher incomes, all economic subjects will ideally be more capable of repaying their debts, translating into lower NPLs ratios.[32] However, the research findings depend on several parameters, including the sample size. The results may be insignificant when derived for a small sample size. Thus, these results certainly provide direction for the jurisdictions, and policymakers may take corrective measures accordingly. We also received mixed results for the UK, India, and Ireland. For instance, with the increase in GDP in the UK and Ireland, NPLs decreased, whereas both moved in the same direction in India. Among the three jurisdictions, the results were ideal for the UK and Ireland than for India.

2.2.2 Unemployment

Now we discuss the relationship between NPLs and the unemployment rate and vice versa, as both are important variables, elucidating the pace of growth and development. The study shows that NPLs and unemployment are closely associated, and unemployment is considered one of the important determinants and predictors of credit risk.[33] The unemployment rate is also closely related to banks' performance, which suffers when unemployment increases. Generally, fewer individuals seek to cooperate with banks due to poor liquidity, resulting in reduced capability to pay for goods and services.[34] A higher unemployment rate implies more people will struggle to pay their debt. Thus, based on the above arguments, there is a positive relationship between the unemployment rate and distressed

[29] Tomak (2013), p. 933.

[30] Alexandria and Santoso (2015), p. 87.

[31] Clementina and Oisu (2014), pp. 87–89.

[32] Hanifah (2015).

[33] Kurumi and Bushpepa (2017).

[34] Mazreku et al. (2018), p. 3.

loans.[35] High unemployment rates usually suggest poor economic conditions and higher NPLs ratios. A poor banking system leads to a weak economy, resulting in the rise of NPLs.

Although unemployment and NPLs have a positive relationship,[35] NPLs also increase with the increase in unemployment. However, the counter-argument advocates the negative relationship between NPLs and unemployment;[36] an increase in the NPL is due to decreased unemployment. A research study[37] identified the factors affecting the NPLs rate in the Eurozone's banking sector between 2000 and 2008, revealed a strong correlation between NPLs and various macroeconomic determinants, including unemployment, and found a statistically significant positive relationship between NPLs and the unemployment rate.

The unemployment rate for the UK ranges from 3.74% to 8.01% over 13 years. There has been a wide fluctuation in the unemployment rate, and the impact of the GFC was visible as it remained at its highest from 2009 to 2013 in the UK. In India, the unemployment rate was highest at 7.11% in 2020, against 5.27% in 2019, experiencing the impact of COVID-19. The unemployment rate in India remained consistently higher during the reference period, deviating from 5.27% to 7.11%. The unemployment rate of Ireland was highest immediately after the GFC at 15.45% in 2012 and reduced significantly to 4.95% in 2018. The unemployment rate of Ireland was relatively higher than that of the UK and India (See Annexure 1 and Fig. 2.2).

The mean value for the UK was 5.93% with SD 1.64, and the correlation between NPLs and unemployment was highly positive, indicating that with the increase in the unemployment rate, NPLs increase significantly. The variation in the unemployment data is less in India compared to the UK, with a mean value of 5.65% and an SD 0.14. The correlation result was positive (+0.17) between NPLs and the unemployment rate. It is interesting to note that the mean value for the unemployment rate was 10.15% for Ireland, which is very high, and the SD value is also very high, with a deviation of 3.90 from the mean value. However, a relatively highly positive (+0.79) correlation between NPLs and the unemployment rate presents a different picture.

This relationship supports the view that unemployment reduces household disposable income and weakens borrowers' ability to pay their loan installments.[37] A study[38] investigating the macroeconomic determinants of credit risk in the banking system of 22 Sub-Saharan African economies concludes that deterioration in the economic environment, including the increasing unemployment rate, leads to increased credit risk in the banking sector, ultimately increasing NPL ratios.

---

[35] Anjom and Karim (2016), p. 84.

[36] Nkusu (2011), p. 93.

[37] Makri et al. (2014), p. 93.

[38] Mpofu and Nikolaidou (2018), p. 141.

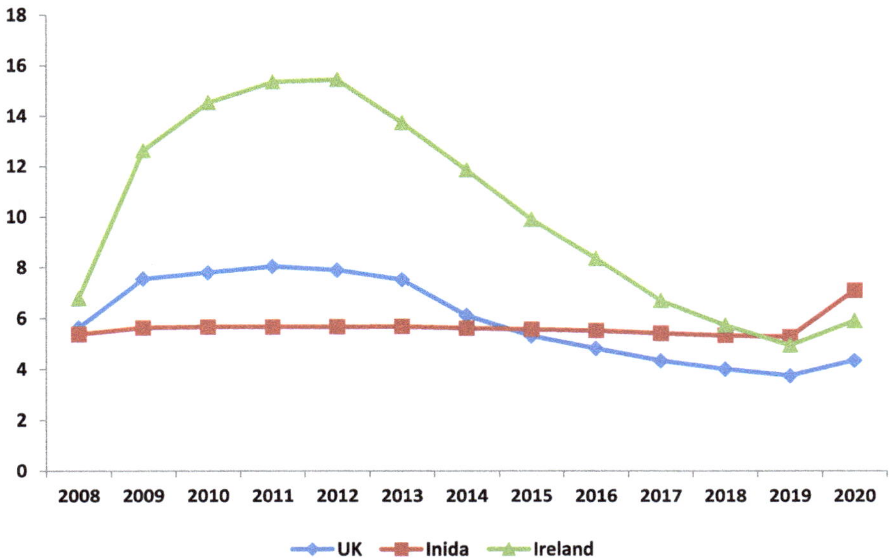

Fig. 2.2 Trend of Unemployment Rate (%). Source: Developed by the researcher using data from the World Development Indicators, World Bank. Data is placed in the Annexure-1

2.2.3 *Inflation*

Inflation is the proxy of monetary policy and measures the general increase in the prices of goods and services. Higher inflation adversely impacts the currency as it decreases its value, directly affecting the banking system. However, due to the rise in prices, the real value of outstanding loans decreases, but at the same time, it also reduces the borrower's paying capacity.[38] The researchers argued that inflation might positively and negatively impact NPLs.[39] The higher inflation rate demands a high-risk premium, resulting in higher interest rates, ultimately affecting the borrowers' cash flow and reducing their ability to repay the loan on time.[40]

NPLs and inflation have positive and negative relationships, and a study on external and internal determinants of NPLs in Indonesia concludes that there is a negative relationship between inflation and NPLs.[41] However, most studies have indicated a positive impact of inflation on NPLs. After surveying 124 banks between 2010 and 2013, an empirical investigation has drawn a positive and significant association between inflation and NPLs.[42] However, inconsistency exists while formulating a hypothesis that draws a negative relation between inflation and NPLs.[42]

[39] Wood and Skinner (2018), p. 44.

[40] Lleshanaku (2015), p. 35.

[41] Mutamimah et al. (2012), p. 49.

[42] Barus (2016), p. 113.

High inflation influences standard interest rates, ultimately reducing the borrowers' loan-servicing capacity. It can also negatively affect borrowers' real income when nominal wages are sticky.[43] If the income does not increase in line with inflation, a rise in inflation increases costs for both households and corporations and thus lowers the available funds for debt repayment,[44] and this would cause NPLs to rise. The inferences drawn in the analysis imply that a rise in inflation is not matched by a commensurate increase in nominal incomes, causing real income to fall and adversely affecting the ability to repay the loan.[31]

While analysing the relationship between inflation and NPLs using the data presented in Annexure 1, it was revealed that the average inflation on consumer prices was 2.08% for the UK, with the highest at 3.86% in 2011; trends varied from 0.37% to 3.86% over a reference period and remained highly inconsistent. The inflation in consumer prices in India was very high in 2010 and 2013, reported at 11.99% and 11.06%, respectively, with the lowest at 3.33% in 2017. There has been a significant variation in the annual inflation rate on consumer prices. The average inflation on the consumer price index was also very high (7.28%), which indicates the real value decreased significantly due to the high inflation rate.

The average inflation rate for consumer prices in Ireland was 0.37%, with the highest at 4.04% in 2008 and the lowest at −4.48% in 2009. The data series suggests that Ireland effectively managed the rising level of prices among the three jurisdictions. The analysis of the reliability and consistency of the data noticed that the SD value for inflation on consumer prices for the UK was 0.989, which is significantly low and indicates that the deviation from the mean value is relatively less, and the data is more consistent and reliable. The deviation is within a range of ±2, and the data is more consistent and unlikely to have a greater impact on NPL ratios. A highly positive correlation between NPLs and inflation on the consumer price index indicates that both variables move in the same direction.

SD value for India was 3.006 for inflation on consumer price, which is significantly higher than the normal value of ±2, showing inconsistency in the data set. The correlation value was also negative, with −0.879 indicating that inflation will decrease with an increase in NPLs, which is inconsistent. Similarly, the SD value was 1.975 for Ireland, within the range of ±2, showing consistency in the data series. However, there was a positive correlation between the two variables (0.280), indicating that inflation also increases with the increase in NPLs.

Among the three jurisdictions, the data set for the UK was more consistent than that for Ireland and India, and the deviation for inflation on consumer prices was significantly higher for India. The impact of inflation on NPLs was relatively less in the UK than in India and Ireland. The correlation value indicates that the change in inflation may not change NPLs; in the case of a price rise, the loan's value will decrease.

---

[43] Ghosh (2015), p. 93.

[44] Louizis and Vouldis (2012), p. 1012.

The negative relationship between the two variables implies that the level of NPLs decreases when inflation increases and vice versa. These findings align with the work of other researchers who concluded that the relationship between inflation and NPLs[40] is insignificant. Some other research studies[45] argued that inflation is statistically insignificant in explaining NPLs, which we have also argued in our analysis.

2.2.4 Exchange Rate

The real exchange rate positively influences the banking sector and NPLs.[44] An increase in the exchange rate means a decline in the domestic currency, while a decrease leads to an appreciation.[46] The reduced exchange rate expands export-oriented enterprises, negatively affecting import enterprises.[47] A real depreciation can even worsen the net value of the enterprise if it has huge liabilities in foreign currencies. Therefore, it will also make it risky for them to credit under depreciation, as they must obtain additional funds in domestic currency to repay the loans. It will also create difficulties for the enterprises to meet their obligations to the banks, leading to the deterioration of bank balance sheets, aggravating the credit crunch, and facing the financial crisis and a crucial decline in economic activities.[48]

The cause of NPLs may result in the slowdown of economic activities, it can also negatively impact economic growth, and a similar link may exist between NPLs and exchange rates. In a comparative study of 75 jurisdictions for 10 years, the authors[22] concluded that the exchange rate significantly affects NPL ratios and other determinants such as real GDP and share prices. The authors further argued that the intensity of the effect depends on the nature of foreign exchange lending. The impact would be more on unhedged borrowers, particularly those with pegged or managed exchange rates.[49]

Regarding currency depreciation,[50] it was argued that depreciation would increase NPLs via negative balance sheet effects for jurisdictions with currency mismatches. Typically, this leads to 'fear of floating' considerations among the authorities, which often maintain tightly managed exchange rates against the dollar or the Euro.[51] During a crisis, the pegged exchange rate collapses due to insufficient foreign exchange reserves, currency depreciation, and increased debt servicing costs in local currency, and terms for borrowers with loans denominated in foreign

[45] Carlos and Bonilla (2012).

[46] Kjosevki et al., (2019), p. 1185.

[47] Nucci and Pozzolo (2001), p. 259.

[48] Pratap and Urrutia (1994), p. 535.

[49] Becker and Fabbro (2006).

[50] Hausmann et al. (2001), p. 387.

[51] Lane and Shambaugh 2010), p. 518.

currency.[52] Suppose these borrowers have no income in foreign currency; defaults on foreign currency-denominated loans will tend to rise under such circumstances, and the level of NPLs will increase.[49]

On the other hand, a depreciation of the local currency can also reduce NPLs through an increase in export volumes and, thus, an improvement of the financial position of the corporate sector. This effect will likely dominate jurisdictions with significant currency mismatches and relatively open economies.[53] Finally, in the case of lending interest rates, the channel to NPLs is likely to work through a rise in the debt service costs of borrowers with variable-rate contracts. Exchange rate depreciations might increase unprotected borrowers' NPLs in countries with high lending in foreign currencies.[53]

The exchange rate trend presented in Annexure 1 for the UK, India, and Ireland demonstrates that currencies depreciated over the reference period in these jurisdictions. However, the deterioration was significantly higher in the Indian currency than in the Euro and GBP compared to the US dollar. The US dollar value per Indian rupee was the lowest at ₹45.56 in 2010 and the highest at ₹74.23 in 2020, registering a decline of 62.93% in Indian currency. Such a change in the currency tends to increase the NPLs, particularly among those borrowers who repay loans in foreign currencies. The depreciation for GBP and Euro was 44.44% and 32.35%, respectively, indicating that the impact was more on Indian borrowers than on the UK and Ireland (see Annexure-1). In this volatile age, ICT plays a crucial role in influencing market forces, and the positive or negative changes in one country will bring global change. Such international market integration will positively and negatively affect NPLs, ultimately influencing the exchange rate.

Our results for mean, SD and correlation show that the average exchange rate for the UK, India and Ireland was £0.68, ₹59.62, and €0.81 with SD values of 0.077, 10.24 and 0.081, respectively, which are highly consistent for GBP and Euro. The SD value for India was 10.24, which was considerably higher, suggesting that the fall in currency value exceeded the permissible limits of SD value ±2 in the Indian currency.

The correlation value was negative for the UK and Ireland, with −0.55 and −0.22, indicating that with the change in exchange rate, NPLs will move in the opposite direction. On the other hand, there was a significant deviation in the Indian currency, and the correlation value was highly positive at 0.91, indicating that both NPLs and exchange rates moved in the same direction. Several factors influence exchange rates, and due to changes in exchange rates, lending, particularly in foreign currency, becomes costlier and burdens borrowers. A decrease in the home currency value will result in costly imported goods, which put pressure on letters of credit issued to traders by commercial banks, thus increasing the risk of default and

[52] Tille (2003), p. 1.

[53] Pavlova and Rigobon (2007), p. 1139.

vice versa[54] The impact of the exchange rate on the NPLs is severe in countries with a high degree of lending in foreign currencies, particularly to unprotected borrowers.

Several studies have also substantiated our findings, and a study conducted in Turkey using exchange rate data from 2005–2015 concluded that euro exchange rates and oil prices have significant positive relationships, while the industrial production index and Istanbul stock index have a negative association with NPLs. The study also revealed that the dollar exchange rate has a strong negative influence on NPLs.[55]

2.2.5 Interest Rate

Interest rate is one of the primary economic determinants of NPLs and is the measure of borrowed funds. An increase in interest rate affects the performing assets in banks as it increases the cost of loans charged to the borrowers and reduces the borrowers' capacity to repay.[56] A research study on NPLs and interest rates established a positive relationship, implying that with an increase in the interest rate, NPLs also increase. A weaker or insignificant relationship between interest rates and NPLs establishes that interest rates are insignificant in affecting the NPLs.[57] Thus, the NPLs level does not necessarily depend on the prime lending rate of the central bank.

However, these findings contrast with the general perception of a significant positive relationship between interest rates and the level of NPLs. As per international evidence, an increase in the Central Bank rate should increase the cost charged on loans, weakening the borrower's debt-servicing capacity, more so if the rates are variable.[56] The sample size also influences the results; for a small sample, the result could be insignificant, and the result will change with a change in sample size. Future studies using a larger sample may provide a significant positive relationship rather than an insignificant relationship between interest rate and the level of NPLs. Other macroeconomic factors also influence the level of NPLs and vice versa. For instance, in the case of share prices, the impact is larger in countries with a large stock market than in GDP. Moreover, interest rate hikes affect the ability to provide debt service, particularly in the case of floating-rate loans. An empirical study on commercial banks in the EU countries[58] confirmed a tight dependency of NPLs on changes in the economic environment of a country.

---

[54] Badarand and Javed (2013), p. 40.

[55] Turan and Koskija (2014), p. 490.

[56] Ombaba (2013), pp. 155–156.

[57] Patnaik and Shah (2004).

[58] Mileris (2014), p. 22.

2.3 Conclusion

This chapter analysed the relationship between macroeconomic determinants and NPLs to gauge how these determinants influenced the level of NPLs in the UK, India, and Ireland. The chapter also analysed the trend of NPLs and macroeconomic determinants from the GFC to the COVID-19 pandemic, covering 13 years after the GFC. Our analysis revealed that GDP has positive and negative relationships with NPLs and vice versa.[59] The GDP and NPLs have a negative relationship in the UK and India, indicating that with the increase in GDP, NPLs decrease, whereas in Ireland, GDP and NPLs moved in a similar direction. The varying results on the relationship between NPLs and GDP depend on these jurisdictions' fundamental economic structures.

The critical analysis of the topic demonstrates that unemployment establishes a negative relationship with NPLs that deteriorates asset quality, thereby increasing NPL ratios; several research studies confirm such dependencies.[60] The unemployment rate and NPLs ratios moved in the same direction for the UK, India, and Ireland. Thus, with the increase in the unemployment rate, NPLs tend to increase, worsening a country's economic conditions due to borrowers' inability to repay loans.

Inflation also influences NPLs to a great extent, and in our analysis, we observed that inflation has a positive and negative correlation with NPLs. Our analysis for the UK, India, and Ireland presented mixed results. For instance, it has a positive correlation for the UK and Ireland and a negative correlation for India. With the rise in prices, the level of unpaid loans regularly increases. Nevertheless, increasing inflation rates also make debt cheaper, which helps improve the quality of life.[61] Several research studies supported our findings; therefore, jurisdictions should develop a mechanism to negate the impact of inflation on NPLs because it has a cascading effect on the economic development of a jurisdiction.

The exchange rate also influences the NPLs ratios; therefore, the UK and Ireland exchange rates fluctuated slowly compared to India. There was a wide variation in India's exchange rate, which indicates that with the increase in the exchange rate, NPLs increased and considerably influenced unhedged borrowers, particularly those who repay the debt in foreign currency. Therefore, NPLs and exchange rates establish negative results for the UK and Ireland and positive results for India, which certainly impact the overall growth of the economy. On the other hand, an increase in interest rate affects the performing assets in banks as it increases the cost of loans charged to the borrowers and reduces the borrowers' capacity to pay.

Thus, these macroeconomic determinants positively and negatively impact the NPLs and vice versa. Many internal and external factors of a particular jurisdiction determine such a relationship. Jurisdictions with strong economic fundamentals

[59] Jakubik and Reininger (2013), p. 3 and Bykova and Pindyuk (2019).

[60] Berge and Boye (2007), p. 65.

[61] Klein (2013).

could control NPLs effectively despite shocks from the GFC and the COVID-19 pandemic. Nevertheless, these macroeconomic determinants are very important, and their impact on NPL ratios is inevitable across jurisdictions. Therefore, jurisdictions must take appropriate policy-level measures to reduce the impact of these determinants on NPLs and ensure financial stability.

References

Abid L, Ouertani MN, Ghorbel SZ (2014) Macroeconomic and bank-specific determinants of household's non-performing loans in Tunisia: a dynamic panel data. Proc Econ Finance 13:58–68

Alexandria MB, Santoso IT (2015) Non-performing loan: impact of internal and external factors (evidence in Indonesia). Int J Human Soc Sci Invent 4(1):87

Anjom W, Karim AM (2016) Relationship between non-performing loans and macroeconomic factors (with specific factors: a case study on loan portfolios-SAARC countries perspective). Asia Pac J Finance Risk Manage 15(3):84

Arham N, Salisi MS, Mohammed RU et al (2020) Impact of macroeconomic cyclical indicators and country governance on bank non-performing loans in emerging Asia. Eurasian Econ Rev 10:707–726

Badarand M, Javed AY (2013) Impact of macroeconomic forces on non-performing loans: an empirical study of commercial banks in Pakistan. WSEAS Trans Bus Econ 1(10):40

Balgova M, Nies N, Plekhanov A (2016) The economic impact of reducing non-performing loans. EBRD Working Paper No. 193 1. https://ssrn.com/abstract=3119677. Accessed 22 July 2023

Barus AC (2016) Analysis of factors influenced the non-performing loans on commercial bank in Indonesia. J Microskill Econ Hero 6(2):113

Bayar Y (2018) Macroeconomic, institutional, and bank-specific determinants of non-performing loans in emerging market economies: a dynamic panel regression analysis. J Central Bank Theory Pract 3:95

Beck R, Jakubík P, Piloiu A (2015) Key determinants of non-performing loans: new evidence from a global sample. Open Econ Rev 26(3):525–550

Beck T, Jakubik P, Piloiu A (2013) Non-performing loans: what matters in addition to the economic cycle? European Central Bank Working Paper 15

Becker C, Fabbro D (2006) Limiting foreign exchange exposure through hedging: the Australian experience. Reserve Bank of Australia Research Discussion Paper 2006–09

Berge TO, Boye KG (2007) An analysis of bank's problem loans. Bank Econ Bull 78(2):65

Bernanke BS, Gertler M, Gilchrist S (1998) The financial accelerator in a quantitative business cycle framework. NBER Working Paper 6455

Boldeanu FT, Constantinescu L (2015) The main determinants affecting economic growth. Bull Transilvania Univ Braşov 8(57):329

Bykova A, Pindyuk O (2019) Non-performing loans in Central and Southeast Europe. https://www.ac.at/non-performingloans-in-central-and-southeast-europe-dlp-4962.pdf. Accessed 20 Feb 2022

Byrne D, Kelly R (2017) Bank asset quality and monetary policy pass-through. Research Technical Papers 11/ RT/17 Central Bank of Ireland

Carlos A, Bonilla O (2012) Macroeconomic determinants of nonperforming loans in Spain and Italy. Dissertation, University of Leicester

Chowdhury SD, Drew S, Smith RK et al (2020) Coronavirus and the effect on the UK GDP. Office of the National. Statistics

Clementina K, Oisu H (2014) The rising incidence of non-performing loans and the nexus of economic performance in Nigeria: an investigation. Eur J Account Audit Finance Res 2(5):87

Donnery S, Fitzpatrick T, Greaney D et al (2018) Resolving non-performing loans in Ireland: 2010–2018. Q Bull 2:54

Endut R, Syuhada N, Ismail F et al (2013) Macroeconomic implications on non-performing loans in Asian Pacific region. World Appl Sci J 57

Faith M (2012) What determines the non-performing loans ratio: evidence from Turkish commercial banks. CEA J Econ 4(1):33

Fajar H, Umanto U (2017) The impact of macroeconomic and bank-specific factors toward non-performing loans: evidence from Indonesian public banks. Banks Bank Syst 12(1):67

Ghosh A (2015) Banking-industry specific and regional economic determinants of non-performing loans: evidence from US states. J Financ Stab 20:93

Graham JR, Harvey CR, Rajgopal S (2005) The economic implications of corporate financial reporting. J Account Econ 40:3–73

Hanifah N (2015) Economic determinants of non-performing loans (NPLs) in Ugandan commercial banks. Taylor's Bus Rev 5(2):137

Hausmann R, Panizza U, Stein E (2001) Why do countries float the way they float? J Dev Econ 66(2):387–414

Jakubik P, Reininger TT (2013) Determinants of nonperforming loans in Central, Eastern and South-Eastern Europe, focus on European economic integration. Oesterreichische Nationalbank 3: 48

Kjosevki J, Petkivski M, Naumovska E (2019) Bank specific and macroeconomic determinants of non-performing loans in the Republic of Macedonia: comparative analysis of enterprise and households of NPLs. Econ Res 132(1):185

Klein N (2013) Non-performing loans in CESEE: determinants and impact on macroeconomic performance. IMF Working Paper 13/7. https://www.imf.org/en/Publications/WP/Issues /2016/12/31/Non-Performing-Loans-in-CESEE-Determinants-and-Impact-on-Macroeconomic-Performance-40413. Accessed 5 Jan 2021

Kurumi L, Bushpepa O (2017) Do macroeconomic variables affect the level of non-performing loans? Sixth conference of students of the agricultural University of Tirana

Lane PR, Shambaugh JC (2010) Financial exchange rates and international currency exposures. Am Econ Rev 100(1):518–540

Lee JM, Chen KH, Chia Chang C et al (2020) Determinants of non-performing loans, firm's corporate governance and macroeconomic factors. Int J Financ Econ 1:11

Leka B, Bajrami E, Duci E (2019) Key macroeconomic drivers on reducing non-performing loans in Albania. AJIS 8(2):88–95

Lleshanaku A (2015) From the perspectives of macroeconomic factors: the past and future of problematic loans in Albania. AJIS 4(1):35

Louizis D, A Vouldis A, Metaxas V (2012) Macroeconomic and bank-specific determinants on non-performing loans in Greece: a comparative study of mortgage, business, and consumer loan portfolios. J of Banking Finance 36:1012

Makri V, Tsagkanos A, Bellas A (2014) Determinants of non-performing loans: the case of Eurozone. Panoeconomicus 61(2):93–206

Mazreku I, Morina F, Misiri V et al (2018) Determinants of the level of non-performing loans in commercial banks of transition countries. Eur Res Stud J 21(3):3

McCann F (2017) Resolving a non-performing loan crisis: the ongoing case of the Irish mortgage market. Central Bank of Ireland Research Technical Paper 10/RT/17

Mileris R (2014) Macroeconomic factors of non-performing loans in commercial banks. Ekonomika 93(1):22–39

Mpofu TR, Nikolaidou E (2018) Determinants of credit risk in the banking system in sub-Saharan Africa. Rev Dev Finance 8(2):141

Mutamimah M, Chasanah Z, Nur S (2012) Internal and external analysis in determining non-performing loans on Shariah compliance bank in Indonesia. J Bus Econ 19(1):49

Nkusu M (2011) Nonperforming loans and macro-financial vulnerabilities in advanced economies. IMF Working Papers 161

Nucci F, Pozzolo AF (2001) Investment and the exchange rate: an analysis with firm-level panel data. Eur Econ Rev 45(2):259–283
Ombaba MKB (2013) Assessing the factors contributing to non–performance loans in Kenyan banks. Eur J Bus Manage 5(32):155
Patnaik I, Shah A (2004) Interest rate volatility and risk in Indian banking (2004) IMF Working Paper 14/17. https://ssrn.com/abstract=878840. Accessed 8 Jan 2022
Pavlova A, Rigobon R (2007) Asset prices and exchange rates. Rev Financ Stud 1139
Poornima SMT (2015) A study on the portfolio of non-performing assets in Indian public sector banks. Int J Appl Res 655
Pratap S, Urrutia C (1994) Firm dynamics, investment, and currency composition of debt: accounting for the real effects of the Mexican crisis of 1994. J Dev Econ 75(2):535
Radivojevic R, Jovovic J (2017) Examining of determinants of non-performing loans. Prague Econ Pap Prague Univ Econ Bus 3:300
Ranjan R, Chandra S (2003) Non-performing loans and terms of credit of public sector banks in India: an empirical assessment. Reserv Bank India Occas Pap 24(3):81
Robert K, Malley TO (2016) The good, the bad and the impaired: a credit risk model of the Irish mortgage market. J Financ Stab 22
Salas V, Saurina J (2002) Credit risk in two institutional regimes: Spanish commercial and savings banks. J Financ Serv Res 22:203
Sapci A, Miles B (2019) Bank size, returns to scale, and cost efficiency. J Econ Bus 105842
Scruton J (2020) GDP monthly estimate, UK. Office for National Statistics–GDP Monthly Estimate https://www.ons.gov.uk/economy/grossdomesticproductgdp. Accessed 22 July 2023
Selma A, Jou MF (2013) Micro and macro determinants of non-performing loans. Int J Econ Financ Issues 3(4):852
Tille C (2003) The impact of exchange rate movements on U S foreign debt. Curr Issues Econ Financ 9(1):1
Tomak S (2013) Determinants of commercial banks' lending behaviour: evidence from Turkey. Asian J Empir Res 3(8):933
Turan G, Koskija A (2014) Non-performing loans in Albania. AJIS 3(3):490
Viswanathan KG (2010) The global financial crisis and its impact on India. J Int Bus Law 91:41
Wood A, Skinner N (2018) Determinants of non-performing loans: evidence from commercial banks in Barbados. Bus Manage Rev 9(3):44
Zaghdoudi T (2020) Threshold effect in the relationship between external debt and economic growth: a dynamic panel threshold specification. J Quant Econ 18:447–456

Chapter 3
Analysis of the Impact of Microeconomic Determinants on NPLs

3.1 Background

The relationship between NPLs and macroeconomic and microeconomic determinants greatly influences a jurisdiction's economic development. The previous chapter critically examined the relationship between macroeconomic determinants and NPLs and vice versa using the data series from 2008 to 2020, which happens to be a period between two major calamities, the GFC and the COVID-19 pandemic. The chapter also presented how the positive and negative relationship between the two variables influences each other, ultimately impacting an economy.

Several microeconomic determinants also influence the NPLs and vice versa, ultimately influencing the economic conditions of a jurisdiction. For instance, bank capitalisation or CAR is vital in lowering the risk of NPLs, and adequately capitalised banks with high RWA tend to experience lower loan losses.[1] On the other hand, higher CAR contributes to the rise in NPLs.[2] Bank profitability also influences credit risk and contributes to increasing NPLs. When banks attempt to boost credit growth, they most likely devote less time scrutinising loan applications to achieve targeted loan disbursement. It is important to pay adequate attention to the borrowers' collateral evaluation, and poor credit scoring and failure to take such measures may lead to loan default. In addition, a lack of monitoring of borrowers' repayment capability also contributes to loan failure, resulting in high loan losses.[3]

On the other hand, poor managerial skills and low efficiency incur high levels of NPLs[4] Deteriorations in cost efficiency increase NPLs; therefore, banking supervision should focus on enhanced cost efficiency to reduce the likelihood of bank

[1] Shrieves and Dahl (1992), p. 439.

[2] Ghosh (2017), p. 93.

[3] Daniel et al. (2010), p. 2929.

[4] Podpiera and Weill (2008), p. 135.

A. Dimri, *Non-Performing Loans*, Ius Gentium: Comparative Perspectives on Law and Justice 125, https://doi.org/10.1007/978-3-031-92952-6_3

failures.[4] Moreover, diversification of the banking business has positive and negative impacts on NPLs, sometimes leading to loan losses. A study between 2003 and 2016 in MENA countries[5] concluded a negative relationship between NPLs and credit growth. Therefore, low-capital banks respond to moral hazards and increase the risk of loan portfolios, resulting in high NPLs.[6]

No clear-cut evidence exists to establish a relationship between bank size and NPLs, and large banks are more likely to incur relatively lower loan losses.[7] Larger banks scrutinise borrowers' financial credibility more rigorously using advanced risk management techniques, preventing them from lending to borrowers with poor credit ratings. We also analyse the z-score, which captures the probability of default in the commercial banking system of a country and compares the buffer, such as capitalisation and returns, with the volatility of those returns.

Banking sector analysts treat NPLs as pollution that destroys the financial ecosystem[8] and substantially impedes economic growth and development. Hence, treating its root cause is essential for a healthy economic environment. In the following sections, we critically examine these microeconomic determinants and their impact on NPLs and vice versa, making a comparative analysis of the prevailing situation in the UK, India, and Ireland. In addition, we also prepared a composite index to assess the overall performance of these jurisdictions and categorise them accordingly (see Table 3.1). The important microeconomic determinants covered in the present chapter include bank capital-to-asset ratio, liquidity ratio, ROA, ROE, NIM, bank size, inefficient bank management, cost efficiency, and Z-score.

3.2 Microeconomic Determinants of NPLs

3.2.1 Bank Capital to Asset Ratio

Asset quality is an important component of banks' profitability that determines the banks' financial health.[9] Asset quality is also related to the quality of loans provided by the banks, and the level of NPLs indicates the banks' soundness. The lower asset quality leads to a credit crunch[10] affecting the profitability of banks and, ultimately, the financial stability of a country. Therefore, lower asset quality or NPLs, known as toxic assets[11] lead to insolvency and bankruptcy, which brings economic

[5] MENA refers to a grouping of countries situated in and around the Middle East and North Africa.

[6] Kjosevski and Petkovski (2020), p. 1009.

[7] Latif et al. (2014), p. 50.

[8] . Barseghyan (2010), p. 873.

[9] Kadioglu et al. (2017), p. 60.

[10] Bernanke et al. (1991), p. 205.

[11] Whalen (1991), p. 1.

slowdown.[12] Thus, measuring the NPL ratios, analysing their effects, and regulating them with the required policies for profitability and growth is crucial.[13] The bank management needs to emphasise evaluating the firms' assets to gauge the credit risk associated with their operation, using it as a micro-prudential determinant in commercial banks' soundness and profitability.[14]

Poor asset quality weakens the local currency and makes it harder to serve the foreign currency debt because it becomes costlier[9] adversely impacting the countries with large amounts of lending in foreign currency and unhedged borrowers.[14] The banks perpetuate lending to fetch good profit during the economic boom, but become vulnerable during a crisis.[15] Under such circumstances, high NPLs influence the banks' profitability, eventually jeopardising asset quality.[16] Thus, lower economic growth, exchange rate depreciation, weaker terms of trade and a fall in debt-creating capital inflows are significant contributors to poor asset quality[17] and negatively impact profitability when measured as LLP over total loans as a proxy for credit risk.

The BCBS has developed several fundamental principles to determine asset quality and loan risk management and suggested necessary changes in related regulations. It even suggested maintaining an 8% capital ratio to RWA to tighten the worldwide banking system; unfortunately, these changes could not prevent the GFC. Nevertheless, RWA rejects possible impairment, improves asset quality, and is considered a better option for measuring asset quality.[18]

The data presented in Annexure 2 and Fig. 3.1 depict the trends of bank CAR[19] and banks' regulatory capital to RWA for the UK, India, and Ireland. The CAR for the UK varied from 4.47% to 7.03%, with mean and SD values of 6.21 and 0.865, respectively. The SD values remained within ±2, indicating that variation was within the normal data distribution range. However, there was a highly negative correlation between NPLs and CAR (−0.64), which shows that with the increase in CAR, NPLs decreased substantially. Interestingly, the UK consistently maintained a higher RWA than prescribed by Basel-I and III, and it varied from 12.9% to 21.60% from 2008 to 2020. The mean and SD values were 18.34 and 2.88, respectively, and the SD value was higher than the normal results of ±2, indicating abnormal data distribution with a high degree of deviation from the mean value. On the other hand, the correlation was also highly negative (−0.622), indicating that with the increase in

[12] Barr and Siems (1994).

[13] Bock and Demyanets (2012).

[14] Lucky and Nwosi (2015), p. 28.

[15] Crockett (1996), p. 168.

[16] Klein (2013).

[17] Abata (2014), p. 39.

[18] Adhikary (2006), p. 75.

[19] It is a ratio of bank capital and reserves to total assets. Capital and reserves include funds contributed by owners, retained earnings, general and special reserves, provisions, and valuation adjustments. Total assets include all nonfinancial and financial assets.

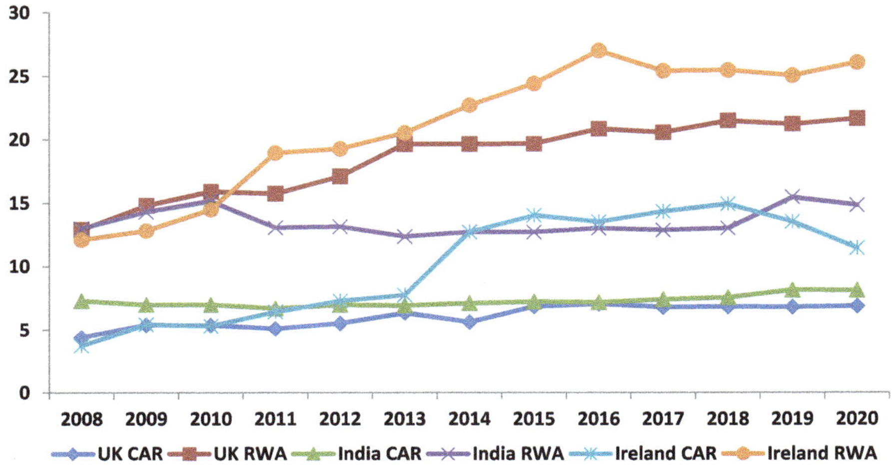

Fig. 3.1 Trend of CAR and RWA (%). Source: Developed by the researcher using data from the World Development Indicators, World Bank. Data is and placed in Annexure 2

the RWA, the NPLs in the UK tend to decrease; thus, high CAR and RWA improved asset quality by reducing NPLs.

The CAR marginally ranges from 6.70% to 8.11% in India, resulting in an almost flat curve (Fig. 3.1). The mean values (7.27) and SD (0.430) show that the data distribution remained within a normal range. A highly positive correlation (0.69) indicates that the CAR could not control NPLs. The value of RWA varied from 12.34% (2013) to 15.42% (2019), with a mean value of 13.47 and SD 1.015, which is within ±2, indicating that variation is not very significant. The positive correlation (0.049) results show that RWA and NPLs moved in the same direction. This situation may be due to several internal factors, including government interference, lending in government-sponsored projects, and a priority sector, and a more in-depth analysis will depict a clear picture.

In Ireland, the trend of CAR was inconsistent and varied from 3.75% in 2008 to 5.32% in 2010. CAR significantly increased from 2013 (7.75%) to 2018 (14.9%), which started falling again in 2019. The SD value of 4.074 was significantly higher than the normal range. Nonetheless, the correlation between NPLs and CAR was −0.12, which was highly negative and was on the expected line. On the other hand, the RWA varied significantly from 12.1% (2008) to 26.94% (2016), and the mean and SD values were 21.06 and 5.205, respectively. The SD value was significantly higher (4.074) than the normal distribution, and the negative correlation (−0.021) between RWA and NPLs suggests that with the increase in RWA, the NPLs ratios decreased in Ireland.

Thus, our analysis shows mixed results for the UK, India, and Ireland. Significant variation in the trends of CAR and RWA for the UK and Ireland resulted in a negative correlation. This indicated that these jurisdictions managed the capital ratios to reduce NPLs. There was a positive correlation between NPLs and CAR and NPLs and RWA. Moreover, a relatively flattened curve suggested that these ratios could not bring NPLs down in India due to several internal factors that need further investigation. Nevertheless, better asset quality is vital for revitalising the banking system.[20] The risk-weighted approach for assessing asset quality has a comparative advantage over the CAR as it presents a better picture of financial stability.

3.2.2 Liquidity Ratio

Liquidity is another microeconomic determinant that is vital in controlling distressed assets. BCBS defines it as the ability of the banks to have available cash or to readily find the cash to meet their obligations when they become due without incurring any unexpected losses.[21] It is the degree of convertibility into cash or the ease of converting assets to cash.[22] The bank's inability to meet its financial obligations leads to current and future risks. Therefore, liquidity creation attempts to avert credit risk and promote economic conditions.

Most importantly, liquidity creation allows banks to increase their credit flow[23] by generating more income. However, researchers argued that liquidity and equity have an opposite relationship. Equity reduces as liquidity expands in an individual bank in each quarter.[24] When the banks convert the deposits into bank equity, it becomes illiquid. Changing deposits into capital also reduces liquidity, putting the banks at severe risk. GFC exposed several drawbacks of banks' liquidity risk management, and the banks worldwide wholly or partially failed to manage liquidity.[24]

In commercial banks, liquid assets play a crucial role because banks operate mainly with the funds of depositors, which are considered essential balance sheet items that can maintain the depositors' confidence.[25] In a healthy bank, the liabilities, including deposits, market funds, and other credits, are important liquidity sources. The Basel Committee has proposed a minimum threshold for short-term liquidity for member countries known as the liquidity coverage ratio (LCR) from January 2015 onwards. Initially, the condition set was at 60%, with a 10% increase annually to reach the systemic disturbance and strengthening of banking systems to finance economic activity. Basel has designed LCR to measure the bank's flexibility when creditors withdraw credit from the market in a crisis.[26]

---

[20] Athanasoglou et al. (2006), p. 121.

[21] Kalanidis (2016).

[22] ObilorIbe (2013), p. 37.

[23] Diamond and Rajan (2010).

[24] Natacha et al. (2006).

[25] Spindt and Tarhan (1980), p. 198.

[26] Hartlage (2012), p. 453.

BCBS addressed structural resilience through the Net Stable Funding Ratio (NSFR), a second liquidity ratio. It advocates adopting alternative liquidity approaches (ALA) if jurisdictions do not have enough assets and liquidity to meet banks' needs for high-quality liquid assets (HQLA).[27] LCR may even cause banks to increase borrowings at an unmanageable level, and even LCR can push banks to engage in regulatory arbitrage, resulting in reduced financial stability.[28] Basel argued that the LCR should ensure that banks hold a sufficient reserve of HQLA to survive liquidity stress lasting 30 calendar days.[28] Adequate liquidity is also needed to avoid the forced sale of the asset with a heavy loss at an unfavourable market condition.[29]

Liquid assets to deposits and short-term funding[30] are essential indicators of financial stability. Liquid assets to deposits and short-term funding proportion remain highly fluctuating for the UK (see Annexure 2). It varied from 36.27% to 69.098% from 2008 to 2020, with a mean value of 55.58. However, the SD value was 7.32, considerably higher than the normal distribution level of ±2. Nevertheless, the correlation was negative (−0.436) between NPLs and liquid assets to deposits and short-term funding, indicating that with the increase in liquid assets to deposits and short-term funding, NPLs will decrease, confirming the arguments presented in the preceding paragraphs.

In India, liquid assets to deposits and short-term funding range from 6.706% in 2013 to 13.285% in 2019, with a marginal variation. The SD value is within the range of ±2, indicating that the distribution was normal. However, the correlation value was positive (+0.755), demonstrating no impact of liquid assets on deposits and short-term funding on NPLs as both variables moved in a similar direction. However, India can also achieve the results obtained by the UK by addressing the issue with systemic improvement and increasing LCR.

The proportion of liquid assets to deposits and short-term funding ratio remained inconsistent for Ireland, and it was highest (40.123%) in 2012 and lowest (26.758%) in 2017. The mean value (34.27) indicates that the variation was highly inconsistent. Moreover, the SD value exceeded the normal distribution range. The correlation between liquid assets to deposits and short-term funding and NPLs was positive (+0.434), indicating that it could not control the NPLs ratio in Ireland. Thus, the variable has a mixed impact on NPLs in these jurisdictions. The impact was positive in the UK and India, and Ireland needs to work on it to improve the results.

[27] Bank for International Settlements (2013).

[28] Leland and Pyle (1997).

[29] Sachs (1997), pp. 1–2.

[30] The ratio of the value of liquid assets (easily converted into cash) to short-term funding plus total deposits. Liquid assets include cash and due from banks, trading securities and at fair value through income, loans and advances to banks, reverse repos and cash collaterals. Deposits and short-term funding include total customer deposits (current, savings and term) and short-term borrowing (money market instruments, CDs and other deposits).

3.2.3 Income Diversification

Income diversification (ID) and NPLs have positive and negative relationships, and banks should not be dependent only on interest income; instead, they should diversify their banking activities in trading, shares, etc., to increase profitability. Banks with diversified incomes are more cautious and try to lower the risks by investing less in high-risk investments.[31] The banks also explore increasing income through investment banking, advisory and brokerage, underwriting fees, and commissions, etc. The traditional income of banks consists of interest income and bank profitability.[32] Banks with higher incomes have better loan performance, showing the inverse relationship between the NPLs and ID. In ID, shifting from interest to non-interest income is imperative to cope with the increasing market competition, and these changes in the income structure may affect the banking sector's stability.

ID is important as it improves banks' profitability and stability, despite the counter-argument suggesting that ID has no significant advantage and does not help to reduce risk.[33] A research study highlighting the relationships between ID and bank stability claims that diversified banks are likely to have positive financial performance, and this is due to economies of scale.[34] The bank's risk-adjusted performance depends on its overall loan portfolio, which may increase with the diversification into non-interest income.[35] There are different benefits that a bank can aid by diversifying into non-interest income, such as increased efficiency and reduction in total risk, which will reduce the volatility in the earnings and increase the bank's market share. The second highlighted benefit is that it generates more revenue and improves bank profitability.[36]

Some researchers argue that ID neither enhances risk-adjusted returns nor improves profitability. It leads to increased costs and vitality in income, and higher diversification leads to lower profitability, efficiency, and stability.[37] Therefore, the indefinite relationship between diversification and profitability (risk) remains confusing, and such unrest persists because most literature considers assets or income diversity alone and has quite different characteristics.[38] The risk will increase if banks generate more interest-based income through loans. Therefore, the loans and other earning assets, such as derivatives and securities, considered risk-based assets, might be more inconsistent than the non-interest income during cyclical downturns.[39]

---

[31] Khan et al. (2020), p. 135.

[32] Tariq et al. (2021), p. 1492.

[33] Williams (2016), p. 16.

[34] Sharma and Anand (2018), p. 1625.

[35] Nisar et al. (2018), p. 60.

[36] Valverde and Fernández (2007), p. 2043.

[37] Adesina (2021), p. 303.

[38] Hsieh et al. (2013), p. 42.

[39] Cavallo and Majnoni (2001).

The issue of ID and bank risk also captured attention in the UK, India, and Ireland. The UK set up the Vickers Commission to suggest reform to the supervisory structure of financial services. It advocated ring-fencing[40] of the UK retail banks, separating deposit and lending functions from investment banking. It emphasised that banks should have an equity ratio of at least 10%. The report highlighted that there should be an internationally indisputable agreed loss-absorbing debt to avoid the crisis. The Commission argued that it sees merits in the UK retail ring-fencing and envisaged that the universal banks should maintain the retail capital ratio in conformity with the UK banks. Therefore, UK banks have separated capitalised retail from other banking activities. It emphasises how interest income and ID impact banks' performance during critical market conditions. The UK banking system is strong enough to control and support household finances, businesses, corporate firms, etc., with the help of the economic recovery programme.[41]

In India, various studies examined the impact of ID and bank performance[42] and argued that the dynamism between ID and bank performance is limited. The study of the effect of diversification on the profitability and insolvency risk measures for the public and private, domestic, and foreign sector banks concludes that ownership does matter in the pursuit of non-interest income.[43] Fee-based income significantly reduces the risk for public sector banks (PSBs) because they pursue more fee-based income when faced with poor loan quality, as evidenced by higher LLP. Moreover, diversification benefits India's PSBs from a regulatory perspective. However, for the private sector banks, both domestic and foreign, the pursuit of fee-based income increases risk, as measured by the volatility of ROA. Non-interest and fee-based income positively impacted the total operating income and bank profitability.[44] Therefore, diversifying public and private domestic banks reduces default and leverage risk while increasing portfolio risk.

A research study concluded that Indian banks have poor ID ranging from 2% to 24.8% in PSBs and 5.45% to 37.73% in private sector banks,[45] severely impacting the market concentration and diversification of bank performance. It further argued that revenue diversification negatively affects cost efficiency, but there was no impact on profit efficiency.[46] Another study confirmed that ID increases returns with relatively less risk for medium and large banks and propagates diversification in small banks.[34]

In evaluating the ID in the European banking sector, the EU Liikanen Report concluded that no business model fared well or badly in the financial crisis. It

---

[40] Ring-fencing is broadly designed for the banks to focus on its traditional interest-generating retail and wholesale financial intermediation activities.

[41] Edmonds (2022).

[42] Horta et al. (2016), p. 172.

[43] Pennathur et al. (2012).

[44] Sarkar (2016), p. 156.

[45] Kaur et al. (2018).

[46] Nguyen and Nghiem (2016), p. 980.

further states that it is necessary to legally separate certain hazardous financial activities from deposit-taking banks within the banking group. The activities to be separated would include proprietary trading of securities and derivatives, and certain other activities closely linked with securities and derivatives markets.[47]

The Central Bank of Ireland report shows that fees and other income arise from diversified business activities, including wealth, bank assurance, foreign exchange, and transactional banking fees.[48] The report also envisaged that the wealth and insurance business was a key driver of this growth, where operating income increased by 11%, new business sales were up 11%, and life market share grew from 2% to 22%. The bank customer base increased from 26% in 2018 to 32% in 2019. It indicates that the system transforms culture and business model and delivers efficiency. Moreover, there was a 4% reduction in operating expenses, excluding levies and regulatory changes, indicating a greater emphasis on working strategically with improved ways, creating capacity to absorb higher depreciation and targeted investment.[48]

The relationship between the NPLs and banks' non-interest income for the UK, India, and Ireland, as presented in Annexure-3, shows that in the UK, the bank's non-interest income was lowest in 2019 (36.28%) and highest at 59.85% in 2011, with a mean value of 47.41 and significantly higher SD (6.25) with abnormal data distribution. The positive correlation value for the UK suggests that non-interest income and NPLs moved in a similar direction, thus establishing no significant relationship between the two variables. In India, the proportion of non-interest income was lowest at 26.23% in 2012 and highest at 35.64% in 2009, with a mean value of 30.06. The SD value was also higher (3.47) than the normal distribution of ±2, indicating a significant deviation in the data distribution. The correlation result was negative with −0.32, indicating that with the increase in non-interest income, the NPLs tend to decrease, supporting ID. The data for Ireland was not available for the entire reference period. However, it is evident that non-interest income in Ireland was significantly higher and ranged from 72.23% to 78.22% during the last 5 years; as a result, the mean value was 60.42, and the SD was +2.47. The correlation result was also positive at 0.023, suggesting no impact of non-interest income on NPLs, as both moved in a similar direction. Based on the prevailing market situation analysis, the banks may opt for ID to fetch more income.

3.2.4 *Inefficient Management and Cost Efficiency*

Banking management is responsible for the bank's failure and the rise in the NPLs ratio; therefore, the bank should focus on effective alternative operational activities to reduce non-productive expenditure. Effectively managing non-productive

[47] Liikanen (2012).

[48] Bank of Ireland (2019).

spending is considered an important task for credit risk management.[49] Policymakers argued that bad management of the banking firm results in the banks' inefficiency, which causes problems in granting loans to the borrowers.[49] Poor evaluation skills result in poor management, where the banks are inefficient enough to check or evaluate the customers' credit applications properly.[50] It leads to lower credit ratings for the approved loans and a high probability of defaults, which increases the level of NPLs. Moreover, banks' inefficiencies decrease profits and increase the chances of high NPLs.[51]

On the other hand, cost efficiency, a ratio between operating expenses and total assets, also helps in improving the NPLs ratio.[4] However, a thin line separates inefficient banking operations and cost-efficiency, and highly profitable banks have an efficient management system and are crucial in lending. The banks should be more critical about the amortisation plan, paying the contract negotiation expenses, calculating the costs to withhold and deposit and disposing of the collateral when loans become non-payable.[52] Effective FinTech may improve cost efficiency, and managers must adopt better technologies for making critical judgments. New marketing and pricing methods would also help to enhance capital by improving profit efficiency. Therefore, an efficient intermediation process is important for reducing NPLs' burden and fostering economic growth.

A research study evaluating the efficiency of FIs has developed four hypotheses: bad luck, bad management, skimping, and moral hazard.[53] The first three hypotheses examined the relationship between bank efficiency and NPLs, and the fourth examined the nexus between bank efficiency and capitalisation.[53] It concluded that problematic loans preceded a reduction in cost efficiency and that cost efficiency preceded problem loans. Thus, the study supported both skimping and bad luck hypotheses. However, the average cost efficiency of banks has increased. It has not harnessed its full potential[54] and such results were due to the slowdown in economic activity after the GFC. Cost efficiency may be considered an important signal for potentially problematic loans. A study.[55] revealed that the banking sector was following the bad management hypothesis. However, the causality between cost efficiency and LLP in banking sectors of CEE countries failed to identify any evidence of a bad management hypothesis, despite identifying a significant negative correlation between problem loans and efficiency.[55]

The study also analysed the relationship between banks' cost-to-income ratio and NPLs and bank overhead cost to total cost and NPLs for the UK, India, and Ireland, based on the data presented in Annexure 3. The bank's cost-to-income ratio

---

[49] Charnes (1978), p. 429.

[50] Karim et al. (2010), p. 118.

[51] Festic et al. (2011).

[52] Konishi and Yukihiro (2004), p. 215.

[53] Berger and Bouwman (2017), p. 139.

[54] Buchs and Mathisen (2005).

[55] Rossi et al. (2005).

was highest in the UK in 2012 (74.28%) and lowest in 2008 (56.44%), with a mean value of 64.49. The higher SD value (5.096) indicates a significant deviation in data distribution. Nevertheless, the negative (−0.168) correlation shows that with the increase in the cost-to-income ratio, NPLs decrease. In India, banks' cost-to-income ratio was highest at 43.44% in 2019 and lowest at 48.09% in 2008, with a mean value of 46.021 (see Fig. 3.2) and an SD value of 1.462, which was within the normal range. However, the correlation value was positive (+0.123). The bank cost-to-income ratio in Ireland was highly inconsistent and varied from 19.37% to 64.12% over 13 years, with a mean value and SD at 45.32% and 15.29%, respectively. SD value was much higher than the normal range of ±2, indicating abnormal distribution. The negative correlation (−0.055) between the two variables indicates that with an increase in cost, the income ratio and NPLs decrease, which is not on the expected line.

On the other hand, the proportion of bank overhead costs for the UK was lowest at 0.39% in 2010 and highest at 1.68% in 2019, with mean, SD, and correlation values of 1.17, 0.39 and −0.86, respectively. For India, the proportion of bank overhead costs to total assets ranges from 1.62% to 2.05%, with a mean and SD value of 1.81 and 0.13, and the correlation results were positive (0.11), which indicates that with an increase in the bank overhead cost NPLs also increases which is not on the expected line. In Ireland, these values have marginal variation ranging from 0.11 to 2.01(see Annexure 3), with mean and SD values of 1.09 and 0.61 within the normal distribution range. The correlation result is also positive with 0.19, indicating that with the increase in overhead bank costs, NPLs also increase. Thus, we have obtained mixed results for the UK, India and Ireland, and these jurisdictions must make efforts to improve the impact of cost, the income ratio, and banks' overhead cost on NPLs.

3.2.5 Return on Assets

On the other hand, ROA measures the ratio of the bank's profitability to its total assets and assesses the bank's efficiency.[56] It measures how efficiently the bank's management generates profit from the total assets on its balance sheet. The higher the ROA, the more efficient the bank management is in managing its balance sheet, and usually, a low ROA has more assets involved in generating profit. It helps to avoid the introduced deformity because of the differences in financial leverage and complications in the tax laws.[57] ROA displays a wide variation across the banks within the quarter and across the banks over time.[57]

[56] Rajan (1994), p. 339.

[57] Kupiec and Lee (2012), p. 1.

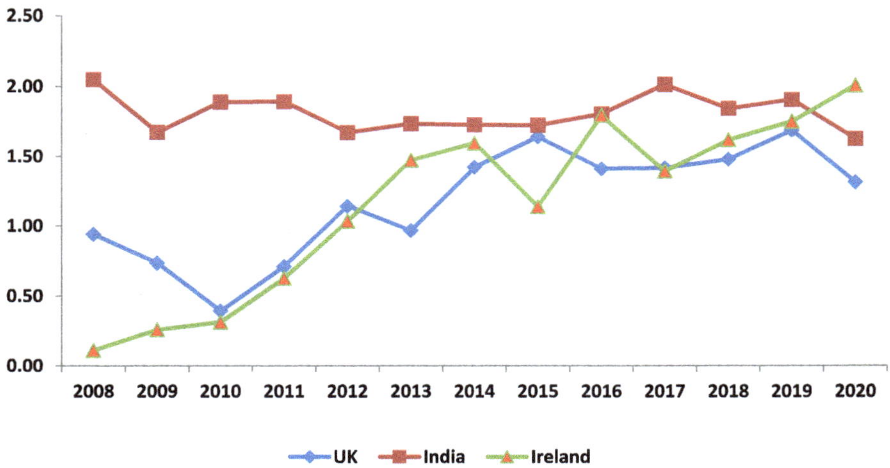

Fig. 3.2 Banks Overhead Costs to Total Assets (%). Source: Developed based on the from the World Development Indicators, World Bank. Data is placed in Annexure 3

Several studies[58] have examined the relationship between ROA and NPLs and concluded a significant and negative relationship. In other words, their findings show that banks with high efficiency and a high rate of profitability have less pressure to make profits and thus less dependence on investing in risk-bearing assets and, therefore, lower NPLs. At the same time, banks with low levels of profitability have more problems with high rates of NPLs. Some research studies derived opposite results and argued that banks with high ROA and ROE were at higher risk and thus faced a higher NPLs rate.[59] Moreover, influential economic conditions generate higher ROAs, and the banks' performance is affected mainly when the market uses the cost of capital to determine the possible return from the investment. The reason is that the interest rate determines the banks' income, which eventually affects ROA.[59] If banks increase the ROA, they must maximise their earning and assets' growth at a certain level and even improve the credit quality.[60]

Now, we examine the relationship between NPLs and ROA for the UK, India, and Ireland using a data series placed in Annexure 2 and depicted in Fig. 3.3. ROA for the UK was lowest (−0.015%) in 2010 and highest (0.672%) in 2015, with a mean value of 0.260 and SD of 0.259 within a normal range of ±2. There was a negative correlation between the NPLs and ROA, which confirms that with the increase in ROA, the NPLs will decrease and demonstrate high profitability with reduced risk. In India, ROA values were lowest (0.177%) in 2019 and highest (1.645%) in 2008, with mean values of 0.201 and SD 0.250, confirming the consistency in data distribution within the normal range. The negative correlation (−0.812)

[58] Stakic (2014), p. 122 and Muhovic and Subic (2019), p. 21.

[59] Tabash (2019), p. 27.

[60] Puspitasari et al. (2021), p. 727.

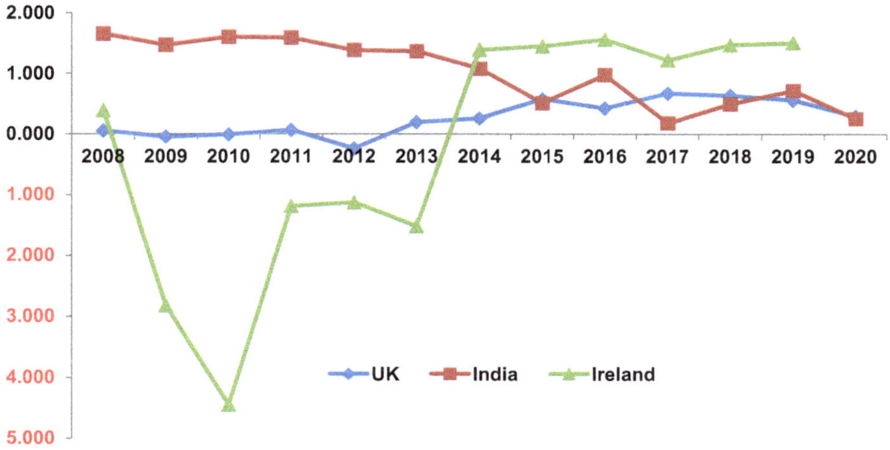

Fig. 3.3 Trend of Return on Assets(%). Source: Developed based on the data from World Development Indicators, World Bank. Data is placed in Annexure 2

results represent that with the increase in the ROA, the NPLs will decrease. ROA in Ireland was lowest (0.177%) in 2017 and highest (1.645%) in 2008, with a mean value of 1.015 and SD of 0.503, and the correlation results were also negative (−0.873). The mean, SD, and correlation results were similar for all three jurisdictions. Research studies on the relationship between NPLs and ROA confirm our findings. Therefore, the jurisdictions should increase ROA and profitability, reducing NPLs.[61]

3.2.6 Return on Equity

ROE is an important indicator for measuring banks' assets and net capital income. It presents the financial performance of a bank and measures its profitability level. Investors and corporate leaders have used this tool to estimate how much profit the owner can hold. ROE is an important indicator for investors because the analysis done by the investors can determine the benefits of the investments.[62] If the value of ROE is higher, the performance of the companies will be better, leading to a rise in stock prices. Also, if the stock prices increase, the stock return of banks will increase,[63] subsequently increasing profitability and reducing NPLs.

---

[61] Yanuardi and Sumiati (2014), p. 274 and Buchory (2015), p. 57.

[62] Purnamasari (2015), p. 80.

[63] Iskandar (2020), p. 704.

As per an estimate, the average ROE in the banks in the EU was significantly higher at the outset of the GFC, at 10.6%. It substantially decreased after reaching a peak in 2013 (25.8%), which was higher than 8% in most markets of the EU Member States.[64] A research study examining the relationship between NPLs and ROE concluded that banks' profitability ratio is closely related to banks' risk-taking behaviour.[61] As highly profitable banks have fewer incentives to engage in high-risk activities, ROE is likely to be negative in such a situation.[65] The authors have established a negative correlation between ROE and NPLs,[66] and this result indicates that deterioration of profitability ratios leads to an increase in NPLs, confirming banks' risk-taking behaviour. This negative relationship also aligns with the argument that bad management leads to riskier activities and weaker performance. Yet another study[67] concluded that individual banks have also identified a significant negative correlation between NPLs and profitability ratios (ROE).

Figure 3.4 and Annexure 2 present the trend of the ROE of the UK, India and Ireland. There has been a significant variation in the ROE of the UK, which was lowest (−1.67%) in 2009 and highest (7.44%) in 2017, with a mean value of 2.94 and the SD of 3.692, and a higher SD value indicates that the data distribution was inconsistent. Nevertheless, the correlation between ROE and NPLs was negative (−0.804), indicating that with an increase in ROE, NPLs decrease.

In India, ROE varied from −5.10% (2012) to 5.95% in 2017, with mean and SD values of 2.29 and 3.20, respectively. The higher SD value indicates an abnormal data distribution, and the correlation between ROE and NPLs for India was highly negative (−0.753), indicating that the rise in the ROE ratio will decrease NPLs. On the other hand, in Ireland, the fluctuation in data was significantly higher, and it came down from 24.74% in 2008 to 1.78% in 2020, with a mean value of 13.61. The SD value was significantly higher (8.52) than the normal data distribution range ±2. Nevertheless, the negative correlation value (−0.918) supports the argument that higher ROE effectively controls the NPLs ratio. Thus, these three jurisdictions have performed on the expected line, and a rise in ROE helped to level down NPLs. Such a trend should persist so that NPLs remain under control.

3.2.7 Net Interest Margin

NIM measures the bank's health and efficiency in storing deposits and sharing the loans. It is considered the most important determinant of an intermediary financial business. It also sees the bank's ability to operate with higher interest rates than

[64] European Commission (2017).

[65] Makri et al. (2014), p. 93.

[66] Boudriga et al. (2009), p. 286.

[67] Cotugno et al. (2010).

Fig. 3.4 Trend of Return to Equity (%). Source: Developed by the researcher based on the data from the World Development Indicators, World Bank. Data is placed in Annexure 2

interest expenses. It is an interest accumulating on the outstanding liabilities and is a crucial indicator of a bank's profitability and growth.[68] One relevant factor that influences the NIM is the average size of the transactions. The economies of scale reduce the average costs, which can have the opposite impact on bank profitability and higher profit results from low loan losses.[69] A research study on two stages of interest margin determination concludes that NIM and NPLs had a negative impact on bank profitability. They further argued that as the NIM increases, the ROA also increases because the profit generated by the banks also increases.[69] Banks usually focus on increasing their NIM to minimise default risk, establishing a direct relationship between the NIM and NPLs.[39]

The data series on NIM presented in Annexure 3 shows that NIM for the UK was highest at 1.32% in 2020 and lowest at 2.13% in 2017, with a mean value of 1.59 and an SD value of 0.26. The correlation value remained positive (0.022), which indicates that with the increase in NIM, the NPLs also increased, which is not on the expected line. The NIM value for India was relatively higher than in the UK, which was 2.72% in 2020 and 3.64% in 2019. The mean and SD values were 3.02 and 0.25, respectively. The lower SD value indicates that the data distribution was normal, and the interest margin remained normal. However, the positive correlation results confirm that NPLs also increase with the increase in NIM. An empirical

[68] Pupitasari et al. (2021), p. 727.

[69] Angori et al. (2019).

study investigating NIM ratios in Indian banks had a considerably high mean value (36) and SD (16.5), concluding that 36% of the NIM comes from fee-based trading activities. It further states that the average MIM for foreign banks was 41%, for private domestic banks 37% and for public banks 31%.[70]

On the other hand, in Ireland, NIM varied from 0.17% in 2008 to 1.50% in 2020, and the variation was insignificant, considering the variation in the UK and India, which was relatively higher. The mean and SD values were 1.01 and 0.33, respectively. However, the correlation between NIM and NPLs was positive. Thus, the NIM and NPLs relationship was positive in all the jurisdictions, indicating that with the increase in NIM, NPLs also increase, possibly due to varying economic factors across jurisdictions and banks, including the quantum of NIM, lending behaviour and pattern and risk-bearing capacity.

3.2.8 Bank Size

The size of the banks was also considered a crucial microeconomic determinant of NPLs, which decides the banks' financial stability.[71] Critics argued that large banks enjoy implicit government subsidies that enable them to undertake more risk.[72] Moreover, there is an argument that large-sized banks are less affected by information asymmetry than small banks.[73] A large bank has substantial total assets and has the availability of funds, effective credit risk management, and a sound evaluation system. Larger banks have better management skills to recover loans from borrowers, and bank size negatively impacts NPLs.

Large assets mean banks have a large volume of credit to distribute and reduce their interest rate.[74] Such a low interest rate means easing down the credit payments and reducing the capacity of the problematic loans faced by the banks. Total assets owned by the banks are an important parameter when judging the size of banks. The banks with more significant assets can generate greater profits, positively affecting the NPLs. However, controlling the bank size is also essential, as large banks may benefit from greater diversification, reducing the risk exposure in their capital.[75] A research study argued that large banks choose more diversification opportunities, which is assumed to be a proxy for diversification.[76] Even the bank's performance

[70] Ahamed (2017), p. 1.

[71] Lu et al. (2005), p. 41.

[72] Gandhi and Lustig (2015), p. 733.

[73] Ranjan and Chandra (2003), p. 81.

[74] Yulianti and Ibrahim (2018), p. 205.

[75] Altunbas et al. (2007), p. 49.

[76] Bardhan and Mukherjee (2016), p. 483.

plays a crucial role in affecting NPLs,[76] and growing bank size is related to bank profitability in a positive sense.[77]

However, these arguments are undoubtedly contrary to the famous theory, the 'too-big-to-fail', which argued that larger banks would tend to undertake more risk, mainly due to the higher liquidity in the form of bonds, compensating for increased credit risk. Therefore, sometimes limiting the bank size helps to ensure stability in a financial system that has always been a focal point of banking supervision and regulation.[78] There are chances of a higher NPLs ratio in the larger banks than the smaller ones because they follow a liberal credit policy. In the agency theory, if the size of the firm/bank increases, it results in managerial empire-building, indicating that large banks sometimes symbolise bad governance. However, counter-arguments suggest that larger banks aren't involved in diversification. Instead, they get involved in risky activities, which increase the level of NPLs.[79]

The UK and the EU are making strong efforts to focus on the size of the banks by demanding more capital and liquidity in addition to the Basel III requirements and trying to restrict the banks from participating in risky activities. The bank size reduces the return volatility associated with the investment risk and is also used to lock in superior returns.[75] However, this effect seems non-linear when the bank size surpasses some thresholds, and bank size positively impacts the volatility of returns.

Several studies revealed that bank size had a negative relationship with NPLs, especially in the case of Spanish banks, Indian PSBs, and Taiwanese banks.[80] Therefore, the size-profitability relationship is still not properly distinguished.[81] So far as risk management is concerned, it has positive and negative effects on NPLs. Lastly, smaller banks differ from large banks in many ways. These differences should not affect the average risk-adjusted returns on bank portfolios unless there is a bank-specific extremity in risk.[72] Thus, bank size and NPLs are strongly associated, and large bank size positively and negatively impacts NPLs. GFC is one example of a situation in which the collapse of large banks led to a financial crisis. Therefore, jurisdictions and banks need to critically analyse the situation before taking any decision because the focus on the bank management should remain on risk reduction, irrespective of the size of the banks.

[77] Smirlock (1985), p. 69.

[78] Adusei (2015), p. 1.

[79] de Hann and Poghosyan (2012), p. 3008.

[80] Louizis and Vouldis (2012), p. 1012.

[81] Pasiouras and Kosmidou (2007), p. 222.

3.2.9 Z-Score

The indicator-based method recommended by the Basel Committee is one of the most common approaches for identifying systemically important banks. There are three main approaches for identifying systemically important banks include the indicator-based measurement approach recommended by the Basel Committee, the bank's contribution to systemic risk assessment, and the network analysis.[82] One of the important statistical measure is z-score, which captures the probability of a default in a commercial banking system and compares the buffer, such as capitalisation and returns, with the volatility of those returns. The z-score is a vital risk indicator in banking, reflecting banks' insolvency probability and measuring the likelihood of failing or going bankrupt.

The z-score generally measures 'how much variability in its returns a bank can absorb by its capital' without becoming insolvent. The SD value of ROA measures the variability in returns, which works as its denominator and the ratio of equity capital to assets plus ROA as a numerator (Z score = ROA + (Equity/Asset) σ (ROA). Where ROA is the return on assets, equity is shareholders' equity or the net assets of a bank, which is the difference between its total assets and total liabilities, asset refers to the total assets of a bank, and σ (ROA) represents the standard deviation of the ROA which measures the variability (deviation) of ROA value from the mean.[83] If the z-score value is high in a bank, the bank will remain a low risk, and a lower value of the z-score indicates a higher risk. A z-score above 3 indicates a low probability and risk of bankruptcy, and a z-score from 1.8–2.0 suggests some financial distress.[84]

A research study examined the relationship between NPLs and z-score, establishing a negative and significant correlation between concentration and bank stability (z-score), indicating that increased market power will increase risks. It revealed that NPLs, as a dependent variable, exhibit a positive and significant relationship with concentration.[85] It was argued[86] that a bank becomes insolvent when its capital falls to zero. However, this assumption is not realistic and practical because a bank needs a positive threshold capital to operate, and it cannot sustain itself below that level. Therefore, the z-score could be considered an accounting-based measure that gauges the distance to default (NPLs).[82]

The trend of the z-score for the UK, India and Ireland presented in Annexure 3 indicates that the z-score for the UK and India was consistently higher. In the UK, it was the lowest at 4.96 in 2008 and the highest at 17.83 in 2018, with a mean value of 12.38 and an SD of 4.85. However, the SD results indicate that the distribution was abnormal and remained higher than ±2. Correlation results suggest that with the

[82] Bengtsson et al. (2013), p. 27.

[83] Xiping et al. (2022).

[84] Altman (2019), p. 31.

[85] Aldomy et al. (2020).

[86] Barry et al. (2011), p. 1327.

increase in z-score, the NPLs ratios declined, and a high z-score indicates a low-risk bank. The higher SD value presents a more significant deviation of data from the mean, and a positive increase will negatively impact NPLs and reduce the chances of insolvency.

In India, the z-score fluctuated from 16.94 (2014) to 23.82 (2018), with a mean value of 19.44 and a relatively higher SD value (2.58). The correlation results between NPLs and z-score were positive (0.92), indicating that with the increase in z-score, NPLs increase, which is not on the expected line, and an in-depth analysis will bring out the real facts. In Ireland, the z-score varies from 0.02 (2010) to 13.72 (2014), with a mean value of 7.87 and an SD of 4.89, which shows abnormal data distribution. However, the correlation between NPLs and z-score was negative. Among the three jurisdictions, the z-score was more consistent for the UK and Ireland, and the positive correlation result for India signified that India should engage in a more in-depth critical analysis.

3.3 Comparative Analysis of Performance

The preceding section analysed the performance of microeconomic indicators for the UK, India, and Ireland using time series data from 2008 to 2020, which the researcher obtained from the World Bank website, which compiles data on development indicators is a reliable source for the robustness and reliability of data (for more detail see Chap. 1, Sect. 1.4.2). Now, based on the mean value of each variable/indicator, we rank them 1, 2 and 3 (Table 3.1). The multiplication of the mean value by the rank obtained the final score for each jurisdiction. A jurisdiction performing relatively better on a particular indicator was awarded the highest weightage of 3. The jurisdiction got a lower average value, ranked one, and accordingly, the rank increases for a higher average value.

The UK has performed better than India and Ireland on two indicators, whereas India on five and Ireland on three. However, the composite score obtained was highest (405.578) for the UK, followed by Ireland (371.931). Among the three jurisdictions, India's performance was relatively lower than that of the UK and Ireland, with a composite value of 322.098. Despite India's comparatively better performance on five indicators, its combined score was relatively lower, which could be due to the lower average score. The performance of the UK was relatively better than that of India and Ireland in terms of many microeconomic indicators. Therefore, India requires more efforts, particularly on the policy and regulatory front, to improve performance so that NPL ratios remain under control.

Table 3.2 consolidates and analyses the results obtained for the UK, India, and Ireland for the SD value and correlation on the ten microeconomic indicators. Table 3.2 indicates that for the UK, the SD value was lower than ±2 on four indicators, including banks' capital-to-assets ratio, ROA, NIM, and overhead bank costs to total assets. SD value was lower for bank capital to assets ratio, regulatory capital to RWA, ROA, NIM, bank cost to income ratio, and overhead bank costs to total

Table 3.1 Comparative Performance of the UK, India, and Ireland on Microeconomic Indicators Using Average Values (2008–2020)

	Countries								
	UK			India			Ireland		
Indicators	Value	Rank	Score	Value	Rank	Score	Value	Rank	Score
Banks' Capital to Assets Ratio	6.21	1	6.21	7.27	2	14.54	10.02	3	30.06
Bank Regulatory Capital to Risk-Weighted Assets	18.34	2	36.68	13.47	1	13.47	21.06	3	63.18
Liquid Assets to Deposits and Short-term Funding	55.48	3	166.44	10.01	1	10.01	34.27	2	68.54
Banks Non-interest Income	47.41	2	94.82	30.06	1	30.06	60.42	3	181.26
Return on Assets	0.26	3	0.78	1.015	2	2.03	−0.18	1	−0.18
Return on Equity	2.94	2	5.88	13.61	3	40.83	−13.02	1	−13.02
Net Interest Margin	1.59	2	3.18	3.11	3	9.33	1.013	1	1.013
Bank Cost to Income Ratio	64.49	1	64.49	46.02	3	138.06	45.32	2	45.32
Bank Overhead Costs to Total Assets	1.169	2	2.338	1.816	3	5.448	1.09	1	1.088
Z- Score	12.38	2	24.76	19.44	3	58.32	7.87	1	7.87
Composite Score	**405.578**			**322.098**			**371.931**		
Overall Rank	**I**			**III**			**II**		

Source: Computed by the researcher based on data placed in Annexure 1 to 3

Table 3.2 Microeconomic Indicators: Comparative Performance

	Countries					
	UK		India		Ireland	
Indicators	SD	Correlation	SD	Correlation	SD	Correlation
Banks' Capital to Assets Ratio	L	N	L	P	H	N
Bank Regulatory Capital to Risk-Weighted Assets	H	N	L	P	H	N
Liquid Assets to Deposits and Short-term Funding	H	N	H	P	H	P
Banks Non- Non-interest Income	H	P	H	N	H	P
Return on Assets	L	N	L	N	L	N
Return on Equity	H	N	H	N	H	N
Net Interest Margin	L	P	L	P	L	P
Bank Cost to Income Ratio	H	N	L	P	H	N
Bank overhead costs to total assets.	L	N	L	P	L	N
Z- Score	H	N	H	P	H	N
Total Low/Negative	**4**	**8**	**6**	**3**	**3**	**7**
Total High/Positive	**6**	**2**	**4**	**7**	**7**	**3**

Note: L = Low, H=High, P = Positive and N = Negative
Source: Developed based on the data placed in Annexures 1, 2 and 3

assets for India. On the other hand, the SD value for Ireland was lower for three variables, including ROA, NIM, and bank overhead costs in total assets. As explained earlier, the SD value presents the deviation in the data from the mean value, and a more consistent series may yield better results.

The correlation presents the positive and negative relationship between two variables, which helps to make a critical argument about the movement of these variables. Out of ten variables for the UK, eight were negative, which indicates that with the increase in these variables, the NPLs ratios decreased, though it may not be the case all the time. In the case of India, the negative correlation value was only for three variables, and for Ireland, it was for seven variables. Finally, the performance of the UK and Ireland was relatively better than India on many variables, and the UK managed its assets effectively and maintained NPL ratios of around 1% once it recovered from the GFC. The problem persisted for a longer period in Ireland, and the impact of the GFC was not visible in India. Nevertheless, NPLs remained a paramount problem in India due to their socioeconomic conditions, which differed from those of the UK and Ireland.

3.4 Conclusion

This chapter examined the relationship between microeconomic determinants and NPLs, using the World Bank data series on world development indicators. Our analysis presents mixed results on banks' CAR and RWA for the UK, India, and Ireland, showing that performance on these indicators was relatively better in the UK and Ireland, as they had negative correlation results, which indicates that with the increase in CAR, NPLs decreased. In contrast, these variables moved in the same direction in India, reflecting more volatility. These jurisdictions have also implemented BCBS guidelines, which envisage adequate capital for effective loan risk management. The EU legalised the criteria developed by Basel banking supervision and regulation, and India also followed the Basel guidelines to strengthen its banking system. CAR and RWA are important parameters that help improve asset quality, making the banks distressed-free.

Moreover, the risk-weighted approach for calculating asset ratio presents a better picture of banks' financial stability, and the jurisdictions should emphasise enhancing the RWA ratio. The liquid capital to asset ratio for short-term funding was relatively higher for the UK; as a result, there was a negative correlation with NPLs, indicating that its improvement reduced NPLs. India needs to increase the liquid capital-to-asset ratio to reduce NPLs.

ID increases the chances of profitability; this section concluded that the Vickers Commission in the UK stressed the ring-fencing of financial activities by separating retail banking from equity and shares, and the EU Liikanen report also recommended separating certain hazardous financial activities from deposit-taking banks legally. Therefore, the UK banking system separated retail banking activities from other income-generating activities. Thus, the UK banking system is strong enough to control and support household finances, businesses, corporate firms, etc., compared to India and Ireland. It is important to assess risk before diversifying banking activities so that banks may avoid possible risks. The relationship between non-interest income and NPLs was positive for the UK and Ireland and negative for India, suggesting that diversification helped to reduce NPLs to some extent.

NPLs become a significant hurdle when it comes to the performance of the banks, and effective bank management reduces the chances of risk by timely visualization of risk and initiating corrective measures. Generally, problematic loans reduce cost efficiency, and banks must address these problems to reduce NPLs. The performance of the UK was relatively better in terms of bank cost-to-income ratio and bank overhead cost-to-total assets than India and Ireland, mainly due to effective management of the banking system. Therefore, Ireland and India must improve these parameters, contributing to reducing NPLs.

The relationship between NPLs, ROA, and ROE measures the banks' profitability and efficiency. The banks must increase the ROA and ROE to maximise their earning and asset growth and improve credit quality.[68] Interestingly, the relationship between NPLs and ROA and ROE was negative for the UK, India, and Ireland, which confirms that with the increase in ROA and ROE, the NPLs decrease. Therefore, the jurisdictions should consistently maintain high ROE and ROA to address the problem of NPLs.

The bank size has a positive and negative relationship with NPLs, and banks need to take a lesson from the GFC, where the crisis started with the failure of 'too big to fail banks'. The banks generally undertake more risk by diversifying their income-generating activities to enhance profit, sometimes resulting in a bank failure. Thus, implicit government subsidies, information asymmetries, credit risk management strategies, income diversification, risk-adjusted returns and bank-specific extremity in risk are some phenomena which need critical examination to assess bank risk-bearing capacity irrespective of their size. Moreover, large banks have a relatively higher risk-taking capacity than small banks. The z-score mainly measures how much risk a bank can absorb with its capital without becoming insolvent. The z-score for all the jurisdictions increased over the reference period, with relatively better performance from the UK. A negative correlation between NPLs and z-score for the UK and Ireland indicates a better impact on asset quality than India.

Finally, the chapter consolidated results to present the comparative picture of all the microeconomic determinants to understand their comparative position. The UK performed relatively better on several microeconomic determinants than India and Ireland. These microeconomic determinants influence the level of NPLs to a great extent. They have direct positive and negative impacts on NPLs, provided other factors, including government interference, internal obstacles, and economic dynamism in the jurisdiction, remain constant and neutral. The jurisdictions should rigorously follow international best practices and ensure effective implementation and monitoring of these determinants to decrease NPLs.

References

Abata MA (2014) Asset quality and bank performance: a study of commercial banks in Nigeria. Res J Finance Account 5(18):39

Adesina SK (2021) How diversification affects bank performance: the role of human capital. Econ Model 94:303

Adhikary BK (2006) Non-performing loans in the banking sector of Bangladesh: realities and challenges. Bangladesh Institute of Bank Management, p 75

Adusei M (2015) The impact of bank size and finding risk on bank stability. Cogent Econ Finance 3(1):1

Ahamed MM (2017) Asset quality, non-interest income, and bank profitability: evidence from Indian banks

Aldomy RF, Thim CK, Lan NTP (2020) Bank concentration and financial risk in Jordan. Montenegrin J Econ 16(3):31

Altman EI (2019) Edward I Altman, PhD: fifty years of z-scores to predict the probability of corporate bankruptcy. J Investment Consult 15. https://ssrn.com/ abstract=3 522672. Accessed 8 Apr 2024

Altunbas Y, Carbo S, Gardener EPM et al (2007) Examining the relationship between capital, risk and efficiency in European banking. Eur Finance Manage 13:49

Angori G, Aristei D, Gallo M (2019) Determinants of banks net interest margin: evidence from the euro area during the crisis and post-crisis period. https://doi.org/10.2139/ssrn.3254362. Accessed 5 July 2022

Athanasoglou PP, Delis MD, Staikouras CK (2006) Bank-specific, industry-specific and macroeconomic determinants of bank profitability. J Int Financ Mark Inst Money 18(2):121

Bank of Ireland (2019) Key performance highlights. http://www.bankofireland.com/app/uploads / assets/strategic-report-2019.pdf. Accessed 24 Apr 2022

Bardhan S, Mukherjee V (2016) Bank-specific determinants of non-performing assets of Indian banks. IEEP 13:483–498

Barr RS, Siems TF (1994) Predicting bank failure using DEA to quantify management quality. In: Sharda R, Stefan VB (eds) Operations research/computer science interfaces series. Kluwer

Barry TA, Lepetit L, Tarazi A (2011) Ownership structure and risk in publicly held and privately owned banks. J Bank Financ 35(5):1327

Barseghyan L (2010) Non-performing loans, prospective bailouts, and Japan's slowdown. J Monet Econ 57(7):873

Bengtsson E, Holmberg H, Jonsson K (2013) Identifying systemically important banks in Sweden–What do quantitative indictators tell us? Sveriges Riksbank Econ Rev 2:27

Berger AN, Bouwman CHS (2017) Bank liquidity creation, monetary policy and financial crisis. J Financ Stab 30:139–155

Bernanke BS, Lown CS, Friedman BM (1991) The credit crunch. Brook Pap Econ Act 2:205

BIS (2013) Basel III: The liquidity coverage ratio and liquidity risk monitoring tools. http://www.bis.org/publ/bcbs238.pdf. Accessed 10 Apr 2022

Bock RD, Demyanets A (2012) Bank asset quality in emerging markets: determinants and spillovers. IMF Working Paper No. 12/71. https://ssrn.com/abstract=2028247. Accessed 22 July 2023

Boudriga AK, Taktak NB, Jellouli S (2009) Banking supervision and nonperforming loans: a cross-country analysis. J Financ Econ Policy 1(4):286

Buchory HA (2015) Banking intermediation, operational efficiency and credit risk in banking profitability. Int Bus Econ Law 4(1):57

Buchs T, Mathisen J (2005) Competition and efficiency in banking: behavioural evidence from Ghana. IMF Working Paper WP/05/17. https://www.imf.org/external/pubs/ft/wp/2005 / wpb0517.pdf. Accessed 25 June 2022

Cavallo M, Majnoni G (2001) Do banks provision for bad loans in good times? Empirical evidence and policy implications. World Bank Policy Research Working Paper No 2619. https://ssrn.com/abstract=632687. Accessed 22 April 2022

Charnes A, Cooper WW, Rhodes E (1978) Measuring efficiency of decision-making units. Eur J Oper Res 2:429

Cotugno M, Stefanelli V, Giuseppe T (2010) Bank intermediation models and portfolio default rates: what's the relation? 23rd Australasian Finance and Banking Conference, Sydney. https://ssrn.com/abstract=1662888. Accessed 25 June 2022

Crockett A (1996) The theory and practice of financial stability. De Economists 144:53168

Daniel F, Lars N, Martin W (2010) Loan growth and riskiness of banks. J Bank Finance 34(12):2929

de Hann J, Poghosyan T (2012) Size and earning volatility of us bank holding companies. J Bank Financ 36:3008

Diamond DW, Rajan RG (2010) Liquidity risk, liquidity creation and financial fragility: a theory of banking. J Polit Econ 109:287

Edmonds T (2022) The independent commission on banking: The Vickers Report' https://research-briefings.files.parliament.uk/documents/SN06171/SN06171.pdf. Accessed 22 Apr 2022

European Commission (2017) European semester thematic factsheet banking sector and financial stability. http://ec.europa.eu/info/sites/default/files/file_import/european-semester_thematic-factsheet_banking-sector-financial-stability_en_0.pd. Accessed 15 Apr 2022

Festic M, Kavkler A, Repina R (2011) The macroeconomic sources of systemic risk in the banking sectors of five new EU member states. J Bank Financ 35:310

Gandhi P, Lustig H (2015) Size anomalies in US Bank stock returns. J Financ 70(2):733

Ghosh A (2017) Sector-specific analysis of non-performing loans in the us banking system and their macroeconomic impact. J Econ Bus 93:29

Hartlage AW (2012) The Basel III liquidity coverage ratio and financial stability. Mich Law Rev 111(3):453

Horta IM, Kapelko M, Lansink AO et al (2016) The impact of internationalisation and diversification on construction industry performance. Int J Strateg Prop Manag 20(2):172

Hsieh MF, Chen PF, Lee CC et al (2013) How does diversification impact bank stability? The role of globalisation, regulations, and governance environments. Asia Pac J Financ Stud 42:813

Iskandar Y (2020) The effects of ROA, ROE, NPL and operating expenses to operating revenues on stock return at commercial banks in Indonesia. J Appl Management 18(4):704

Kadioglu E, Telceken N, Ocal N (2017) Effect of assets quality on the bank profitability. Int J Econ Finance 9(7):60

Kalanidis D (2016) The impact of liquidity on bank profitability: post-crisis evidence from European banks. International Hellenic University

Karim MZA, Chan SG, Hassan S (2010) Bank efficiency and non-performing loans: evidence from Malaysia and Singapore. Prague Econ Pap 2:118

Kaur N, Srivatsav S, Jadiyappa, N et al. (2018) Income diversification and bank stability: evidence from India. https://doi.org/10.2139/ssrn.3340806. Accessed 18 June 2022

Khan MA, Siddique A, Sarwar Z (2020) Determinants of non-performing loans in the banking sector in developing state Asian J Account Res 5(1):135

Kjosevski J, Petkovski M (2020) Macroeconomic and bank-specific determinants of non-performing loans: the case of Baltic states. Empirica 1009:48–1028

Klein N (2013) Non-performing loans in CESEE: determinants and impact on macroeconomic performance. IMF Working Paper 13/7. https://www.imf.org/en/Publications/WP/Issues /2016/12/31/Non-Performing-Loans-in-CESEE-Determinants-and-Impact-on-Macroeconomic-Performance-40413. Accessed 5 Jan 2021

Konishi M, Yukihiro Y (2004) Factors affecting the bank risk taking: evidence from Japan. J Bank Financ 28:215

Kupiec P, Lee T (2012) What factors explain the differences in return of assets among community banks? Federal Deposit Insurance Corporation. https://www.fdic.gov/regulations/resources/cbi/report/cbi-roa.pdf. Accessed 30 June 2022

Latif AA, Coleman AK, Charles A (2014) Asset quality in a crisis period: an empirical examination of Ghanaian banks. Rev Dev Finance 4(1):50–62

Leland HE, Pyle DH (1997) Informational asymmetries, financial structure and financial. Intermed J Finance 32(2):371

Liikanen E (2012) High-level expert group on reforming the structure of the EU banking sector. https://ec.europa.eu/info/sites/default/files/liikanen-report-02102012_en.pdf. Accessed 23 Apr 2022

Louizis D, A Vouldis A, Metaxas V (2012) Macroeconomic and bank-specific determinants on non-performing loans in Greece: a comparative study of mortgage, business and consumer loan portfolios. J Bank Finance 36:1012, 1027

Lu D, Thangavelu MS, Qing H (2005) Biased lending and non-performing loans in China's banking sector. J Dev Stud 41:1071–1091

Lucky LA, Nwosi AA (2015) Asset quality and profitability of commercial banks: evidence from Nigeria. Res J Finance Account 18:26

Makri V, Tsagkanos A, Bellas A (2014) Determinants of non-performing loans: the case of Eurozone. Panoeconomicus 61(2):93–206

Muhovic A, Subic J (2019) Analysis and impact of main macro and microeconomic factors on the growth of NPLs in the emerging financial markets. Ekonomika 65(4):21–30

Natacha V, Escorbaic BS, Tiesset M (2006) Bank liquidity and financial stability. Banque de France Financial Stability Review 9. https://www.bis.org/ifc/publ/ifcb28g.pd. Accessed 11 Mar 2022

Nguyen TPT, Nghiem SH (2016) Market concentration, diversification and bank performance in China and India: an application of the two-stage approach with double bootstrap. Manag Financ 42(10):980–998

Nisar S, Peng K, Wang S (2018) The impact of revenue diversification on bank profitability and stability: empirical evidence from the south Asian countries. Int J Financ Stud 6(2):40

ObilorIbe S (2013) The impact of liquidity management on the profitability of banks in Nigeria. J Finance Bank Manage 37

Pasiouras F, Kosmidou K (2007) Factors influencing the profitability of domestic and foreign commercial banks in the European Union. Res Int Bus Financ 21(2):222–237

Pennathur AK, Subrahmanyam V, Vishwasrao S (2012) Income diversification and risk: does ownership matter? An empirical examination of Indian banks. J Bank Financ 36(8):2203–2215

Podpiera J, Weill L (2008) Bad luck or bad management? Emerging banking market experience. J Financ Stab 4(2):135–148

Pupitasari E, Sudiyatno B, Hartoto WE et al (2021) Net interest margin and return on assets: a case in Indonesia. J Asian Finance Econ Bus 8(4):727

Purnamasari D (2015) The effect of changes in return on assets, return on equity and economic value added to the stock price changes and its impact on earnings per share. Res J Finance Account 6(6):80

Puspitasari E, Sudiyatno B, Hartoto WE et al (2021) Net interest margin and return on assets: a case study on Indonesia. J Asian Finance Econ Bus 8(4):727

Rajan RG (1994) Why bank credit policies fluctuate. Q J Econ 2(109):399

Ranjan R, Chandra S (2003) Non-performing loans and terms of credit of public sector banks in India: an empirical assessment. Reserv Bank India Occas Pap 24(3):81

Rossi SPS, Schwaiger M, Winkler G (2005) Managerial behaviour and cost/profit efficiency in the banking sectors of central and eastern European countries. Working Paper https://ssrn.com/abstract=676365. Accessed 28 June 2022

Sachs JD (1997) Alternative approaches to the financial crisis in emerging markets. Harvard University

Sarkar S (2016) The dynamics of the revenue diversification and efficiency of banks in India. IIM Kozhikode Soc Manage Rev 5(2):156–172

Sharma S, Anand A (2018) Income diversification and bank performance: evidence from BRICS nations. Int J Product Perform Manag 67(9):1625

Shrieves RE, Dahl D (1992) The relationship between risk and capital in commercial banks. J Bank Finance 16(2):439–457
Smirlock M (1985) Evidence on the non-relationship between concentration and profitability in banking. J Money Credit Bank 17(1):69
Spindt PA, Tarhan V (1980) Liquidity structure adjustment behavior of large money center banks. J Money Credit Bank 12(2):198
Stakic N (2014) Determinants of trends in the level of non-performing loans in the banking sector in Serbia. Aust Bank 4:122
Tabash M I (2019) An empirical investigation on the relationship between disclosure and financial performance of Islamic banks in The United Arab Emirates. J Asian Finance Econ Bus 6(4):27
Tariq W, Usman M, Tariq A et al (2021) Bank maturity, income diversification and bank stability. J Econ Manage 22(6):1492–1511
Valverde SC, Fernández FR (2007) The determinants of bank margin in European banking. J Bank Financ 31(7):2043–2063
Whalen G (1991) A proportional hazards model of bank failure: an examination of its usefulness as an early warning tool. Econ Rev-Federal Reserve Bank Cleveland 27(1):1
Williams B (2016) The impact of non-interest income on bank risk in Australia. 73. J Bank Financ 73:16–37
Xiping L, Tripe D, Malone C (2022) Measuring bank risk: an exploration of z-score. https://www.efmaefm.org/0EFMSYMPOSIUM/2017/papers/Measuring%20Bank%20Risk_An%20exploration%20of%20z-score.pdf. Accessed 4 May 2022
Yanuardi A, Sumiati DH (2014) Determinants factor for the profitability of banks listed on the Indonesian stock exchange. J Account Multiparadigm 5(2):274
Yulianti E, Ibrahim AR (2018) The effect of capital adequacy and bank size on non-performing loans in Indonesian banks. J Account Res Org Econ 1(2):205–214

Chapter 4
Non-Performing Loans and Regulatory and Supervisory Responses

4.1 Introduction

The previous chapter analysed the impact of the microeconomic determinants on NPLs and vice versa, covering a wide range of determinants, and noticed the positive and negative impact of these determinants on NPLs, which ultimately affect the financial stability of a country. Therefore, it is imperative to provide a suitable and effective regulatory and supervisory response to reduce the impact of these determinants on NPLs. The global organisations dealing with financial sectors, such as the IMF, OECD, EU, etc. and individual jurisdictions have made committed efforts to regulate and supervise the financial sector, including banks, by enacting several regulations, directives, codes, decrees, acts, statutes, etc. In addition, the older and decaying regulatory and policy instruments were replaced with new ones to match the requirements of a diversified banking sector, so that the problem of NPLs was dealt with effectively and to ensure financial stability.

The banking sector witnessed the disastrous event of the GFC in 2008, which erupted so strongly and influenced policies, regulations, and popular opinion across the globe.[1] The phrases 'bank bailouts, "systemic risk,' and 'too big to fail' became common utterances among scholars, researchers, legal experts, and policymakers. The international discussion forum regularly grappled with complex regulatory decisions for specialist regulators.[1] The arguments on the cross-border application of financial regulation that stabilises geopolitics have also become the focal point of discussion.[2] The impact of the GFC was enormous, and the implication of weak regulation was a reality, resulting in regular debate in the parliaments worldwide for carefully crafting new financial regulations that 'matter now as never before'.[1] Therefore, the GFC casts a very long shadow on the shape of current financial

[1] Partnoy (2017).

[2] Aspinwall (1993), p. 53.

A. Dimri, *Non-Performing Loans*, Ius Gentium: Comparative Perspectives on Law and Justice 125, https://doi.org/10.1007/978-3-031-92952-6_4

regulation and scholars continue to debate fundamental questions on the role of the State in the construction and regulation of the financial system as they continue to grapple with persistent and troubling regulatory conundrums, including the complexity and uncertainty in the financial system.[3]

Consequently, the UK, India, and Ireland strengthened their regulatory system and enacted legislation addressing financial sector issues. For instance, the UK replaced the existing system with PRA, FCA, BoE, and HMT, making them responsible for regulating the financial market and ensuring smooth business conduct.[4] Being the EU Member States, the UK and Ireland transposed EU legislation from financial sectors into their domestic law to regulate the financial market and banking business. Brexit prompted the UK to enact the UK Financial Services Act 2021 to make necessary amendments to the EU legal instruments that the UK transposed into domestic law. The UK efforts continued, and in 2023, a new legislation viz-a-viz. the Financial Services and Markets Act (FSMA 2023) was enacted to address the issues of the financial market in the post-Brexit era.

India has multiple regulators to regulate and supervise the financial services and banking business; for instance, the RBI regulates the banking business, SEBI securities, IRDA insurance, FMC forward and futures markets, such as food and public distribution, and the Pension Fund Regulatory and Development Authority (PFRDA) pension funds.[5] The important legislation dealing with financial sector includes the Sick Industrial Companies (Special Provisions) Act 1985, SARFAESI Act 2002 and IBC 2016. In addition, the RBI has also issued guidelines on asset classification, debt restructuring strategies, the provision of loans for long-term projects and infrastructure, etc.

In Ireland, the CBI and ECB regulate and supervise financial sector-related activities and work closely with each other, following the Single Supervisory Mechanism (SSM).[6] Thus, the ECB is the lead regulator, delegating several activities to the CBI as the competent authority in Ireland. Besides transposing EU legislation, the Central Bank Act enforced many codes of conduct and other legislation to regulate the financial market and banking business, including CCMA, ISI, MART, etc.[7]

Hence, the present chapter examines the effectiveness of all these legislation in addressing the problem of NPLs. The chapter also presents a comparative analysis of the legal and supervisory architecture of the UK, India, and Ireland to answer the research questions raised in the first chapter of this book on the competencies of the existing regulations and directives to deal effectively with the issues pertaining to distress in the financial market and banking business.

---

[3] Butler and Macey (1988), p. 677.

[4] Lovegrove and Bainbridge (2019).

[5] Nachane (2022).

[6] Council Regulation (EU) No 1024/2013 of 15 October 2013 conferring specific tasks on the European Central Bank concerning policies relating to the prudential supervision of credit institutions (2013) OJ L 287/63.

[7] Sibley (2019).

4.2 Regulatory and Supervisory System: Global Scenario

The GFC and COVID-19 pandemic prompted global jurisdictions to tighten financial regulatory architecture to control NPLs; accordingly, the USA replaced its multiple federal agencies that regulated the financial system in the USA with the Federal Reserve, the OCC, and the FDIC after enacting the Dodd-Frank Act in 2010. The fragility of the US financial market during the COVID-19 pandemic ripped through the economy, which brought the banks to the 'brink of failure' mainly due to the fragile regulatory model, poorly suited to match its design[8] and warrants suitable changes to match the existing requirements. The EU banking system adopted the bail-in resolution tool and public financial support as a precautionary recapitalisation, along with the SSM and SREP frameworks, to address wide divergences at the national level. ECB principle-based regulations and directives included a preventive restructuring framework that provided a substantial degree of harmonisation. Such legislation permitted cross-border comparison and provided a unified concept of loan classification and the definition of NPLs. The failure of several banks has raised fundamental questions on the resolution mechanism and insolvency processes for EU banks to address the problem of NPLs.[9]

Similarly, Greece introduced a new legal regime in 2010 known as *Katselis Law*[10] to harmonise the framework for NPEs designing an APS ('Hercules') to reduce NPLs cases without state aid intervention. Greek law does not contain a provision for challenges on the grounds of insolvency, and it does not introduce a regulatory framework that provides a floor for the sale price that could protect the seller from litigation. The Italian Guarantee on Securitisation of NPLs aimed to dismantle NPLs with the support of the EC,[11] but it also received criticism. Cyprus amended its bankruptcy code in 2015 and even introduced a new procedure with personal payment schemes for secured and unsecured loans. The Central Bank of the Russian Federation imposed new regulations to manage banks' income, strengthening its oversight by revoking the license of many banks, resulting in a considerable decrease in the number of banks, and Russia received mixed results with these efforts.[12] Despite several efforts, the profitability in the banking sector has been negative due to low-interest rates for a long time, coupled with the increased burden of bad loans and the impact of the COVID-19 pandemic.

[8] Singh (2007).

[9] Huertas (2019), p. 225.

[10] Bazinas and Sakkas (2012).

[11] Amador et al. (2013), p. 365.

[12] Ahmed et al. (1999), p. 1.

4.3 United Kingdom: Overview of Banking Regulations

The UK's banking regulatory and supervisory system evolved gradually until the Western Bank of Glasgow failed in 1857.[13] In 1878, many shareholders were bankrupt due to the collapse of the City of Glasgow Bank,[14] which led to the enactment of the Companies Act 1889. Due to a peculiar self-regulation and external control on interest payable on deposits, the banks lost public confidence in the banking system, and people withdrew their deposits, causing over 20 banks to fail from 1860 to 1890.[15]

The banking crisis[16] erupted, from the Western Bank of Glasgow's collapse in 1857 to the GFC 2008 with Northern Rock Bank, which prompted the regulator and policymakers to make the system compatible and robust. Therefore, in 1979, the Banking Act came into existence, and until then, the BoE had no statutory responsibility to supervise banking activities.[17] The BoE has bail-in and other resolution powers and was responsible for developing resolution strategies and plans, and their execution.[18] However, the innovation in the banking sector and the entry of foreign banks posed challenges and disrupted the relationship between the BoE and the financial sector.[19]

In 1971, the BoE enhanced competition in the banking system by allowing foreign banks and other FIs to compete directly with commercial banks in a range of products in retail markets.[20] This period of deregulation contributed to volatile property markets and a surge in lending without adequate prudential supervision[21] prompting a 'secondary banking crisis' in 1973–1974, where BoE acted as a last resort for the lenders.[22] The impact of the secondary banking crisis was huge and mainly responsible for the dramatic crash in British property prices that caused dozens of small lending banks to face the threat of insolvency and bankruptcy .[23] The increasing pressure from the EEC for greater harmonisation of banking regulation prompted a general overhaul of the banking system governance in the UK.

---

[13] Bagehot (1873).

[14] Acheson and Turner (2008), p. 235.

[15] Mahate (1994), p. 1.

[16] Baker and Collins (1999), p. 428.

[17] Burn (2006).

[18] Gracie et al. (2014), p. 4.

[19] Helleiner (1994).

[20] Schenk (2014), p. 1129.

[21] Schenk (2010).

[22] Capie (2010).

[23] Reid (1982).

4.4 Regulators for the Financial Sector in the UK

In the UK, prudential supervision activities remained with the institutions that supervise banks, securities, insurance, etc., and this proliferation was ineffective in regulating and supervising banking activities. The UK Government abolished the 'plethora of specialist regulatory and supervisory agencies 'by merging all regulations' into a single agency in 1997, considering it one of the most radical changes in the financial institutional structure. Therefore, the Integrated Financial Services Authority (FSA) came into existence, combining nine supervisory agencies. It developed a 'tripartite' shared responsibility structure between the BoE and HMT. The FSA undertook micro-prudential supervision, while the BoE was responsible for overseeing payment methods and maintaining a broad overview of the financial system.[18] The tripartite system continued, necessitating several financial innovations, and was considered one of the healthy mechanisms to ensure financial stability and avert crisis. Despite having such a robust mechanism, the risk continuously accumulated and prompted the regulatory authority to think differently.

Moreover, the effectiveness of the FSA in dealing with the GFC remained questionable, and many flaws became visible in regulatory and supervisory policies that did not go far enough. Critics argued that failures of coordination and information asymmetry among the agencies frustrated systemic oversight.[22] The FSA developed its supervisory approach of treating customers fairly, assuming that most firms intend to deal with customers reasonably. However, the firms focused on increasing profits and grossly violating FSA guidelines on fair treatment, and even sometimes mis-selling the products. This experience led to initiating a process to wind up FSA, and more power was vested in the BoE. Consequently, under the FPC, PRA and FCA, in line with the 'Twin Peaks Model' were established in 2012.[24]

Thus, the PRA and FCA have major responsibilities for regulating banking activities in the UK. PRA authorises banks and building societies in the UK to undertake activities such as arranging, safeguarding, and administering investments and certain residential mortgage lending. These two agencies work closely in the authorisation process, and the PRA is required to obtain the consent of the FCA before granting any permission. In addition, FPC has a macro-prudential mandate that helps to identify the imbalances, risks, and vulnerabilities in the UK financial system.

It directs the PRA and FCA to take appropriate actions to reduce risks.[25] In the UK, if a person is involved in any regulated activity by way of business without permission, it is considered a criminal offence under FSMA [ss (20) (1) (a-b) and (2) (a-c)].[26] PRA and FCA can act against such a person or firm that fails to comply with a conduct rule involved in an infringement by imposing criminal liability for

[24] Twin Peaks Model, the two agencies have clearly defined objectives enabling them to carry out their work expediently and creating an obligation of accountability on the part of each agency.

[25] Putnis et al. (2023).

[26] Financial Services and Markets Act [2000].

misconduct that leads to the failure of a bank, building society or investment firm.[27] But this can be ruled out if it is an authorised person or exempted from the authorisation requirement [ss19 (1) (a-b) and (2)].

The PRA has a three-pronged approach for regulating and supervising firms, including a judgement-based approach, a forward-looking approach[28] and a key-risk-focused approach (see Fig. 4.1). These approaches ensure that the firms do not fall into a financial crisis trap.[29] Thus, it helps them in such a way by avoiding significant disruption to all the critical financial services and reducing the actual and potential systemic risk. The PRA even ensures that firms conduct their business smoothly so that the UK's financial system is not affected and remains stable.

On the other hand, the key role of the HMT is to control public spending, set the direction of the UK's economic policy and work to achieve strong and sustainable economic growth. The HMT is responsible for the UK's financial services and the regulatory framework. Its constitutional duty and responsibility are to ensure that set standards are executed properly and effectively according to the established framework.[30] It also ensures easier access and use of financial services for people

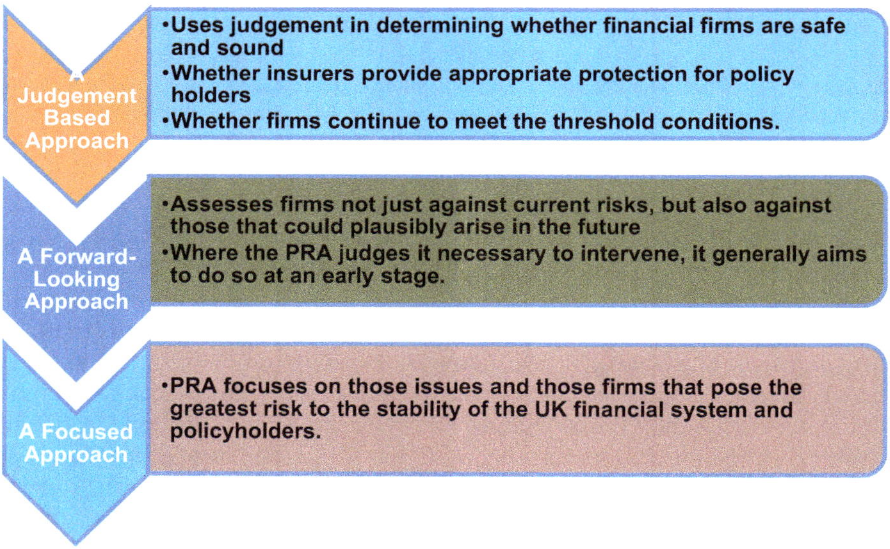

Fig. 4.1 PRA's Approach to Regulation and Supervision. Source: Developed by the researcher based on the information available in existing literature, including Jan Putnis et al. (2021) and Bank of England website

---

[27] Council Regulation (EU) No 575/2013 of 6 July 2013 on prudential requirements for credit institutions and investment firms and amending Regulation (EU) No 648/2012 [2013] *OJ L176/1*.

[28] Lastra (2013), p. 221.

[29] Bank of England (2023).

[30] HMT (2021).

and improves financial sector regulation to protect customers and the economy. Thus, its objectives are to place the public finances on a sustainable footing, ensure the financial systems' stability and increase employment, productivity, and competitiveness.[30]

It is evident that the PRA supervises prudential matters, and the FCA ensures the conduct of these matters.[31] The overlaps persist in the supervision and conduct of activities regulated by the PRA and the FCA. Therefore, the appropriate level of coordination between these entities is essential. Moreover, a debate on the appropriate form of regulatory and supervisory mechanisms continues as financial markets evolve and develop. The obstacles to coherent, effective, and harmonised regulations and supervision have become a point of discussion internationally.[32] The following section analyses the regulations and directives pertaining to financial sectors implemented by the UK to ensure financial stability and to reduce NPLs.

4.5 Directives and Regulations to Regulate the UK Financial Market

The legal system of the UK is integrated with the EU, particularly after the '*acquis communautaire*'[33] in 1957. It has become cohesive under the European Community Act (ECA) 1972, legislation allowing the UK entry into the EU. Under such circumstances, the UK transposed the EU regulations and directives into UK law. This proliferation was criticised by a segment of people who argued that the UK's move to join EEA/EU was a 'posture of hope and optimism or head-shaking despair'.[34] The adoption and continuation of the EU legislation into domestic law persisted even though some were less effective and have put an 'excessive burden on the UK legal system'.[35] The frequent interpretation of ECJ decisions in domestic court cases to decide legal matters reflected the influence of the ECJ on the UK domestic courts.[36]

Many directives and regulations in the EU regulate the currency, emissions, and binary contracts. Until Brexit, the UK transposed the EU directives and regulations into domestic law. Accordingly, MiFID I and II, MiFIR, CRD, PSD AML, etc., have also been transposed into UK domestic law. However, the Financial Services Act 2021 clarifies the legal position of these legislation in the post-Brexit scenario. The following section analyses the role of these financial sector directives and

[31] IMF (2022).

[32] Havrylchyk and Kierzenkowski (2015).

[33] It refers to treaties, EU legislation, international agreements, standards, court verdicts, fundamental rights provisions, and horizontal principles in the treaties.

[34] McMIE, Barker (1973), para 2.

[35] Gordon (2016), p. 511.

[36] Basedow (2023), p. 550.

regulations, how these instruments control the UK banking sector, and to what extent they will remain effective post-Brexit after enacting the Financial Services Act 2021 and FSMA 2023.

4.5.1 Market in Financial Instrument Directive and Market in Financial Instruments Regulation

The Market in Financial Instrument Directive (MiFID) was enacted by the EU in 2004 to ensure transparency, investors' protection, competition and information symmetry among the market participants.[37] The directive improves the investment ecosystem in the EU by increasing competition among the firms. It also intends to increase the accessibility of markets to informed and uninformed investors by narrowing the information asymmetry. MiFID abolishes the 'concentration rule' to improve liquidity and market quality and to foster competition. Thus, the directive aimed to make the financial market 'efficient, resilient and transparent and to strengthen investor protection'.[38]

The directive has provided pre-trade transparency by ensuring accurate time availability of current orders and quotes relating to shares to the public (arts 27, 29 and 44). It also focuses on post-trade transparency by disclosing all market intermediaries' details about executed trades to the public (arts 28, 30, and 45). Similarly, art 31 classifies the investors as retail, professional, and eligible counterparties with varying degrees of protection.[39] Despite having several merits, the regulatory framework suffered a mis-selling crisis.[40] MiFID-I addressed the gaps and weaknesses by making relevant changes and replacing them with MiFID II and MiFIR.[39] This legislation also marks up the selling processes of the FIs by adopting the rules governing the organisational requirements and the conduct of the business provisions.[41]

Article 1 (1), the EU directive[39] deals with third-country firms providing investment services or performing investment activities by establishing a branch in the union.[39] Arts 5, 6 (1) and 7 clarify authorisation for establishing one or more branches or ancillaries to cover the whole of the EU. Despite strict provisions in the legislation, sometimes firms violate them. Therefore, the European Securities and Markets Authority (ESMA) has been made responsible for monitoring the proper use of authorisation, including a penalty for involvement in 'systematic infringement' (arts 70–73) with the right to appeal (art 74).[39] The services and activities that

[37] Daniel et al. (2020), p. 113.

[38] Ferrarini and Wymeersch (2006).

[39] Council Directive 2014/65/EU of 15 May 2014 on markets in financial instruments and amending Directive 2002/92/EC and Directive 2011/61/EU (recast) Text with EEA relevance [2014] OJ L173/349.

[40] Alexander (2019).

[41] Busch and Ferrarini (2017), p. 124.

come under the authorisation, also known as the European passport,[42] and an investment firm must fulfil extensive authorisation requirements to obtain such a passport.[43]

Therefore, MiFID I was considered strict, and MiFID II/MiFIR even tightened the reins, mainly due to the gaps regarding investors' protection and transparency.[44] MiFID II states that the Member States may require third-country firms to provide investment services and activities to retail and elective professional clients from local branches, which are authorised and supervised under specified criteria. A third-country firm can establish a branch in a Member State provided it has authorisation under MiFID II, MiFIR, and the firm can 'passport' any investment services or activities into the other Member States. However, the third-country branch regime in MiFID II is optional, and the UK has not implemented this clause. Therefore, its existing domestic regime for third-country branches remains unresolved. The UK has retained its key exemption under the RAO.[39] the 'overseas person' exclusion. This exclusion plays an important part in the access of third-country firms to the London market.

This legal instrument received criticism for not considering market regulation or promoting financial products. It also has ambiguity in its concern to protect the clients, primarily due to the lack of a standardised information disclosure system for the customers. It also lacks a consistent format for presenting information on costs, charges, and risks from financial service providers.[45] The legislation does not clarify specific needs regarding the strict supervision of organisational governance to stop a conflict of interest in designing and selling financial instruments and products.[40] Therefore, in 2018, MiFID II and MiFIR were replaced by MiFID.

MiFID rules clarify the position of business operations in the UK and the EU, allowing EU firms to trade their equity from the EU-recognised stock exchange. The MiFIR, art 23, limited the trading scope to the EU firms and envisaged that permission would be required to undertake financial activities. Therefore, without obtaining permission, trading would be treated 'as non-systematic, ad-hoc, irregular and infrequent'.[46] Moreover, the London-based stock exchange will not have 'equivalence status'.[47] Several stocks have a market share in the UK and the EU trading venues, and trading will solely depend on the type and nature of authorisation.

Thus, EU firms may use the provision of the third-country regime. In addition, 'EU discretion on equivalence assessment' would delay the permission process for trading with third countries. Moreover, critics argued that such permission would be highly 'susceptive to political interference and influence'.[48] Thus, an agreement on

[42] Council Directive (2014) arts 6 (3) (31), (32), (34) and (35).

[43] Council Directive (2014) arts 9–13 and arts 9–16.

[44] Busch (2017), p. 340.

[45] Franke (2016).

[46] ESEM (2019), 3.

[47] Holt, (2019), para 3.

[48] Currie (2018), p. 32.

equivalence is warranted for firms to conduct business smoothly. Without equivalence, the UK and EU branches could not establish and operate across the border, having a cascading effect on the business on both sides, which will have larger implications on the economy of these jurisdictions.

The Financial Services Act 2021 amended the UK's MiFIR equivalence regime for third-country investment firms to broadly reflect the changes introduced by the EU. The Act allows the FCA to specify reporting requirements for the firms that register under this regime. It also amended the equivalence assessment criteria to reflect the changes for incorporating in the UK's prudential rules. It has made provision of additional powers to the FCA to impose temporary restrictions or prohibitions or withdraw the registration of the firms that register under this regime if they fails to comply with the provisions of the Act. In the larger interest of the UK and EU, the ease of doing banking and financial business will help the economy on both sides, so the UK and EU legislation should focus on easing the regulatory burden.

4.5.2 Payment Services Directive

In 2007, the EU enforced the PSD[49] to consolidate the fragmented law across its Member States. It became binding for the EU Member States to implement this legislation to harmonise the payment system across the EU[50] and replace the older version to provide the legal foundation for the EU single market for safer payments and more innovative payment services. The main objective of the directive was to make cross-border payments easy, efficient, and secure. It also promoted innovation, competition, and efficiency, as envisaged in art (2) ss (1–5). This directive brought several benefits to the EU economy, such as easy access to new markets, offering consumers more choices, and avoiding possible risks. The PSD[51] offered more transparency and was much more informative to the consumers regarding the execution of payment, time, and fees (arts 38–49).

It even helped to strengthen refund rights and clarify the liability of the consumers and the payment institutions, resulting in easier and quicker payments throughout the EU. Although its objective was to ensure a harmonised approach across the EU, there were significant differences between the structures of payment services,

[49] Council Directive 2007/64/EC of 13 November 2007 on payment services in the internal market amending Directives 97/7/EC, 2002/65/EC, 2005/60/EC and 2006/48/EC and repealing Directive 97/5/EC [2007] OJ L 319/1.

[50] Council Directive (EU) 2015/2366 of 25 November 2015 on payment services in the internal market, amending Directives 2002/65/EC, 2009/110/EC and 2013/36/EU and Regulation (EU) No 1093/2010, and repealing Directive 2007/64/EC [2015] OJ L 337/35.

[51] Council Directive 2007/64/EC of 13 November 2007 on payment services in the internal market amending Directives 97/7/EC, 2002/65/EC, 2005/60/EC and 2006/48/EC and repealing Directive 97/5/EC [2007] OJ L 319/1.

passporting payment services and equal charges for domestic and cross-border payments across the EU.[52] Moreover, there was confusion on the exemption and liability for unauthorised payments and arrangements for registering complaints at the national level. EC published a 'Green Paper' to integrate the EU market for card, internet, and mobile payments to resolve these issues to some extent.[53]

Subsequently, the wide use of innovative digital payment methods worldwide and their positive and negative impact on the FinTech market prompted the EU to revisit PSD provisions. Accordingly, PSD II was enacted in 2015 'to launch innovative, safe and easy-to-use digital payment services and to provide consumers and retailers with effective, convenient and secure payment methods'.[52] With the enactment of PSD II, the EU encouraged its banking system to develop a new payment system with reduced cost to compete with the emerging FinTech market. Therefore, with the enactment of PSD II, the EU has 'fired the starting gun for banks vs. FinTech fights overpayments'.[54] The new 'rules will guide all market players, old and new, to offer better payment services' to consumers, besides ensuring their security.[55] In addition, it will also increase security measures to protect the payments from scams and fraud, which directly impact financial stability.

The directive also recognises the payment (art 2) services outside the EEA, which will be covered even if payment is in non-EEA currencies. The authorisation of payment services remained the same in both directives. However, Article 15 clarifies that the EBA will publish a central public register of authorised payment services firms to avoid possible financial crime. The directive also leaves scope for the host member to take preventive measures to address large-scale fraud (art 30). In addition, it also provides clarity on incorrect or unauthorised payments and provides such information to regulatory authorities to reduce the impact on financial stability (arts 78–79).[50]

Thus, PSD II aimed to promote FinTech development by collecting and analysing transaction information and providing a software bridge between the merchant's website and the customer's online banking platform.[50] However, critics argued that the legislation would pose a significant challenge for small innovators and provide greater opportunities for prominent players such as Apple and Amazon to gain margins.[56] In the UK, the FCA amended its rules and guidance to adopt the provisions in the PDS in the post-Brexit scenario to make the payment system robust and avoid possible distress in the financial market. Although the PDS has made several provisions to regulate the payment system to prevent possible financial crime, considering the evolution of several alternative online payment platforms and a more versatile approach will help to make the system vigorous and avoid potential impact on the banking sector.

---

[52] Brener (2018), p. 103.

[53] EU (2012).

[54] Johns (2017), para 1.

[55] Eurasia Review (2017).

[56] Romanova et al. (2018).

4.5.3 Anti-Money Laundering Directive (AMLD)

The fifth Anti-Money Laundering Directive (AMLD) came into existence in 2018,[57] and the UK adopted it on 10 January 2020 with some exceptions related to customer due diligence on random credit cards, account information, and safe deposit. The objective of the fifth AMLD was to reinforce the EU's AMLD/CFT regime to address the ongoing compliance issue, increase transparency, beneficial ownership of companies, and enhance ownership cooperation and information sharing.

This directive requires EU Member States to ensure that the 'national registers of the beneficial ownership of the legal persons introduced by the fourth AMLD are easily accessible to the public.[58] The fifth AMLD is also important in strengthening cooperation and information sharing between the financial supervisors. While implementing the fifth AMLD, the UK decided to go beyond the minimum requirements, strengthening its position and thus having the most comprehensive and advanced AMLD regime.[59]

The directive also creates a hostile environment for criminals hoping for banks to manage finances through non-transparent structures. The fifth AMLD targets virtual currency, particularly those providers involved in the exchange services between crypto assets and fiat currencies, which are not transparent. It also provides services to safeguard private cryptographic keys on behalf of the customers to hold, store and transfer virtual currencies.[60] It also deals with peer-to-peer providers, custodian wallet providers, and issuers of new crypto assets, such as ICO, IEO, etc.

The UK banks were considering implementing the EU rules and regulations to strengthen the financial system, particularly in dealing with money laundering. However, the situation has changed considerably since Brexit. As discussed earlier, the UK government is inclined to change the rules and regulations to suit its requirements. Such a move might affect the allocation of responsibilities and even the content of the banking regime.[59] The UK government has decided to return to the British regulation style, which believes that the regulators must make the rules rather than set out in law.[61] As a rule-maker, the PRA is trying to introduce a proportionally greater and differentiated regulatory framework for firms that are not so important.

---

[57] Council Directive (EU) 2018/843 018 on the prevention of the use of the financial system for the purposes of money laundering or terrorist financing and amending Directives 2009/138/EC and 2013/36/EU [2018] OJ L 156/43.

[58] Council Directive (EU) 2015/849 of 20 May 2015 on the prevention of the use of the financial system for the purposes of money laundering or terrorist financing, amending Regulation (EU) No 648/2012 of the European Parliament and of the Council, and repealing Directive 2005/60/EC of the European Parliament and of the Council and Commission Directive 2006/70/EC(EU) 2015/849 [2015] OJ L 141/73 art 3 para 6 (a) (i).

[59] Alshaleel (2020), p. 123.

[60] Witney (2020).

[61] BoE (2020).

The PRA believes that if strict prudential requirements are made applicable to all firms, problems can arise amongst them. The motive is to introduce a strong and simple framework fully aligned with the Basel Core Principles, which should be simpler than the Basel standards applied to larger and internationally active banks.[62] Hence, the directive will certainly provide checks and balances on the activities undertaken through the extensive use of FinTech. It will also help to regulate online platforms and alternative currencies, including crypto.

4.5.4 Capital Requirement Directive

CRD IV[63] and CRR[27] are the most important legal instruments dealing with the regulatory requirements of capital buffers against RWA.[64] The UK transposed these legal instruments into its domestic law, mainly in line with Basel III capital standards. The PRA made many amendments to CRR, except where it has discretion over applying a rule. The provisions made in the regulation make it an effective legal instrument to deal with capital requirements. The directive emphasised that the Member States shall ensure appropriate measures are in place to obtain the information needed to assess the institutions' compliance and smooth flow of information [art 6, sub-ss (a-e)]. In addition, credit institutions must obtain authorisation before commencing the activities (arts 10–14). Before granting authorisation to a credit institution, the competent authority will consult another Member State where the credit institution plans to establish a subsidiary of a credit institution and insurance firm. The directive also has provisions for the withdrawal of authorisation and the requirement of initial capital for investment firms and local firms.

The directive has made provision for FIs to compulsorily maintain minimum regulatory capital and the Common Equity Tier 1 (CET) capital requirement to meet the funds. Figure 4.2 clarifies the total capital requirement under CRD to mitigate the possible risk. Tier 1 capital consists of 'high-quality capital, displaying permanence, deep subordination and discretionary and mandatory cancellation of distributions.' It consists of CET 1 and additional Tier 1 capital. On the other hand, Tier 2 capital under Basel III is 'hybrid instruments with a maturity of not less than five years.'[65] It is ineffective in dealing with the risk in a crisis. The CET1 also has two more components, including a CCB of CET 1 capital equal to 2.5% of their total risk exposure as provisioned in art 92(3) of the regulation on an individual and consolidated basis.[27] However, small, and medium-sized investment firms are exempted from such requirements. In addition, the regulation also emphasised that institutions

---

[62] BoE (2021).

[63] Council Directive (EC) 2013/36/EU of 26 June 2013 on access to the activity of credit institutions and the prudential supervision of credit institutions and investment firms, amending Directive 2002/87/EC and repealing Directives 2006/48/EC and 2006/49/EC [2013] OJ L 176. 27.

[64] Council Regulation (2013).

[65] Sumpter (2014).

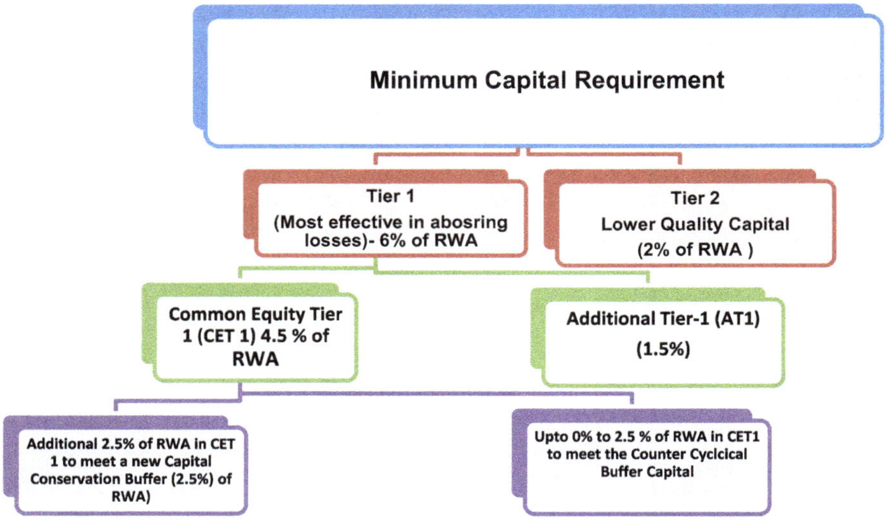

Fig. 4.2 Flow Chart of Minimum Capital Requirement. Source: Developed by the researcher based on the information available in Sumpter et al. (2014)

'must maintain an institution-specific countercyclical capital buffer (CCyB) equivalent to their total risk exposure amount (up to 0.0% –2.5% of RWA) as provisioned in art 92(3) of EU regulation.[27]

Later, in 2016, CRD V came into existence to strengthen the bank capital requirements as per the recommendation of the Basel Committee and the financial stability report to address Europe-specific issues. However, despite several rounds of negotiation, the EU could not find a conscientious agreement on the requirement of buffer capital for the entire EU. Therefore, on the advice of the EBA, the European Parliament provisioned for a new prudential regime for investment firms.

The UK's stance on the implementation of CRD V is very clear, and it states that the UK will transpose parts of the CRD V but will apply discretion on some aspects.[66] The PRA currently imposes a 'PRA buffer' on the CRD IV buffer requirements, and in the UK, banks must hold over 10.5% of regulatory capital which include 6%. Therefore, CRR tightened the definition of CET 1 and increased the requirements to at least 4.5% of RWA, besides emphasising additional Tier 1 Capital and Tier 2 capital, subordinated debt with a maturity of at least 5 years.[65] It creates a new class of regulatory capital in cases where resolution authorities require subordination to ordinary liabilities. Thus, the UK has made the provisions of capital requirement more meticulous than suggested by the EU and Basel to meet the liquidity requirement, particularly in the financial crunch.

[66] Pugsley (2020).

4.5.5 *Financial Services Act 2021*

After Brexit, the UK enacted the Financial Services Act 2021[67] significant landmark legislation towards controlling the financial services in the post-Brexit scenario and ensuring that the UK remains an 'open and dynamic financial centre' to provide technologically embodied financial services. While most of the Act seeks to shape the regulatory framework for the UK financial services outside of the EU, the legislation also 'contains a broad range of measures unconnected to Brexit', affecting firms across the financial sector. Nevertheless, John Glen, Economic Secretary to the Treasury, envisaged that 'for the first time in decades, the UK has full control of its financial services regulation.'[68] He further states that 'this Act will protect people who rely on financial services daily and boost the competitiveness of the UK dynamic global financial centre'. It is 'a major milestone' in the UK's plans to develop a regulatory system that works for the UK and helps the UK to seize new opportunities in the global economy.[69]

Thus, this Act enhances the UK's world-leading prudential standards and promotes financial stability. Secondly, it establishes control over the UK financial services regulations, which were otherwise transposed EU directives into domestic law and largely influenced by the EBA and relied on the ECJ for clarity on a specific matter. Thirdly, the Act will protect customers and help the UK develop as a global financial hub that provides financial services and promotes openness between the UK and jurisdictions worldwide.[68]

The Act also empowers the HMT and the PRA to repeal CRR to update and implement the Basel standards. Moreover, the power of authorisation and equivalence rests with HMT under s 27 sub-ss (1) (2) of the act.[66] The FCA introduced a new procedure to cancel the authorisation of inactive firms to perform certain regulated activities, and the power for such action is allowed through s 28.

Thus, the UK has strong regulatory and supervisory mechanisms to regulate and supervise the financial services market, including the banking business. The proactive role of the PRA and the FCA in effectively regulating the regulated activities reduced the impact of the GFC, and in a short span of 4 years, it brought the NPLs level to less than one per cent. Moreover, the transposition of EU regulations and directives related to the financial market and banking business into domestic law made the financial activities effective, transparent, and symmetric and protected the customer's interest. The UK also amended certain provisions in the EU legislation through the Financial Services Act 2021 to suit its requirements and geared up to make further amendments to ensure financial stability.

[67] Financial Services Act 2021, Chap 22 [2021].

[68] Davies (2021), p. 1.

[69] Shalchi (2021).

4.5.6 Financial Services and Market Act 2023(FSMA 2023)

FSMA 2023 makes significant changes to the framework for financial services regulation in order to reflect the United Kingdom's (UK) position outside of the EU.[70] It aimed to enhance the UK's position as a leading financial hub by reforming the capital markets regime and regulating the coins which are being used as a method of a new payment system across the globe. It also strengthens by amending the objectives of the financial services regulators to include advancing international competitiveness and ensuring medium to long-term growth of the UK economy. The FSMA mainly revoked retained EU law related to financial services (s 1 of FSMA, 20223),[70] establish a new designated activities regime, conferring powers on the UK regulatory authorities such as PRA, FCA, BoE and HMT to designate and oversee activities of critical third parties that provide services to financial firms. It also introduced a new regulatory gateway for approving the financial promotions of firms that are, otherwise not authorised by the UK regulatory authority.[71]

When the UK decided to leave the EU, a significant portion of the EU law was incorporated into the UK law by EU (Withdrawal) Act 2018, which was referred to as retained EU law to ensure that the UK continued to enjoy the privilege of a stable regulatory framework, nevertheless, these laws were subject to amendments for removing deficiencies, if any rise. Since the UK was no longer a member of the EU, it was free to make necessary amendments to the EU-regained legislation. Thus, a long list of retained EU laws was revoked, including EU regulations, directives, delegated regulations, acts, and UK subordinate legislation.[71] Accordingly, EU legislation related to a financial sector that was likely to be revoked included the Prospectus Regulation, MAR, CRR and MiFID. The objective of repealing retained EU law was to establish a comprehensive FSMA model for financial services regulation. However, this legislation will be revoked once regulatory authorities replace it with a new law.

There are several regulated activities pertaining to the financial market that are subject to EU retained law regulation, including listing shares, entering derivative contracts for commercial hedging and short selling, etc. The activities continue to be regulated by the EU retained law. However, the government feels that bringing these activities under the RAO umbrella would be disproportionate. For this purpose, FSMA 2023 established a designated activities regime (DAR) which does not require authorisation. However, it must fulfil certain regulatory requirements, and HMT, as empowered by the act, decides which activity falls within the purview of DAR. In addition, HMT also monitor that the activities are carried out within the rules unless they are exemptions. FSMA 2023 also provides a new schedule 6B[70] of regulated activities unless they are exempted, which limits the power of HMT to determine the scope of DAR, which regulated activities.[71]

---

[70] Financial Services and Markets Act 2023.

[71] Polk (2023).

FSMA 2023 also emphasised regulating e-money and payment services firms as an important third party and authorised HMT to designate a person that provides services to one or more authorised persons to monitor these services to avoid challenges to financial stability. The designated third parties are subject to the regulations of PRA, FCA and BoE, which must enable them to put in place minimum resilience of the services provided by the third parties. In addition, FSMA2023 also introduces new regulatory gateways to ensure that authorised firms, before approving financial promotions for unauthorised firms emphasising that it must pass through and obtain specific permission from the FCA. FCA has the power to apply restrictions on financial promotions; thus, this gateway will improve the quality of financial promotions in the customers' interest.[71]

Although it is too early to offer criticism on the provision of FSMA 2023, it is considered both evolutionary and revolutionary. The extent of reforms is unprecedented, primarily extending existing models of regulating financial services with an effort to revoke the EU rule-making functions. There is some uncertainty on how the power will be used, likely changes in the long term, and to what extent it will influence policy implementation. Albeit, it provides a great opportunity for firms operating in the financial sector to achieve greater efficiencies and provide innovative financial services[72] making London a major global financial hub.

4.6 India: An Overview of Banking Regulations

In India, the banking system started with the functioning of the Bank of Hindustan in 1770, which stopped its operation by 1832. More than 600 banks came into existence during this period, and a few were able to succeed. Later, during the British reign in India, the East India Company established three banks viz-a-viz the Bank of Bengal, the Bank of Bombay and Bank of Madras and later renamed them the Presidential Banks.[73] These three banks merged into a single bank in 1921 and were named 'Imperial Bank of India'. The Imperial Bank of India was later nationalised in 1955 and is now known as the SBI, the largest public sector bank in the country. Since then, along with SBI, many public and private sector banks have been established and are working in India.[69] However, in terms of asset composition, PSBs dominate, accounting for almost three-fourths of the banking system assets.[74] The share of private banks has increased gradually, and the total banking assets of PSBs were around 90% in 1991 and reduced to 70% in 2017.[74]

---

[72] Yeo et al. (2023).

[73] Burton (2016).

[74] RBI (2023).

4.7 Financial Sector Regulators

In India, several bodies are responsible for regulatory and supervisory mandates for the financial sector with clearly delineated domains and objectives (Fig. 4.3). These regulators include the RBI, which regulates banks, non-banking financial companies (NBFCs) and micro-FIs. The Securities and Exchange Board of India (SEBI) regulates securities markets, and the Insurance Regulatory and Development Authority (IRDA) regulates the insurance sector. In addition, the Forward Markets Commission (FMC) regulates forward markets, and the PFRDA regulates pension funds.[5] The Ministry of Finance is also a key player in the finance sector regulation, responsible for financial planning and legislation.

However, among these regulatory bodies, the Hilton Yong Commission's recommendation laid the foundation for establishing the RBI, the country's central bank and main regulator. It plays a significant role in ensuring financial stability. The RBI Act 1934 provides the statutory basis for its functioning. The main objective of the

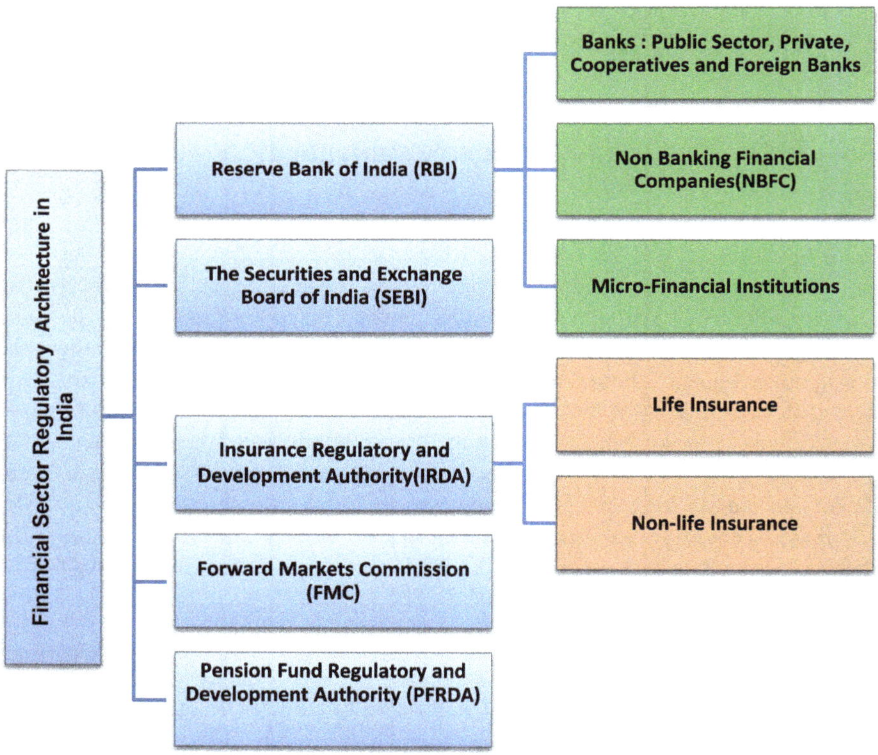

Fig. 4.3 Financial Sector Regulatory Architecture in India. Source: Developed by the researcher using literature from RBI Annual Reports of 2011–2012, 2018–2019 and 2021–2022 (see pages 308 and 309 for details)

RBI is to conduct consolidated supervision of the financial sector in India, which comprises commercial banks, FIs, and non-banking finance firms.[75] The RBI formulates, implements, and monitors India's monetary policy to maintain financial stability and ensure credit flows to productive economic sectors. The RBI also manages all foreign exchange under the Foreign Exchange Management Act 1999.

The Banking Regulation Act of 1949 monitored the activities of all commercial banks in India and empowered RBI the authority to grant and revoke bank licenses. Section 17(1) of the Act envisaged that every banking company incorporated in India should create a reserve fund. It clarified that the fund should be 20% of its profit and loss account, prepared under s 29.[76] As per the provision in BRA 1949, the RBI becomes a bank shareholder and obtains voting rights, and it has the power to remove and appoint a board of directors and modify banking policies.[72] RBI issues time-to-time guidelines to make the financial system and banking business stringent to avoid financial distress. RBI also constituted several committees for reforms in the banking system.

4.8 Regulations and Guidelines to Control NPLs

The ever-increasing NPAs in the Indian banking sector seriously threatened financial stability, and policymakers provided suitable regulatory and policy prescriptions to deal with the problem effectively. For speedy, time-bound resolution, liquidation of stressed assets, de-clogging bank balance sheets, and efficient reallocation of capital, the government, Insolvency and Bankruptcy Board of India (IBBI), and the RBI are working together to address the challenges through a multi-pronged approach.[77] The recent measures taken at the policy and regulatory level included strengthening the legal framework by enacting legislation and evolving the regulatory and supervisory mechanisms in the country.

To ensure a transparent debt resolution system, the Central Repository of Information on Large Credits (CRILC) bridges the gap by 'addressing the issues of information asymmetry. In addition, these institutions also emphasised undertaking Asset Quality Reviews (AQR) and initiating PCA to strengthen banks' fundamentals and improve the institutional framework. RBI also promoted JLF and addressed the problem associated with coordination to a great extent. All these efforts aimed to strengthen the review process followed by banks for restructuring debt. [73]Thus, the following section deals with the efforts made by India through its regulatory and policy initiatives to address the issue of NPA during the last four decades.

Sick Industrial Companies Act 1985 The Indian parliament approved the Sick Industrial Companies Act (SICA) in 1985, intending to revive the sick industrial

[75] Yoo (2005), p. 167.

[76] Banking Regulation Act [1949] (India).

[77] Patel (2011).

units and refer them as non-viable companies to the High Court (HC) for liquidation.[78] Under SICA, the Board of Industrial and Financial Reconstruction (BIFR) became the first step towards evolving insolvency and bankruptcy law in the country, which has leapt forward over the last four decades. However, the efforts taken under SICA for revival and liquidation remained ineffective mainly due to cumbersome legal proceedings. The BIFR and sometimes the HC could not take the broader view of the implications of their judgments, and mostly protected the interest of the workers, proving heaven for debtor companies to seek shelter from their creditors. As a result, more than 1.5 million PSBs involving 662.2 million cases remained pending in various courts.[79]

Recovery of Debts Dues to Bank and Financial Institutions Act 1993 The effectiveness of SICA remained questionable mainly due to delay in settlement of cases and conservative approach, resulting in the enactment of the RDBFI Act 1993 to expedite adjudication and recovery of debts due to banks and FIs. The DRTs were authorised to deal with the NPAs of secured and unsecured borrowers with loans exceeding ₹ one million. The effective implementation of DRT remained challenging as many cases were pending before the civil court, and chances of delay in the recovery process were inevitable.

Moreover, the timeline for DRTs to settle the cases was within 180 days, and the loopholes in the system prompted the advocates to seek more time to file documents. The absence of the advocate on the hearing date and the adjournment of the hearing delayed the process abnormally.[80] Moreover, the banks might delay the process, expecting the borrowers to wilt under pressure and be willing to negotiate, but this tactic could not yield the desired result. The repeated delays, increasing costs, and the wastage of precious time and resources exposed the limitations of the settlement process through the judiciary. Therefore, a penalty for the delay and an incentive for early disposal would help overcome the RDBFI's shortcomings to some extent.

Corporate Debt Restructuring Cell 2001 The failure of the RDBFI to effectively resolve NPLs cases prompted the introduction of CDR, a scheme evolved by the RBI for implementation by banks and FIs for the realisation of the amount of debt from the debtors who were not able to pay the amount in full. It was a voluntary agreement between the debtor and creditor or the creditor and the creditor whereby approval of 75% of creditors was mandatory. It covered multiple banking accounts and consortium or syndication of accounts with ₹100 million aggregate outstanding. It is a three-tier structure consisting of the CDR Standing Forum, CDR Empowered Group (EG), and CDR Cell. The restructuring plan is submitted to the CDR cell and approved by the EG within 180 days, which is mandatory.

---

[78] Ministry of Finance (2015).

[79] Zwieten (2015).

[80] Regy et al. (2016).

The debtor-creditor and inter-creditor agreements have legal standing and are binding on debtors and creditors.[81] However, some concerns include validity issues, delay, and non-implementation of the restructuring plan despite legal binding and the right of compensation cropped up.[81] The foreign creditor's unwillingness to associate with the CDR loan restructuring mechanism limited its scope. They considered this mechanism biased towards local debtors, which was undoubtedly a limitation of the CDR process.

SARFAESI Act 2002 The drawbacks in earlier regulatory and policy instruments realised the need to enforce the SARFAESI Act to deal with the problem of loan restructuring. The NPAs in the banking sector was continuously rising in the early part of the twenty-first century. As per RBI estimates, the gross NPAs of Scheduled Commercial Banks (SCB) were 15.7% in 1997.[82] It became a significant policy concern, and accordingly, the Naraimham Committee I, II, and Andhyarujina Committee suggested enacting legislation, namely, the SARFAESI Act, which empowered banks and FIs to take possession of securities and dispose of them without the court's intervention.[83]. There was a dispute and argument about pending cases of BIFR, and the apex courts' judgment (Madras High Court) settled the same in the case of *'Petrochemicals v BIFR'*, which gave precedence to the SARFAESI Act over SICA.

Another equally important recommendation of the Narasimham Committee II was the establishment of ARCs so that NPAs could be transferred from the banks' balance sheets to ARCs to develop markets for the securitisation of loans. Consequently, Asset Reconstruction Companies India Limited (ARCIL) started working in 2002 with SBI, IDBI, ICICI Bank, and PNB sponsorship. Subsequently, several such ARCs cropped up in the public and private sectors, bringing their number to 29. In addition, the act also advocates for hearing and the resolution of cases through Debt Recovery Tribunals (DRTs).

There was extreme ambiguity in the provision of the Act, which envisaged that 'no reference shall be made to BIFR'. Based on the provisions in SICA, the borrowers challenged the SARFAESI Act in court, delaying the restructuring process. However, in *Noble Aqua Pvt Ltd v State Bank of Indian*[84] and *Kanakadhara Spinning Mills v the Registrar*[85] it has been argued that the creditors' banks are not entitled to enforce the SARFAESI Act. It was a severe jolt to the effective implementation of the Act and the restructuring plan of the RBI. Nevertheless, the Supreme Court (SC)

[81] Banerjee (2018).

[82] RBI (2009).

[83] The Securitisation and Reconstruction of Financial Assets and Enforcement of Security Interest Act [2002] (India).

[84] Noble Aqua Pvt. Ltd. and Ors v State Bank of India and Ors 4815 (2007).

[85] M/S Kanakadhara Spinning Mills v the Registrar 10600 (2007).

in *Madras Petrochemicals v BIFR*[86] clarified the SARFAESI Act's supremacy over SICA, greatly relieving the regulator and supervisor.

However, the progress of debt recovery was not very encouraging, and the number of default cases and the corresponding amount increased significantly. In 2012–2013, the number of cases referred to was 1,044,636, involving ₹1057 billion, with a recovery of ₹233 billion, 22% of the amount involved.[87] On the other hand, the total number of cases referred in 2017–2018 was 3,439,477, with a recovery of ₹2956 billion and a total recovery of ₹404 billion, which is 13.7% of the total amount.[88] Such dismal results on the recovery front put severe pressure on the regulator and supervisor to think differently. As a result, the RBI issued new guidelines for the classification and restructuring of loans in 2014.

Framework for Revitalising Distressed Assets 2014 The RBI issued guidelines[89] to all banks to classify the assets as Special Mentioned Accounts (SMA) based on the quality of the assets. The RBI clarified that if the principal or interest payment is overdue for more than 30 days; the account shows signs of incipient stress and is classified as SMA0. Similarly, the loan amount is classified as SMA01 if a principal or interest payment is overdue between 31–60 days. When the principal or interest payment is overdue between 61–91 days, it falls under category SMA02. It is the responsibility of CRILC to collect, store, and disseminate lenders' credit data to understand the loan portfolio of the lenders, which helps to categorise them accordingly.

The guidelines categorically state that once an asset falls into a category of SMA-2, the banks should form a JLF mandatorily and prepare a Corrective Action Plan (CAP). For the formation of JLF, the lenders' aggregate exposure (AE) should be ₹1000 million and above. However, the lender can also form a JLF even if the AE is less than ₹1000 million and the AE falls under the SMA0 and SMA01 categories, respectively. The IBA will be responsible for formulating a master JLF agreement incorporating the rules for the functioning of JLF, which lenders sign.

RBI has played a proactive role in visualising the possible distressed assets; however, critics argued[90] that regulatory forbearance is not a panacea for the troubles that disturbed the credit management environment in the banking sector. Moreover, the guidelines do not clarify whether signing an inter-creditor agreement is mandatory or the possible consequences of not agreeing on a restructuring package. Although the lenders trust the JLF process, they are at the mercy of the other lenders to reach an agreement and avoid accelerated provisioning, highlighting its limitation. Despite several reservations by the critics, the RBI's attempt to categorise the

[86] M/S Madras Petrochem Ltd. and Anr v BIFIR and Ors [2016] SC (CA) 614–615.

[87] RBI (2012–13).

[88] RBI (2017–18).

[89] RBI (2014b).

[90] Sivaprakasam and Roy (2014).

assets and suggest a solution for its restructuring provides direction to the banks struggling with relatively high NPAs.

Flexible Structuring of Long-Term Project Loans to Infrastructure and Core Industries 2014 RBI's efforts to provide a sound environment for the economy to grow continuously, and it also intervenes to provide guidelines for the banks providing credit to the projects dealing with infrastructure and core industries for their sustainability whose life usually runs 20–30 years. Commercial banks are the primary source of long-term debt financing for long-term projects that require significant capital for investments. While granting loans for such projects and infrastructure, the initial construction period and the date of commencement of commercial operation (DCCO) are deciding factors.

The RBI realises that such a long gestation asset repayment should start from DCCO. The banks invariably restrict the maximum period of 10–12 years to address the asset-liability mismatch[91] severely affecting the project's viability. Therefore, the RBI advised the banks to fix a more extended amortisation period with periodical financing of 5 years, considering the project's economic life and concession period.

Thus, the RBI envisaged that there is no ceiling on the repayment period of such loans, except in the case of special regulatory treatment for asset classification on restructuring. Therefore, banks should fix realistic repayment schedules after critically assessing the borrowers' cash flow. However, the RBI clarifies that if a bank refinances any existing infrastructure through 'take out financing' without a predetermined agreement with other banks, such financing does not come under restructuring, as certain terms and conditions are applicable for restructuring.

The bank that offers an initial debt facility may sanction the loan for a medium term of 5–7 years, taking care of the initial construction period and DCCO. If the initial debt facility or refinancing debt facilities become NPAs, banks should stop refinancing. Therefore, the RBI has provided explicit instructions for financing long-term infrastructure projects by assessing its pros and cons to avoid the possible accumulation of NPLs.

The RBI instruction regarding the constitution of a JLF envisaged that as soon as the AE of ₹1000 million shows a sign of distress, JLF should come into action. The objective was to provide opportunities for lenders to restructure distressed loans by exploring the possibility of alternative equity and strategic investors. However, these options could not produce the desired result.[92]

Strategic Debt Restructuring 2015 In 2015, the RBI developed an SDR scheme that allowed JLF to convert borrowers' part or all debt into equity shares with the condition that JLF must possess 51% equity collectively.[93] Lenders must find a buyer within 18 months to avoid slipping such assets under the NPA. Under this

[91] RBI (2014b).

[92] Khullar (2016).

[93] RBI (2014).

scheme, the JLF implements a CAP focusing on three R, viz-a-viz rectification, restructuring and recovery. The creditors may also consider restructuring the borrower's account if the account is viable and the borrower is not a willful defaulter.

The JLF should also consider the techno-economic viability study for restructuring the assets. Moreover, the JLF should also give the borrowers an option on whether the entire or partial loan amount needs to be restructured into the company's share if the borrowers do not meet the 'critical conditions' stipulated in the duly approved restructuring package.[94] There are detailed guidelines for declaring an asset as NPLs and measures taken to restructure the loans by following this debt-equity swap. If these options are not feasible, the bank initiates the recovery process, considering various legal and other options. However, the decision to invoke SDR rests with JLF. It further envisaged that a minimum of 75% of creditors with 60% of their values be involved while invoking SDR, and JLF should hold a 51% equity share of the ailing company. The banks seek several relaxations under SDR; if unable to sell the company to a new promoter within 18 months, all the regulatory relaxations automatically cease.

However, the scheme has several flaws; it does not clarify the basis for arriving at the restructuring plans for multiple creditors and converting debt into equity on 'Fair Value' seems vague. The market price and conversion price issue always persists, as the market price will remain lower than the conversion price. The critics[89] argued that 18 months is too short for the banks to wrap up the entire process of initiating, running the business and finding a buyer; therefore, it must be re-looked. However, later, the RBI concluded that SDR also remained ineffective in addressing the problem of NPAs[95] as it was challenging to find a new buyer for the distressed assets.

Sustainable Structuring of Stressed Assets 2016 The RBI introduced a Scheme for the Sustainable Structuring of Stressed Assets (S4A) in 2016.[96] The important conditions RBI imposed for the debt to qualify under the scheme included the commencement of commercial activities in the project, AE of more than ₹5000 million, and the debt meeting the sustainability test. The power to declare a sustainable debt rests with the JLF, which acts based on independent techno-economic viability and considers several factors before deciding.[91]

The banks were highly optimistic and looked at S4A as an opportunity to clean their balance sheet; the scheme was applicable for operational projects, not for projects under construction, which was one of the major weaknesses of S4A. Moreover, a few borrowers had met the RBI's condition of half the loan being recoverable.[97] However, there are encouraging instances where Piramal Enterprises Ltd. joined

[94] Jaiswal (2015).

[95] Nair (2016).

[96] RBI (2016).

[97] The Hindu Business Line (2016).

hands with Bain Capital Credit to invest up to $1 billion in stressed debt and restructured assets to fetch a profit.

Similarly, ICICI Bank Ltd. and Apollo Global Management looked at multiple ways of investing in troubled firms to make an addition to their income. Finally, Brookfield Asset Management Inc. signed an MOU with the SBI to invest in stressed assets.[98] Thus, despite several criticisms and loopholes in the circular, these examples prove its usefulness for banks dealing with stressed assets. It establishes that there are market players for distressed assets and buys them to earn a profit.

Guidelines on Sale of Stressed Assets by Banks Despite extensive efforts, the problem of NPAs in India persisted at concerning levels. In response, the RBI issued new guidelines in 2016 for selling NPAs to securitisation companies (SCs) and asset reconstruction companies (ARCs). Under these guidelines, banks must identify stressed assets, especially those classified as "doubtful" above a defined threshold. Unlike earlier processes, these asset sales are now open to participation not only by SCs and ARCs but also by other banks and NBFCs with expertise in resolving distressed assets. This approach, emphasising wide publicity of bids and e-auctions, aims to attract a larger pool of buyers and make the bidding process more competitive, ultimately driving better outcomes.

However, these guidelines conflicted with the existing Joint Lenders' Forum (JLF) approach for resolving stressed assets. Banks also faced limitations in negotiating the sale of complex and unique assets, which could shift their focus from core lending activities to managing distressed assets. The success of this scheme, therefore, depends on how actively banks engage in trading these assets (KGMP 2016).

Insolvency and Bankruptcy Code 2016 A significant breakthrough in dealing with stressed assets came by enacting the IBC 2016, a deep structural reform with a far-reaching impact on the Indian economy. After extensive consultation with stakeholders, it has been crafted with extreme care to ensure it delivers on its sustainability objectives without unintended consequences. The IBC has been continuously evolving to address the deficiencies arising from its implementation so that it synchronises with emerging market realities.[99] IBC also consolidated and amended the laws relating to reorganisation and insolvency resolution of corporate persons, partnership firms, and individuals in a time-bound manner to maximise the value of the assets.[100]

The purpose of the IBC was to promote entrepreneurship, make credit available and provide comprehensive law for insolvent loans. Section 12 (1) (2) of the IBC emphasised completing the corporate insolvency resolution process (CIRP) within 180 days of the application admission. The focus of the IBC lies on the completion of the process in a time-bound manner to maximise the value of assets.[96] The code

---

[98] Nair (2016).

[99] Sahoo (2019).

[100] RBI (2016).

has a regulatory framework for the CIRP, individual and partnership entities, a fast-track insolvency resolution process, corporate liquidation and voluntary liquidation.[96] The IBC has made the insolvency resolution process smooth, which has improved India's ranking on the insolvency parameter from 136 in 2016 to 108 in 2018[101] and 52 in 2020.[95]

Under IBC, an applicant submits a resolution plan that the resolution officer examines. The committee approves the same with a two-thirds majority of creditors. The Adjudicating Authority (AA) finally approves it and appoints a resolution professional, provided it meets the requirement stipulated in s 30 (2) of the code. If the insolvency resolution plan remains incomplete within the deadline, the AA may initiate the liquidation process, as explained in section 31 of the code. The Act also has a provision for an insolvency resolution process for individual and partnership firms, with DRT as the AA.

Thus, the IBC 2016 provides legislation relating to bankruptcy, insolvency, and liquidation for individual firms and corporate entities. The Code also boosts direct foreign investment in India by improving India's ranking on the 'Ease of Doing Business' index.[102] The code does not provide any safeguard for the leave petition and the order of DRT and NCLT, which can be challenged in the courts, limiting the scope of the IBC.[98] The provision in s 7 violates principles of natural justice as it empowers the AA to reject a CIRP application without a hearing. The court opined on the issues where the act remains silent on the right of hearing and does not oust the principles of natural justice. Hence, the court held that the AA should hear the corporate debtor (CD) before admitting or rejecting any matter.[103]

The validity of ss 7, 8 and 9 of the code remained questionable and challenging due to the differentiation between operational creditors(OCs) and financial creditors(FCs), which violates the constitutional guarantees of equality. Rejecting this argument, the Kolkata HC accepted the rationale given by the Bankruptcy Law Reforms Committee (BLRC) that the FCs were better suited, on various counts, to decide the fate of the CDs. The HC rejected the challenge to these sections and upheld the constitutional validity of the code.[104] Such a decision further boosts the efforts to resolve the insolvency and bankruptcy issues.[99]

On the other hand, in Mittal v Gupta (2021)[105] SC clarifies the roles of CD and resolution applicants while giving judgment. Moreover, SC also clarified the challenge to clause (d) of s 29 A and its applicability to a juristic person.[106] Similarly, the SC held the relevant rules in Uttara Foods v Mona Pharmacham.[107] Therefore, it is

---

[101] World Bank (2018).

[102] Goyal (2017), p. 1724.

[103] Sri Metalikas Ltd. v Union of India Writ Petition, [2017] HC WP 7144.

[104] Swiss Ribbons v Union of India, 99 (2018)

[105] Arcelor Mittal India Pvt. Ltd. and Ors. v Satish Kumar Gupta 9402–9405 (2021).

[106] Renaissance Steel India Pvt. Ltd. & Ors v Electrosteels Steel India Ltd. & Ors 175 902-1905 (2018).

[107] Uttara Foods and Feeds Pvt Ltd v Mona Pharmacham 18520 (2017).

argued that the Code needs revision because some sections and sub-sections are ambiguous and continuously challenged, exposing its limitations.[95] Despite several limitations, the Code has effectively dealt with insolvency and bankruptcy cases. The government and regulatory authorities also look at the criticism openly and make necessary amendments to strengthen the IBC.

Prudent Framework of Resolution of Distressed Assets (2019) The RBI developed guidelines on the Prudent Framework of Resolutions of Distressed Assets in 2019 to further guide banks in managing their distressed assets. However, the SC quashed these guidelines[108] because it opined that the Central Bank is not empowered to issue such a general circular under section 35AA of the RBI Act. Moreover, several companies pleaded that the time given by the Central Bank was insufficient to tackle the bad debt.

Therefore, the RBI came out with a new circular and emphasised that it is voluntary for the banks to declare default to NCLT and complete the resolution process in 180 days. The circular also provides a 30-day review period for the lenders once the borrower has been declared bankrupt. The coverage of the new circular is more comprehensive as it covers commercial banks, NBFC, small finance banks, and term finance institutions.

Thus, India took several initiatives on the regulatory and supervisory front to control NPLs and achieved partial success. The debtors and creditors challenged the provisions of the acts and code in the respective courts, which greatly delayed the restructuring process. However, the loopholes in the legal instruments were corrected by making necessary amendments, which strengthened the insolvency and bankruptcy process to some extent and improved credibility. Nevertheless, there is tremendous scope for improvement in the provisions of the code. A more rigorous resolution process would certainly contribute to reducing the cases of NPLs and subsequently contribute to the financial stability, economic growth and prosperity of the country.

4.9 Financial Sector Regulators in Ireland

With the evolution of the banking sector, the regulatory system also evolved, and Ireland adopted many regulations to regulate the banking sector. The first such initiative could be traced to 1447 when Ireland passed a rule against chipped and other unlawful money.[109] Since then, Ireland has enforced several acts to regulate banking activities, including the legal interest of money, better payment of inland bills of exchange, making promissory notes more obligatory, changing interest rates, etc. However, along with the evolution of banking regulations, the number of bankruptcy

[108] Jose (2021).

[109] Gilbart (1836), p. 6.

cases also cropped up, resulting in the enactment of the first Bankruptcy Act in 1871. The bankers whose activities led to bankruptcy might be made bankrupt, and their affairs were settled according to the Banking Act of 1759. Subsequently, the Bank of Ireland came into force in 1873 and the Bank of Belfast in 1808.[105]

While developing commercial resources, Ireland faced several obstacles and realised the importance of secured banking. The evidence suggests that the strike by most of the banks in 1820 and the refusal of the Bank of Ireland to comply with the government's instruction to establish bank branches to extricate the country from difficulties gave a strong signal to the Government.[105] The challenges posed by the Joint Stock Banking Companies resulted in enforcing an agreement between the government and the banks to make the system more transparent.[105]

In Ireland, the ECB is the main regulator for financial sector-related activities. It works as a Single Supervisory Mechanism Regulation (SSMR) in close coordination with the CBI.[6] Thus, the ECB is the lead regulator, delegating activities to the CBI. Ireland categorises FIs as significant and less significant institutions, and the ECB supervises significant institutions operating in Ireland, while the CBI supervises the less significant institutions.

The main objective of SSMR is to ensure the safety and soundness of credit institutions, to maintain financial stability without disregarding the unity and integrity of the internal market, based on equal treatment of credit institutions, to prevent regulatory arbitrage.[6] In addition, the ESMA, European Insurance and Occupational Pensions Authority (EIOPA) and European Systemic Risk Board (ESRB) also regulate various financial sector activities.[6]

The EU has assigned the ECB all the activities related to supervisors, including compliance, monitoring, review, recovery plans, and early intervention where credit is likely to breach the applicable prudential requirements.[6] These roles empower the ECB to act as a supervisory authority, watch the banking system and take corrective measures to avoid insolvency. The ECB is responsible for providing a report on the financial stability in Ireland. ECB can issue guidance and instructions to CBI to make the supervision effective and vigilant. On the direction of the ECB, CBI introduced the 'Probability on Banks Risk Impact System' (PRISM) to determine the risk and its potential impact on banks, and it has categorised the banks as high impact, medium impact, medium-low impact, and low impact. Thus, the ECB has immense regulatory and supervisory power to ensure the activities of FIs are as per the EU regulations and directives.

In Ireland, the Central Bank Act of 1942[110] empowers the banks to 'safeguard the integrity of currency and ensure the control of credit, with the constant and predominant aim for the welfare of the people.[106] Art 7 (1) (a-m) and (2) (a-b) provide detailed functions that empower the CBI to control the financial system. The banks in Ireland are not permitted to be engaged in activities for which they have not sought authorisation from the CBI/ECB. Therefore, these two regulators work closely to ensure financial stability in Ireland. The following section examines the regulations, directives, acts, codes, etc., substantially impacting the Irish financial sector.

[110] Central Bank of Ireland (1942).

4.9.1 Bank Recovery and Resolution Directive

In 2015, Ireland transposed the EU Bank Recovery and Resolution Directive (BRRD)[111] into Irish law, which empowered CBI to act as a National Resolution Authority. It also resolves the problem of failing banks, credit unions, and investment firms through a Single Resolution Mechanism (SRM) and Single Resolution Board (SRB). This framework enhances the resilience and resolvability of institutions, which will be better prepared to deal with and recover from a crisis. It focuses on minimising the impact of failure on an institution and suggests that all credit institutions and investments must prepare a recovery plan.

Article 4(5) of the BRRD requires the resolution authority to cooperate closely with the competent authority involved in supervising functions and preparing, planning, and applying resolution decisions. Regulation 7(4) of the BRRD requires the CBI to ensure adequate structural arrangements and operational independence and avoid conflicts of interest between its resolution authority and other functions. Banks prepare a recovery plan with suitable implementation options in case of significant financial deterioration. The BRRD empowers the supervisor to choose executive recovery options, remove management, and change the structure of the institutions. Thus, the resolution activities are taken in advance by the CBI or SRB to avoid failure and ensure effective management of the resolution process. They are also empowered to apply resolution tools to failing institutions to minimise their impact on the financial system.

Thus, CBI has established the National Resolution Authority Internal Rules (NRAIR) and works in concurrence with SSRM. However, the EU introduced the institution's Bank Recovery and BCHD Resolution[112] to absorb losses effectively. The purpose of this legislation was to introduce greater harmonisation. BRRD2 and SRMR2 further strengthened the process with refined power and discretion about minimum requirements for own funds and eligible liabilities (MREL). However, its success in dealing with the FIs operating in multinationals depends on the legal system, which may slow the resolution process.

---

[111] Council Directive 2014/59/EU of 15 May 2014 establishing a framework for the recovery and resolution of credit institutions and investment firms and amending Council Directive 82/891/EEC, and Directives 2001/24/EC, 2002/47/EC, 2004/25/EC, 2005/56/EC, 2007/36/EC, 2011/35/EU, 2012/30/EU and 2013/36/EU, and Regulations (EU) No 1093/2010 and (EU) No 648/2012 of the European Parliament and of the Council [2014] OJ L*173*.

[112] Council Directive (EU) 2017/2399 of 12 December 2017 amending Directive 2014/59/EU as regards the ranking of unsecured debt instruments in insolvency hierarchy *OJ L 345/96.*

Council Regulation (EU) No 1024/2013 of 15 October 2013 conferring specific tasks on the European Central Bank concerning policies relating to the prudential supervision of credit institutions [2013] OJ L 287/63.

4.9.2 Credit Reporting Act 2013

The Credit Reporting Act 2013 was considered significant for introducing the Central Credit Registrar, which covered many loans such as credit cards, overdrafts, mortgages, and business loans. It helps to provide comprehensive information on borrowers. It also helps to bestow the CBI macro-prudential tools to assess the trend of lending, which is helpful in a crisis because both the creditors and lenders get adequate information to identify the risk concentrations.[113]

The information in the register is useful for evaluating risk for extending credit, changes to the nature of credit arrangement, monitoring credit failure under the credit agreement and analysing the portfolio of credit agreements [s 16 (a-f)]. The act also made provisions to deal with credit information if there is an impersonation. The act has also ensured that credit information providers should know their rights and duties. Thus, the Credit Reporting Act ensures that all the information about 'credit applications, credit agreements and parties' are maintained in the register and effectively used to assess the risk when required. This act provides comprehensive information on the regulated activities of lenders, borrowers, and associated businesses and protects data, but the authenticity of the correct information remains questionable.

4.9.3 Consumer Protection Code

The Consumer Protection Code,[114] initially introduced in 2006, took the final shape in 2012 to provide a consistent level of consumer protection to enhance confidence and trust in the financial system for all financial services offered by the jurisdictions.[115] The CBI uses several methods to monitor consumer protection activities, including inspections, general reviews on a particular topic, mystery shopping, financial services advertising, social media monitoring and guides to consumer protection risk assessments[115] Ireland made several changes in the CPC to strengthen the legislation. The Code's provisions are binding on 'regulated entities' and must be complied with while providing financial services for the regulated activities.[115]

The code also emphasises preventing information asymmetry between regulated entities and customers. Therefore, a regulated entity must ensure that all information it provides to a consumer is clear, accurate, and up-to-date. The code ensures that customers should have up-to-date information. The code also envisaged that the regulated entities should ensure that the design, presentation, and content are clear, fair, accurate and not misleading while issuing the advertisement. Thus, the Irish

---

[113] Credit Reporting Act 45 (2013) No 45 (Ireland).

[114] Consumer Protection Code 2012 (2012) (Ireland).

[115] Central Bank of Ireland.

CPC has made sufficient provisions to protect the customer's interest and it undoubtedly positively impacts financial stability and the economy.

The CPC mainly focuses on 'securing customers' best interest' by using international best regulatory practices. The act explores best available practices for the customers, from effective marketing services, changes in financial services, new delivery channels, and the impact of regulation and innovation in financial services. It also discusses customer protection principles, including innovation and disruption, digitisation, unregulated activities, pricing matters, effective information, vulnerability, etc.[116] Thus, the code ensures that customers' interests are protected when regulated financial service providers cannot meet their obligations, so that market speculations do not affect the customers and they can meet their financial obligations.

4.9.4 Code of Conduct on Mortgage Arrears

The CBI was committed to ensuring 'prudential and consumer protection mandates', which prompted it to adopt appropriate strategies and operations to resolve NPLs effectively.[117] Therefore, in February 2009, for the benefit of mortgage lenders, the CCMA came into being, with a revision in 2013. Section 117 of the Central Bank Act has a provision to enact such a code, and lenders abide by the code's provisions as a matter of law. CCMA aimed to ensure fair and transparent treatment of distressed borrowings and to recognise mortgage arrears as unique compared to other assets.

An important part of CCMA is the Mortgage Arrears Resolution Process (MARP), which follows the resolution based on the merit of each case. The act also emphasises adopting a flexible approach while initiating MTRP because the resolution process aims to assist the borrowers [ch 3 s (3) (a)].[118] It also collects information about arrears, staff dealing with mortgage resolution and nonpayment of mortgage arrears. The lenders should proactively determine the reasons for the financial difficulties preventing the borrowers from repaying mortgage arrears [ch (3) (10)].[118]

Under the MARP, the lender is responsible for establishing communication with the borrowers, providing financial information, assessing the mortgage arrears, and suggesting a resolution plan. The MARP applies when the mortgage arrear remains outstanding for more than 31 days from the date of declaring arrear, the alternative payment system is also not working, and its term has expired. Thus, the lender should follow due procedure before suggesting a resolution plan, and even while suggesting a resolution plan, explore all the possible repayment possibilities.[118]

---

[116] Maher et al. (2022).

[117] Sharon (2018).

[118] Code of Conduct on Mortgage Arrears [2013] (Ireland).

The CBI issued a direction that regulated entities will provide each borrower with complete information on the assessment of mortgage arrears and the reasons for considering alternative repayment arrangements.[118] While the provision of this information does not apply retrospectively, regulated entities should act in the best interests of consumers and facilitate requests for this information from such borrowers.[119] However, these arrangements were inappropriate and unsustainable for borrowers' circumstances. The CBI's prudential and consumer protection mandates ensure that the banks have proper strategies and operations to resolve the NPLs problem. CCMA applies to the security holder that the CBI regulates. If the security holder is unregulated, then the CCMA applies to the servicers whose role is to manage and administer these mortgage loans for the security holder in those situations where the unregulated entity holds the loans originated by regulated entities.[120]

The motive of CCMA is to ensure fair and transparent treatment of financially distressed borrowers. It even helps to acknowledge that mortgage arrears are unique compared to the other classes of assets. However, critics argue that merit is essential when considering each mortgage arrears case[121] The Irish government and its legal system consistently tried to resolve the mortgage arrears crisis. Thus, making necessary changes in conveyance law, establishing ISI and PIA, and shortening bankruptcy terms were some of the CBI's actions to control NPLs.[117]

Mortgage Arrears Resolution Targets The initiatives of the Government of Ireland resulted in significant progress through these Central Bank interventions, but the mortgage arrears continued to increase rapidly. CBI was dissatisfied with the quality of the response of regulated lenders[119] and introduced MART to improve the arrears. With the help of MART, the Central Bank imposed quarterly quantitative targets on the six main mortgage lenders. Some critical considerations behind implementing MART were the continuous deterioration of the account in late arrears, a lack of sustainable solutions, and a lack of apparent plans to deal with the crisis.[119]

However, after the implementation of MART, the restructuring mix began to broaden and change. The banks implemented sustainable solutions to solve the distressed mortgage accounts. The central banks also introduced sustainable guidelines to deal with important factors and solutions for resolving mortgage arrears cases. On-site credit inspections by the Central Bank helped to examine the samples of these sustainable solutions during the MART programme.[119] MART even sets out a schedule for the banks to resolve the problem of non-performing mortgage loans, which ultimately helps resolve NPL cases.

[119] Report on Mortgage Arrear (2016).

[120] Houlihan (2018).

[121] Sharon et al. (2018), p. 54.

4.9.5 *Insolvency Service of Ireland*

ISI of Ireland is an independent statutory body introduced in 2013, and its role is to restore insolvent persons to solvency. It monitors the operations of arrangements relating to personal insolvency, the Debt Relief Notice (DRN), the Debt Settlement Arrangement (DSA) and the Personal Insolvency Arrangement (PIA), as provisioned in the PIA 2012.[122] It also considers the DRN applications and processes them for the protective certificate for DSAs and PIAs, which ultimately protects the borrowers from legal actions [s 96 (1) (a-h)]. It maintains the DRN, DSA and PIA registers, which are crucial to the settlement process.

It also provides information to the public on the workings of the Act. It supervises and regulates a person or class of persons to perform the functions of an approved intermediary. It also authorises, supervises, and regulates individuals to carry on practice as insolvency practitioners.[122]

The ISI also manages and processes the timely resolution of bankruptcy and insolvency solutions. It also helps regulate and monitor the performance of personal insolvency practitioners and adopt innovative insolvency services recognised as Ireland's leading authority on personal insolvency. It also helps to design, plan, and implement an effective communication strategy, raising awareness of bankruptcy and insolvency solutions amongst the target audience. It ensures effective corporate governance, helps develop the staff, and enhances organisational capability.

Personal Insolvency Arrangement PIA is an insolvency resolution for people with unsecured and secured debts.[122] It is a three-bet resolution mechanism introduced by the PIA Act 2012. When a debtor satisfies the eligibility criteria under s 91 of the Act, the debtor may propose the PIA with one or more creditors to pay and restructure debts. [122]Under s 90 of the Act, the debtor can enter PIA once only.[123] Moreover, a debtor cannot avail of the PIA if involved in other debt resolution processes introduced by the Act.[120] It is a formal agreement with the creditors that write off unsecured debts. It even helps to restructure the remaining secured debt. However, debtors applying for the loan must cooperate with the creditors for at least 6 months regarding the rescheduled mortgage loans.[122]

PIA allows both the secured and unsecured debts to be re-negotiated, but only with the approval of 65% of creditors, including the support of over half of the unsecured and secured creditors.[123] These approval criteria were satisfied by only half of the cases that passed through the initial application stage.[123] Also, the legislation protects the secured creditor's rights, provided they take the initiative to participate in a PIA.[124] PIA usually lasts up to 5 years and can be extended to 6 years in certain circumstances,[122] and this period is known as the supervision period. The consent of the involved parties is required to finalise the agreement's length. The PIA proposal

---

[122] Insolvency Service of Ireland (2016).

[123] ISI (ss 91 and 111).

[124] Spooner (2018), p. 790.

must get the approval of borrowers and creditors.[122] Once PIA supervision expires, the remaining debts of unsecured creditors are written off. Thus, it means that the borrower no longer owes money. However, when the PIA ends, the borrower still must pay the outstanding amount on secured debts, such as a mortgage.

Thus, through CBI, Ireland took several initiatives at the regulatory and supervisory levels to control NPLs and ensure financial stability. Ireland also adopted a transparent approach while implementing these resolutions. It also took borrowers' consent on all aspects of mortgage arrears, including information on the resolution plan. The magnitude of the problem was so high, and despite all these efforts, the problem of high NPLs continues and persists in the short run. Nonetheless, these sustained efforts yielded visible positive results, and NPLs, which touched the highest of 22.37% in 2013, have dropped to 2.48% in 2020 (refer to Table 1.1, Chap. 1).

4.10 Comparative Analysis of Insolvency and Bankruptcy Laws

The following paragraphs present a comparative analysis of the insolvency and bankruptcy laws/codes of the UK, India, and Ireland for restructuring NPLs. The UK, India and Ireland enforced these Codes/Acts in 1996, 2016 and 2012, respectively (Table 4.1). After liquidation, the UK insolvency and bankruptcy law has provisions for acquiring the assets and distributing the proceeds among the creditors as per their eligibility. The UK law also has a winding- up procedure in case of very bleak chances for survival, and if the court is satisfied with the grounds set for winding up. UK law recognises creditors' rights, and the debtor company completes this process. The director of the debtor company calls a shareholders' meeting to nominate a liquidator. The law has four important pillars: voluntary company arrangements, administrative receiverships, liquidations and administrations.[125]

In the UK, the court appoints an administrator to restructure the debt of companies facing financial difficulty and unable, or likely to become unable, to pay debts. When a court assesses that a company is likely to become insolvent, it appoints an administrator, hoping for its survival, on the recommendation of a director, shareholder, and creditor. AA appoints resolution professionals in India, and personal insolvency practitioners perform such actions in Ireland.

Creditors are comfortably positioned in the UK as they can access the company's assets once insolvency proceedings begin. However, the replacement of administrative receiverships significantly affects the position of most secured lenders. One of the important criticisms of UK law lies in its encouraging approach for the creditors to liquidate the firm without giving them opportunities to initiate action.[126] The

[125] Coles and Pullen (2013).

[126] Kaiser (1996), p. 67.

Table 4.1 The UK, India, and Ireland: Insolvency and Bankruptcy Laws

Variable	UK	India	Ireland
Law	Insolvency Act 1986.	Insolvency and Bankruptcy Code of India 2016.	Bankruptcy Code 1986 Personal Insolvency Code 2012.
Scope and applicability	Applicable to the UK.	India, Part I (1) applies to India except for Part III, which is related to individual and partnership firms.	Ireland domiciled in the State or within one year before the application date s 26 (2). (i) Resided in the State, or (ii) had a place of business in the State.
Responsibility for insolvency proceeding	Insolvency monitor or administrator (A 13) (1–3) A15 for Scotland on the recommendations of the director and creditors	Insolvency resolution professional appointed by AA (s 16)	Personal insolvency practitioner (under part 5)
Major thrust	On the survival of the company [(pts 2) (8) (3) (1)] rather than liquidation.	Liquidation of CDs under s33 (b) (1–3).	Debt settlement arrangement with a focus on survival.
Responsibility to initiate proceedings	Director of the debtors' company with relevant documents A2 (2).	FCs (s7), Operation creditors (s 9) CD (s 10).	Official Assignee and the Creditors' Assignee.
Time for settlement	Administrative period will expire after 12 months unless creditors consent and the court extends it up to 6 months.	The time limit for completion of CIRP is 180 days with a maximum of 90-day. for a one-time extension (s 12).	Protective certificate for a period of 70 days(s 47(5) with an extension of 40 days by the court after satisfying some conditions.
Moratorium	Yes A moratorium is between the filing of an application, the appointment of an administrator, and the actual appointment.	Yes In exceptional cases, an automatic moratorium against any debt recovery actions of 180 days by the creditors may be extendable by 90 days.	Yes
Sale of assets	The administrator has the power to sell any of the debtors' property without permission.	RP may do so after the approval of CoC (s 28).	DSA will not sell assets necessary for debtors' employment, business or vocation unless the debtor explicitly consents to such a sale.

(continued)

Table 4.1 (continued)

Variable	UK	India	Ireland
Debt settlement arrangement or resolution plan	08 weeks of administrator appointment or extended period as the court may allow. The resolution plan approval requires a simple majority.	Based on the information memo (s 29), a resolution plan can be submitted (s 30.4), and the plan is to be approved by the CoC by a 75% voting share. As per s 31, the resolution plan by CoC should be approved by AA.	As per s 2 (a), 60 months can be extended to 12 months.
Priority rules	It prioritises the settlement of claims to secured creditors and later to all other parties.	Secured creditors' claims are settled in priority after settlement of all the costs associated with insolvency, followed by unsecured creditors.	No such rule is in existence.

Source: Compiled from various sources, including respective insolvency and bankruptcy laws/codes

increasing trend of outside reorganisation of resolution also encourages privatisation of the bankruptcy process,[127] which is also not received well in the corporate arena.

However, the insolvency processes in Ireland and the UK are similar in several parameters, including compulsory and voluntary liquidations, receiverships and examinership processes.[128] Under s 1417, the Irish code, the HC can wind up unregistered companies, even those incorporated outside Ireland, for undertaking business.[129] The UK also has similar power under s 426, Insolvency Act 1986. Moreover, compulsory winding up commenced in the UK is automatically recognised by Ireland, and these provisions need careful examination in the post-Brexit scenario.

There is a similar provision to appoint a liquidator, with some exceptions, mainly when the proceeding is not considered final and might be in breach of natural justice, particularly when it is contrary to public policy.[130] Moreover, recognition of collecting proceedings on winding up is somewhat unclear and analogous to the UK and Ireland Acts.[131] Another similar example is the law, where the Irish SC acknowledged the authority of Cambridge Gas in Re Flight Lease (Ireland) Limited.[130] Similarly, the UK SC judgement[132] recognises the Irish SC judgement. Thus, insolvency proceedings in the UK and Ireland demonstrate several similarities, with some exceptions.

[127] Jensen (1989), p. 67.

[128] Umfreville et al. (2014), p. 412.

[129] Fannon and Murphy (2012).

[130] Cambridge Gas Transport Corporation v The Official Committee of Unsecured Creditors of Navigator Holdings PLC and others 26 689 (2006).

[131] Fletcher (1999).

[132] Rubin and other v. Eurofinance and other 895 (2012).

While comparing UK law with that of India, the UK initiated the insolvency proceedings based on clear evidence for restructuring and liquidation. In India, the creditor or the CD on loan default can start the insolvency resolution. Moreover, in the UK, a pre-packaged rescue with the consent of creditors and the debtor company in agreement decides on selling the company's business before initiating formal insolvency proceedings, IBC does not provide such a provision.

In the UK, an administrator takes over the company's management, plays a central role in the rescue process and is empowered to manage the company's affairs, business, and property. In India, AA suspends the powers of the CD's board of directors and appoints an interim resolution professional with the approval of the creditors' committee.[133] In the UK, the creditors' consent is mandatory to approve a resolution proposal, whereas, in India, the creditors' committee takes all the decisions.

The UK law grants a moratorium to a company for a specific period of 20 days, extending up to 15 days. This period falls from application submission until the appointment of an administrator. The IBC ensures an automatic moratorium for the debts under recovery actions. Such a moratorium remains effective for 180 days, extendable up to 90 days in exceptional cases. UK and Indian insolvency laws do not provide superior creditors with funding for distressed companies through specific legislation like the US.

In the UK and Ireland, the major focus is on the company's survival and debt settlement, whereas in India, the major focus is on liquidating corporate debt. Moreover, in the UK, the director of the debtor company is responsible for initiating the debt settlement process. In India, the responsibilities lie jointly with FCs, operation creditors and CD; in Ireland, it is the official assignee and creditors' assignee. In the UK and India, the priority is to settle claims. Thus, these legislations have similarities and dissimilarities in the resolution process. In contrast, in the UK and Ireland, referring to the court cases of each other, confirms more similarity in their laws.

4.11 Comparative Analysis of Regulatory and Supervisory Response

The regulators in the UK and Ireland have considerable flexibility with the least government interference. In India, too much government interference prevents financial regulators from making timely decisions. These jurisdictions have many regulations, directives, acts and statutes, and the UK and Ireland transposed the EU directives and regulations into their national law, which are largely common rules. Thus, consolidating these legal instruments is essential to strengthening the legal system of the banking and financial sectors. An integrated regulatory mechanism

[133] Kishnan (2018), p. 100.

Table 4.2 Regulatory and Supervisory Response: Comparative Analysis

Variables	UK	India	Ireland
Regulators	Multiple (FCA, PRA, HM, Treasury, BoE)	Multiple (SBI, SEBI, IRDA, FMC, PFRDA	Single supervisory mechanism through ECB and CBI
Important regulations	MiFID I and II, MiFIR CRD, CRR AMLD, PDS, BRRD, Financial Services Act 2021	SICA 1985, RDBFI 1993, SARFAESI 2002, IBC 2016	MiFID I and II, MiFIR, CRD, CRR, AMLD, PDS, BRRD, CPC, CCMA, MART
Intervention of the government	Moderate	High	Moderate
Regulatory architecture	Strong	Moderate	Moderate
Supervisory authority	Multiple	Multiple	Single
National resolution authority	Yes Insolvency service board	Yes Insolvency and bankruptcy Board of India	Yes National Resolution Authority
Insolvency act	UK Law Insolvency Act 1986	Insolvency & Bankruptcy Code 2016	Bankruptcy Code 1986 Personal Insolvency Code 2012
Basel III norms for capital requirement	Yes	Yes	Yes

Source: Compiled from the UK, India, and Ireland legal documents

dealing with the financial services market, including banks, in a much more coordinated and effective manner would yield better results (see Table 4.2).

Based on the analysis of the regulatory and supervisory provisions, the regulatory architecture of the UK and Ireland is much stronger than that of India. PRA, FCA, and BoE have considerable independence in regulating financial sectors' 'regulated activities.' These jurisdictions have insolvency service boards with different nomenclatures to deal with issues related to insolvent banks. These jurisdictions also have insolvency acts and codes to deal with the problems of NPLs. EU has brought several directives and regulations to regulate financial sector activities, including addressing the problem of NPLs, and accordingly, all these legislations become binding for the UK and Ireland to transpose into domestic law, which the UK discontinued after Brexit—the Indian efforts continued by enacting legislation to strengthen her insolvency and bankruptcy reign.

The RBI play a proactive role in issuing guidelines on various issues, including debt classification, CDR, sustainable debt restructuring, provision of loans for long-term projects and infrastructure, and enforcing the law. Besides implementing the EU regulations and directives, Ireland has implemented several debt resolution strategies to deal with mortgage arrears. Thus, these jurisdictions took several initiatives, but the problem in India and Ireland persisted for longer and warrants a change in the debt resolution approach.

4.12 Concluding Remarks

This chapter depicts a comprehensive picture of the regulatory and supervisory ecosystem of the UK, India, and Ireland. It also critically examined and compared the role of regulatory authorities in regulating the financial market to level down NPLs. The chapter also examined the effectiveness of the legal instruments in addressing the problem of NPLs. The intended objective of this analysis was to gauge the suitability of existing legislation for resolving distressed assets, besides delineating a critical overview of their consolidation and integration. The chapter also gauged whether the existing laws are enough to address the problem of NPLs and whether a new regulatory framework is warranted.

The UK has strong and integrated regulatory mechanisms consisting of PRA, FCA, BoE and HMT to regulate the financial market, including the banking sector. The UK reformed its financial sector regulations by combining many supervisory agencies and developing a 'tripartite' structure of shared responsibility between the BoE, the HMT, and the FSA to link micro-prudential and macro-prudential supervision and regulation. The loopholes in the FSA brought the PRA and the FCA into the picture in 2012 to strengthen the regulatory system in the UK.

The PRA and the FCA work in close coordination as the PRA promotes the safety and soundness of the firms it regulates and ensures that policyholders are appropriately protected. In contrast, the FCA also regulates PRA-regulated firms regarding business matters. Therefore, UK firms are 'dual regulated' or follow a twin peak approach in regulating the financial sector. Moreover, the PRA has three-pronged approaches to regulate and supervise the financial market, reducing NPLs to a manageable level (see Table 1.1 Chap. 1).

Moreover, before Brexit, the UK transposed EU regulations and directives into domestic law. PRA played an important role in carefully crafting these laws, and FCA ensured the effective implementation of these regulations. Brexit posed a serious challenge and prompted the UK to introduce the Financial Services Act 2021, making necessary amendments to the EU financial sector regulations and directives, including CRD, MIFID, MIFIR, PSD, BRRD, and AMLD, to strengthen them. However, FSMA 2023 focused on revoking retained EU law and strengthened the financial sector regulations appropriately. In addition, the UK also has the effective Insolvency Act 1996, which deals with cases of insolvency and bankruptcy and has provisions to provide an effective resolution to insolvency cases.

In India, in addition to the RBI, sector-specific regulators such as SEBI, IRDA, FMC, and PFRDA play important roles in regulating financial sector activities. India has made consistent efforts at the regulatory and supervisory levels to provide effective legislation to deal with the problem of high levels of NPLs. Indian Parliament approved SICA to revive sick industrial units; however, due to several pitfalls in the system and cumbersome legal proceedings, revival and liquidation remained ineffective, and SICA miserably failed to achieve its intended objective. India again enacted legislation, namely RDBFI, but it also had a similar fate, mainly due to the monotonous legal system, which considerably delayed the settlement of cases.

The reforms in the banking sector continued, resulting in the enactment of the SARFAESI Act 2002, which achieved partial success for the securitisation of distressed assets through ARCs, prompting the supervisor and regulator to think differently. The act also promoted the settlement of recovery of loans through the *Lok Adalats* and DRTs, but they also remained ineffective in recovering NPLs.

Subsequently, RBI issued guidelines to classify the debt SMA0, SMA1 and SMA2 based on the number of days the principal and interest payment is overdue. It was a good move from the RBI to categorise the debt and provide restructuring solutions to the banks with high NPAs. In addition, the RBI also issued guidelines for restructuring loans for long-term projects and infrastructure, suggesting the repayment of loans from DCCO. It also provided explicit instructions for financing such a project, so the loan does not fall under the forbearance or NPLs category. RBI also issued guidelines on SDR, sustainable structuring of stressed assets and sales of stressed assets to improve the quality of assets and bring a qualitative and quantitative reduction in NPAs. However, these initiatives failed to attain the intended objective without protection from suitable legal instruments.

Finally, the Government of India enacted IBC 2016, a major landmark in the insolvency and bankruptcy regime with a far-reaching impact on the legal system for loan restructuring. The objective of the code was to provide comprehensive law for insolvent loans, complete the restructuring process in a time bound manner, and maximise the asset value. This code significantly smoothened the restructuring process with the help of the adjudicating authority and legal professionals who were responsible for implementing the resolution plan. However, cavities in the code were challenged in the HCs and the SC of India, which certainly limited the scope of the code. Accordingly, several amendments to the IBC have already been made to strengthen various provisions. Nevertheless, the provisions in the IBC will likely play an important role in addressing the issue of distressed assets in India. Despite all these efforts, NPLs in India were highest in 2017–2018.

Ireland's regulatory ecosystem evolved gradually, where the ECB is the main regulator for financial sector-related activities and closely coordinates with the CBI. Ireland has already adopted SSM and SSMR to regulate the financial sector, including the banking business. Thus, the ECB is the lead regulator, and the CBI is the competent authority in Ireland to regulate financial sectors and banking business. The FIs in Ireland have been categorised as significant and less significant institutions and regulated by the ECB and CBI, respectively.

Ireland has enacted many codes of conduct and other legal instruments to regulate and supervise the financial market and banking business. Ireland became more vigilant since it was trapped in a crisis during the GFC due to the collapse of the retail estate and SMEs and increasing individual insolvencies. The crisis also prompted Ireland to strengthen its domestic law, enacting CPC 2012, CCMA, MART, PIA, etc. However, the NPL ratios remain very high due to several deficiencies in these legislations which needs to be addressed effectively.

As a Member State of the EU, Ireland transposed EU legislation into domestic law, and all the directives and regulations of the financial sector applicable to the UK before Brexit were also binding on Ireland to implement them. Ireland also enacted the Bankruptcy Code 1986 and the Personal Insolvency Code 2012 to address insolvency and bankruptcy proceedings. However, it is argued that the chances of insolvencies will be less if unified, high-quality supervision by the ECB and national supervisor works effectively in close coordination.[134] Therefore, reducing NPLs and the success of unified supervision, dismantling the sovereign debt vicious circle and financial market segmentation is essential.

Finally, this chapter concludes that the UK, India, and Ireland have made strong provisions to regulate the financial market and mitigate the impact of financial crises like the GFC and COVID-19. The regulators, supervisors, and policymakers have played significant roles by enacting legislation, issuing guidelines, crafting suitable policies, and promptly implementing and monitoring them to address the problem of NPLs effectively. The analysis of insolvency and bankruptcy acts/codes revealed various similarities and divergences across these jurisdictions. Therefore, they can harness the strength of each legislation to make the regulatory system stronger.

Nonetheless, despite all these efforts, the problem of NPLs remained challenging; mainly, it was more acute in India and Ireland, from the GFC to COVID-19, despite the impact of the GFC was minimal on the Indian financial sector. Therefore, a more proactive supervisory and regulatory approach is required to deal with the problem of NPLs and level it down by designing an integrated approach. Moreover, the widespread use of online technologies has also posed serious challenges to curb the percolation of problems across the globe in no time; therefore, while crafting a new legislation, these challenges also need to be addressed effectively.

References

Acheson GG, Turner JD (2008) The death blow to unlimited liability in Victorian Britain: the city of Glasgow failure. Expl Econ Hist 45(3):235. https://doi.org/10.1016/j.eeh.2007.10.001. Accessed 14 July 2022

Ahmed AS, Takeda C, Thomas S (1999) Bank loan loss provisions: a re-examination of capital management, earnings management and signalling effects. J Account Econ 28:1–25

Alexander K (2019) Principles of banking regulation. Cambridge University Press

Alshaleel MK (2020) The UK and EU'S fifth anti-money laundering directive: exceeding expectations. Eur Comp Law 17(4):123

Amador JS, Gonzalez JEG, Pabon AM (2013) Loan growth and bank risk: new evidence. Fin Mkts Portfolio Mgmt 27(4):365

Aspinwall R (1993) Conflicting objectives of financial regulation. Challenge 36(6):53

Bagehot W (1873) Lombard street: a description of the money market. Wiley

Baker M, Collins M (1999) Financial crisis and structural change in English commercial bank assets 1860–1913. Explor Econ Hist 36:428. https://doi.org/10.1006/exeh.1999.0727. Accessed 18 June 2022

Banerjee S (2018) Corporate debt restructuring. https://www.centrik.in/tag/corporate-debt-restructuring. Accessed 20 Mar 2022

[134] Soskic (2015), p. 385.

Bank of England (2020, 12 November) Strong and simple, speech by Sam Wood. https://www.bankofengland.co.uk/-/media/boe/files/speech/2020/strong-and-simple-speech-by-sam-woods.pdf. Accessed 8 July 2023

Bank of England (2021) A strong and simple prudential framework for non-systemic banks and building societies. Discussion paper DP1/21. https://www.bankofengland.co.uk/-/media/boe/files/prudential-regulation/discussion-paper/2021/dp121.pdf?la=en&hash=BAF03DB89BF248EE72D75096249C. Accessed 9 July 2023

Bank of England (2023) Prudential regulation authority's to approach to banking supervision. https://www.bankofengland.co.uk. Accessed 10 July 2023

Basedow JR (2023) A theory of external judicial politics: the ECJ as cautious gatekeeper in external relations. West Eur Polit 46(3):550

Bazinas G, Sakkas Y (2012) The introduction of consumer bankruptcy proceedings in the Greek legal order: law 3869/2010. Insolv Restruct Int 6(1):9. https://www.bazinas.com/media/5b31f3f11e13b.pdf. Accessed 18 July 2021

Brener A (2018) Payment service directive II and its implications. In: John TL, Pierangelo GM, Cummins RM (eds) Disrupting finance, fintech and strategy in the 21st century. Palgrave Macmillan, p 103

Burn G (2006) The re-emergence of global finance. Palgrave

Burton D (2016) Discipline, self-discipline, and legacy: military and regimental savings banks in India. J Imp Commonw Hist 44(1):1–22

Busch D (2017) MiFID II: stricter conduct of business rules for investment firms. Cap Mark Law J 12(3):340

Busch D, Ferrarini G (2017) Product governance and product intervention under MiFID II/MiFIR. Oxford University Press

Butler HN, Macey JR (1988) The myth of competition in the dual banking system. Cornell Law Rev 73:677

Capie F (2010) The Bank of England 1950s to 1979. Cambridge University Press

Coles I, Pullen S (2013) Key differences between the US bankruptcy code and the UK insolvency act 1986. Bank Financ Serv Policy Rep 22(9)

Currie C, O'Brien J, Yonge W (2018) EU update: the latest developments on Brexit, MAR, MiFID II. The Investment Lawyer 1:32. https://www.morganlewis.com/-/media/files/publication/outside-publication/article/investmentlawyer-eu-update-jan2017.pdf?rev=2fe234b98c4e48bcab22ee8348e81932&hash=71008E31E66571DBF1B994244C84D7 B9. Accessed 15 June 2019

Daniel D, Agarwal V, Poshakwale S (2020) Market in financial instruments directive (MiFID) stock price informativeness and liquidity. J Bank Financ 113

Davies C (2021) What does taking back control mean for financial services? European Future May 17. https://www.europeanfutures.ed.ac.uk/what-does-taking-back-control-mean-for-financial-services/. Accessed 5 July 2022

ESEM (2019) Impact of Brexit on market obligation of share. Public Statement 3

EU (2012) Consultation on green paper–towards an integrated European market for card, internet, and mobile payments. https://ec.europa.eu/finance/consultations/2012/card-internet-mobile-ayments/docs/privacy_statement_en.pdf. Accessed 10 July 2022

Eurasia Review (2017, 17 November) Consumers to benefit from safer and more innovative electronic payments. https://www.eurasiareview.com/28112017-eu-consumers-to-benefit-from-safer-and-more-innovative-electronic-payments/. Accessed 11 July 2022

Fannon IL, Murphy G (2012) Corporate insolvency and rescue, 2nd edn. Bloomsbury Professional

Ferrarini G, Wymeersch E (2006) Investor protection in Europe: corporate law making, MiFID and beyond. Oxford University Press

Fletcher I (1999) Insolvency in private international law, 1st edn. Oxford University Press

Franke G, Mosk T, Schnebel E (2016) Fair retail banking: how to prevent mis-selling by banks. http://safe-frankfurt.de/fileadmin/user_upload/editor_common/PolicyCenter/Franke-Mosk-Schnebel-Fair_Retail_Banking.pdf. Accessed 4 May 2022

Gilbart JM (1836) The history of banking in Ireland. Longman

Gordon R (2016) The courts after Brexit. J Int Bank Financ Law 511

Goyal S (2017) Insolvency and bankruptcy code, 2016: problems and challenges. Imp J Interdiscip Res 3(1):1724

Gracie A, Chennells L, Menary M (2014) The Bank of England's approach to resolving failed institutions. Bank Engl Quart Bull 54:4

Havrylchyk O, Kierzenkowski R (2015) Enhancing the financing of the real economy and financial stability in the United Kingdom. OECD Economics Department Working Papers No. 1245. https://www.oecd-ilibrary.org/docserver/5jrxqbk75c43-en.pdf?expires=1690817679&i=id&accname=guest &checksum=6FF71CBDAFA79D67641DC215880B9AE0. Accessed 11 May 2022

Helleiner E (1994). States and the re-emergence of global finance: from Bretton Woods to the 1990s. Cornell University Press

HM Treasury (2021) Financial services future regulatory framework review call for evidence: Regulatory coordination. https://assets.publishing.service.gov.uk/government/uploa ds/system/uploads/attachment_data/file/1032075/FRFReviewConsultation_2021-_Final.pdf. Accessed 10 May 2022

Holt A (2019) Hundreds of stocks at risk from Brexit and MiFID II trading rule. IR Magazine, 14 Feb para 3. https://www.irmagazine.com/regulation-mifid-ii/hundreds-stocks-risk-brexit-and-mifid -ii-trading-rule. Accessed 12 June 2019

Houlihan C, Colleran JH, Ensor J (2018) Recent cases on enforcement of security of interest to owners and prospective purchases of Irish NPLs portfolios. Dillon Eustance. https://www.dilloneustace.com/uploads/files/Recent20Cases20on20Enforcement20of20Mortgages20for20Owners20of20NPL20Portfolios_7931335_5203.pdf. Accessed 13 July 2022

https://rbidocs.rbi.org.in/rdocs/notification/PDFs/330NT250216EFF71EF8EC454943A584E9DD0A3E 77FB.PDF. Accessed 15 February 2022

Huertas TF (2019) Will bust banks be born again by bail-in? Butterworths J Int Bank Financ Law 39:225

Insolvency Service of Ireland (2016) <https://www.isi.gov.ie/EN/ISI/PAGES/ABOUT_THE_ISI> Accessed 7 July 2022

International Monetary Fund (2022) Banking supervision and issues in financial stability (2022) Financial Sector Assessment Program, International Monetary Fund (IMF) Country Report No. 22/10. https://www.imf.org/en/Publications/fssa. Accessed 11 Apr 2022

Jaiswal, RK (2015). Strategic debt restructuring scheme–RBI circular. SIRC of the Institute of Chartered Accountants of India. https://www.bangaloreicai.org/images/icons/2015/SpecialArticle/1507july01.pdf. Accessed 21 Mar 2022

Jensen MC (1989) Active investors, LBO, and privatisation of bankruptcy. J Appl Corp Financ 22(1):77. https://ssrn.com/abstract=1581817. Accessed 10 July 2022

Johns H (2017 May 22) EU fires starting gun for banks vs. Fintech fight over payments Reuters para 1. https://www.reuters.com/article/us-eu-payments-regulations/eu-fres-starting-gun-for-banks-vs-fntech-fght-over-payments-idUSKBN1DR1AZ. Accessed 4 Apr 2022

Jose T (2021 June 8) RBI prudent framework for resolution of stressed assets 2019, Indian Economy: Economy and Finance. https://www.indianeconomy.net/splclassroom/rbis-prudential-framework-for-resolution-of-stressed-assets-2019. Accessed 30 Mar 2022

Kaiser KMJ (1996) European bankruptcy laws: implications for corporations facing financial distress. Financ Manag 25(3):67

Khullar V (2016) Rise of non-performing assets in India. The PRS, May 11. https://prsindia.org/theprsblog/the-rise-of-non-performing-assets-in-india. Accessed 11 Feb 2022

Kishnan N (2018) Insolvency and bankruptcy code 2016–a critical review for resolving increasing NPA's in Indian banking industry. Wealth 7(3):100

KPMG (2016) Guidelines on sale of stressed assets by banks. KPMG, October 5. Accessed 23 Mar 2022

Lastra RM (2013) Defining forward looking, judgement-based supervision. J Bank Regul 14:221
Lovegrove S, Bainbridge A (2019) Banking regulation 2019. Global Legal Insights. https://www.globallegalinsights.com/practice-areas/banking-and-finance-laws-and-regulations/united-kingdom. Accessed 28 Jan 2020
Mahate AA (1994) Contagion effects of three late nineteenth century British banks failure. Bus Econ Hist 33:1
Maher D, Callanan G, Dobbyn L et al. (2022) Central Bank of Ireland launches review of the consumer protection code. https://www.lexology.com/library/detail.aspx?g=d5f9b71b-256b-4733-aef2-5872a12dcfd9. Accessed 10 July 2023
McMIE D, Barker D (1973) We are in-but without the fireworks. The Guardian, Manchester, 1 January, para 2
Ministry of Finance (2015) The report of the bankruptcy law reforms committee: Rationale and design. https://www.ibbi.gov.in/BLRCReportVol1_04112015.pdf. Accessed 15 May 2022
Nachane D M (2022) India's financial sector: the regulatory and supervisory landscape. Wiley Online Library. https://onlinelibrary.wiley.com/toc/14679701/2012/35/1. Accessed 31 July 2023
Nair V (2016) Has the strategic debt restructuring experiment run aground? Mint, August 20. https://www.livemint.com/Industry/jlQ90MUEd8nVVEf9O3brDI/Has-the-strategic-debt-restructuring-experiment-run-aground.html. Accessed 21 Mar 2021
Nair V., RBI allows banks to sell stressed assets to NBFCs, other lenders. https://www.livemint.com/Industry/VZHDNd1epJoxIljoRIjIGN/RBI-releases-guidelines-on-sale-of-stressed-assets-by-banks.html. Accessed 22 Mar 2022
Partnoy F (2017) Financial systems, crises, and regulation. In: Moloney N, Ferran F, Jennifer Payne J (eds) The Oxford handbook of financial regulation. Oxford University Press
Patel UR (2011) Resolution of stressed assets: towards the endgame. RBI Bulletin HTTPS://RBIDOCS.RBI.ORG.IN/RDOCS/BULLETIN/PDFS/01SP1109175A4B2A255253477FBB25696E95633563.PDF. Accessed 10 May 2022
Polk D (2023, July 20) The financial services and markets act 2023 ushers in an era of major regulatory change in the UK. Insight https://www.davispolk.com/insights/client-update/financial-services-and-markets-act-2023-ushers-era-major-regulatory-change. Accessed 25 Oct 2024
Pugsley J (2020) Glimpse of post-Brexit UK reveals nothing radical. The Banker August 3. https://www.thebanker.com/Analysis-Opinion/Reg-ageGlimpse-of-post-Brexit-UK-regime-reveals-nothing-radical. Accessed 6 July 2022
Putnis J, Bonsall N, Shone S (2023) The banking regulation review: United Kingdom. The Law Reviews. https://thelawreviews.co.uk/title/the-banking-regulation-review/united-kingdom. Accessed 10 July 2023
RBI (2014) Review of prudential guidelines-revitalising stressed assets in the economy
RBI (2016) Insolvency and bankruptcy code 2016. https://legislative.gov.in/sites/default/files/The%20Insolvency%20and%20Bankruptcy%20Code%2C%202016.pdf. Accessed 23 Mar 2022
Regy P, Roy S, Sane R (2016) Understanding judicial delays in India: Evidence from debt recovery tribunals. The Leap Blog, 18 May 18. https://blog.heleapjournal.org/2016/05/understanding-judicial-delays-in-india.html. Accessed 11 July 2022
Reid M (1982) The secondary banking crisis, 1973–75: its causes and course, 2nd edn. Macmillan
Report on Mortgage Arrears (2016). https://www.centralbank.ie/docs/default-source/publi cations/correspondence/finance-reports/mortgage-arrears-report.pdf?sfvrsn=2. Accessed on 4 July 2022
Reserve Bank of India (2009) Gross and net NPAs of scheduled commercial banks-Bank group-wise (2009). https://www.rbi.org.in/scripts/PublicationsView.aspx?id=19791. Accessed 21 Jan 2022
Reserve Bank of India (2012–13) Report on trend and progress of banking in India. https://rbidocs.rbi.org.in/rdocs/Publications/PDFs/0RTP21112013_F.pdf. Accessed 11 January 2022
Reserve Bank of India (2014a) Flexible structuring of long-term project loans to infrastructure and core industries. https://rbidocs.rbi.org.in/rdocs/notification/PDFs/CDB150714FP.pdf. Accessed 18 March 2022

Reserve Bank of India (2014b) Framework for revitalizing distressed assets in the economy–Guidelines on joint lenders forum (JLF) and corrective action plan (CAP). https://rbidocs.rbi.org.in/rdocs/notification/PDFs/503ACF260214F.pdf. Accessed 2 Jan 2022

Reserve Bank of India (2016) Scheme for sustainable structuring of stressed assets. https://rbidocs.rbi.org.in/rdocs/notification/PDFs/NT422B1EE9DF2D4B5484487065B8FB94B5EC9.PDF. Accessed 11 Jan 2022

Reserve Bank of India (2017–18) Report on trend and progress of banking in India. https://rbidocs.rbi.org.in/rdocs/Publications/PDFs/0RTP2018_FE9E97E7AF7024A4B94321734CD76DD4F.PDF. Accessed 11 January 2022

Reserve Bank of India (2023) Websites of banks in India. https://rbi.org.in/scripts/bank links.aspx. Accessed 22 July 2022

Romanova I, Grima S, Spiteri J (2018) The payment service directive II and competitiveness: the perspective of European fintech companies. Eur Res Stud J 21(2):5–22

Sahoo MS (2019) A journey of endless hope. In IBBI (eds) Insolvency and bankruptcy code: a miscellany of perspectives. IBBI. https://ibbi.gov.in/uploads/whatsnew/2019-10-11-191223-exc18-2456194a119394217a926e595b537437.pdf. Accessed 22 Mar 2022

Schenk C (2014) Summer in the city: banking failures of 1974 and the development of international banking supervision. Engl Hist Rev 129(540):1129

Schenk CR (2010) The decline of sterling: managing the retreat of an international currency 1945–1992. Cambridge University Press

Shalchi A (2021) Financial Services Act 2021: a briefing paper. House of Commons Library May 7. https://commonslibrary.parliament.uk/research-briefings/cbp-8705/. Accessed 18 July 2022

Sharon D, Fitzpatrick T, Greaney D (2018) Resolving non-performing loans in Ireland: 2010-2018. Q Bull 2:54

Sibley Ed (2019) Monetary and financial stability: the implications for prudential supervision. In: Conference on European Economic and Monetary Union: The First and The Next 20 Years, Vienna

Singh D (2007) Banking regulations in UK and US financial markets. Ashgate Publishing Company

Sivaprakasam B, Roy D (2014) Analysis of framework to revitalize distressed assets. Indian Business Law Journal September 16. https://law.asia/analysis-of-framework-to-revitalize-distressed-assets/. Accessed 15 March 2022

Soskic D (2015) Global financial reform since 2008: achievements and shortcomings. Panoeconomicus 62(3):385

Spooner J (2018) The quiet-loud-quiet politics of post-crisis consumer bankruptcy law: the case of Ireland and the troika. Mod Law Rev 81(5):790–824

Sumpter K (2014) Capital requirements directive IV framework capital and capital adequacy. Allen & Overy Client Briefing Paper 2

The Hindu Business (2016, October 21) All you wanted to know about S4A. The Hindu Buniness, Line 21. https://www.thehindubusinessline.com/opinion/columns/slate/all-you-wanted-to-know-about-s4a/article64539157.ece. Accessed 21 Mar 2022

Umfreville C, Omar P, Lucke H (2014) Recognition of UK insolvency proceedings post-Brexit: the impact of a 'no deal' scenario. International Insolvency Review 27:412. https://www.onlinelibrary.wiley.com/doi/epdf/10.1002/iir.1325. Accessed 11 July 2022

Witney S, Lee A, Burnett A (2020) The UK's implementation of the EU's 5th money laundering directive. https://www.debevoise.com/insights/publications/2020/01/the-uks-implementation. Accessed 3 June 2022

World Bank (2018) Resolving insolvency: The challenges of successfully implementing insolvency reforms. https://documents1.worldbank.org/curated/en/935691513855172936/ pdf/122196-WP-DB18-Resolving-insolvency.pdf. Accessed 23 Mar 2022

Yeo A, McEneny G, Cooke J (2023, July 3). Overview of the Financial Services and Markets Act. Dentons. https://www.dentons.com/en/insights/newsletters/2023/july/3/the-financial-services-and-markets-act-2023/overview-of-the-financial-services-and-markets-act. Accessed 26 Oct 2024

Yoo TH (2005) Indian banking sector reform: review and prospect. Int Area Rev 8(2):167–189

Zwieten KV (2015) Corporate rescue in India: the influence of the courts. J Corp Law Stud 1(2). https://ssrn.com/abstract=2466329. Accessed 16 May 2023

Chapter 5
Resolution of Non-Performing Loans: Policy Response

5.1 Introduction

The preceding chapter examined and discussed the regulatory and supervisory initiatives undertaken by the UK, India, and Ireland to control the level of NPLs. A comparative analysis of regulatory and supervisory initiatives to assess their effectiveness presented a comprehensive picture of existing regulatory and supervisory efforts. This chapter critically examines the policy interventions adopted by these jurisdictions. The US savings and loan (S&L) crisis in the 1980s,[1] the Asian[2] and Nordic[3] financial crisis of the 1990s, and the GFC of 2008 have incited the global economy to develop some policy resolutions to control NPLs.[1] However, their success varies across jurisdictions, largely depending on 'macroeconomic and structural banking sector conditions, the type of problem assets, the fiscal space for public sector intervention, and legal and judicial frameworks' for NPLs resolution.[1]

It is evident that NPLs substantially reduce the allocation of resources for economic development and reduce the banks' profitability. Therefore, suitable policy interventions address the problem of NPLs and push up the country's economic growth. The jurisdictions frequently adopt write-downs and write-off approaches to address the high NPLs that deplete capital buffers. Consequently, the banks end up in a situation where they have reduced capacity to extend new credit and expand their business, ultimately dragging down the growth prospects.[4] It is imperative to adopt a comprehensive policy to resolve the issues of NPLs. The fragmented approach applied from bank to bank would not yield the desired result in the long

[1] Baudino and Yun (2017).

[2] Fung et al. (2004).

[3] Borio (2010).

[4] Aiyar et al. (2015).

A. Dimri, *Non-Performing Loans*, Ius Gentium: Comparative Perspectives on Law and Justice 125, https://doi.org/10.1007/978-3-031-92952-6_5

run, despite having several advantages, including an acquaintance with the customers' profiles.[5] The centralised resolution to successfully restructure a large build-up of NPLs would be a successful venture.

The NPLs resolution policies consist of bank-specific (decentralised) and country-specific (centralised) approaches. The centralised AMC serves all or some distressed financial institutions and ensures economies of scale and enhanced bargaining power, whereas, under a decentralised approach, a separate individual AMC is established for individual distressed financial institutions, including banks. The decentralised approach allows AMC to tap a better knowledge base relating to the loans and assets transferred to them from originating institutions, which is more flexible in the management of assets.[6] Centralised AMC caters to a broader clientele and offers a range of loan restructuring and resolution options. The important decentralised resolution tools include 'individual bank-specific restructuring, bank-internal bad-bank units, and bank-specific asset management companies'.[7]

Some important NPLs resolution policies the jurisdictions have applied include debt restructuring-out-of-court workouts, write-offs, direct sales, securitisation, APS, and public AMCs. In addition, the jurisdictions also use mergers and acquisitions and purchase and assumption transactions as NPLs resolution strategies (see Fig. 5.1). The following section analyses the pros and cons of these policies to control NPLs in the jurisdictions under the purview of this study. The chapter also briefly touched upon the policy responses of some global jurisdictions to understand the historical milieu of NPLs resolution strategies.

5.2 Policy Responses to Address the Problem of NPLs: An Overview

The problem of NPLs becomes more severe without a well-designed resolution plan, and jurisdictions worldwide have sincerely tried to deal with the problem with appropriate policy responses. Japan came up with the Takenaka plan to present an accurate estimate of the size of the problem[8] and restructured NPLs through AMCs, recapitalisation programmes and resolution mechanisms. Japan also enforced the Financial Revitalisation Act in 1998 to clean up the banks' balance sheets and recapitalise them to resolve the credit crunch problem.[9]

---

[5] Constancio (2017).

[6] Woo (2000).

[7] Fell et al. (2017).

[8] Hoshi and Kashyap (2010).

[9] Diamond and Rajan (2009).

This restructuring model had several deficiencies, and many smaller banks were closed with apparent hesitation to admit government assistance publicly. In addition, it also lacked a resolution procedure for complex financial holding companies.[10] Moreover, instead of taking over the companies, the government preferred to continue running relatively costlier swap contracts, and critics argued that the government should assume the contracts and continue making and receiving payments rather than closing them out.[11]

On the other hand, the Swedish crisis of the early 1990s posed a considerable economic threat, and policymakers responded more perpetually despite piecemeal resolution strategies in the initial phase.[12] The important characteristics of a Swedish banking crisis and its resolution strategies[13] was political unity to defend the pegged exchange rate of the krona. However, critics doubted maintaining the pegged krona rate for an extended period.[14] Moreover, despite political differences, the Swedish leadership understood the gravity of the problem and strongly supported blanket guarantees for bank deposits and liabilities. The *Riksbank* immediately took 'Swift Action' to restore depositors' confidence throughout the resolution process.

The banks were divided into three categories, depending on the statutory CAR, to restore them to solvency through a temporary guarantee from the banking support authority. Banks in crisis were also encouraged to look for private support. Sweden established AMCs, namely Securum and Retriva, and transferred 'bad' assets to the bad bank for restructuring. The Swedish bank resolution policy measures were regarded as successful internationally because the banking system was reasonably intact and hardly showed signs of a credit crunch. Moreover, Swedish crisis management was also a domestic affair, and no international organisations like the IMF were involved, which helped build trust.[14]

After the failure of Lehman Brothers, the US Treasury recommended the purchase of the troubled assets to stabilise the financial system. Accordingly, the US implemented the Troubled Asset Relief Programme (TARP), Capital Purchase Programme (CPP), Emergency Economic Stabilisation Act, and Dodd-Frank Wall Street Reform and Consumer Protection Act 2010. Nine major banks availed assistance under TARP and CPP, and later, the government decided to conduct the 'Stress Test' of distressed banks to assess capital adequacy. The banks that received government assistance could repay their debts by selling their assets for securitisation. The NPLs resolution policy of the US government received criticism and was considered a 'schizophrenic approach'[8] because it tried to resolve the credit crisis without changing the existing legislation. The Federal Reserve and the Treasury did not

[10] Caballero et al. (2008).

[11] Cargill et al. (2000).

[12] Englund and Vihriala (2009).

[13] Jonung (2009).

[14] Laeven and Valencia (2008).

possess the power to bail out Lehman from bankruptcy[15] by illegally using government money for its acquisition.[16] Similarly, the lack of a proper resolution mechanism led to misunderstandings among the Treasury, Federal Reserve, and Congress.[17] The stress test modalities focused on the banks' future and income generation and received appreciation, but their long-run success was questionable.

Moreover, there was considerable heterogeneity in the earnings forecast, and Wells Fargo Bank argued that it could earn much more than suggested in the stress test.[18] On the other hand, Bank of America ended up experiencing a shortage of money after the acquisition of Merrill Lynch, using TARP because it was not transparent while disclosing its financial standing. The banks hesitated to use government money for solvency because the stress test suggests a relatively higher compulsory threshold of regulatory capital after meeting the minimum level of absorbing losses. The following section analyses various policy options adopted by the UK, India, and Ireland using the centralised and decentralised NPLs resolution approach.

5.3 Decentralised NPLs Resolution Policies (Bank-Specific Restructuring)

The decentralised NPLs resolution policy has four basic structures determined by the 'legal structure and degree of balance sheet consolidation.' The entities are simpler to set up and are legally separated with a clean balance sheet. The four types of bank-specific structures are on-balance sheet guarantee, internal structuring unit, off-balance sheet SPE and bad bank spinoff.[19]

5.3.1 On Balance Sheet Guarantee

This important structuring solution allows the banks to protect the parts of their portfolios with the government's help against losses. This scheme aims to recapitalise the banks to minimise the capital requirement. This scheme provides an

[15] Izzo et al. (2009).

[16] Swagel (2009).

[17] Wessel (2009).

[18] Goldberg (2009).

[19] Martini et al. (2009).

immediate solution to the banks, so they may consider using alternative available policies to restructure their distressed assets. The bank's separation approach was not transparent without a balance sheet de-consolidation and assets separation.[19] The approach has also been implemented in the UK, India, and Ireland to 'quickly recapitalise the banks.'

It remained a popular approach during the GFC and COVID-19 because the respective governments proactively decided to maintain bank capital. As a result, the NPLs ratio in these jurisdictions remained stable, particularly during COVID-19 (see Table 1.1, Chap. 1). However, this scheme has some flaws regarding balance sheet de-consolidation and clarity on the asset separation approach, limiting investors' attraction. The approach may provide a short-term solution, but the banks may look for an alternative restructuring plan in the long term.

5.3.2 Internal Restructuring Units

Under this scheme, some banks assign the responsibility of loan restructuring to a separate unit to ensure effective management, efficiency, and clarity on the incentives. For instance, Dresdner Bank established an internal restructuring unit dedicated to asset restructuring. Similarly, in the UK, HSBC has a special asset management division, and Barclays has a special situation group. In India, many banks have special units, including the corporate account group of SBI, which deals with debt restructuring. In Ireland, the Bank of Ireland and Allied Irish Bank have such units. This approach lacks efficient risk transfer; however, it increases the transparency of the core banking performance.

5.3.3 Off-Balance Sheet SPE

Under this scheme, the banks shift parts of their bad portfolio to SPE for restructuring, mainly to the government-sponsored SPE. The SPE removes bad loans from the balance sheet and is considered a valuable tool for small and homogeneous assets. This scheme is more prevalent in the UK and Ireland than in India. We should not forget that converting distressed assets into an SPE is complex and unfeasible. The assets are generally heterogeneous, and funding is insufficient, ultimately influencing the restructuring plan.

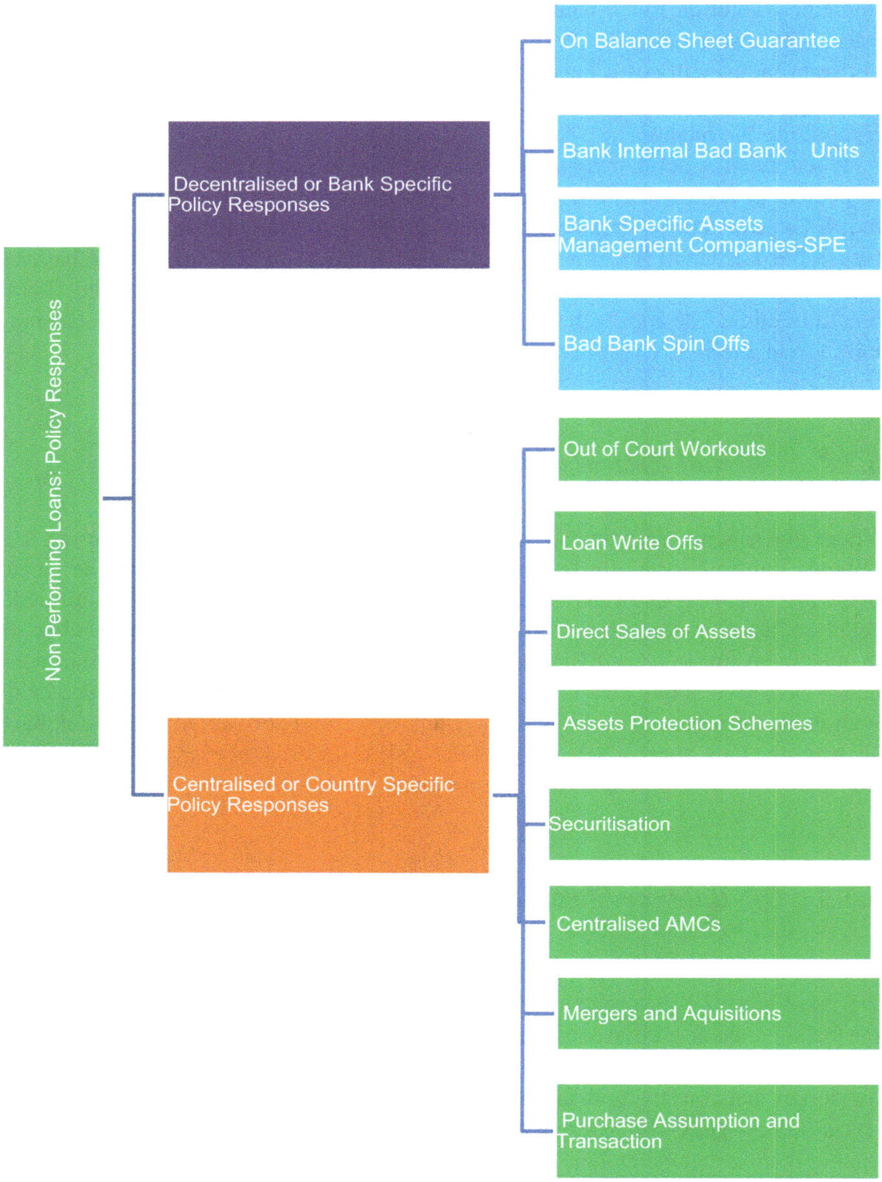

Fig. 5.1 Non performing loans: policy responses [Source: Developed by the researcher based on the information available in Baudino and Yun (2017)]

5.3.4 *Bad Bank Spin-Off*

Under this scheme of bad bank resolution, the assets are disposed of to the legally separated entity, ensuring maximum risk transfer and increasing core bank flexibility. The resolution plan also focuses on attracting outside investors. Moreover, the scheme increases complexity and transaction costs as it often requires a banking licence, thus making operational costs very high. The asset valuation transfer and funding process is also very complex and not readily available. Moreover, the readily available legal and accounting system is also not suitable for separating balance sheets into bad bank entities. Therefore, critics argued that this method should be a last resort when other asset management methods are insufficient.[1]

5.4 Centralised NPLs Resolution Policies (Country-Specific Restructuring)

The weak financial system and a relatively higher level of lending are generally held responsible for the rising level of NPLs, which ultimately erode the banks' profitability and solvency. The problem percolates across jurisdictions; consequently, many banks and FIs collapse due to a financial crisis, which eventually impedes the growth of an economy. This situation warrants an immediate policy response from the supervisory authority on the policy and regulatory front to reduce the impact of the crisis. Under such circumstances, to fetch a better result, the supervisory authority deploys various resolution strategies that require enormous resources and take time to deliver results.

Jurisdictions worldwide have adopted several options to resolve the problem of increasing NPLs (Fig. 5.1). However, the success of a particular resolution plan depends on a conclusive assessment of asset quality and proper estimation of the magnitude of the problem. The success of these policies varies considerably across jurisdictions and banks. The following section analyses the pros and cons of these NPLs resolution policies adopted in the UK, India, and Ireland.

5.4.1 *Debt Restructuring and Out-of-Court Workouts*

Out-of-court workouts (OCWs), a relatively cheaper and faster debt restructuring mechanism, do not involve a judicial process[20] while restructuring NPLs. The UK used the OCWs plan known as the London Approach,[21] which became a popular

[20] Claessens (2005).

[21] Pen Kent, explains that London Approach is a voluntary, collective approach, adopted by banks in the United Kingdom, when faced financial difficulty. It essentially helps the financial community to preserve value and allowed many businesses to survive which might otherwise have been wholly or partially closed.

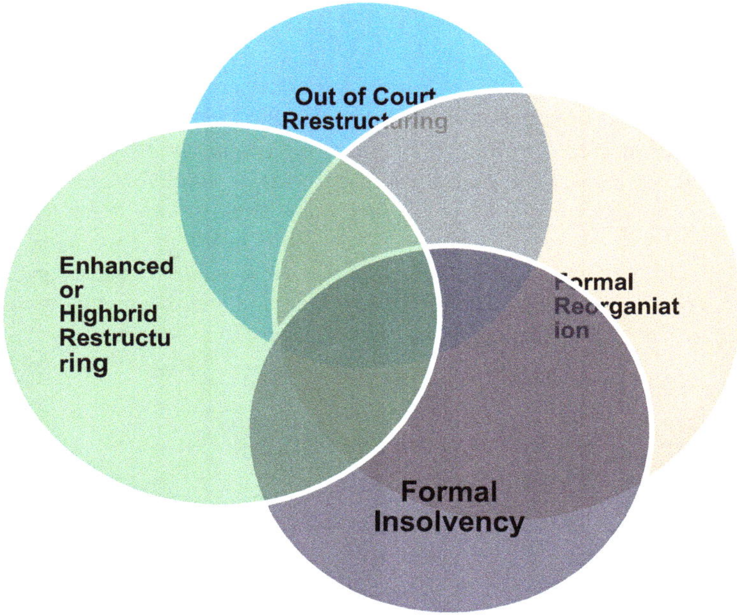

Fig. 5.2 Overlapping relationship between out-of-court workouts and formal insolvency proceedings (Source: Based on World Bank out-of-court debt restructuring model)

restructuring tool during the AFC. The BoE strongly supported the London Approach as a reasonable way of addressing corporate financial difficulties.[22] Under OCWs, the creditors prepare a detailed workout plan and submit it to the court for its approval, and the court has no role in the design of the restructuring plan. This hybrid, cost-effective debt restructuring approach became popular in several jurisdictions, including the UK, India, and Ireland, which have successfully adopted it, allowing companies to continue operations during the restructuring process.[23]

This pre-packed tool received appreciation from policymakers, FIs, insolvency representatives, and enterprises. However, critics argued that finding a restructuring tool with a 'one size fits all' approach is very difficult.[23] Therefore, jurisdictions may develop and adopt flexible tools to meet their specific financial sector requirements after assessing the gravity of the problem.

The OCWs are considered an informal approach to bad debt restructuring, an alternative to formal insolvency procedures. There is no clear-cut dividing line between formal insolvency proceedings and informal restructuring processes. A hybrid procedure might find a point of contact between informal and formal debt workouts.[23] Figure 5.2 depicts a clear overlap between formal, informal, and hybrid

[22] Kent (1993).

[23] Garrido (2012).

restructuring, and this continuum depends on the degree of judicial intervention and formality while undertaking the restructuring task.

Thus, the UK and India used a blended restructuring plan, having informal (OCWs) and formal resolution proceedings. In contrast, Ireland concentrated on the mortgages of individuals, SMEs and CREs. Therefore, it came out with the targeted intervention of Debt Relief Notice for discharging relatively small amounts of unsecured debt, subject to conditions, for persons with essentially no income or assets, subject to a supervision period of 3 years. Debt Settlement Arrangements (DSA) attempt to settle unsecured debt generally over 5 years. Personal Insolvency Arrangement (PIA) makes settlement of secured debt up to €3 million and unlimited unsecured debt over a 6-to-7-year period.[24]

The debt restructuring programme received criticism for several reasons, including the relationship between cost efficiency and NPLs restructuring,[25] the volume of debt, and the time taken for loan recovery. The chances of recovery are higher if a smaller volume of debt goes through a restructuring process. Nevertheless, OCW is widely used in the UK and India as it is a mutual, speedy, cost-effective, semi-formal and less intervening framework for insolvency.

5.4.2 *Loans Write-Offs*

The loan write-off is usual and routine, which helps wipe out the build-up of NPLs from the bank balance sheet. It is the most common and simplest way to dispose of NPLs and is prevalent across jurisdictions. In a financial crisis, jurisdictions have frequently used write-offs as a mandatory emergency measure for addressing the problem of NPLs.[1] Write-off significantly impacts the bank's profitability, resulting in hesitation among banks to write off NPLs from their balance sheet. They presume that the balance sheet will automatically improve with improvements in macroeconomic conditions. Generally, jurisdictions adopt the option of NPLs' write-off when they believe that the chances of recovery are minimal and the comparative cost of the loan restructuring is relatively higher.[26] Capital level and low provisioning are important considerations for loan write-offs because the banks' capital buffers and provisions should be significantly high to absorb loan losses.[1]

The UK, India and Ireland have adopted this policy option as an effective resolution mechanism. Figure 5.3 presents the trend of loan write-offs in the UK since the GFC, and it is evident that the loan write-off in the UK was highest during 2009–2011 and even increased by 185.68% in 2009. Jurisdictions worldwide implemented several policy options to address the problem of NPLs, and the UK was no exception. However, the situation improved gradually, and the loan write-off has fallen

[24] IMF (2013).

[25] Gibler and Black (2004), p. 137.

[26] Ingves (2011).

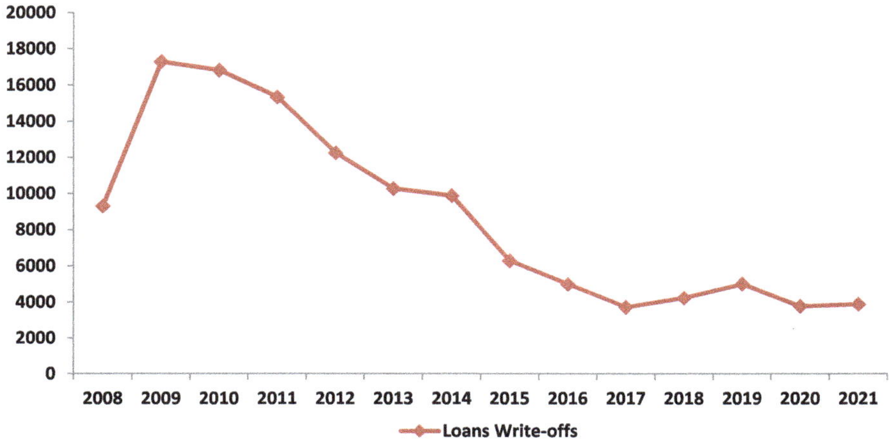

Fig. 5.3 Trend of loans write-offs in the UK (£ million) (Source: Developed by the researcher based on the information available in the Annual Reports of the BoE)

significantly since 2012. The declining trend continued except in 2019, when a marginal increase was due to the impact of COVID-19.

The decline trend was due to a change in the portfolio behaviour of banks after the GFC.[27] Due to the change in the banks' portfolio behaviour, the independent banks diverted their lending to UK residents to avert the risk. Moreover, non-resident loan write-offs impacted UK resident lending. A fall in the capital brought about a significant drop in lending, particularly to private nonfinancial corporations. In contrast, household lending increased with reduced capital, indicating that banks substituted less risky assets due to capital shortage after the GFC. Thus, a capital crunch was a primary reason for a fall in lending after the crisis, ultimately influencing the growth and creating a problem for overall economic output.[28]

Figure 5.4 presents the trend of NPLs write-offs in India, and it is evident that from 2012–2013, there was a sudden rise in loan write-offs, which was 279.07% over previous years. In 2016–2017, loan write-offs recorded an abnormal increase of 904.17%. Critics argued that after evaluating and considering the impact of NPLs, the banks, under the guidelines of the RBI, write off bad loans as part of their regular exercise to clean up their balance sheet, avail tax benefits and optimise capital.[29] Nevertheless, the borrowers of written-off loans continue to be liable for repayment, and the recovery process of dues from such borrowers in written-off loan accounts remains unchanged. As discussed, the large-scale write-off could be attributed to the state policy to keep the balance sheet clean and stimulate growth.[30]

[27] Moraa and Logan (2012), p. 1103.

[28] Fisher (1933), p. 337.

[29] See, The Economics Times (2021).

[30] Dutta (2018).

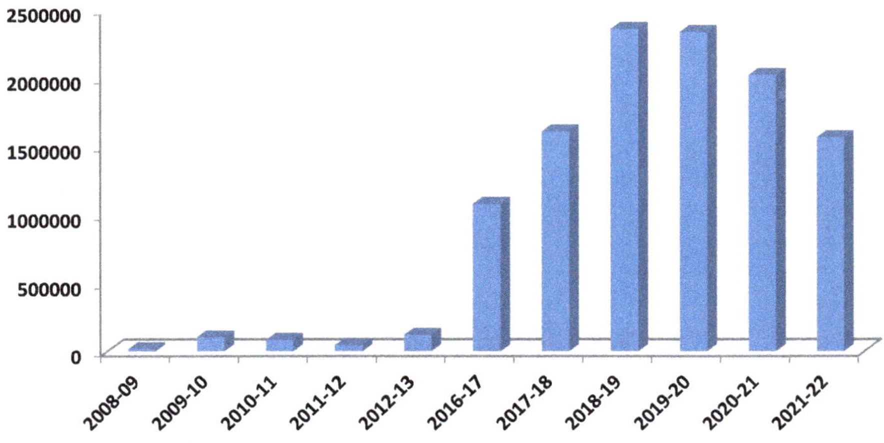

Fig. 5.4 Loans write offs in India (₹ million) (Source: Developed by the researcher based on the various issues of RBI Reports)

Critics argued that the write-off helped to release the amount set aside for provisioning. This amount becomes available to the bank for the business undertaking, ultimately benefiting the economy.[29]

On the other hand, in the EU, EBA does not provide mandatory NPLs write-off rules. Nonetheless, Ireland and other jurisdictions have introduced principles-based local guidelines for loan write-offs.[31] The ECB has issued a guidance manual on prudential provisioning backstop to facilitate complete provisioning and write-off. The guidelines envisaged full provisioning of unsecured loans after 2 years and secured loans after 7 years of identification. As per ECB guidelines, the write-off practices comprise part of banks' NPL resolution strategies.

On the other hand, CBI stressed that loan arrears for more than 53 weeks are considered significant when writing off bank balance sheets. However, after write-offs, banks should continuously pursue recovery and prioritise loans with prolonged arrears. A formal agreement with creditors allows debt write-offs under DSA; the debtor agrees to pay a percentage of their overall debt over a specified period so that debtors become solvent after payment of the full debts.[31]

Critics argued that policymakers injected significant equity into the banking system to mitigate the adverse effects of bank de-leveraging.[32] The UK, India, and Ireland have made it mandatory to write off NPLs and book the loss after a set of period.[33] However, banks always remained reluctant and expressed apprehension in writing off distressed debt from their balance sheet, mainly due to its implications on the profits and capital of the banks.[34] They presume that the positive change in

[31] ECB (2017).

[32] Bernanke (1983), p. 257.

[33] Kim and Haque (2002), p. 1.

[34] Fabian and Arranz (2013).

the macroeconomic conditions will improve the situation of the borrowers and enable them to repay the borrowings. Therefore, they keep the entire loan on their balance sheet, hoping to restructure it in future.[35] The arguments suggest that too little risk-bearing capacity and poor-quality capital with deficiencies in the regulations caused the GFC to spread 'across the globe like wildfire' and prevented write-offs in some jurisdictions.[35]

Moreover, write-offs contribute to the immediate reduction in bank capital, and low provisioning will discourage banks from adopting this approach. Even if they opt for it, the write-off amount is likely to be small, which may not help the jurisdictions and banks to overcome the NPLs problem. However, the IMF reports pointed out that a considerable increase in the write-off reduced the bad debt in Italy and brought it down to the pre-crisis level.[36] The study also identified some important demand and supply-side factors responsible for slow write-offs. Demand-side factors include low provisioning and capital buffers, heavy reliance on collateral, close relationships with borrowers, and tax disincentives to provisioning.[37] The supply side factors are a lengthy and inefficient judicial process and a small investor base with limited risk capital. These factors ultimately contribute to significantly high NPLs, which impact banks' profitability, new lending, lower bank valuation, and increased funding costs.[36] Thus, the UK, India and Ireland should use these policy instruments to help banks relieve themselves from NPLs through timely write-offs, which will positively impact the country's economic growth.

5.4.3 Sales of Assets

Direct sale of assets to bad banks[38] and investment firms is another equally important NPLs resolution plan. Selling NPLs to AMCs follows the process with due diligence and provides sufficient information to prospective buyers to ensure information symmetry and transparency. Several jurisdictions have adopted this approach, and recent examples of direct sales of distressed debts have come from Ireland, Spain, and the United Kingdom.[39] The authors argued that direct sales generally cover loan packages in place of individual loans and, by doing so, take advantage of the diversification of risks through asset pooling.[1]

As discussed earlier, after the GFC, NPLs piled on the bank balance sheet, and the UK, Ireland, and India were no exception. The bad banks in Ireland and the UK have made significant inroads with their wind-down strategies. The

[35] Eis et al. (2013).

[36] Jassaud and Kang (2015).

[37] Gaston and Song (2014).

[38] A bad bank is an asset reconstruction company (ARC), involved in management and recovery of bad loans or NPAs of other banks.

[39] Jenke and Colman (2016).

government of Ireland established the National Asset Management Agency (NAMA) in 2009. Similarly, the United Kingdom Asset Resolution Limited (UKAR), wholly owned by the HMT for asset sales, was established in 2010. These initiatives aimed to salvage the failed banks and building societies, such as the Irish Bank Resolution Corporation (IBRC), formerly the Anglo-Irish Bank of Ireland and the Dunfermline Building Society in the UK.[39] During the last decade, the bad banks carried considerable transactions and have become important policy instruments for addressing the NPLs resolution challenges. For instance, since its inception, UKAR has made significant progress towards its long-term objectives by reducing arrears, repaying government loans, shifting the balance sheet burden, and driving cost-effectiveness.[39]

On the other hand, the RBI also issued comprehensive guidelines in 2005 for selling NPAs to other banks and NBFCs. These guidelines do not entail NPLs sales to securitisation and RCs.[40] RBI guidelines suggest that before displaying an asset for sale, the banks should follow certain norms duly approved by the board of the respective banks. The exercise aims to ensure that banks have the skills to sell and purchase NPLs. While assessment of the value, the purchasing bank offers for the asset and deciding whether to accept or reject the offer would be at the bank's discretion, and banks should avoid accepting such an offer at a contingent price.[40]

NPA placed for purchase should fall under the standard category. Once the bank sells NPA to other banks, the balance sheet becomes clean, and in case the sale price is below net book value, debit the shortfall from the profit and loss account of the selling banks, and a higher NVA will be used to meet the shortfall. After adjusting the recovery of NPA against acquisition cost, the access amount turns into profit. The bank should also consider capital adequacy and assign 100% RWA to mitigate risk.[40]

Since its incorporation, NAMA has realised €18.7 billion from overall disposal proceeds in Ireland, a major chunk of 42% of sales in 2014. Two major loan sales include Project Eagle to Cerberus and Project Tower to Blackstone. After disposing of its bond debt, NAMA planned to wind down its activities completely by 2020. Irish retail banks sold €7.8 billion of mortgages and corporate loans, contributing to NPLs reductions. Central Bank research suggests that many NPLs still on bank balance sheets may be difficult to cure. It implies that loan sales will likely remain part of the toolkit available to lenders to reduce NPLs.[41]

Ireland has learned the lesson from the crisis and is now focusing on the mortgages that guarantee 'sustainable lending standards in the mortgage market'. Therefore, Ireland tried to 'prevent the emergence of an unsustainable relationship between credit and house prices' because it would provide resilience support to the borrowers and lenders, ultimately improving the economic base. While doing so, the CBI will ensure the implementation of these goals by assessing the

[40] RBI (2005).

[41] Kelly and Mazza (2019).

macroeconomic benefits and costs involved in the performance of these measures.[42] Ireland also introduced new regulations in 2015 that suggest that mortgage lending should be the outcome of a high loan-to-value and loan-to-income ratio [s (5) and (6) (1) (a) (b)].[43] Thus, asset sales remained a vital policy instrument for resolving NPLs problems, and it has been applied successfully by several jurisdictions, including the UK and Ireland.

5.4.4 Securitisation

Asset securitisation[44] is another policy response that jurisdictions use to restructure NPLs. Although it is a relatively more complex method, it nonetheless broadens the potential buyer base for asset disposal. The first asset-backed security issues came into the market in the United States in the 1970s. The UK used this method of loan restructuring for the first time in 1985. In a real sense, a small amount of UK lending was securitised in 1993 through this method.[45] It diversifies the risk away from a single credit and allows the investors to choose a combination of risk-reward that best reflects their preferences. Therefore, the securitisation process intends to convert NPLs into marketable securities, which could attract more buyers, including foreign institutional buyers.

The cost of restructuring NPLs under securitisation is relatively low compared to other options, and it fetches higher NPLs prices than direct sales.[46] Critics have argued that the cost factor plays a prominent role in dealing with the securitisation of small NPLs, including households, individuals, and SMEs, and selling these NPLs incurs high transaction costs.[4] There are several examples where jurisdictions have used securitisation as a practical policy resolution tool for treating NPLs. For instance, the US used RTC during the S&L crisis of the late 1980s, Italy used GACS, and Greece used the Hellenic Asset Protection Scheme (HAPS) to securitise NPLs through SPV.[47]

In addition, the UK, India, and Ireland have also enforced legislation to bring securitisation into the legal framework. The EU regulation[48] categorically states that 'due diligence, risk-retention and transparency requirements' are vital for the securitisation of loans of a retail client (art 1). It also advocates simple, transparent, and standardised (STS) securitisation with a ban on re-securitisation (arts 5–8). The regulation has provisions (art 7) for the requirements of securitisation special pur-

[42] Bank of Ireland (2021).

[43] Central Bank (Supervision and Enforcement) Act 2013 (Section 48) (Housing Loan Requirements) Regulations [2015] (Ireland).

[44] Securitisation is the pooling of assets to repackage them into interest-bearing securities.

[45] Twinn (1995), p. 123.

[46] Fell et al. (2017).

[47] Deloitte (2020).

[48] The Securitisation (Amendment) (EU Exit) Regulations (2019) (UK).

Table 5.1 Comparison of EU Securitisation Regulation with the UK Withdrawal Act

Variables	UK	Ireland (EU Regulation)
Regulations	Securitisation (Amendment) (EU Exit) Regulations 2019	REGULATION (EU) 2017/2402
Sponsors	Credit Institutions, whether located in the UK or a third country	No clarity on the operational location of credit institutions
Portfolio management entity	To operate from the jurisdiction in which it is established	To operate from the EU only
Securitisation	Non-ABCP securitisation, the SSPE does not need to be in the UK	STS only if the originator, sponsor, and SSPEs are established in the EU
Transparency requirement	Transparency requirements have been amended and applied in the case of originators, sponsors, and SSPEs established in the UK-art 5(1) (f)	Institutional investors must verify compliance with certain requirements before investing in a securitisation position by originators, sponsors and SSPEs-art 5(1) (e)
Risk-retention	Direct obligation on the originator, sponsor or original lender of a securitisation	Direct obligation on the originator, sponsor or original lender of a securitisation

Source: Compiled after referring to the UK Securitisation Act and EU Regulation

pose entities (SSPEs) to dispose of assets. It also provides the information relating to the transaction to investors when requested, and this responsibility lies with originators, sponsors and SSPEs. Art 5 provides specific conditions for establishing SSPEs in a third country. Article 6 states that originators, sponsors, or original lenders are under a 'direct' obligation to satisfy the risk retention requirements.[48] ESMA has supervisory power to monitor and secure assets and withdraw licences.

On the other hand, the UK securitisation[48] regulation empowers the PRA to supervise and monitor securitisation activities. It has a provision to give direction to the originator, sponsor, and SSPE for private securitisation. The regulation also focuses on the fact that STS securitisation should be easier for investors to understand so that effective asset securitisation occurs. Table 5.1 presents a comparative picture of the provisions of the UK and the EU Securitisation Act. There are certain asymmetries besides replacing ESMA, the EBA and EIOPA with PRA and FCA.

Moreover, EU regulation is unclear about the sponsor or investment firm and whether an investment firm needs to be established in the EU to be a sponsor. In contrast, the UK regulation clearly states that an 'investment firm is, in principle, capable of being a sponsor, whether located in the UK or a third country.[49] The EU securitisation regulation is relatively rigid in the operational area of the originator, sponsor, and SSPE. It restricts its operation within the EU to make securitisation STS. However, in the case of the UK, it gives flexibility and states that for non-ABCP securitisation, the SSPE is not required to be in the UK only.

[49] Griffiths and O'Connor (2021).

Similarly, Article 5 of the EU securitisation regulation puts certain compliance conditions for the investors on transparency requirements, and the UK regulation has amended the same. As per art 5 of the EU Securitisation Regulation, the investors must verify compliance with certain requirements before investing in a securitisation. Similarly, risk retention and credit- granting conditions have been provisioned depending on whether the originator or other relevant entity is also established in the EU or a third country. The UK securitisation regulation has also amended the requirement to verify compliance with transparency.

Article 5(1) (e) of the EU Securitisation Regulation provides that institutional investors must verify the information on non-EU entities, including originator, sponsor or SSPE. Article 5(1) (e) does not specify the jurisdictional scope of the investor and the due diligence requirement. In the case of the UK Securitisation Regulation, it amends art 5(1) (e) to apply to originators, sponsors and SSPEs established in the UK. In addition, a new art 5(1) (f) states that the investor must verify that an originator, sponsor or SSPE has also been established in a third country. Financial Vehicle Corporations (FVCs) carried out securitisation activities in Ireland as per EU regulations.[50] The Irish SPV has made remarkable progress in securitising CLOC, RMBS, CBCS and ABCP.[51]

The SRFAESI Act of 2002 provided several provisions for NPLs' securitisation in India. Nonetheless, the ecosystem for such a market is still developing. RBI issued guidelines in 2006[52] with subsequent revisions in 2012,[53] and to counter COVID-19 measures, the RBI completely revamped the guidelines in 2021[54] so that these could match with the developed market.[55] RBI, Master Direction on Securitisation of Standard Assets Directions, 2021, is the latest guideline for securitising NPLs.[55] Thus, the RBI is the main regulator, and SEBI exercises oversight with listed instruments for securitisation transactions. Banks and NBFCs are originators for NPLs, and ARCs undertake the securitisation of assets.[55]

The guidelines also specify that the originators must comply with the retention/holding period requirement specified before securitisation and follow due diligence. The RBI and SEBI can levy penalties in case of a breach of regulatory obligations, and the penalty amount will depend on the nature of the violation. SPEs, or SPVs, are also subject to the restriction provisioned in the respective regulation.

Thus, securitisation helps provide a clean balance sheet that involves risk transfer to other investors, but such a transfer fails to diversify the portfolios.[56] In securitisation, very large portfolios are used for asset restructuring, and in the case of a single

[50] Council Regulation (EC) of the European Central Bank of 18 October 2013 concerning statistics on the assets and liabilities of financial vehicle corporations engaged in securitisation transactions (recast) (ECB/2013/40) [2013] EN L 297/107.

[51] CLOC stands for collateralised loan obligations category, RMBS for residential mortgage-backed securities CABC for corporate asset-backed securities and ABCP for asset-backed commercial paper.

[52] RBI (2006).

[53] RBI (2012).

[54] RBI (2021).

[55] Mashruwala and Kumar (2022).

[56] Bisky (1986), p. 35.

asset, benefits are never likely to materialise, and a diversified portfolio fetches more benefits.[57] In addition, scholars opined that there is a 'separation of ultimate risk from the source of the risk in securitisation, and asset-backed securities have limited information about such assets, which may lead to sub-optimal investment decisions.[58]

Due to their uncertain performance, the underdeveloped local capital markets impede the use of securitisation tools to dispose of NPLs. Moreover, a deficiency in direct sales valuation and the difference will likely intensify this problem. The world has examples of how the US debt crisis percolated, and local capital markets jeopardised securitisation.[59] Therefore, with an integrated application of securitisation, the sales of assets and AMCs may derive better results. The UK, India and Ireland should promote asset restructuring using securitisation to maximise the gain from NPLs.

5.4.5 *Asset Protection Scheme*

APS is another equally important debt resolution policy intervention implemented by the UK to support banks.[1] This scheme is generally used in acute financial crises and credit crunches when risk remains unmanageable. Under such an acute financial crunch, APS provides a recess to distressed banks by extending bank-specific support, covering entities with a high level of NPLs, and intending to support the entire banking sector and the selected entities. Sometimes, banks do not meet the criteria APS sets, so they raise capital from private sources to strengthen their balance sheets. Nevertheless, the programme's feasibility relies on several factors, including the effective use of the guarantee scheme by the officials and the confidence of the market participants.

In the UK, HMT implemented APS to rescue major banks after the GFC by purchasing the shareholdings of Royal Bank of Scotland (RBS) and LBG, amounting to £37 billion.[60] It protected these banks from exceptional loans, mortgages, and other financial losses. The HMT placed the assets worth £282 billion in the APS and injected £25.5 billion in RBS with a commitment of an additional £8 billion if required.[61] The target lending for Lloyds and RBS was £14 billion, and both banks surpassed their lending target. However, Lloyds withdrew from the scheme after paying a fee of £2.5 billion with a promise that it would raise additional capital from the shareholders. While joining the scheme, the banks were required to make legal commitments to increase lending, and the commitment for RBS was £25 billion. The efforts taken by the Treasury helped to develop positive market sentiments towards supported banks, and such capital injection also avoided possible insolvency.

[57] Ibbotson and Sinquefield (2021).

[58] Jassur et al. (2009), p. 400.

[59] Ashcraft and Schuermann (2008).

[60] Grosen et al. (2014), p. 568.

[61] HM Treasury (2010).

The study conducted to assess the impact of APS revealed that it is a convenient resolution tool to reduce asymmetric information and support the banks in raising new equity. More importantly, APS also mitigate the risk of a credit crunch by decreasing the economic capital of the distressed banks.[60] The Head of the UK National Audit, Amyas Morse, states that APS successfully maintained financial stability and prevented the failure of major banks. Success was partial,[62] and with this, HMT also acquired valuable practical knowledge on dealing with the banks in difficulties. The jurisdictions should use this tool to bail out banks if the problems remain in the limited banks.

5.4.6 Asset Management Company

AMC is also an effective debt resolution tool used in the US S&L crisis and later in the AFC and European Sovereign Debt crises.[6] AMCs, a money management firm, is a public or private entity that acquires impaired loans and assets from an insolvent bank to own, manage and sell to improve the loan recoveries. It is the 'most widely used and accepted method internationally' for dealing with NPLs, particularly in systemic banking crises.[63] AMCs facilitate the restructuring of financial assets, ensure a high recovery rate, provide prompt and speedy resolution, and normalise the asset market by crowding out good assets.[64] It identifies and organises assets before selling, recovering, restructuring, and writing off to maximise the operational gains by separating assets from distressed banks to an independent entity outside the bank.

There are two types of AMCs viz-a-viz centralised and decentralised resolution tools, based on the work assigned and performed during the crisis with the help of disposition vehicles. Nonetheless, there were no clear-cut rules regarding the superiority of the approaches[65] and the jurisdictions used them for their suitability and convenience, despite their advantages and disadvantages, having cross-country adoption and implementation.[66]

The decentralised management of impaired loans provides a learning experience for bank officials, which they can replicate in future lending. However, the success of the centralised and decentralised loan restructuring system depends on their legal power to deal with distressed assets.[67] The decentralised approach is more flexible in managing assets and analysing the asset profile.[6] Table 5.2 presents a comparative picture of decentralised (devolved) and centralised (integrated) AMCs. Both

---

[62] National Audit Office (2010).

[63] Campbell (2008), p. 211.

[64] Takatoshi and Yuko (2007).

[65] Hagiwara and Pasadilla (2004).

[66] Seelig et al. (2004).

[67] Gareia (1997).

Table 5.2 Types of AMCs with key assessment indicators

Variables	Types of AMCs with key assessment indicators	
	Devolved (decentralised)	Integrated (centralised)
Institution/level	Banks	AMCs
Monitoring activities	Better	No monitoring
Understanding of borrowers' profile	Strong	Weak
Relations with borrowers	Strong	Weak
Assessment of assets	Market value	Book value
Profit	Higher	Less
Flexibility	More	Less
Bargaining power	Less	Higher
Value maximisation	Less	Higher
Tenure	No rigidity	Fixed
Government interferences	Less	High
Links between the banks and corporate	Intact	broken
Workout plan	Uneven	Uniform

Source: Developed from the existing literature, such as Woo (2000) and Seelig et al. (2004) and also used in Dimri et al. (2024)

approaches have a certain edge over each other, and success would depend on the restructuring time, volume, and quality of assets provided for resolution.[68]

As discussed in the preceding section, UKAR is a government-managed AMC owned by HMT. The foundation of UKAR lies in the UK Banking (Special Provisions) Act,[69] ch 2, s(2) (a), which empowers the HMT to transfer securities issued by an authorised UK deposit-taker (banks and building societies) for maintaining the stability of the UK financial system. The Treasury also has the power to avert serious threats to financial stability by taking appropriate measures. It is also empowered to provide financial assistance to deposit-takers to maintain financial stability [s (2) (b)].

The Act has several other provisions, including the transfer of securities to BoE or its nominee [sch (3)] and compensates shareholders [sch 5 (1) (a–c)]. Such transfer should be free from all trusts, liabilities, and encumbrances [sch 1 (1) (a)].[69] Thus, the Act provides comprehensive guidance for the transfer of securities from the UK deposit takers in the case of a financial crisis like the GFC. Accordingly, UKAR replaced Bradford & Bingley (B&B) and Northern Rock Asset Management (NRAM) with their assets and liabilities to restructure them and salvage the country from the financial crisis.[69]

UKAR aimed to manage the mortgage portfolios and assets of B&B and NRAM by following a wind-down approach to maximise the taxpayers' values. UK Financial Investments Limited (UKFI) managed these entities before their

[68] Dimri et al. (2024), pp. 338–358.

[69] UK Banking (Special Provisions) Act [2008] (UK).

nationalisation in 2010.[70] B&B and Northern Rock faced pressure from the housing and financial markets and encountered severe funding problems due to the GFC. However, UKAR successfully reduced the size of mortgage portfolios over the years, and its latest report suggests that the balance sheet assets were down by 95% from 2010 to 2021 (Fig. 5.5)[71] UKAR made a repayment of a significant proportion of government loans in 2019, resulting in a 96% reduction in arrears. Accordingly, the expenses of UKAR also decreased considerably by 86% from 2010 to 2021.[70]

Thus, it reduced its balance sheet substantially and became a profit-making company every year since its inception. Despite not having a sunset date, by the end of 2021, UKAR sold off all its assets and equity interest, thus ending government ownership of B&B and Northern Rock.[72] Thus, UKAR successfully restructured the stressed debt, which was possible with constant monitoring and supervision. Therefore, UKAR has made significant progress in resolving NPLs-related problems by disposing of shareholdings in B&B and NRAM logically and actively.[73]

[70] Lawson (2021), p. 641.

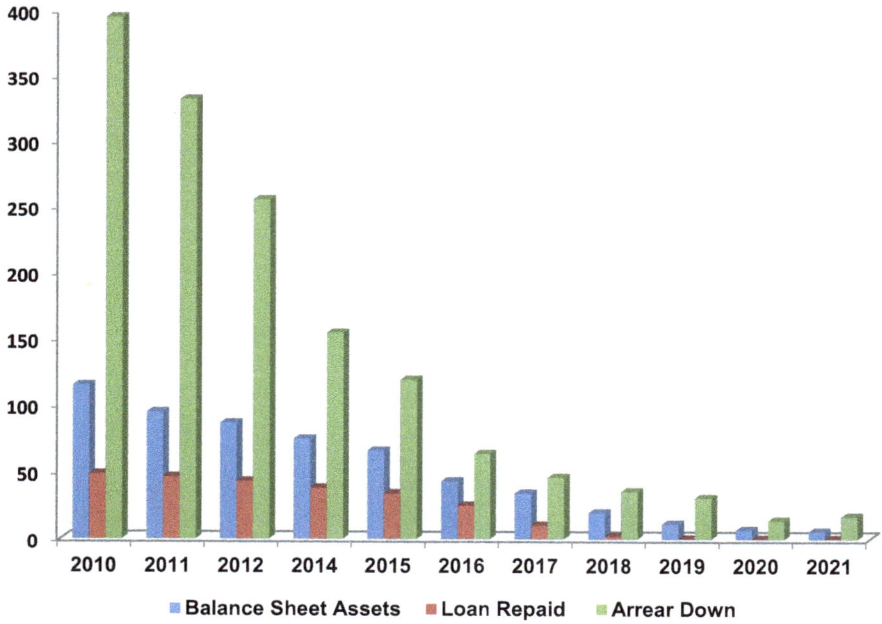

Fig. 5.5 Progress of UKAR on sale of assets (£m) (Source: Developed by the researcher based on the information available in various issues of Annual Report of UKAR)

[71] UKAR (2021).

[72] UKAR (2010b), p. 9848.

[73] UKAR (2010a).

Thus, the UKAR played a vital role in protecting and creating value, providing financial support, and preserving financial stability in the UK.

On the other hand, the RBI issued guidelines for establishing ARCs in 2003 under the SARFAESI Act of 2002; accordingly, ARCIL was the first ARC and SBI, and ICICI Bank were the main shareholders.[74] India also used AMCs for loan restructuring, which is considered one of the standard policy prescriptions for resolving the banking crisis.[75] AMCs undertake such action to exploit the accounting guidelines and manage their reported earnings.[76]

Despite the partial success, the role played by ARCs in managing NPAs in the Indian banking sector is considered significant. The guidelines issued by SBI envisaged that ARCs must spend 15% of the security receipts (SRs).[77] The ARCs are also empowered to raise funds from qualified institutional buyers, as explained in s 2(1)(u) of the Act.[78] The bank can sell NPLs to ARCs by paying cash or issuing debentures, bonds, or other securities. Sections 3 (1)(a) to 3(6) have made explicit provisions for obtaining a certificate of registration (CoR), which stands cancelled as provisioned in s 4 due to non-compliance with the RBI guidelines. Thus, after obtaining the CoR from the RBI, the ARCs conduct securitisation and reconstruction activities, and in the absence of the CoR, such activities are outside the scope of the RBI.

The banks auction NPAs to ARCs with 20% of their book value and, instead of paying full acquisition costs upfront, issue SRs. As per RBI guidelines, ARCs invest 5% of each SR, and the recent guidelines enhanced the investment limit to 15%. However, assessment of the performance of ARCs in the context of different models of the ARCs used at the national and international levels to address the problem of NPLs needs critical examination.[79] Figure 5.6 presents the trend of financial assets securitised by ARCs, banks, FIIs and other entities in India. The share of subscriptions by ARCs to security receipts (SRs) has shown an increasing trend. The share of subscriptions by ARCs was initially insignificant and gradually improved.

The banks' policy to diversify the investor base in SRs declined the share of bank subscriptions in SRs. Nonetheless, ARCs have expanded in size and number, and 29 such ARCs are currently operational in the country. However, there was a considerable reduction in the capital at the disposal of AMCs compared to the size of NPLs.[80]

Ireland set up NAMA under the National Assets Management Agency Act 2009 due to the severe impact of the GFC on the banking sector. Section 11 (a–d) of the Act provides for acquiring eligible bank assets and holding, managing, and realising

---

[74] Bhagwati et al. (2017), p. 338.

[75] Narang and Kaveri (2016), p. 16.

[76] Pandey and Guhathakurta (2019), p. 1.

[77] Jana and Thakur (2015), p. 16.

[78] The Securitisation and Reconstruction of Financial Assets and Enforcement of Security Interest Act [2002] (India).

[79] Kothari (2017).

[80] Sinha (2016).

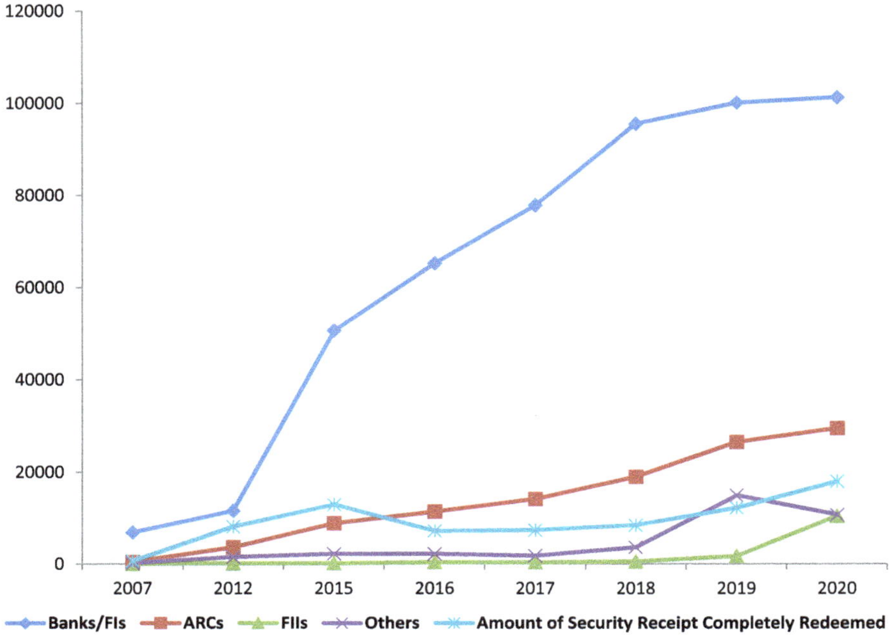

Fig. 5.6 Trend of details of financial assets securitised by carious channels in India (₹m) (Source: Developed by the researcher using data from various issues of Reports on Trend and Progress issues by the RBI)

acquired bank assets and takes all steps to protect, enhance, or realise their best value.[81] It acquired the real estate debt that escalated due to the financial and property crisis. The main motive for removing assets from the banks was to 'optimise the returns for the Irish public, stabilise the Irish banking sector, restore the flow of credit, and minimise the risk to the taxpayers'.[82] It has the following functions [s 11 (d) (i) (ii) (iii)]:

- 'The disposal of loans or portfolios of loans in the market for the best achievable price;
- securitisation or refinancing of a portfolio of loans and
- holding, refinancing, realising, and disposing of any relevant security'.[81]

NAMA identifies and buys eligible impaired assets from participating credit institutions and gets the best possible financial return.[83] Section 41 (1) (2) of the Act explicitly states the role of NTMA in providing NAMA business, support services, resources, and systems as determined by the board. After acquiring assets, NAMA

[81] National Asset Management Agency Act [2009] (Ireland).

[82] Lenihan (2018).

[83] Nye (2021), p. 546.

asks each borrower to provide a business plan and strategy for repaying the loans.[84] NAMA assigns its asset management duties to its participants and only manages the assets related to the largest borrowers.[84] NAMA adopted a twofold approach to maximise the recovery from property-backed loans. It includes strategic asset management and investment to improve the assets' income-generating potential' and enhance their future disposal value. Therefore, it releases assets for sale in a phased manner, considering market demand and credit absorption capacity.[84]

NAMA has made significant progress since its inception, and during 2021, it accumulated a profit of €195 million and a transfer of €3 billion to the exchequer with a lifetime surplus of €4.5 billion. By the end of 2021, 98% of its acquired portfolio was de-leveraged, generating total cash of €46.9 billion (see Fig. 5.7). Since the progress in cash generation was remarkable, NAMA could repay €31.8 billion in debt, with the repayment of €30.2 billion in government-guaranteed debt. It also generated €6.5 billion in rental income from secured properties and proceeds from loan refinancing. Figure 5.8 presents sector-wise disposal of debts, which was the highest (33%) from residential, followed by retail (20%) and land development (18%).

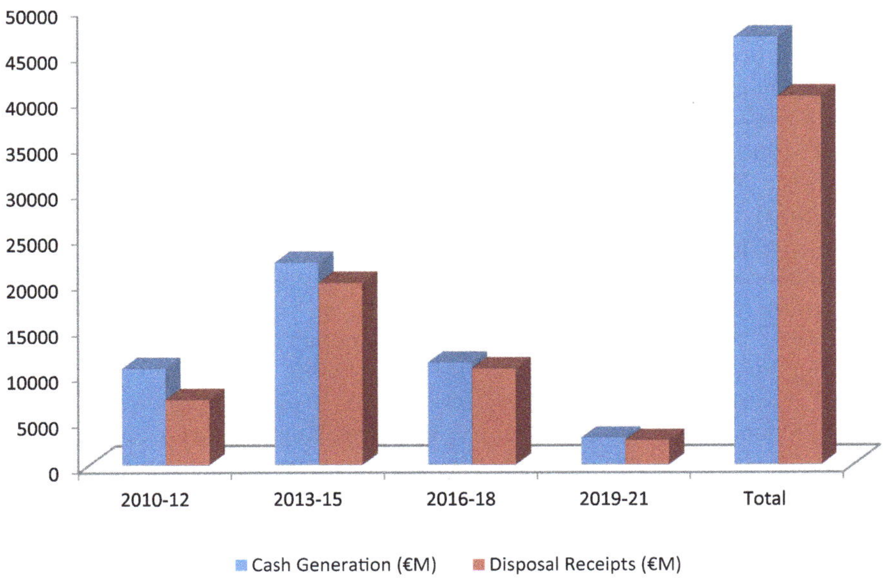

Fig. 5.7 NAMA: Cash generation and disposal receipts (Source: Developed by the researcher using data from various issues of Annual Reports of NAMA)

[84] Buckley (2012).

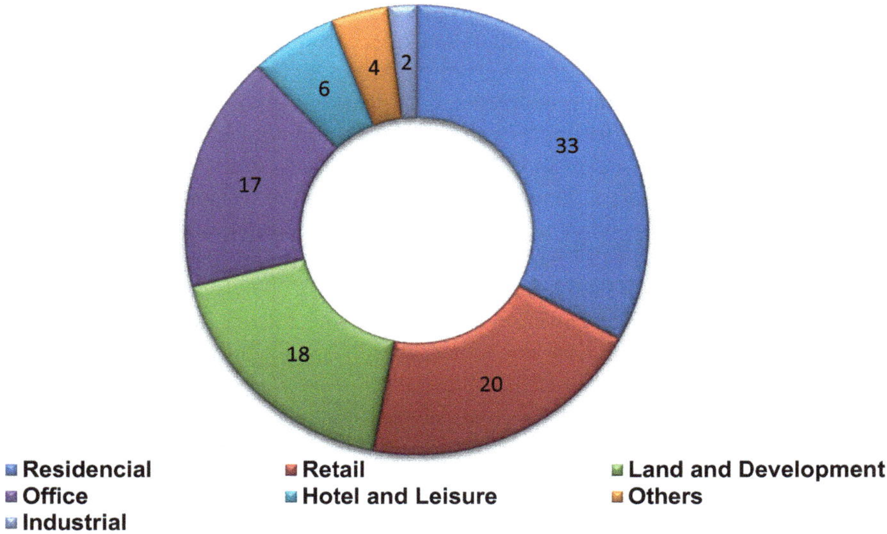

Fig. 5.8 Sector wise disposal of loans since inception of NAMA (%) (Source: Developed by the researcher using data from Annual Report NAMA 2021)

NAMA adopted effective strategies to handle distressed debt and achieved significant success. For instance, in the early years, the condition of the Irish market was continuously deteriorating. It focused on the UK market to dispose of assets, which was optimistic about generating cash and meeting the debt recovery target. However, once the Irish market improved, it pursued an intensive asset management programme. NAMA accelerated the sales of Irish assets in 2013 after enhancing the Irish market situation.[81] It also made tailored portfolios of properties to generate interest among the investors and released them in the market in a phased manner.[81] This helped to create a positive environment in the Irish market and enabled NAMA to maximise the return.

However, despite avoiding the credit crunch, improving banks' efficiency, and attracting new equity into the banks, the restructuring approaches of the banks invited criticism.[85] The critics argued that NAMA would have handled the NPLs resolution more efficiently and effectively by establishing a link with the borrowers. The banks would have developed better workout plans to speed the recovery by improving monitoring mechanisms.[6] If loan restructuring completely lies with AMCs and limits the ownership of banks, and they also do not get the required support and cooperation, it would prevent the banks from taking responsibility and with little or no chance of taking precautions in future lending. Moreover, considerable risk is also associated with private AMCs assessing the transferred assets, with a dilemma of evaluating them on the book or market value. However, centralised

[85] Dziobeck and Pazarbasioglu (1997), p. 161.

AMCs instantly relieve the banks by transferring their balance sheets and restructuring them independently through SPVs.

The UK and Ireland established AMCs to restructure NPLs piled on the bank balance sheet after the GFCs. This loan restructuring model was highly successful in the UK, where UKAR repaid government shares in a time-bound manner. The problem was more acute in Ireland; NAMA also took time, but it successfully restructured the distressed loans. In India, the mushrooming of AMCs diluted the purpose, and the success was not up to the expectations. India needs to look differently to revamp AMCs so that they can also significantly contribute to NPLs resolution. Nevertheless, AMCs are a powerful tool for restructuring NPLs, and jurisdictions should use them to dispose of bad assets, maximise profit, and ensure financial stability.

5.4.7 Mergers and Acquisitions

Mergers and acquisitions (M&A) of failed entities have been prevalent in the corporate sector. This strategy in the banking sector successfully bails out banks with distressed assets by consolidating the banking business and combining two or more banks.[86] With M&A, larger commercial banks take over small credit institutions to resolve the NPLs problem.[87] Some jurisdictions introduced the Bank Mergers Act and the Bank Holding Company Act to facilitate the process. M&A improves banking efficiencies and productivity and provides an effective policy response to control NPLs. The loan quality and cost influence the M&A process, and banks with poorer loan quality have significantly higher costs.

Similarly, deposit rates have positive and negative impacts on M&A, and some critics argue that deposit rates fall for the banks involved in M&A.[88] Some conclude that deposit rates do not significantly change the market concentration.[89] Banks' profitability, efficiency, and size also positively and negatively impact the M&A. The UK, India, and Ireland have a long history of using M&A to consolidate banking businesses to avoid financial crises.

M&A started in British banking in 1826 when BoE lost its monopoly in Wales and England. In the UK, 122 joint-stock banks controlled two-thirds of national deposits by 1875.[90] Later, banks started consolidating their activities, and peak banking mergers took place from 1880 to 1890. However, in the largest merger in 1918, five big groups, including Lloyds, Barclays, National Provincial, Midland, and Westminster, were formed and continued to shape the British banking market.

---

[86] Rameshbhai (2017), p. 62.

[87] Peng and Wang (2004).

[88] Prager and Hannan (1998), p. 21.

[89] Rhoades (1998), p. 273.

[90] Collins (1998).

Barclays and Lloyds are still amongst the largest five British banks, whereas National Provincial and Westminster constituted NatWest within the RBS, and the Midland Bank became part of HSBC in 1992.[91]

However, critics argue that amalgamations increase expenses and reduce profits, leading to complications due to inflated staff and diluted quality. On the other hand, a study concluded that bank mergers positively impact the banking business, increasing liquid assets and market concentration, consequently raising the banks' returns.[92] M&A also leads to bank failure, and one such example is the acquisition of ABN Amro bank by the RBS in 2007, which led to the failure of RBS and invited government intervention for its nationalisation and raised several questions on the benefits of M&A, and demand for enacting a proper regulation also cropped up.[93] In the recent M&A attempts, Lloyds TSB acquired HBOS, and RBS acquired ABN Amro, which also failed to improve the performance through economies of scale, increased market share, ROAs, cost efficiency, etc.[94]

M&A in the UK is subject to law and regulations, and the City Code on Takeovers and Mergers, known as the Takeover Code, governs public companies.[95] This code also applies to transactions involving private and dual-listed companies. In addition to the Takeover Code, the Companies Act of 2006 also plays an important role in the M&A process. The UK Takeover Code is quite comprehensive, prohibits dealings by persons other than the offeror (r 4), and restricts the offeree company from accepting the offer (r 4.5). It also has provisions on the transparency of information and payment of compensation [r (9) (b), (24) (3) and r (10) (c)].

Moreover, rule 94 (6) (4) provides financial collateral arrangements, and rule 5 puts several restrictions and some exceptions for the acquisitions of firms. The code also provides the right of withdrawal as a provision in r 34, where a shareholder is entitled to withdraw the acceptance within 21 days. However, critics argued that the code does not deal adequately with the growing role of private equity firms and sovereign wealth funds in investment banks.[96]

While assessing the impact of M&A in the UK, authors concluded that a high level of total institutional ownership is positively related to cross-border M&A deals. It suggests that institutional ownership concentration can help to protect shareholders' interests, particularly in cross-border M&A.[97] Nevertheless, besides the takeover code, other legislation also deals with the various aspects of M&A in the UK, and such dependence exposed its weakness, making the process relatively complicated. Therefore, the need to re-visit the existing code seems inevitable from

---

[91] Matthews et al. (2007), p. 2025.

[92] Grossman (1999), p. 323.

[93] Catley (2008).

[94] Yang (2017).

[95] The City Code on Takeovers and Mergers [2008] (UK).

[96] Sheridan (2008), p. 42

[97] DeYoung et al. (2009), p. 87.

the point of view of consolidating several sections and subsections of other regulations to make it more practical.

The banks in India have a long history of reorganisation, which led to mergers of banks to bail out weaker banks, protect customer interests, and create larger banks to be competitive globally[98] based on the recommendation of the M Narasimham Committee,[99] Verma Committee,[100] Khan Committee[101] and PJ Nayak Committee (2014) suggested the merger or privatisation of state-run banks, resulting in large-scale mergers from 2019 onwards (Table 5.3).

The mergers in Indian banks are grouped into three categories, viz-a-viz mergers for weak banks for restructuring, achieving economies of scale, and expanding scale (Table 5.4). The objective of mergers is to enhance the capacity to increase credit, national presence, and international reach, reduce cost, have next-generation technology, and speed up economic development. Thus, mergers would lead to a greater synergy among banks and may reduce the bad quality assets to some extent.[102]

The Company Act 2013 and its amendments, rules, subsequent notifications, and circulars regulate M&A in India. Sections 230–240 of the Act[103] are guiding principles for the enforcement of M&A. Therefore, s 230 (1) (a) provided for a compromise or arrangement for M&A between a company and its creditors under the supervision of the National Company Law Appellate Tribunal (NCLAT) to reorganise the company's share capital by consolidating shares (s 231). Suppose there is a problem with satisfactorily implementing the compromise or arrangement, and the company cannot pay its debts, the NCLAT may order the winding up of the company under section 273. Section 232 deals with mergers and amalgamations of companies; the tribunal grants sanctions for a compromise or an arrangement proposed between companies. The compromise or arrangement constitutes a merger or the amalgamation of two or more companies to reconstruct the company or companies as per s 232(1) (a). Thus, under this provision, the whole or part of the company's assets and liabilities are transferred to another company.[102]

The Act also has provisions for mergers of foreign companies and vice versa under s 234 (2) with the prior approval of the RBI. The compromise, arrangements, and amalgamation rules of 2016[104] also play an important role in the smooth conduct of M&A. For instance, NCLAT may wind up the company if the debt is unpaid. On the other hand, s 233 provisioned for fast-track mergers so that the company could be relieved from the lengthy procedures provided in s 332 with the condition of having the approval of shareholders, directors, and creditors. Finally, s 237

98 Dhmeja et al. (2021), p. 423.

99 RBI (1991).

100 RBI (1996).

101 RBI (1997).

102 Rai (2019).

103 The Companies Act [2013] (India).

104 Companies (Compromises, Arrangements and Amalgamations) Rules [2016] (India).

Table 5.3 Bank mergers and acquisitions in India

Reasons for mergers and acquisitions					
Restructuring of weak banks			To achieve scale & times bank scale of economies		
Acquirer by	Year	Bank merged	Acquirer by	Year	Bank merged
Canara Bank	1985	Lakshmi Commercial Bank	HDFC Bank	2000	Times Bank
PNB	1993 2003	New Bank of India Nedungadi Bank Ltd	ICICI Bank	2001 2002	Bank of Madura ICICI ltd
Bank of India	1993	Bank of Karad Ltd	Centurion Bank	2005	Bank of Punjab
SBI	1995	Kashinath Seth Bank	Indian Overseas Bank	2007	Bharat Overseas Bank
OBC	1997 1998 2004	Punjab Co-op Bank and Ban Doab Bank Ltd Global Trust Bank	**Expansion of scale**		
BOB	1998 2002 2004	Bareilly Corporation Bank Banaras State Bank Ltd South Gujarat Local Area Bank	Kotak Mahindra Bank	2014	SBI of Indore
Union Bank of India	1999	Sikkim Bank Ltd	SBI	2009 2020 2010 2017	SBI of Saurashtra Bank of Rajasthan SBI of Indore Bharatiya Mahila Bank (BMB) SBI: Associates Bikaner & Jaipur Hyderabad Mysore Patiala Travancore
Federal Bank	2006	Ganesh Bank of Kurundwad	Centurion Bank	2006	Lord Krishna Bank
IDBI Bank	2006	United Western Bank	HDFC Bank	2008	Centurion Bank
			ICICI	2007	Sangli Bank

Source: Compiled based on various issues of Trends and Progress of Banking in India, RBI and research paper by Dhmeja et al. (2021)

envisages that the central government can amalgamate the companies in the public interest and lays down the procedure for the same.

Moreover, the NCLAT deals with all grievances under company law. Thus, the Act has sufficient provisions for dealing with M& A, its processes and violations to protect the interests of the shareholders. Nonetheless, the main objectives of banks' mergers in India were to reduce operational costs, maximise the utilisation of human resources, reduce the risk of insolvency and bankruptcy, and rationalise resources.

Table 5.4 Five mega-mergers in the recent times

Acquirer bank	Year	Target banks	Purpose of mergers	Type of mergers
Bank of Baroda	2018	Dena bank Vijaya Bank	**Expansion**	**Voluntary mergers**
PNB	2020	Oriental Bank of Commerce United Bank of India		
Allahabad Bank	2020	Indian Bank		
Union Bank	2020	Andhra Bank & Corporation Bank		
Canara Bank	2020	Syndicate Bank		

Source: Developed by the researcher based on the information available in Dhmeja et al. (2021) & Strategic Policy Issues and based on India Today Report, 31st August 2019

In Ireland, M&A is governed by many EU and domestic laws and regulations, including the Companies Act 2014, as amended.[105] This Act provides a legislative basis for the scheme of arrangement both for public and private companies. The Irish Takeover Panel Act 1997 (as amended),[106] the European Communities Takeover Bids, Regulations 2006 (as amended),[107] Substantial Acquisition Rules 2007 (SAR) and Irish Takeover Rules 2013 are some important regulatory instruments that govern M&A in Ireland. In addition to Council Regulations, the Central Bank's investment market conduct also provides certain disclosure requirements that must be complied with while acquiring shares of an Irish public limited company to ensure information transparency.[108] The Irish Takeover Panel monitors and supervises takeovers in Ireland and directs companies for non-compliance with rules and general principles. Generally, there are no restrictions on foreign buyers in Ireland. The principal means of acquiring an Irish public company include a takeover offer, arrangement scheme, and cross-border or domestic mergers.

While analysing the mergers and acquisitions legislation of the UK, India, and Ireland, it is realised that in addition to principal regulations, many supplementary regulations, laws, circulars, and notifications also govern the process of M&A. For instance, in Table 5.5, the City Code on the takeovers is the principal regulation surrounded by six supplementary regulations and rules that govern the M&A in the UK. Similarly, along with the Company Act 2013, five auxiliary laws govern the M&A in India, and the situation in Ireland is nonetheless the same. Therefore, concentrated efforts are required to consolidate these regulations, and the jurisdictions should develop much stronger regulations to deal with the process of M&A.

[105] Companies Act 2014 Number 38 of [2014] (Ireland).

[106] Irish Takeover Panel Act [1997] (Ireland).

[107] Council Directive 2004/25/EC of 21 April 2004 on Takeover Bids [2004] L 142/12.

[108] Cullen and Given (2022).

5.4.8 Purchase and Assumption Transaction

Purchase and Assumption Transaction (PAT) is another policy instrument several jurisdictions use to prevent weak banks from insolvency and bankruptcy. In the USA, the FDIC used PAT to bail out banks with distressed assets and liabilities, deposit payoffs, and open bank assistance transactions. A comprehensive purchase

Table 5.5 Comparative status of mergers and acquisitions legislation

Principal law regulation	Supplementary regulations, directives, laws and circulars	Functions
UK		
City Code on Takeovers	–	Principal law that governs public and private M&A
	Company Act (CA)	It governs the 'squeeze-out' procedure, which allows majority shareholders (minority shareholders) to squeeze out from the minimum threshold using the compulsory acquisition procedure under CA
	FSMA	Under which FCA regulates the issuer and the financial market. The takeover of companies whose shares are admitted for trading is subject to an obligation under the FCA
	Withdrawal Act	Rules that govern the offer of shares to the public
	Market Abuse Regulation (MAR)	Enforced by the FCA and the Criminal Justice Act governing insider dealing and market abuse
	The Enterprise Act 2002, Competition and Markets Authority	Acts as a UK merger control authority
	National Security and Investment Act 2021	Creates a stand-alone foreign direct investment
India		
Company Act 2013	–	Regulates companies in India
	Indian Contact Act 1872	Governs contracts and the rights that parties can agree to be contractually under Indian law
	Competition Act 2002	Regulates combinations and prohibits anti-competitive agreements
	Foreign Exchange Management Act 1999 and circulars, directions and rules issued by RBI	Regulate foreign investment in India
	Income Tax Act 1961	Direct tax-related considerations with respect to M&A in India and transactions that have cross-border elements
	Securities and Exchange Board of India Act 1992	Regulates securities markets in India, including acquisitions involving companies listed on stock exchanges in India

(continued)

Table 5.5 (continued)

Principal law regulation	Supplementary regulations, directives, laws and circulars	Functions
Ireland		
Irish Takeover Panel Act 1997 (Takeover Bids)	–	Principal law that governs public and private M&A
	Companies Act 2014	Governs private and public M&A activity and provides the legislative basis for schemes of arrangement
	Competition Act 2002	Certain takeovers must be notified of and approved by the CCPC and EC Merger Regulation, which governs joint ventures and acquisitions
	Regulations (EU Market Abuse Regulation)	Impose obligations on companies whose securities are listed on regulated markets and regulate insider dealing and market manipulation
	Transparency (Directive 2004/109/EC) Regulations 2007	The CBI's guidance on the Irish Transparency Rule 2018. Central Bank Investment Market Conduct Rules 2019 contain certain disclosure requirements that must be complied with to acquire shares

Source: Compiled after referring to regulations such as the UK City Code on Takeover, the Company Act 2013, and the Irish Takeover Panel Act 1997

and assumption contract agreement between healthy and unhealthy banks is usually signed and enforced. Under PAT, the healthy bank takes over some or all of the unhealthy bank's assets and liabilities and assumes some or all of its responsibilities.[63] Thus, the unhealthy bank is relieved from the responsibilities of the enforcement contract. Moreover, the depositors of the unhealthy bank transferred to the healthy bank automatically, and their funds remained intact. However, healthy banks can change the interest rates, fees, etc.

PATs have several benefits; they avoid adverse deposit insurance payout results. It protects all the failed bank's depositors and other creditors by assuming their deposits and debts from the assuming bank.[63] As an insurer of deposits, the regulator is relieved from the difficult and time-consuming obligation of paying off hundreds or thousands of depositors. Moreover, the banking services previously served by the failed bank continue uninterrupted as the assuming bank agrees to reopen all the failed bank's offices.

5.5 Suitability of NPLs Resolution Tools: A Comparative Analysis

Table 5.6 presents a comparative picture of the NPLs resolution policies adopted by the UK, India, and Ireland. The success of NPLs resolution depends on several factors, including country-specific macroeconomic conditions, asset types, financial

Table 5.6 Comparison of policy options across the UK, India and Ireland

Policy option	UK	India	Ireland
Debt restructuring & out-of-court workouts	**Yes**	**Yes**	No
Write-offs	**Yes**	**Yes**	**Yes**
Direct sales	**Yes**	**Yes**	**Yes**
Asset protection scheme	**Yes**	No	No
Securitisation/law	**Yes** Securitisation (Amendment) (EU Exit) Regulations 2019	**Yes** Guidelines on Securitisation of Standard Assets 2006 and 2012 RBI, Master Direction—(Securitisation of Standard Assets) Directions (2021)	**Yes** Council Regulation (EU) 2017/2402
AMC	**Yes** UKAR (Public Govt Owned)	**Yes** ARCIL-28 other ARCs (Public and Private)	**Yes** NAMA (Public Govt Owned)
M&A	**Yes** City Code on Takeovers and Mergers Companies Act 2006	**Yes** Company Act 2013	**Yes** Takeover Panel Act 1997 Companies Act 2014
PAT	No	No	No

Source: Developed based on the information available in existing literature including Baudino and Yun (2017), and Jassaud and Kang (2015)

space, and legal and judicial constraints.[1] For instance, in the case of slow growth, the NPLs resolution option may not yield the desired result. However, for homogeneous NPLs, the collateral valuation would be easy, and direct sales, AMC, and securitisation could prove vital resolution methods that the UK and Ireland used effectively during crises. Moreover, individual direct sales, workouts for individual and corporate debt, and debt-to-equity exchange are preferred methods of loan restructuring for individual loans and large corporate and highly specialised assets.[36] Securitisation and write-off are considered better policy options for restructuring SMEs and corporate loans, provided the legal system allows such restructuring.[46] These restructuring tools best suit Ireland, considering the nature of bad debts.

On the other hand, direct sales and securitisation could be highly effective resolution tools for unsecured and less complicated loans and remain prevalent in these jurisdictions.[46] However, a jurisdiction with a negative fiscal balance, like India, would not like to use resolution tools involving public sector expenditure. AMCs are considered the most suitable resolution tools for such jurisdictions. On the other hand, write-offs, private AMCs, and direct sales may not be suitable for jurisdictions with negative fiscal balances. Moreover, the jurisdictions adopt bailout plans to ensure financial stability by injecting considerable capital. The success of these resolution tools depends on the debtor-focused resolution methods. Moreover, the legal and judicial framework also impacts bank-oriented resolution tools. For instance, legal problems may arise while implementing direct sales and securitisation.[1]

Scholars have also argued that AMC would be a better option for jurisdictions with a credit boom, asset overvaluation, and high-leverage banks[1, 36] and Ireland is one such example. In a 'low growth situation like in India, 'write-offs, direct sales, securitisation, and debt restructuring' would be highly suitable. There are some essential prerequisites for NPLs resolutions, including creating buffers for NPLs absorption, information symmetry, legislation to support NPLs resolution plans, adequate supervision, and the use of private sector resources deployed without prescribed policy options. Thus, combining macroeconomic and macro-prudential policy options would greatly alleviate the NPLs problem.[1]

The UK successfully implemented the APS to bail out RBS and Lloyds Bank as a one-time NPLs resolution plan. However, very few jurisdictions have applied this policy option, and India and Ireland have not made such attempts. The M&A got effective legal support through the respective regulations and helped to consolidate banks to ensure economies of scale. These jurisdictions effectively used the existing policy measures to treat, restructure and resolve NPLs piled on the bank balance sheet.

5.6 Conclusion

This chapter examined the policy response that the UK, India, and Ireland implemented to control NPLs. It also discussed the pros and cons of centralised and decentralised resolution approaches. It also pointed out how these approaches effectively level down ever-increasing NPLs despite having a fragmented opinion of the critics on the suitability and sustainability of these policy responses.[1] The decentralised loan restructuring approaches focused on making the bank responsible for resolving NPLs. The banks are in a relatively better position than centralised AMCs to restructure distressed assets. They know the borrowers' loan profiles and can quickly establish a link with them and develop a better workout plan to speed up the recovery of distressed assets.[7] However, we also feel that the scope and mandate of these resolution tools are narrow, and their effectiveness remains limited to individual banks or branches. In the present scenario, where banks have diversified their activities, the problem percolates very quickly, and the sustainability and effectiveness of these tools will remain questionable.

On the other hand, the centralised approach ensures economies of scale and enhanced bargaining power, permits the 'consolidation of skills and resources and is considered more efficient in recovering the maximum possible value of assets'. Therefore, instead of a piecemeal approach, integrated policy resolution effectively addresses the problem of NPLs. Nevertheless, the critics' opinions are sharply fragmented, and they advocate both approaches depending on the size of the distressed assets.[1] Therefore, the conclusion derived from the analysis of several centralised approaches that addressed the problem of NPLs is that their success varied considerably across jurisdictions and banks, depending on the regulatory protection and sovereign support they enjoyed.

The jurisdictions also used OCWs, a relatively cheaper and faster debt restructuring tool that does not involve a judicial process while restructuring NPLs. It is a mutual, speedy, cost-effective, semi-formal, and less intervening framework that is faster than a comprehensive judicial process. It has also proved effective in corporate debt insolvency and bankruptcy resolution. The UK, India and Ireland adopted this approach, and the UK government even responded to the crisis that emerged with the COVID-19 pandemic through hybrid OCWs. On the other hand, India adopted a blended approach with formal and informal resolution proceedings. Due to the varying nature of loan profiles in Ireland, the focus was on resolving individual mortgages, SMEs, and CREs.

The loan write-off and liquidity injection increase the prospect of a high growth rate and mitigate the adverse effects of bank de-leveraging. However, low provisioning and poor capital levels are considered significant hurdles for writing off the NPLs and banks with sufficient capital buffers and provisions can absorb the loan losses. The UK and India have effectively used loan write-off; the UK used it to subside the impact of the GFC, whereas, in India, such instances were more frequent after 2016 because the new reign at the national level intended to provide a clean balance sheet to the banks as a part of policy measures. Ireland uses principles-based local guidelines for loan write-offs.[31] Moreover, it envisaged that unsecured loans should have full provisions after 2 years and secured loans after 7 years. Ireland also issued guidelines stating that loan arrears for more than 53 weeks are significant for write-offs, banks should continuously recover such amounts, and DSA formally consented with creditors to allow debt write-offs.

The bad banks in the UK and India have made significant inroads with their wind-down strategies. The AMCs, including UKAR, NAMA, and ARCs, salvaged failed banks and building societies in these jurisdictions. For instance, after repaying government loans, the IBRC in Ireland and the Dunfermline Building Society in the UK shifted the balance sheet burden to NAMA and UKAR. The UKAR made significant progress, and its balance sheet assets were considerably down from 2010 to 2021, resulting in a significant reduction (96%) in arrears. In India, the RBI provided detailed guidelines for the banks, which need respective boards' approval for disposal through sale. The ARCs successfully restructured bad debts, but the success was not very promising. NAMA has realised a considerable amount from overall disposal proceeds in Ireland, and by 2021, it restructured more than 80% of its loans. The pace of restructuring was relatively slower in Ireland than in the UK, and India needs to review and revamp asset disposal through ARCs.

Moreover, the UK also introduced and implemented APS to support banks. HMT purchased considerable shareholdings of the RBS, Northern Rock, and LBG for financial stability, providing a successful bailout plan to its banks. Such an effort created positive market sentiments towards supported banks, besides avoiding bankruptcy and insolvency. The scheme was successful; banks returned the debt and reduced the government's shareholdings to negligible.

The UK, India, and Ireland also used securitisation measures to restructure debts and accordingly made strong provisions in their respective laws. The EU regulation 2017 was incorporated into Irish law, and the UK made necessary amendments to securitisation regulations. RBI also issued guidelines for securitising standard assets through its master circular. On the other hand, securitisation laws are similar in the UK, India, and Ireland. These regulations and guidelines advocated STS securitisation with reliance on SSPEs and used them effectively to restructure NPLs.

M&A of failed entities have been prevalent in the corporate sector, and the UK, India, and Ireland have used this tool to salvage weak banks. These jurisdictions have strong regulations for implementing M&A, but consolidating regulatory architecture is imperative to strengthen the M&A process in these jurisdictions. For instance, the UK Takeover Code is the principal regulation governing public companies and several other regulations are required to complete the process. Nonetheless, M&A continues to shape the British banking market despite bank amalgamations increasing expenses and consequently reducing profits in the short run. In India, the recent M&A resulted in the recommendation of several committees with the intended objective of merging weak banks for restructuring, achieving economies, and expanding scale. An in-depth study will suggest the extent to which amalgamation achieved the intended objectives. Ireland also has several regulations and directives to control M&A, including the Irish Takeover Panel Act and the European Communities Takeover Bids. It has used them to consolidate the banking system for financial stability.

Finally, the chapter has presented a comparative analysis of the pros and cons of these policy instruments. It concluded that the suitability of a particular resolution tool depends on the macroeconomic conditions, asset qualities, fiscal space and legal and judicial constraints prevailing for a specific jurisdiction. Nonetheless, these resolution tools achieved the intended objectives of NPLs restructuring. While comparing the achievements of these jurisdictions, the resolution plans achieved mixed results, which varied from jurisdiction to jurisdiction. A bouquet of resolution tools based on the prevailing practices would help to consolidate policy options. International institutions like the IMF, EBA, OECD, and Basel may play a proactive role in making them effective instruments of loan restructuring and resolution. Nevertheless, country-specific efforts to innovate efficient and effective NPLs resolution tools must continue to provide suitable policy options for the jurisdictions and banks to deal with NPLs.

References

Aiyar S, Bergthaler W, Jose M et al (2015) A strategy for resolving Europe's problem loans. IMF staff discussion note. https://www.imf.org/en/Publications/Staff-Discussion-Notes/Issues/2016/12/31A-Strategy-for-Resolving-Europe-s-Problem-Loans-43286. Accessed 21 Dec 2020

Ashcraft AB, Schuermann T (2008) Understanding the securitisation of subprime mortgage credit. Federal Reserve Bank of New York. https://doi.org/10.2139/ssrn.1071189. Accessed 30 Oct 2022

Bank of Ireland (2021) Mortgage measures framework review. Consultation paper 146. https://www.centralbank.ie/docs/default-source/publications/consultation-papers/cp146/cp146-mortgage-measures-framework-review.pdf?sfvrsn=329c921d_5. Accessed 1 Dec 2022

Baudino P, Yun H (2017) Resolution of non- performing loans–policy options. Bank for International Settlements. https://www.bis.org/fsi/publ/insights3.pdf. Accessed 10 Dec 2022

Bernanke BS (1983) Nonmonetary effects of the financial crisis in the propagation of the great depression. Am Econ Rev 73:257

Bhagwati J, Khan MS, Bogathi RR (2017) Can asset reconstruction companies (ARCs) be part solution to the Indian debt problem? Indian Council for Research on International Economic Relations working paper 338. https://icrier.org/pdf/WorkingPaper338.pdf. Accessed 6 Nov 2022

Bisky T (1986) Securitisation gives new meaning to car pools. ABA Bank J 78(8):35

Borio C, Bent B, Peter GV (2010) Resolving the financial crisis: are we heeding the lessons from the Nordics? BIS working papers no 311. https://www.bis.org/publ/work311.pdf. Accessed 11 Dec 2023

Buckley J (2012) National asset management agency management of loans. Report of the comptroller and auditor general. https://www.nama.ie/uploads/documents/NAMAAnnualReport2012.pdf.3,15,28,51. Accessed 19 Apr 2021

Caballero RJ, Hoshi T, Kashyap AK (2008) Zombie lending and depressed restructuring in Japan. Am Econ Rev 98(5): 1943.

Campbell A (2008) Bank insolvency and the problem of non-performing loans. In: Omar PJ (ed) International insolvency law, themes and perspectives. Ashgate, p 211

Cargill TF, Hutchison MM, Ito T (2000) Financial policy and central banking in Japan. MIT

Catley S (2008) Battle of the banks: RBS wins ABN Amro. Practicallaw. https://uk.practicallaw.thomsonreuters.com/0-381-3289?contextData=(sc.Default)&transitionType=Default&firstPage=true. Accessed 13 Nov 2023

Claessens S (2005) Policy approaches to corporate restructuring around the world: what worked, what failed? In: Pomerleano M, Shaw W (eds) Corporate restructuring, lessons from experience. World Bank

Collins M (1998) Money and banking in the UK: a history. Routledge

Constancio V (2017) Resolving Europe's NPL burden: challenges and benefits: keynote speech ECB. https://www.ecb.europa.eu/press/key/date/2017/html/sp170203.en.html. Accessed 12 Dec 2022

Cullen I, Given J (2022) Mergers and acquisitions laws and regulations Ireland. https://www.iclg.com/practice-areas/mergers-and-acquisitions-laws-and-regulations/ireland

Deloitte (2020) NPL securitisation and related governmental guarantee schemes in Europe. https://www2.deloitte.com/uk/en/pages/financial-advisory/articles/securitisation-of-npls-rpls-and-supporting-governmental-schemes.html. Accessed 15 Oct 2022

DeYoung R, Evanoff DD, Molyneux P (2009) Mergers and acquisitions of financial institutions: a review of the post-2000 literature. J Financ Serv Res 36:87

Dhmeja LN, Hazarika DD, Dhameja M (2021) Banks mergers in India: historical perspective and strategic policy Issues. Indian J Ind Relat 56(3):423

Diamond D, Rajan R (2009) Fear of fire sales and the credit freeze. University of Chicago

Dimri A, Cairns SM, Campbell A (2024) Restructuring non-performing loans through assets management companies: global scenario. Int Commercial Company Law Rev (ICCLR) 33(6):338–358

Dutta KP (2018) What is loan write-off and how it helps Banks' India Today. https://www.indiatoday.in/india/story/what-is-loan-write-off-and-how-it-helps-banks-1353388-2018-10-01. Accessed 17 November 2022

Dziobeck C, Pazarbasioglu C (1997) Lessons from systemic bank restructuring: a survey of 24 countries. IMF working paper 161. https://www.imf.org/external/pubs/ft/issues/issues14/. Accessed 8 Nov 2021

Economics Times (2021) Banks write off Rs 46,382 Crore NPA in H1. The Economic Times, New Delhi, 29 April 2021. https://economictimes.indiatimes.com//industry/banking/finance/banking/banks-write-off-rs-46382-crore-npa-in-h1/articleshow/87987512.cms?utmsource=contentofinterest&utmmedium=text&utmcampaign=cppst. Accessed 13 Oct 2022

Eis HK, Passaris G, Tappi A (2013) SME loan securitisation 2.0 market assessment and policy options. Working paper 2013/19. EIF Research & Market Analysis. https://www.eif.org/news_centre/publications/eif_wp_2013_19.pdf. Accessed 14 Oct 2022

Englund PP, Vihriala V (2009) Financial crisis in Finland and Sweden: similar but not quite the same. In: Jonung L, Kiander L, Vartia P (eds) The crisis of the 1990s in Finland and Sweden, The Nordic experience of financial liberalisation. Edward Elgar

European Central Bank (2017) Stocktake of national supervisory practices and legal frameworks related to NPLs. https://www.bankingsupervision.europa.eu/ecb/pub/pdf/ssm.stock_taking2017.en.pdf. Accessed 13 Oct 2022

Fabian B, Arranz MR (2013) Indebtedness and deleveraging in the euro area country report 13/232. International Monetary Fund

Fell J, Grodzicki M, Martin R et al (2017) A role for systemic asset management companies in solving Europe's non-performing loan problems. Eur Econ 1:71

Fisher I (1933) The debt-deflation theory of great depressions. Econometrica 1:337

Fung Siu-Cheong Ben and others (2004) 'Public Asset. Occasional paper no 3. https://www.bis.org/fsi/fsipapers03.pdf. Accessed 10 December 2023

Gareia G (1997) A framework for analysis and assessment. In: Alexander WE, Davis JM, Ebrill LP et al (eds) Systemic bank restructuring and macroeconomic policy. International Monetary Fund

Garrido J (2012) Out of court debt restructuring. The World Bank

Gaston E, Song W (2014) Supervisory roles in loan loss provisioning in countries implementing IFRS. IMF working paper 14/170. https://www.imf.org/external/pubs/ft/wp/2014/wp14170.pdf. Accessed 19 Oct 2023

Gibler KM, Black RT (2004) Agency risks in outsourcing corporate real estate functions. J Real Estate Res 26(2):137

Goldberg J (2009) Large-cap banks: industry overview, stress test results on the horizon. Barclays Capital Equity Research

Griffiths D, O'Connor D (2021) The revised securitisation regulation regime in the UK. https://www.mayerbrown.com/en/perspectives-events/publications/2021/02/the-revised-securitisation-regulation-regime-in-the-uk. Accessed 23 Nov 2022

Grosen A, Jessen P, Kokholm T (2014) An asset protection scheme for banks exposed to troubled loan portfolios. J Econ Financ 38:568

Grossman RS (1999) Rearranging deck chairs on the Titanic: English banking concentration and efficiency 1870–1914. Eur Rev Econ Hist 3(3):323

Hagiwara AT, Pasadilla G (2004) Experience of Asian asset management companies: do they increase moral hazard? Evidence from Thailand. Asian Development Bank, ERD working paper no 55. https://www.adb.org/sites/default/files/publication/28188/wp055.pdf. Accessed 15 Aug 2023

HM Treasury (2010) The asset protection scheme (2010). https://www.nao.org.uk/wp-content/uploads/2010/12/1011567es.pdf. Accessed 7 Nov 2022

Hoshi T, Kashyap AK (2010) Will the US bank recapitalisation succeed? Eight lessons from Japan. J Financ Econ 97:398

Ibbotson RG, Sinquefield R (2021) Stocks, bonds, bulls, and inflation. CFA Institute Research Foundation. https://doi.org/10.2139/ssrn.3893876. Accessed 30 Oct 2022

Ingves S (2011) Basel III–much-needed regulations for a safer banking sector. Speech at the Swedish Society of Financial Analysts, Stockholm, 1 February 2011. https://www.bis.org/review/r110202b.pdf. Accessed 17 Oct 2022

International Monetary Fund (2013) IMF country report no. 13/93. www.imf.org/external/pubs/ft/scr/2013/cr1393.pdf. Accessed 16 Oct 2022

Izzo P, Murray S, Lahart J (2009) Economic confidence rebounds. The Wall Street Journal, New York, 11 September 2009. https://www.wsj.com/articles/SB125261100485400509. Accessed 14 Dec 2022

Jana MM, Thakur MK (2015) An overview of non-performing assets management and banking performance - an empirical analysis. Manag Account 50(1):42

Jassaud N, Kang K (2015) A strategy for developing a market for nonperforming loans in Italy. IMF working paper 15/24. https://www.imf.org/external/pubs/ft/wp/2015/wp1524.pdf. Accessed 18 Oct 2023

Jassur L, Favato G, Print C (2009) The flaws of securitisation. Int J Corp Gov 1(4):400

Jenke A, Colman N (2016) European debt sales, loan portfolio advisory. KGMG. https://assets.kpmg.com/content/dam/kpmg/pdf/2016/03/european-debt-sales2.pdf. Accessed 24 Oct 2023

Jonung L (2009) The Swedish model for resolving the banking crisis of 1991–93: seven reasons why it was successful. Economic paper no. 360. European Commission

Kelly K, Mazza E (2019) Mortgage affordability across the income distribution. Central Bank of Ireland Financial Stability Note No. 15. https://www.centralbank.ie/docs/default-source/publications/financial-stability-notes/no-15-mortgage-repayment-affordability-across-the-income-distribution-(kelly-and-mazza).pdf?sfvrsn=4. Accessed 20 Oct 2022

Kent P (1993) The London approach: Bank of England. Quarterly bulletin. https://www.bankofengland.co.uk/quarterly-bulletin/1993/q1/the-london-approach%2D%2D-speech-given-by-mr-pen-kent-to-the-chartered-institute-of-bankers. Accessed 15 Dec 2023

Kim S, Haque HM (2002) The Asian financial crisis of 1997: causes and policy responses. Multinational Bus Rev 10(1):1

Kothari V (2017) Asset reconstruction companies-making good misuse of the law. https://www.indiafinancing.com/AnalysisonAssetReconstructionCompanies-MakingGoodMisuseoftheLaw.pdf. Accessed 17 Dec 2023

Laeven L, Valencia F (2008) The use of blanket guarantees in banking crises. IMF working paper WP/08/250. https://ssrn.com/abstract=1316718. Accessed 15 Dec 2022

Lawson A (2021) United Kingdom Asset Resolution Limited (UKAR). J Financ Crises 3(2):641

Lenihan B (2018) National Asset Management Agency Act 2009. https://revisedacts.lawreform.ie/eli/2009/act/34/revised/en/pdf?annotations=true. Accessed 10 Sept 2021

Martini L, Heuser M, Fest M (2009) Bad banks, finding the right exit from the financial crisis. McKinsey working papers on risk. https://www.mckinseycom/~/media/mckinsey/dotcom/client_service/risk/working%20papers/12_bad_banks_finding_the_right_exit_from_the_financia_crisis.ashx. Accessed 26 Nov 2022

Mashruwala A, Kumar P (2022) India: securitisation. JSA Law, 4 March 2022. https://www.jsalaw.com/articles-publications/india-securitisation/. Accessed 5 Nov 2022

Matthews K, Murinde V, Zha T (2007) Competitive conditions among the major British banks. J Bank Financ 31:2025

Moraa N, Logan A (2012) Shocks to bank capital: evidence from UK banks at home and away. Appl Econ 44:1103

Narang D, Kaveri VS (2016) Perspectives on sale of NPAs to ARCs under security receipt. Vinimaya 37(1):16

National Audit Office (2010) HM Treasury: asset protection scheme, 21 July 2010. https://www.nao.org.uk/reports/hm-treasury-the-asset-protection-scheme/. Accessed 8 Nov 2022

Nye A (2021) National Assets Management Agency (NAMA). J Financ Crises 3(2):546. https://ssrn.com/abstract=3904302. Accessed 15 Aug 2023

Pandey A, Guhathakurta K (2019) Nonperforming loan auction: prudent policy response or earnings management? Wiley Online J 1:1

Peng YH, Wang K (2004) Cost efficiency and the effect of mergers on the Taiwanese banking industry. Serv Ind J 21

Prager RA, Hannan TH (1998) Do substantial horizontal mergers generate significant price effects? Evidence from banking industry. J Ind Econ 46(4):433

Rai V (2019) Banks mergers a good move. Financial Express, New Delhi, 11 September 2019. https://www.financialexpress.com/industry/banking-finance/banks-mergers-a-good-move-says-vinod-rai/1702542/. Accessed 22 Nov 2022

Rameshbhai GM (2017) Mergers and acquisitions in banking sector. Int J Adv Res Comput Sci Manag Stud 4(12):62

Reserve Bank of India (1991) Report of the Committee on the Financial System (M Narasimham Committee)

Reserve Bank of India (1996) Report of the working group on restructuring weak public sector banks (Verma Committee)

Reserve Bank of India (1997) Allow banks to pledge corporate bonds as collateral with RBI (Khan Committee)

Reserve Bank of India (2005) Guidelines on purchase/sale of non-performing financial assets. https://rbidocs.rbi.org.in/rdocs/Notification/PDFs/64686.pdf. Accessed 10 Oct 2022

Reserve Bank of India (2006) Guidelines on securitisation of standard assets. https://rbidocs.rbi.org.in/rdocs/notification/PDFs/68628.pdf. Accessed 04 Nov 2022

Reserve Bank of India (2012) Revisions to the guidelines on securitisation transactions. (2012). https://rbidocs.rbi.org.inb/rdocsb/notification/PDFs/C170RG21082012.pdf. Accessed 4 Nov 2022

Reserve Bank of India (2021) Master direction – Reserve Bank of India (Securitisation of Standard Assets). (2021). https://rbidocs.rbi.org.in/rdocs/notification/PDFs/85MDSTANDARDASSETSBE149B86CD3A4B368A5D24471DAD2300.PDF. Accessed 4 Nov 2022

Rhoades SA (1998) The efficiency effects of bank mergers: an overview of case studies of nine mergers. J Bank Financ 22:273

Seelig IS, Steven A, Dong H (2004) Issues in the establishment of asset management companies. International Monetary Fund. https://www.imf.org/external/pubs/ft/pdp/2004/pdp03.pdf. Accessed 16 Oct 2022

Sheridan I (2008) The impact of bank stakes. Int Financ Law Rev 42

Sinha A (2016) Non-performing assets in Indian banking and the role of assets reconstruction companies. ICTACT J Manag Stud

Swagel P (2009) The financial crisis: an inside view. The Brookings Institution. https://www.brookings.edu/wp-ontent/uploads/2009/03/2009abpeaswagel.pdf. Accessed 25 Nov 2022

Takatoshi I, Yuko H (2007) Bank restructuring in Asia: crisis management in the aftermath of the Asian financial crisis and prospects for crisis prevention–Korea. RIETI discussion paper series 07-E-038. https://www.rieti.go.jp/jp/publications/dp/07e039.pdf. Accessed 22 Oct 2022

Twinn CI (1995) Asset-backed securitisation in the United Kingdom. Bank of England Quarterly Bulletin, 134

UK Asset Resolution (2010a) Northern Rock Renamed Northern Rock (Asset Management) Plc. https://ypfs.som.yale.edu/library/northern-rock-renamed-northern-rock-assetmanagement-plc. Accessed 21 Nov 2021

UK Asset Resolution (2010b) Bradford & Bingley Plc annual report and accounts 2009. YPFS Documents (Series 1) 9848. https://elischolar.library.yale.edu/ypfs-documents/9848. Accessed 18 Nov 2022

UKAR (2021) UK asset resolution limited annual report and accounts. https://www.ukar.co.uk/wp-content/uploads/2021/08/UK-Asset-Resolution-Limited_ARA_2020-21_Web-Accessible_UA.pdf. Accessed 08 Oct 2021

Wessel D (2009) In Fed we trust: Ben Bernanke's war on the great panic. Three Rivers Press

Woo D (2000) Two approaches to resolving nonperforming assets during financial crisis. IMF working paper WP/33. https://www.imf.org/en/Publications/WP/Issues/2016/12/30/Two-Approaches-to-Resolving-Nonperforming-Assets-During-Financial-Crises-3460. Accessed 15 Oct 2022

Yang P (2017) Mergers and acquisitions in UK banking industry: performance analysis. https://www.academia.edu/51829146/MergersandAcquisitionsinUKBankingIndustryPerformanceAnalysis. Accessed 12 Nov 2022

Chapter 6
Empirical Analysis of NPLs Through Case Studies of Commercial Banks from the UK, India, and Ireland

6.1 Introduction

Analysis of the effectiveness of various NPLs resolution policy responses adopted by the jurisdictions to deal with the problem of NPLs has presented mixed results. The present chapter evaluates three unique case studies involving LBG, PNB, and BIG to assess their risk management system from the GFC to the post-COVID-19 pandemic. The GFC and the COVID-19 pandemic jeopardised risk management efforts and seriously threatened the banking business due to the economic downturn. The GFC significantly increased corporate and household debt defaults, eroding the asset quality across banks.[1] Under such circumstances, a substantial increase in NPLs was inevitable, and the banks had no option but to increase LLP due to deterioration in asset quality and poor earnings. The bank's ability to absorb more loan losses remains grim, and the only option was immediate support from supervisors and fiscal authorities.[1] The respective governments and central banks adopted several policies to ease the challenges faced by the banks due to the induced stress of crises, whether the GFC or COVID-19. Government support helped to mitigate the negative impact of the crisis to a great extent. There was considerable uncertainty in economic recovery, particularly in the long run, because capital adequacy might not suffice to meet future challenges, and banks may face problems due to the impact of the crisis.[1]

This chapter evaluates these banks' financial performance, asset quality, regulatory and supervisory measures, and micro-level risk management systems to comprehend the ground realities. LBG and BIG were provided government bailouts from 2009–2011 to avoid possible insolvency, and the government of India provided bail-out support to scam-ridden PNB in 2018. During COVID-19, sovereign support was enormous to save the banks from a potential crisis. In addition, the

[1] OECD (2021).

A. Dimri, *Non-Performing Loans*, Ius Gentium: Comparative Perspectives on Law and Justice 125, https://doi.org/10.1007/978-3-031-92952-6_6

chapter focuses on analysing COVID-19 initiatives to put banks on the path of recovery. Finally, the chapter presented a comparative analysis of these case studies on several asset quality indicators to determine whether the existing system could address and mitigate future risks.

6.2 Lloyds Banking Group

Lloyds Bank was established in 1765 and later merged with TBS Group, forming Lloyds TSB Group in 1995.[2] It also acquired Scottish Windows a mutual life-assurance company, in 2000, making Lloyds Bank the second-largest life-assurance and pension provider in the UK.[3] In the same year, Lloyds-TSB purchased Chartered Trust from Standard Chartered Bank to form Lloyds-TSB Asset Finance Division, which provides motor, retail and personal finance in collaboration with Black Horse.[4] Finally, Lloyds TBS acquired HBOS, establishing LBG in 2009.[5]

LBG is actively involved in retail, commercial, and corporate banking, as well as general and life insurance, pensions, and investments. LBG expanded its international banking business in 40 countries, with 26 million customers accessing its leading digital presence globally.[6] It provides services through different names, including Lloyds-TSB, Halifax, Bank of Scotland, Scottish Widows, Clerical Medical and Cheltenham and Gloucester. LBG is quoted on the London Stock Exchange (LSE) and the New York Stock Exchange (NYSE) and is one of the largest companies within the FTSE 100.

Financial Achievements Market disruption after the GFC largely impacted the asset quality of the banks, which had a consequential adverse impact on the financial performance of LBG, resulting in a reduction in profit before tax (PBT) to 80% in 2008.[7] Due to market dislocation, it grew by only 9%, and the impairment losses also increased by 68% in 2009, reflecting the significant impact of the GFC. The slowdown in the UK economic environment and the effect of falling housing prices were the main reasons for such a dismal performance.[7]

Nonetheless, LBG maintained a robust capital ratio and strong liquidity throughout the global financial market turbulence. Despite the adverse economic environment, LBG also acquired HBOS in 2008, resulting in a shoot-up in impairment. The then chairman of LBG, Sir Victor Blank, admitted that LBG was aware of the bad

[2] New York Times (1995).

[3] Miller (1999).

[4] Garfield (2000).

[5] Warner (2009).

[6] Lloyds Banking Group (2021b).

[7] Lloyds Banking Group (2009).

loans on HBOS' balance sheet and its impact on asset quality to some extent.[8] The speed of the economic downturn contributed to the drastic collapse, and losses were at the worst end of expectations.[9] The anticipated loss of around £10 billion negatively contributed to the 32% fall in LBG's share prices.[10]

Lloyds continued its efforts to consolidate its financial position and planned to sell its 60% stake in St James Place Wealth Management to raise funds. This decision was taken well before the financial crisis. However, the Bank's spokesperson stated it was 'a good business that was performing well' and was 'comfortable' with its shareholdings.[11] The LBG retail Spanish business also incurred a £43 million loss in a year. Therefore, in 2013, LBG decided to sell its loss-making Spanish retail operation and local investment management business to Banco Halifax Hispania and Banco de Sabadell, respectively and incurred a loss of £250 million.[12]

Under such circumstances, FCA instructed the banks to initiate the stress test, suggesting 'peak-to-trough' criteria,[13] and in case of adverse results, LBG would require additional funding. However, the LBG agreed with the redemption of preference shares to avoid payment of £480 million annual interest to the Treasury. LBG encountered many specific losses during the economic slowdown that forced LBG to participate in the HMT-launched APS to salvage the banks from possible insolvency and bankruptcy[14] The FCA was ready to provide additional government capital to Lloyds-TSB if it had not taken over HBOS.[15] During the crisis, the LBG also disposed of its retail banking business of 600 branches, constituting 19% of its mortgaged assets. Gradually, a sign of recovery started, and the LBG business returned to profitability.

The Government provided a recapitalisation plan by injecting billions of pounds in return for equity.[16] Therefore, it negotiated a restructuring plan with the EC as it was necessary to receive state aid. After the recapitalisation and acquisition of HBOS, the government stake in LBG was 43.4%, with a 57.9% stake in HBOS alone.[17] Thus, the Government's investment in LBG amounted to £20.3 billion. However, in 2013, it started sales of its shares to recover the invested amount, which continued until 2017 with a final tranche of 0.5%. The government made a small

[8] Robert (2009).

[9] Johnson and Johnson (2002)

[10] The Telegraph (2002).

[11] Reuters (2012).

[12] BBC News (2013).

[13] For instance, a fall in UK GDP of over 6% with no growth until 2011 and a return of growth in 2012, a 12% rise in the unemployment rate, a fall in UK house prices with a 50% peak-to-trough and a fall in commercial property prices with a 60% peak-to-trough.

[14] Sharp (2009).

[15] Griffiths (2009).

[16] Darling (2011), p. 11.

[17] Kennedy (2009).

profit from the sales, realising £21.2 billion.[18] The LBG became the first European Bank to repay the government for its credit crunch investment performance.[7]

Assessment of Asset Quality The banking sector across the globe passed through a challenging phase, and the asset values of banks, including LBG, deteriorated significantly. Incidentally, the Lloyds-TSB decision to acquire HBOS coincided with the GFC,[19] and this move brought a further deterioration in asset quality, resulting in the highest NPLs (10.6%) in 2010, significantly higher than the overall NPLs ratio of the UK (3.96%). Due to the impact of the GFC, the impairment losses[20] increased to 20%.

The government support provided respite to the group, and NPLs started receding with the improvement in the financial conditions of the UK. Therefore, with a bailout plan, the financial condition started improving from 2011 onwards, and the NPLs ratio marginally came down to 8.69% in 2012. Such a trend persisted, resulting in a substantial decrease in NPLs, which was 1.28% in 2018, marginally higher than the average NPL ratio of the UK (1.11%).[21] However, despite significant improvement in NPLs, there was considerable variation in other parameters (see Fig. 6.1), which may be due to the final decision on Brexit and the outbreak of the COVID-19 pandemic.

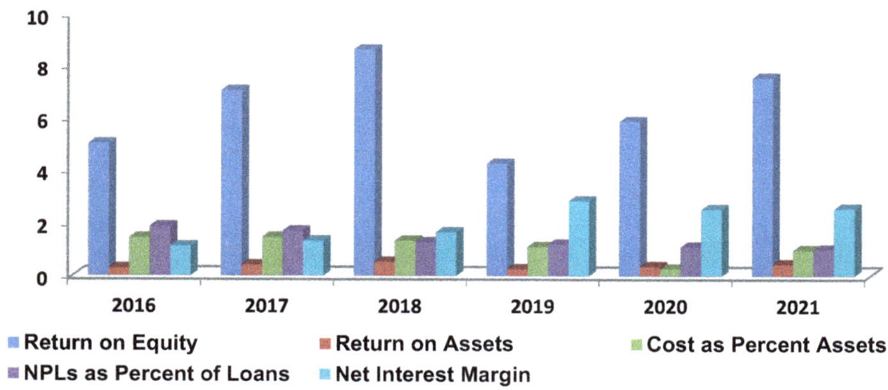

Fig. 6.1 Performance of asset quality indicators (Source: Developed by the researcher based on the various issues of Annual Reports of LBG)

---

[18] Kleinman (2017).

[19] Lloyds Banking Group (2008).

[20] An impairment loss refers to a recognised reduction in the carrying amount of an asset that is triggered by a decline in its fair value. When the fair value of an asset declines below its carrying amount, the difference is written off. Carrying amount is the acquisition cost of an asset, less any subsequent depreciation and impairment charges.

[21] Helgi Library (2019).

However, due to a marginal improvement in financial performance, impairment was reduced to 26% in 2011, which persisted until 2019. LBG strictly followed CRD IV guidelines and made the balance sheet risk-free. In addition, it also ensured a higher CET1 ratio (10.3%) and core Tier 1 ratio (14.0%), improving its loan-to-deposit ratio to 113% and core ratio to 100%.[22] All these measures improved the financial condition of LBG, and growth in the overall lending situation, particularly SME net lending, grew by 4% against a shrinking market. The balance sheet also showed improvement with a significant reduction in the impairment despite the integration of HBOS.[22]

In difficult situations, LBG remains a strong institution focused on building deeper customer relationships. The combination of Lloyds, TSB and HBOS developed into a stronger organisation and contributed to ensuring financial stability. There was a gradual improvement in asset quality. For instance, RWA improved by 3.02% in 2014, and the leverage ratio became stronger (4.1%). SME lending grew for the fourth consecutive year, and LBG actively participated in 'Britain Prosper Drive'.[23] Consequently, the government started selling its share in phases, completing the process by 2017, and LBG became a private entity.[24]

However, some critics argued that the lost interest remained unsettled even after injecting the taxpayers' money into the LBG, and heavy losses suffered by Lloyds hit the Government's stake.[25] Contrary to these arguments, Lloyds' chief executive claimed that the LBG expected the government to make £500 million from the bailout; the figure was close to £900 million, earning more money than it invested.[26] The persistent policy and supervisory efforts decreased the NPLs from 10.6% in 2010 to 1.28% in 2018, showing LBG's commitment to ensuring financial stability.[21] Therefore, a significant business transformation and improved performance made LBG a low-risk bank with a strategic balance sheet and funding position.

Impact of COVID-19 Pandemic There was a severe jolt to LBG's efforts due to the outbreak of the COVID-19 pandemic, which caused unprecedented economic contraction due to lockdown and a series of guidelines by the government to stop the spread of the virus. The LBG works with the stakeholders in the crisis environment to ensure the sustainable recovery of debts. It provided a 1.3 million moratorium across mortgages, loans, credit cards and motor finance products. The pandemic has significantly impacted the performance of LBG and reduced its profit after tax (PAT) by 54%, earnings by 66% and increased impairment charges by 23% in 2020.[27]

[22] Lloyds Banking Group (2012).

[23] Lloyds Banking Group (2014).

[24] Scuffham (2013).

[25] Dunkley (2017).

[26] BBC News (2013).

[27] Lloyds Banking Group (2020).

LBG supported over a million customers with payment holidays across mortgages, credit cards, loans, and motor finance. Such an initiative has allowed customers to get back on track without impacting individual credit quality. In addition, it also supported businesses facing hardship during the lockdown. Due to the lockdown, many firms 'closed and furloughed their staff, while others have incorporated and adapted to external changes as a contingent measure'. LBG supported these entities, obtaining over £12 billion through government-backed lending schemes HMT implemented during COVID-19 and granting them capital repayment holidays.[27]

The impact of COVID-19 continued in the following year, prompting LBG to extend payment holidays so that customers could re-plan their business strategies. LBG also established connections with society, providing practical support to the most vulnerable segment through door-to-door service.[27] Thus, LBG provided time and space for customers to recover from the impact of the pandemic without losing their businesses, homes, and other valuables. The 3-month interest-free buffer on the overdraft also helped the customers to recover and rethink restarting their businesses. All these efforts help the LBG reduce the cases of NPLs, improve asset quality, and help the UK grow and prosper.[28] Thus, LBG's COVID-19 policy, which supports customers, community, individuals, and businesses (Fig. 6.2), helped LBG win the customers' faith and helped the Group recover from the pandemic.

Return to Recovery After the Pandemic The efforts taken during the peak period of COVID-19 helped the speedy recovery of LBG from its impact. As a result, its financial performance has significantly improved, substantially reducing the impairment in 2021. The LBG expanded the availability of affordable and quality homes and helped many SMEs boost their digital capability. Thus, the LBG earned a profit and reinstated dividend payments after COVID-19.[29] Realising the importance of the Environment, Social and Governance (ESG), the LBG supported the green finance initiative to support green growth to reduce carbon emissions to 50% by 2030 and move toward net zero emissions as early as possible, but not later than 2050.[30]

The LBG progress continued in 2023 as its profit increased £0.5 billion, and the return on tangible equity was 15.8%. The bank is making strong progress in deepening and innovating and becoming the UK's largest digital bank, as 87% were using digital services. In 2023, the bank completed the acquisition of Tusker, a stand-out business in the salary sacrifice market for predominantly ultra-low emission vehicles, helping the bank to meet its net zero ambitions, and Tusker has already met the 60% target since its acquisition. The bank has made good progress on mass affluent business by launching 'Lloyds Bank 360', a mobile-first proposition with a holistic view of wealth, educational materials, and financial coaching.[30]

---

[28] Lloyds Bank (2020).

[29] Makortoff (2021).

[30] Lloyds Banking Group (2021a, 2023).

Fig. 6.2 COVID-19 responses (Source: Developed by the researcher based on the information available in the Annual Report 2021, Lloyds Banking Group)

LBG made a provision of £2.4 billion in 2020 to cover possible defaults on lending as a cushion for potential bad debts of businesses and households due to the fallout from COVID-19. It also promoted inclusive and equitable economic and social recovery involving communities across the UK. It helped those facing homelessness and financial abuse and provided them with respite during the pandemic. Thus, LBG considerably helped in rebuilding household financial health and well-being.[30] The asset quality with credit performance across portfolios is broadly at or favourable to pre-pandemic levels.[30] All these efforts gradually improve the asset quality of the LBG with a reduction in impairments and NPLs.[29]

Risk Management Strategy of LBG Despite turbulence in the financial sector, LBG followed strong corporate governance practices, professional standards, and corporate values[29] at all levels of risk management. Senior management designed strategic policies and procedures to promote a risk-free environment, professionalism, and integrity, and the executive authorities avoid risk oversight. The risk management framework ensured transparency while identifying possible risks, sharing experiences, and pointing out root causes when things go wrong.[30] Figure 6.3 presents its robust risk management framework, which consists of risk culture and customers, risk appetite, risk governance, risk control and self-assessment and three lines of defence.

Fig. 6.3 Risk Management Framework (Source: Developed by the researcher based on the information available in the Annual Reports of LBG)

LBG also focuses on developing group-wise portfolio risk appetite, critically discussing possible risks regularly, and providing possible oversight to the grassroots management on specific business areas and activities. The main emphasis was identifying, measuring, and controlling risks and undertaking self-assessment to discover lapses. LBG follows a consistent approach to identifying enterprise-based risk behaviour and follows the Enterprise Risk Management Framework (ERMF)[6] to initiate the corrective measures to avoid possible distress.

LBG implemented three lines of defence, viz-a-viz the business line, risk division, and internal audit line, defining clear accountabilities. LBG has divided and grouped risk into different categories for effective control, including market, credit, funding, liquidity, capital, operational, regulatory, strategic, and climatic risks. LBG critically assessed these risks and developed monitoring and mitigation systems through high-level groups and committees.[6]

Regulatory Response LBG adhered to the international standard for measuring capital adequacy, implemented Basel guidelines and maintained a satisfactory capital ratio throughout the transaction.[19] The FSA has set up Individual Capital Guidance (ICG) for each bank in the UK and made it clear that ICG remains confidential between the banks and the FSA, and LBG strictly adheres to these guidelines.[31] LBG also followed the UK's regulations and directives to protect the customers, including the EU Unfair Commercial Practices Directive, Unfair Trading

[31] Lloyds-TSB Group (2007).

Regulations, Payment Services Directive, and Consumer Credit Directive. Moreover, LBG adapted to the new liquidity regime based on the Individual Liquidity Adequacy Standards of the FSA to meet the reporting requirements. Thus, LBG advocates maintaining high levels of compliance with regulatory requirements.[7] LBG also endorsed the application of a regulatory ring fence in retail banking operations under the Financial Services Act 2021.

LBG was subject to a stress test suggested by EBA and PRA, and it exceeded the capital threshold in both tests.[23] The UK Financial Stability Report proposed a new capital framework, and the BoE implemented the same for the banks in the UK.[32] LCR became the key ratio for cash and liquid assets a bank must hold, and the group comfortably met these requirements.

The regulatory response in 2021 primarily focused on addressing COVID-19 strategic transformation and uncertainty arising from the UK's departure from the EU and other changes in regulatory standards. The regulatory authority increased RWA, resulting in a marginal decrease in CET 1 in 2022. Moreover, FPC announced that the UK CCyB rate would increase to 1% by December 2022, and LBG made matching changes to the CCyB by increasing it to 0.9%.[6]

PRA increased its focus to enhance the quality of regulatory reporting, emphasising timely and accurate independent reviews of governance, controls and risk management processes within firms. The LBG has made matching changes to strengthen the control environment in the financial and regulatory reporting system by establishing a Regulatory Reporting Review, which reviews current regulatory reporting activities and enhances them where necessary.[6] Thus, LBG made several changes on the regulatory front to match the guidelines suggested by the UK regulatory and supervisory authorities. These initiatives helped the group to develop robust mechanisms to address the risk and avoid a possible financial crunch. Moreover, LBG successfully managed GFC and COVID-19 by taking several initiatives through its robust risk management system and effective regulatory, policy and supervisory environment.

6.3 Punjab National Bank

PNB was founded in 1894 under the Indian Companies Act as an off-shoot of the *Swadeshi Movement* (an Indian independence movement which emphasised self-sufficiency and developing nationalism) and was regulated by the RBI Act 1934 and the Banking Regulation Act 1949.[33] It is India's second-largest government-owned bank in terms of its business volumes and network, having over 180 million customers and 12,248 branches with an international presence. It caters to various audiences through various services, including corporate and personal banking, industrial finance, agricultural finance, and international finance.[34] As per the decision of the

[32] Bank of England (2015), p. 8.

[33] Tandon (1989).

[34] Pandey (2018).

Government of India to consolidate the banking system, the Oriental Bank of Commerce and United Bank of India amalgamated with PNB in 2019.[35]

Since its inception, PNB has made steady progress and shown resilience to surge over many crises. The merger of other banks in PNB started in 1940 with the merger of Bhagwan Dass Bank.[33] Several banks amalgamated in PNB, including Bharat Bank in 1951, the Universal Bank of India, Indo Commercial Bank in 1961, and the Nedungadi Bank.[36] In 2020, the Oriental Bank of Commerce and the United Bank of India also merged into PNB. The Government of India nationalised major commercial banks, along with PNB, in 1969 to have absolute control over the functioning of banks. The bank recently came into the limelight for a major fraud involving US$1.4 billion related to a fraudulent Letter of Undertaking (LoU) issued by its Brady House branch in Fort Mumbai, which made the PNB liable for the amount.[37] The impact of the fraud was so huge that it significantly impacted the bank's asset quality, and NPA's increased considerably.

Performance of PNB India has emerged relatively untouched by the GFC, mainly due to its 'conservative regulatory framework' and public ownership in the banks, emphasising financial prudence and avoiding high risk.[38] Thus, due to stringent regulatory and supervisory mechanisms, India's comparative position remained stronger than several other jurisdictions. Its systematic planning has admirably fought the downward spiral of recession, demonstrating its flexibility and strength. Therefore, PNB was ranked 250th amongst the top 1000 global banks as per 'The Banker Magazine' (London) in 2009 and 31st among the top 500 Indian companies by 'The Economic Times' Intelligence Group Survey.[39]

While analysing the performance of PNB during the last 14 years, the bank's net profit increased by 50.9% during 2008–2009 due to an increase in the banking business by 25.3%, and the market environment remained conducive. Consequently, the bank registered substantial credit growth of 29.5% during the peak period of the GFC. The operating profit also increased by 43.4%, with a 50.9% increase in earnings per share. The cost-to-income ratio was 42.27%, with an improvement of 4.54% over previous years.[39]

The total business of PNB increased by 73.94% from 2011–2016 with an average increase of 15% per year. However, its net profit remained fluctuating and registered the highest decrease of 29.59% in 2014, mainly due to a substantial increase in Gross Non-Performing Assets (GNPA) from 1.79% to 12.90%. NPA also increased from 0.85% to 8.61% during the same period. There was a significant increase in provisions from 24.02% in 2011–2012 to 88.07% in 2015–2016 to counter the problem of increasing GNPA and NNPA. GNPA and NNPA also affected the operative profit, which was 17.20% in 2011 and significantly decreased to 2.76% in

[35] The Times of India (2019).

[36] Turnell (2009).

[37] The Economic Times (2018).

[38] Eichengreen and Gupta (2013).

[39] Punjab National Bank (2008–2009).

2013 and 2.18% in 2016, respectively.[40] The net and operative profits remained negative, and the GNPA and NNPA were highest at 18.38% and 11.24%, respectively, showing deterioration in the bank's financial performance in 2017–2018.[41]

However, there was a marginal improvement in net profit, which increased by 3.39% in 2018–2019, and net investment also increased by 7.27%. The major contribution was from the domestic market, and government securities and deposits also rose by 3.3%.[41] Despite the challenges of the COVID-19 pandemic, the bank's domestic business increased by 3.2%, its operating profit by 13.4%, and its cost to deposit by 5.16%.[41] Such progress continued, and the bank was on the path of recovery in 2021–2022. Thus, the deposits and operating profit of PNB, OBC and UNI combined were 57.18% and 55.91%, respectively.[42]

Asset Quality As discussed earlier, the GFC had a mild impact on India's banking sector compared to other countries. The PNB 2008–2009 annual reports also substantiate this fact by releasing data on asset quality and arguing that despite the 'global financial turmoil and stress in the domestic banking sector, the PNB has performed exceedingly well'.[37] Thus, NIM increased by 3.62%, ROA by 0.24% to 1.39%, and CAR under Basel II was 14.03% against 13.46% in 2007–2008.[37] Annexure 4 and Fig. 6.4 clarify the movement of various asset quality parameters from 2008 to 2022.

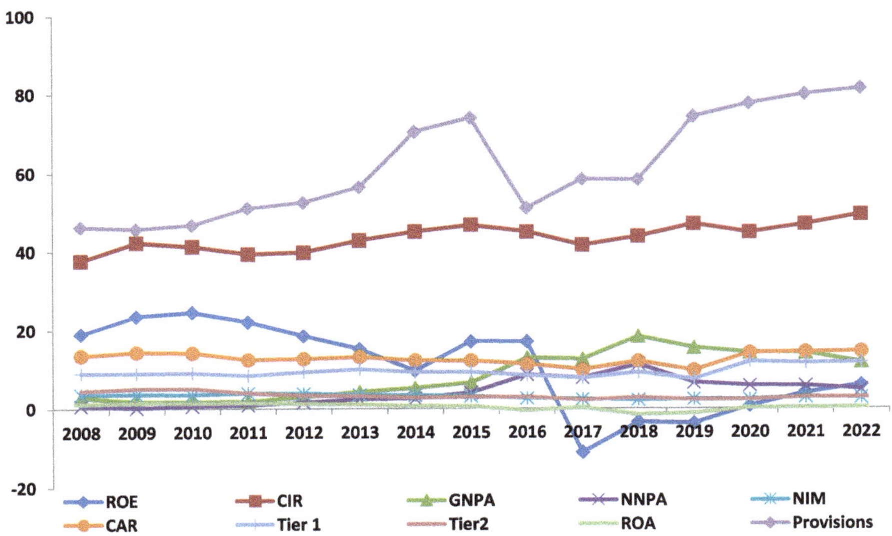

Fig. 6.4 Performance trend of PNB on asset quality variables (Source: Developed by the researcher based on the data available in the various issues of PNB Annual Reports)

40 Punjab National Bank (2015–2016).

41 Punjab National Bank (2020).

42 Punjab National Bank (2022, 2024).

There was significant variation in ROE over the years, with the highest (24.52%) in 2010 and the lowest (3.83%) in 2019. The fluctuation in CIR and NIM was relatively less, and the CIR ratio was highest in 2022, at 49.38%, and the lowest was 37.73% in 2008. The CAR remained strong except in 2017 (8.98%) and 2019 (9.73%). The trend of NIM remained consistent, with marginal variation ranging from 2.16% in 2018 to 3.96% in 2011. There was considerable variation in ROA, which was highest in 2008 (1.39%) and lowest in 2018 (−1.60%).

The ROA remained more than 1% between 2008 and 2013, less than 1% from 2014 onwards, and negative in 2016 (−0.61%), 2018 (−1.60%) and 2019 (−1.25%), respectively. The return on assets started improving from 2021 onwards (0.15%), and it was 0.55% in 2023–2034.[42] There was a substantial increase in the provisions, from 46.18% in 2008 to 81.60% in 2022, indicating that the bank has enough capital to meet potential financial distress. Thus, most asset quality indicators have performed as per the banks' expectations, and deviation was due to internal and external factors, including the impact of banking fraud, COVID-19, internal and external economic factors, etc. Nonetheless, PNB effectively addressed the difficulties due to the GFC, the COVID-19 pandemic, and counterfeiting activities. Consequently, after touching the peak, the GNPA and NNPA started receding due to several efforts' banks initiated (discussed in the following section), and it was 11.78% and 4.80%, respectively, in 2022.[42] The reduction in GNPA and NNPA continued, and in 2023–2024, it was 2.72% and 0.73%, respectively.[42]

Banking Fraud, Impact on Asset Quality and Regulatory Response Despite several risk redressal measures, PNB recently came across a major fraud by Nirav Modi, Mehul Choksi, and others to the tune of ₹2.81 billion (roughly $1.8 billion), one of the biggest frauds in the banking industry in India.[43] This fraud occurred due to counterfeiting LoUs to the overseas branches of other Indian Banks using SWIFT,[44] an international financial communication system. In doing so, the bank bypassed the regulatory reporting system and issued LoUs without authorisation and without submitting any security (collateral) mandatory for the obtained LoUs.[45] The regulatory guidelines suggest that the issuance of LoUs to the gems and jewellery sector be for 90 days, not 365 days. The impact of the fraud was so enormous that it significantly impacted the bank's asset quality.[46] The bank started legal proceedings against the culprit once an employee detected the fraud. ED recovered some of its finances with 'immediate confiscation' of about ₹7000 crore assets, promulgating the fugitive economic offenders' ordinance.[46]

[43] The Hindu (2021).

[44] SWIFT is a Society for Worldwide Interbank Financial Telecommunications with its headquartered in Belgium. It carries secure financial messages from one bank to the other in a safe and secure manner. SWIFT is not involved in settling or clearing fund transfers, which is generally misunderstood.

[45] First Post (2018).

[46] The Hindustan Times (2018).

The offender and his associates' actions violated section 17 of the Contract Act, forcing the Government to enact the Fugitive Economic Offenders Act (2018)[47] to prevent economic offenders from escaping the country. The act empowers the courts to confiscate all assets and properties of the offenders with a default of over ₹1000 million. It applies to offenders who evade the charges by wilfully remaining outside the jurisdiction of the Indian judiciary. The government investigated the alleged scam, and the Enforcement Directorate (ED) seized a cumulative ₹56.74 billion worth of diamonds, gold and jewellery from the offenders' homes and offices. On the persuasion of the Indian government, the UK court in Nirav Deepak Modi v Government of India ruled his extradition to India to face fraud and money laundering charges.[48]

It severely impacts the bank's credibility despite an assurance to the participating banks for immediate payment. In addition, the mechanism developed by regulators like the RBI and SEBI to address such issues invited criticism. Nevertheless, as a corrective measure, the RBI banned the banks from issuing LoU guarantees and connected the core banking systems with SWIFT.[49] The value of the fraudulent transaction was 50 times more than PNB's net worth for the third quarter, ₹2300.11 million. The immediate impact was the reduction in the market capitalisation by 5.8% for Union Bank of India, 9.9% for Allahabad Bank, 3.4% for Axis Bank and 3.35% for SBI and NNPA also increased to 10.35% in 2018.[49]

The scam was a learning lesson and provided opportunities for the bank to reform the internal system, resulting in an improved and strong performance in the credit position, including better management of credit, market, and operational risks.[50] RBI must strengthen its credit, operations, and market risk guidelines and promote better discipline among the banks. RBI's over-dependence on banks does not delve into the details that need critical examination. Moreover, the RBI did not impose a mandatory condition on the banks to link their core banking software with SWIFT[51] However, RBI also emphasised that the 'Red Flagged Accounts' need effective and constant monitoring.[52] Fraud also raises questions about the disclosure and compliance mechanisms developed by the Ministry of Finance and the Ministry of Company Affairs.[53] Although PNB took several corrective measures, a more vigilant watch on foreign transactions is desirable to avoid such instances in the future, and effective monitoring is necessary to avoid fraudulent engagement.

NPAs Management Initiatives PNB took several initiatives at the micro-level to manage NPLs, including establishing specialised NPA management branches, known as Asset Recovery Management Branches and specialised cells, known as

[47] The Fugitive Economic Offenders Act [2018] (India).

[48] Nirav Deepak Modi v Government of India [2021] EWHC 2257 (Admin).

[49] Muthalaly (2020).

[50] Punjab National Bank (2018).

[51] Reuters (2018).

[52] Gayathri and Mangaiyarkarasi (2018), p. 12.

[53] Pandey (2018).

Special Asset Recovery Cells.[50] The bank regularly monitors all NPA cases and has developed account-specific resolution strategies for upgrading NPAs to the performing category within the scope of the SARFAESI Act and has achieved considerable success. Consequently, the ratio of GNPAs reached 1.77% in 2009 against 2.74% in 2008. The net NPAs to net advance ratio was 0.17% in 2009, which also reduced to 0.64% in 2008.[50] Such reduction was possible due to its continuous efforts to rehabilitate the potentially viable sick units through BIFR, mainly through debt restructuring and OTS.[50]

The bank also implemented account-specific resolution strategies to upgrade NPAs to the performing category and convert accounts into the standard category. The bank also adjusted its policy on the recovery of loans and NPA management to improve the quality of its asset portfolio in compliance with the regulatory guidelines. Later, the bank also engaged ARCs and retired bank officials to resolve assets for micro-level management of NPAs. PNB also adopted the Internal Rating Based Approach and Models Approach for Market Risk and the Advanced Management Approach for operational risk as recommended by the RBI.[50]

The bank launched a special recovery drive to improve asset quality by launching a PPF campaign and a Pan India Recovery Drive (PIRD). The pan-India drives successfully improved the recovery of small advances. It organised Mega *Rin Mukti Shivirs* (Debt Relief Camps) for the wilful defaulters as per RBI guidelines to expedite the pace of settlement.[50] In 2017, it assigned Key Responsibility Areas for the staff working in ARMBs. Under the mission, *Gandhigiri* initiated a peaceful dharna (demonstration) to put moral pressure on the defaulters to clear the dues. Moreover, the bank successfully initiated an e-auction portal to dispose of bad assets and realised the sale of the securitised assets.

Despite the COVID-19 pandemic, banks' efforts to curtail NPAs continued. As part of the loan restructuring strategies, a SASTRA[54] portal and PNB LenS lending solutions were launched for retail, agriculture and MSME loans up to ₹250 million and for corporate sectors above ₹250 million. The Bank's CAR stood at 14.32%, with Tier-I capital at 11.50% and CET1 at 10.62%. The Common recovery portal, SASTRA, was further strengthened and integrated with OTS, SARFAESI, DRTs, NCLT and wilful defaulters. The bank also strengthened the DRT and SARFAESI portals by re-configuring the NCLT with them. The bank also prepared a database of the wilful defaulter loaded through a separate module.[50]

PNB also integrated its Pride App with SASTRA across the branches for effective monitoring and follow-up of NPAs. It also made Geo-Tagging to monitor the activities and location of field-level functionaries and their efforts to address NPA cases at a micro level by linking field operations with SASTRA. Thus, PNB has made several policy-level efforts to level down NPAs and achieved considerable success with the help of micro-level management.

---

[54] SASTRA stands for Stressed Assets Targeted Resolution Action—a scheme launched by the Bank to address the problem of NPAs.

Risk Management The bank focused on ensuring sustained growth and upkeep of its asset portfolio in a healthy condition by understanding, measuring and managing risk. The focus was primarily on identifying high-risk areas and emphasising a balance between risk and ROA to increase shareholders' value.[50] Therefore, the credit risk framework of the bank is highly vigorous, and its central server, PNB TRAC, is a scientific method of assessing clients' credit risk ratings. Moreover, the bank's central server embodied score-based ratings for retail loans to achieve faster and more accurate processing and delivery of credit,[50] bring uniformity to the system, and facilitate accurate data analysis to categorise the credit.

The bank closely monitors the interest rate and liquidity risk through its well-established organisational structure, exclusively dedicated to risk management functions. It uses stress testing, modified duration,[55] and VaR[56] for treasury operations. The bank has a well-defined organisational structure for risk management functions (Fig. 6.5). It investigates the overall market risk management, including interest rate and liquidity risk.

The bank is proactive and undertakes regular validation exercises of its rating models in addition to migration and default rate analysis to test the appropriateness of its rating models. The bank uses these results in its credit portfolio management, categorises the asset portfolio into low, medium, and high risk, and places them before the Risk Management Committee.[40,41,42] The central server scoring model

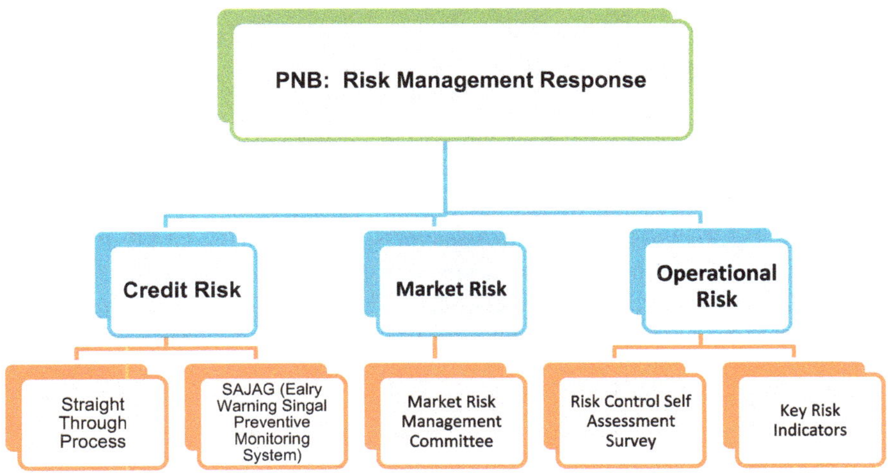

Fig. 6.5 Risk management response in PNB (Source: Developed by the researcher based on the information available in the PNB Annual Reports)

[55] Modified duration is a formula that expresses the measurable change in the value of a security. It measures the change in the value of a bond in response to a change in 100-basis-point (1%) change in interest rates.

[56] Value at Risk (VaR) measures and quantifies the level of financial risk within a firm, portfolio or position over a specific time frame.

monitors the performance of retail banking and SME advances. These mechanisms help the bank achieve quick and accurate credit delivery and bring uniformity to portfolio management.

The bank strictly follows RBI guidelines and relevant risk management policies, including risk management philosophy and policy, credit management and risk policy, operational risk management policy, credit risk mitigation and collateral management policy, Internal Capital Adequacy Assessment Process (ICAAP), etc. In addition, the bank has also implemented various requirements of the Basel III guidelines on capital adequacy.[40,41,42]

Thus, PNB faces several challenges, including major banking fraud, which has cost millions of dollars and contributed to an abnormal increase in GNPA and NNPA despite the government bailout plan. In addition, uncertainty loomed all around due to the spread of the COVID-19 pandemic. However, PNB took several regulatory, policy and supervisory initiatives to address the problem effectively. Its micro-management of loan recovery and extensive use and integration of ICT to monitor field-level activities and robust risk management system helped the bank to bring substantial reduction in GNPA and NNPA, which was highest in 2017–2018 (18.38% and 11.24%) and came down to 8.74% and 2.72% respectively in 2022.[50] Therefore, coordinated efforts from the field to the policy level help to mitigate the problem of NPLs to a great extent. Nevertheless, future success depends on sustained efforts following an integrated and coordinated approach at all levels.

6.4 Bank of Ireland Group

Royal Charter established the Bank of Ireland in 1783, and its first branch started operation at Mary's Abbey. The number of branches increased gradually to 58 by 1883.[57] The bank had a long history of mergers and acquisitions. In 1926, it acquired National Land Bank and changed its name to National City Bank Ltd[58] It acquired the share capital of Hibernian Bank Limited in 1958, renamed it National Bank of Ireland Ltd in 1965, and finally incorporated it into the Bank of Ireland. In the same year, Investment Bank of Ireland and Bank of Ireland Asset Management came into existence, having British branches, and afterwards, were acquired by Williams & Glyn's .[59] Bank of Ireland Group (BIG) plays a significant role in the banking business and provides diversified banking services to its customers.

BIG acquired several firms to consolidate its position and doubled the size of its asset management business.[60,61] The BIG announced the acquisition of Burdale

[57] Bank of Ireland Act (1781) (Ireland).

[58] Bank of Ireland (2022).

[59] McCabe (2011).

[60] English (2000).

[61] Reid (2002).

Financial Holdings in 2004 and, later in 2005, sold Bristol and West to Britannia Building Society to consolidate its financial position.[62] The Government of Ireland and the EC took several steps to support the Bank of Ireland after the GFC, including approving a restructuring plan in 2010 under the EC recapitalisation scheme of €3.5 billion to the Irish Government.[63] The NPLs in Ireland, including in the BIG, remained significantly higher after the global downturn and with its prolonged after-effects.

Financial Progress Despite the global downturn, BIG's final dividend was 53.6% in 2007–2008, showing an increase of 5%. The underlying PBT also increased by 5%,[64] and the profit of the BIG was 21% in 2008 compared to 23% in 2007, reflecting a marginal decrease in the profits.[64] Due to market dislocation, underlying operating profit before impairment charges on loans decreased by 28% in 2009 compared with the previous year. Due to deterioration in the financial performance and a significant reduction in overall profitability, 2008–2009 remained the year of greatest vulnerability and extreme difficulty.[64]

However, BIG successfully managed the challenges of volatile global markets and delivered a satisfactory underlying performance in 2010, resulting in an increase in earnings per share by 4% and PBT by 6%.[65] The lending and deposit growth also remained strong, and the cost-income ratio was down due to an effective cost management system. Moreover, the asset quality remained strong, and there was a reduction in the impairment charges, strengthening the funding position despite global market dislocation.[65] Gradually, there was an improvement in the BIG's financial performance, and in 2011, there was a substantial reduction in losses. Total operating income was 27% lower, reflecting the continuity of a low-interest rate environment, intense competition for deposits in the Irish market, and the elevated wholesale funding cost.[66] However, total operating expenses were reduced by 8%, reflecting continued rigorous cost management and effective delivery of operational efficiencies.[67]

In 2014, there was further improvement in BIG's financial performance, and the NIM increased by 2.11% from 1.84%, PBT also increased by 96.92%, and average interest-earning increased by 5.5%.[68] There was a substantial improvement in the financial performance in 2018, and its profit increased by 13% over the previous year. Gradually, there was an improvement in the financial performance of the Group and its lending increased by 3% in 2018. The market share of new mortgage lending was 24%, and it also grew for SME lending. There was a continuous reduc-

[62] Osborne (2005).

[63] The Irish Times (2009).

[64] Bank of Ireland (2008).

[65] Bank of Ireland (2010).

[66] Bank of Ireland (2011).

[67] Bank of Ireland (2011).

[68] Bank of Ireland (2014).

tion in NPEs, which was 4.4% of gross loans, and the BIG was the first Irish bank to get NPEs below 5% after the GFC.[68]

Asset Quality The Bank of Ireland faced serious liquidity constraints due to disruption in the international financial markets in the latter half of 2008, mainly due to 'recession and rapid deterioration in credit conditions and asset prices'. During this period, ROE was 21%, capital ratios equity Tier-1 and core Tier 1 were 5.7% and 8.1%, respectively, and the NIM was 1.66%. The Group successfully managed the challenges of volatile global markets and delivered a relatively satisfactory performance in 2009. The slump in the Irish economy was due to exacerbated wholesale funding and over-reliance on CRE. Irish banks, including the BIG, took an optimistic view of future economic prospects and entered the downturn over-leveraged. Consequently, the Irish government supported banks in Ireland, including the Bank of Ireland, with decisive actions.[69] The capital ratios also remained strong, resulting in 11.1% total capital, 8.1% core Tier 1, and 5.7% equity Tier 1 ratios, respectively.[70]

The impact of the GFC was very severe in Ireland, and several initiatives were taken with the help of external financial support to ensure financial stability, including bilateral loans, which are considered extremely important for sustainable economic growth and to ensure the proper functioning of a healthy banking system.[71] The government took several measures, including investment in national pension reserve funds and the introduction of ELG for credit institutions in 2009, to facilitate institutions issuing debt securities and securing deposits due to maturity.[72] The government suggested support programmes to the banks, including BIG, reconstructing and recognising fiscal policy and structural reforms. The EC and IMF also approved such a move.[73] BIG also became part of the PCAR and PLAR to remove vulnerable land, development, and restructuring loans.[73]

The problem continued in 2010 due to the severity of the sovereign debt, its compliance, and the economic downturn. Despite this pressure, the equity and core Tier 1 ratios were more than 7% and 8%, respectively. The bank losses on the disposal of assets to NAMA and impairment provisions to non-NAMA portfolios remained relatively higher and were within the expected line. The EU and IMF emphasised downsizing and reorganising the banking sector, and new regulatory requirements of Tier-1 capital put BIG under stress.[65] Despite these factors, the core Tier 1 ratio was maintained at 10.3% in BIG from 2011 to 2013.[66] In addition, the group also prepared a deleveraging plan to reduce reliance on liquidity support from monetary agencies and state funding[74] Thus, the contraction in the Irish economy,

[69] O'Carroll (2010).

[70] Tier 1 capital, comprising CET1 and AT1, and Tier 2 capital.

[71] Credit Institutions (Financial Support) Act (2008) No 18 (Ireland).

[72] Molloy (2009), para 2.

[73] Brown (2022), p. 214.

[74] Bank of Ireland (2012).

the fiscal adjustment programme, and high unemployment levels contributed to the increase in insolvencies. There was a sharp fall in property value, which also increased illiquidity and adversely affected the banking business.

Although the volatility in Europe and the international market continued, a steady recovery started in BIG in 2012 due to momentum in the strategic priority of achieving sustainable profitability.[68] The significant improvement in the financial market conditions in the last leg of 2012 prompted the group to diversify its funding by issuing Irish Mortgage Asset-Backed Securities and Tier 2 debt.[68] The trend continued in 2013 and was a turning point for the Irish economy as it took a path of recovery.

The Irish economy continued the path of speedy recovery in 2014, and Ireland became the fastest-growing economy in Europe, and the international market endorsed it. BIG announced its buyback plan of € 50 million shares in phases, which was a positive sign for recovery and returning to private ownership.[68] The BIG achieved a 2% NIM in 2013 and also took the initiative to optimise asset prices and funding, effectively managing the balance sheet and generating sustainable returns.[75] The group continues to generate substantial capital, as the CET1 ratio was 11.3%, transitional CET 13.3%, and TCR 18.8% in 2018 before the pandemic (see Table 6.1).

Impact of COVID-19 The progress of the BIG remained stable until COVID-19, and it posted significantly higher underlying LBT in 2020, with COVID-19 having a material effect on financial performance. Total income was 8% lower than in 2019, with a decrease in return to profitability in the second half of 2020. The BIG's loan book deteriorated due to foreign exchange and stable net lending. The total new lending volume was 19% lower than in 2019, reflecting reduced activity in core markets. Net interest income (NII) was 2% lower than in 2019. The BIG's impairment coverage increased to 2.9% from 1.6% in 2019. The NPE exposure also increased to 5.7% of gross customer loans. The regulatory CET1 capital ratio of 14.9% and fully loaded CET1 capital ratio of 13.4% in December 2020 and 14.3% in December 2023 remain strong despite elevated impairment charges.[76] However,

Table 6.1 Trend of some important indicators of asset quality

Year	ROE	NPE	CET 1 regulatory	CET 1 fully loaded	Total capital regulatory
2016	7.4	9.4	14.2	12.3	18.5
2017	6.3	6.5	15.8	13.8	20.2
2018	7.2	6.3	15	13.4	18.8
2019	6.8	4.4	13.4	14.9	18.6
2020	4.1	5.7	15	13.8	19.2
2021	12.8	5.5	17	16.0	12.3

Source: Compiled from the various issues of the Annual Report of the Bank of Ireland

[75] Boucher (2013).

[76] Bank of Ireland (2020, 2023).

the impact of COVID-19 gradually disappeared, and BIG's underlying operating profit was at the pre-COVID level, increasing by 53% compared to 25% in 2019. Despite the challenges presented by COVID-19, BIG's activities substantially transformed in 2021, and its operating profit was 25% more than in 2019. COVID-19 was, in fact, a real-life stress test and had a severe impact on the performance of the banks, including LBG. In addition to the impact of COVID-19, the UK's decision to leave the EU has considerably impacted its credit formation, and its consequences have continued to endure for some time.[77] The low-interest rate environment negatively impacted BIG's revenue. It was coupled with the prolonged negotiation of final Brexit terms, creating significant uncertainties. The business relationship between the UK and Ireland is so interrelated that Ireland exports 16% of Irish services and 9% of Irish goods to the UK. However, the innovative digital enhancements also helped BIG to deliver its objectives and maintain strong momentum on key priorities.

Despite the pandemic, the group ended the year with a strong capital position. Moreover, it also benefited from the support provided by the regulators, such as lowering the risk weightage for SME loans.[78] Therefore, by 2021, the Group recovered from the impact of COVID-19, and two significant acquisitions took place, KBCI's performing loan portfolios and deposits and J&E Davy (Davy).[79] During 2009 and 2011, the Bank of Ireland received €4.8 billion in support from the Irish State. The Group reduced the state share from 13.9% to below 6% in 2021, mainly due to its strong financial position and continuous sell-down of the state shareholdings. Thus, Ireland became the first Eurozone jurisdiction to successfully emerge from the EU and IMF support programme due to significant progress and strong economic recovery.[80] Hence, NPE was 5.5% in 2022 due to a gradual improvement in asset quality, and this reduced by 50 basis points to 3.1% of gross customer loans in 2023 despite the increase in the loan book by 23% as €8 billion of loans were acquired from KBCI.[81]

Risk Management BIG undertook several steps to manage the risk arising from its business activities. The Central Bank and Credit Institutions (Resolution) Act[82] and the Credit Institutions (Stabilisation) Act 2010[83] have created a mechanism for state intervention in the banking industry, which could significantly impact banking operations, including the BIG. The Act also provides funding for financial instability as per art 10 (2). Under the Resolution Act, the Central Bank will take over, run, and break up troubled FIs to minimise the cost of a bank failure for taxpayers. A

[77] Helm et al. (2021).

[78] McDonagh (2020).

[79] Reuters (2021).

[80] Brennan (2022).

[81] Bank of Ireland (2021, 2023).

[82] Central Bank and Credit Institutions (Resolution) Act [2011] (Ireland).

[83] Credit Institutions (Stabilisation) Act [2010] No 36 (Ireland).

special resolution fund is also to be set up, with a levy to be placed on banks to cover the cost of the Central Bank assuming control of a financial institution. The Resolution Act and the Stabilisation Act allow the Central Bank to manage banks in the national interest rather than the shareholders' interest. The Resolution Act empowers the Central Bank to apply to the HC to appoint a special manager to run a troubled bank.[84] These two acts provide sufficient safeguards to avoid insolvency and bankruptcy and strengthen the Irish regulatory system to resolve FIs. However, there are instances where banks and building societies approached the court on the commencement of the regulatory investigation.

In Purcell v Central Bank of Ireland & Ors.,[85] the Central Bank commenced a regulatory investigation into commercial lending and credit risk management procedures at the Irish Nationwide Building Society, which collapsed during the financial crisis. The court protects the right of the Central Bank, citing the example of Fingleton v Central Bank of Ireland & Ors,[86] where the judge observed that it was non-compliant with regulatory measures for credit risk management. In addition, the Central Bank can also create a bridge bank to take control of deposits and loans of a failed institution pending their transfer to another bank.

The BIG has made a robust mechanism to address any risk banks are likely to face. Its risk management system consists of three-tier support systems: line management in individual businesses and relevant group functions, central risk management functions, and Group Internal Audit (GIA).[76] This system is like the system developed and implemented by LBG in the UK. Under the three-tier support system, several committees operate under Group Risk Policy Committees (GRPCs), as presented in Fig. 6.6. The roles and responsibilities of these committees are well defined to oversee all risk categories, formulate risk appetite recommendations, develop policies, and establish integrated mechanisms for risk measurement and management standards.[76]

The BIG has made mechanisms to identify, monitor and mitigate risks and categorise them based on their intensity. Important risks include credit, funding, business, regulatory, market, operational, people, insurance, and strategy. The group has also provided three levels of defence to mitigate the risk. In the first line of defence, line management is responsible for identifying, controlling, reporting, and implementing individual business and group functions. The second level, the nominated risk owner, is responsible for formulating risk strategy, policy, and process, assessing risk exposure correctly and managing identified risk appropriately by providing independent risk oversight and analysis. In the third line of defence, an internal audit critically assesses the business and function. It assigns an appropriate rating, providing information to senior management on various aspects, including remediation plans monitored for progress and completion dates as agreed.[76] The group

[84] Central Bank and Credit Institutions (Resolution) Act [2011] (Ireland).

[85] Purcell v Central Bank of Ireland & ors [2016] IEHC 514.

[86] Fingleton v The Central Bank of Ireland [2018] IECA 105.

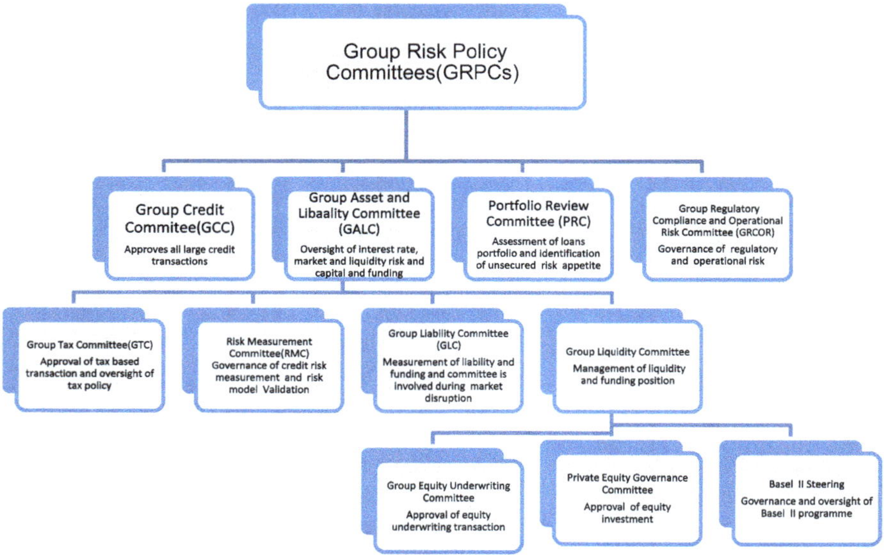

Fig. 6.6 Group Risk Policy Committees (GRPCs) (Source: Developed by the researcher based on information available in Annual Reports of the Bank of Ireland)

monitors capital and leverage ratios to meet all regulatory requirements and internal targets.[76] It also prepares comprehensive stress tests and forward-looking financial projections and reviews them to ensure capital adequacy, liquidity, and leverage positions.[76]

BIG has identified a comprehensive risk taxonomy (see Fig. 6.7) and ensures robust governance through a matured risk management lifecycle built on the foundation of the key enablers. The major risk taxonomy includes credit, funding, business, market, regulatory, operational, people, insurance, and strategic risks. Its well-designed mechanism facilitates the reporting and intensifying of risk concerns from the business units. The identified risk was reported to the Board and its appointed committees, immediately prompting the business unit to adopt the approved risk management policies and decisions.[76]

Thus, individual responsibility is a key ideology of risk management in the BIG, and the BIG remained successful in risk management to a great extent. BIG is aware of external market shocks that emerged during the GFC and the COVID-19 pandemic. Geopolitical event risks like the UK's departure from the EU, the recent Russia-Ukraine war and other emerging risks could substantially impact earnings, capital adequacy, and trade prospects in the future. Nevertheless, BIG has made sufficient provisions to address the various types of risks, and its effective monitoring will make its ecosystem more robust.

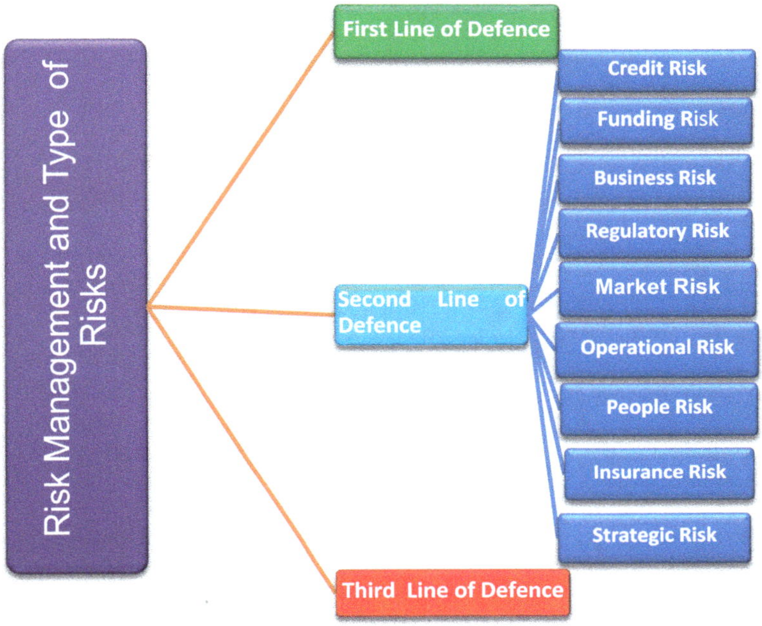

Fig. 6.7 Risk management and type of risks (Source: Developed by the researcher base on the information available in the Annual Reports of Bank of Ireland)

6.5 Comparative Analysis of Banking Risk Management Approach

The preceding sections examined the progress of the LBG, PNB, and BIG on asset quality, financial performance, and the regulatory and risk management initiatives they took to address the NPLs-related issues since the global downturn in 2008. The impact of the GFC was visible on LBG and BIG, but the impact was relatively less on PNB. In PNB, the internal risk management system was inadequate, resulting in the most extensive banking fraud that sniffed huge capital from the bank through an unverified LoU. Moreover, the COVID-19 pandemic aggravated the problem, and the recovery was slow due to measures taken by the jurisdictions announcing a moratorium to relieve the customers. The impact of the final agreement on the UK's departure from the EU was also visible on LBG and BIG. The relative position of asset quality of a particular group/bank in addressing the NPLs problem that emerged due to several factors, including market dislocation due to the GFC, banking fraud, the COVID-19 pandemic, Brexit and the Russia-Ukraine war is presented in Table 6.2.

While analysing the NPLs data, the NPLs of PNB were 11.78% in 2021 compared to 5.5% and 1.28% for BIG and LBG, respectively. There was a significant improvement in the NPA of PNB, and it was 0.73% in 2023–2034. Interestingly, the

Table 6.2 Comparative analysis of bank's performance

Variables	LBG	PNB	BIG
NPLs/NPA current rate	1.28 (2018)	11.78	5.5
Highest after GFC	10.6% (2010)	18.38 (2018)	9.4 (2010)
Lowest NPLs/NPAs	0.889% (2003)	1.71	4.4 (2018)
ROA	1.07 (2020), 2.65 (2019)	0.15 (2021)	0.21 (2021)
ROE	2.3% (2020) 13.8 (2021)	3.88 (2021)	12.8 (2021) 4.1 (2020)
NIM	2.54 (2021)	2.88	1.34
CET-I	16.3 (2021)	11.73 (2021)	17 (2021)
Bailout scheme adopted after GFC	Yes-GFC	No—GFC Yes—Fraud	Yes—GFC
Risk management system	Robust	Robust	Robust
Regulatory mechanism	Strong-PRA-FCA, HMT	Strong-RBI	Strong-EBA—SSM and CBI
Govt interference	Moderate	High	Moderate
Response to crisis	Prompt	Moderate	Prompt

Source: Compiled by the researcher based on the information in the Annual Reports of LBG, PNB and BIG

NPLs ratio of PNB remained relatively lower after the GFC, 1.71% in 2010, than in the UK and Ireland, and such a trend persisted until 2012; thus, the impact of the GFC on PNB was minimal. There was a sharp increase in the GNPA ratio of PNB, and in 2018, it was the highest (18.38%). A sharp rise in the NPLs ratio was due to uncertainty looming after banking fraud, despite the immediate injection of funds as a bailout plan.[87]

The ROE was significantly higher for LBG (13.08%) and BIG (12.08%) in 2020 and 2021, respectively, indicating a faster recovery from the impact of the COVID-19 pandemic, and it was significantly low for PNB (3.88%). The ROE was significantly low for both groups in the previous financial year, with 2.3% (LBG) and 4.1% (BIG). On the other hand, ROA was 1.07% for the LBG, which was marginally higher compared to 0.15% for PNB and 0.25% for BIG. The NIM of LBG and PNB was 2.88% and 2.54%, respectively, and marginally lower (1.34%) for BIG compared to PNB and LBG. Similarly, CET- I was also highest for LBG (16.3%) and BIG (17%), and it was significantly low (11.73%) for PNB.

LBG and BIG participated in the bailout plan of the respective governments to save them from possible insolvency, and both groups successfully paid the government shares. The government recouped £20.3 billion it ploughed into LBG during the financial crisis, and LBG became a private entity in 2017. BIG also achieved the

[87] Bloomberg (2018).

target in 2022 and returned €2 billion more than the bailout amount to the government.[80] The COVID-19 pandemic struck the profitability, and it reported losses in 2020. In addition, BIG also made provisions to cover loan amounts that were expected to default due to the pandemic.[80]

On the other hand, the government of India infused $290 million into PNB to help it meet dues on its perpetual bonds and restore capital to the level needed to pay the coupon.[88] PNB must pay ₹1.35 billion to cover the 8.98% annual interest. It cannot make the payment because an unprecedented loan fraud wiped out its profits and pushed the bank's capital below mandated levels. PNB's core Tier I capital was 5.96%, below the RBI limits of 7.375% in 2018.[85]

The risk management system in LBG, BIG and PNB is multi-layer and strong, and the responsibility at each level is assigned to identify risk and report it to the next level, providing solutions to overcome the risk. In addition, there are a dozen GRPCs to monitor the risk. On the other hand, PNB strictly follows RBI guidelines and relevant risk management policies, including operational risk, credit risk mitigation, collateral management, ICAAP, etc.[89] In PNB, micro-level risk management is very strong, and grassroots-level activities are linked with the central portal for effective monitoring.

The supervisory, regulatory, and policy mechanisms of LBG, BIG, and PNB appear to be very strong on paper but need attention in early risk identification assessment and timely resolution. This assessment of regulatory response is based on the critical review of existing literature discussed in the preceding sections of this chapter and the regulatory response by the respective regulator. For instance, during the GFC, the Central Banks of the UK and Ireland immediately infused funds and issued directions to the banks facing financial difficulties. In India, during banking fraud, several lapses were noticed on the part of the RBI to handle a crisis, prompting the researcher to categorise a moderate regulatory response for India and a strong one for the UK and Ireland.

6.6 Conclusion

This chapter mainly focused on the strategies LBG, PNB and BIG adopted to address the problem of NPLs. Their asset quality, financial progress, risk management system, and institutions' regulatory and supervisory response to manage the financial crisis due to GFC, Brexit, the COVID-19 pandemic, and the Russia-Ukraine war positively impacted NPLs management. A comparative picture of these FIs concluded that there are several similarities and dissimilarities in risk

[88] It's the annual interest payment made by the issuer of a bond to the bondholder until it reaches maturity.

[89] Reserve Bank of India (2023).

management systems. Respective governments and regulators took prompt action to salvage the banks from possible insolvency, particularly during the financial crisis.

The NPLs remained a cause of concern in LBG, PNB, and BIG, and the performance of LBG was relatively better than that of PNB and BIG. The reasons for higher NPLs in LBG and BIG were market dislocation and downturn after the GFC. These groups would have been on the verge of insolvencies if the respective governments had not taken prompt action. The bailout plan gave them an appetite and gradually improved their asset quality. Consequently, the government sold its stake in LBG and BIG in phases to recover the bailout amount, and finally, they became purely private entities.

The impact of the GFC on the PNB was insignificant due to the conservative approach of the Government of India, which restricted the bank from international financial market exposure, and most of the investment was in the domestic market. Thus, the Indian banks had limited direct exposure to the US mortgage market.[90] Despite this, the NPLs were highest in PNB mainly due to the macroeconomic and microeconomic determinants coupled with banking fraud, which sniffed off a huge amount of the bank's profit and resulted in a bailout package from the Government of India. Moreover, it has raised doubts over internal safety operations in financial firms.

These institutions have made robust mechanisms for mitigating the risk, and even LBG and BIG have developed a three-level risk management system. Moreover, the groups put sincere efforts to categorise the risk into credit, market, liquidity, and operation to regulatory and strategic and developed and implemented mitigation strategies accordingly. PNB focused on micro-level management of risks and adopted APMS, PMS, and PIRD, besides organising mega debt relief camps for wilful defaulters, *Gandhigiri* approach to put defaulters under pressure. Moreover, these FIs work in a strong regulatory and supervisory ecosystem with constant support and guidance from the regulators on capital adequacy so that banks remain liquid.

Despite all these mechanisms, financial crises and large banking fraud always loom over them and instantly percolate across the globe, jeopardising the robust mechanisms developed and implemented so far. The international expansion of the banking business has made them more vulnerable and risk-prone. Therefore, the system needs to be developed and made more watchful to identify the risks and resolve the issues at the branch level before they percolate across the branches and jurisdictions and turn into a national or global crisis. Critical assessment of bank/jurisdiction-specific macroeconomic and microeconomic (bank-specific) parameters at the policy level will contribute to ensuring financial stability. Finally, these case studies helped us understand the micro-management of risk and the efforts these institutions took to motivate the wilful defaulters to reduce the cases of NPLs/NPAs.

[90] Mukher (2023).

References

Bank of England (2015) The financial stability report of the UK. https://www.bankofengland.co.uk/-/media/boe/files/financial-stability-report/2015/december-2015.Pdf?la=en&hash=7D815F673187E150A4DB75159EBF82E991E332F. Accessed 11 Feb 2023

Bank of Ireland (2008) Annual report 2008. https://www.annualreports.com/HostedData/AnnualReportArchive/b/bank-of-ireland-group-plc_2008.pdf. Accessed 5 Feb 2023

Bank of Ireland (2010) Annual report 2010. https://www.annualreports.com/HostedData/AnnualReportArchive/b/bank-of-ireland-group-plc_2010.pdf. Accessed 5 Feb 2023

Bank of Ireland (2011) Annual report 2011. https://www.annualreports.com/HostedData/AnnualReportArchive/b/bank-of-ireland-group-plc_2011.pdf. Accessed 5 Feb 2023

Bank of Ireland (2012) Annual report 2012. https://investorrelations.Bankofireland.com/app/uploads/bank-of-ireland-annual-report-for-the-year-ended-31-december-2012.pdf. Accessed 7 Feb 2023

Bank of Ireland (2014) Annual report 2014. https://www.annualreports.co.uk/HostedData/AnnualReportArchive/b/bank-of-ireland-group-plc2014.pdf. Accessed 23 Apr 2023

Bank of Ireland (2020) Annual report 2020. https://www.annualreports.com/HostedData/AnnualReportArchive/b/bank-of-ireland-group-plc_2020.pdf. Accessed 5 Feb 2023

Bank of Ireland (2021) 2021 results announcement. https://investorrelations.bankofireland.com/app/uploads/Bank-of-Ireland-Investor-Presentation-Year-End-2021-March-2022.pdf. Accessed 25 July 2023

Bank of Ireland (2022) Bank of Ireland history. http://www.bankofireland.com/about-BIG-group/about-the-group/company-overview/BIG-history/. Accessed 21 Feb 2023

Bank of Ireland (2023) Bank of Ireland buys KBC's Irish assets in 5-billion-euro deal. Reuters, 22 October 2021. https://www.reuters.com/business/finance/bank-ireland-buys-kbcs-irish-assets-5-billion-euro-deal-2021-10-22/. Accessed 21 Feb 2023

BBC News (2013) Lloyds to sell Spanish retail division to Sabadell. BBC News, 19 April 2013. https://www.bbc.com/news/business-22335045. Accessed 11 Jan 2023

Bloomberg (2018) Bailout for scam-hit PNB: government to infuse Rs 2000 crore to help bond. Financial Express, 17 July 2018. https://www.financialexpress.com/industry/banking-finance/bailout-for-scam-hit-pnb-government-to-infuse-rs-2000-crore-to-help-bond-payment/1247885/. Accessed 16 Feb 2023

Boucher R (2013) Group chief executive review. Bank of Ireland annual report. https://www.annualreports.com/HostedData/AnnualReportArchive/b/bank-of-ireland-group-plc_2013.pdf. Accessed 6 Feb 2023

Brennan J (2022) State return on crisis-era bailout to Bank of Ireland now stands at €1.8bn so far. The Irish Times, 7 April 2022. https://www.irishtimes.com/business/financial-services/state-return-on-crisis-era-bailout-to-bank-of-ireland-now-stands-at-1-8bn-so-far-1.4847005. Accessed 9 Feb 2023

Brown SS (2022) Ireland: Credit Institution (Financial Support) Scheme, 2008. J Financ Crisis 4(4):214

Darling A (2011) Back from the brink: 1000 days at number. Atlantic Books, p 11

Dunkley E (2017) UK government sells remaining stake in Lloyds. Financial Express, London, 16 May 2017. https://www.ft.com/content/4fe7e528-8ef9-3382-aa26-51fed63e1422. Accessed 19 Feb 2023

Eichengreen E, Gupta P (2013) The financial crisis and Indian banks: survival of the fittest. J Int Money Financ 39:138. https://doi.org/10.1016/j.jimonfin.2013.06.022. Accessed 23 July 2023

English S (2000) Ireland Bank Buys Chase de Vere. The Telegraph, 29 July 2000

First Post (2018) PNB fraud: ED to seek immediate confiscation of Nirav Modi's assets under fugitive economic offenders' ordinance. First Post, 27 May 2018. https://www.firstpost.com/india/pnb-fraud-ed-to-seek-immediate-confiscation-of-nirav-modis-assets-under-fugitive-economic-offenders-ordinance-4484551.html. Accessed 21 Jan 2022

Garfield A (2000) Standard Chartered wins $1.3bn chase deal. Independent, 2 September 2000. https://www.independent.co.uk/news/business/news/standard-chartered-wins-1-3bn-chase-deal-700061.html. Accessed 30 Dec 2022

Gayathri S, Mangaiyarkarasi T (2018) A critical analysis of the Punjab National Bank scam and its implications. Int J Pure Appl Math 119:12. https://ssrn.com/abstract=3274568. Accessed 15 June 2023

Griffiths K (2009) Britain's banking crisis: how it happened. The Times, 3 October 2009. https://www.thetimes.co.uk/article/britains-banking-crisis-how-it-happened-tp9fbm0cm3m. Accessed 12 Jan 2023

Helgi Library (2019) Lloyds banking group-asset quality. Helgi Library, 22 December 2019. https://www.helgilibrary.com/charts/lloyds-banking-group-asset-quality/. Accessed 10 Jan 2023

Helm T, O'Carroll L, Browne M (2021) The growing Brexit threat to Ireland. The Guardian, 19 January 2021. https://www.theguardian.com/politics/2021/feb/07/the-growing-brexit-threat-to-ireland. Accessed 09 Feb 2023

Hindustan Times (2018) PNB gives CBI list of 150 fraudulent LoUs issued to Nirav Modi. Hindustan Times, 20 February 2018

Johnson S, Johnson S (2002) HBOS was 'finished' before Lloyds takeover. The Telegraph, 2 December 2002. https://www.telegraph.co.uk/news/uknews/scotland/6710682/HBOS-was-finished-before-Lloyds-takeover.html. Accessed 14 Jan 2023

Kennedy S (2009) UK government to take 43.4% in combined Lloyds, HBOS. Market Watch, 12 January 2009. https://www.marketwatch.com/story/uk-government-to-take-434-in-combined-lloydshbos-group. Accessed 15 Jan 2022

Kleinman M (2017) Lloyds free of taxpayer ownership as ministers sell final shares. Sky News, 17 May 2017. https://news.sky.com/story/lloyds-free-of-taxpayer-ownership-as-ministers-sell-final-shares-10880324. Accessed 15 Jan 2022

Lloyds Bank (2020) UK financial institutions show resilience despite COVID-19 and Brexit uncertainty. https://www.lloydsbankinggroup.com/media/press-releases/2020/Lloyds-bank/uk-financial–instituteons-show-resilience-despite-covid-19-and-brexit-uncertainty.html. Accessed 19 Feb 2023

Lloyds Banking Group (2008) Annual review. https://www.lloydsbankinggroup.com/assets/pdfs/investors/annual-report/2008-download-links/2008_lbg_annual_review.pdf. Accessed 20 Jan 2023

Lloyds Banking Group (2009) Annual report and accounts 2009. https://www.lloydsbankinggroup.com/assets/pdfs/investors/financial-performance/lloyds-banking-group-plc/2009/q4/2009-lbg-annual-report.pdf. Accessed 14 Jan 2022

Lloyds Banking Group (2012) Annual report and accounts 2012. https://www.lloydsbankinggroup.com/assets/pdfs/investors/financial-performance/lloyds-banking-group-plc/2012/q4/2012-lbg-annual-report.pdf. Accessed 24 Dec 2022

Lloyds Banking Group (2014) Annual report and accounts 2014

Lloyds Banking Group (2020) Annual report and accounts 2020. https://www.lloydsbanking-group.com/assets/pdfs/investors/financial-performance/lloyds-banking-group-plc/2020/q4/2020-lbg-annual-report.pdf. Accessed 24 December 2022

Lloyds Banking Group (2021a) ESG report 2021. https://www.lloydsbankinggroup.com/assets/pdfs/investors/financial-performance/lloyds-banking-group-plc/2021/q4/2021-lbg-esg-report.pd. Accessed 24 Dec 2022

Lloyds Banking Group (2021b) Annual report and accounts 2021. https://www.lloydsbanking-group.com/assets/pdfs/investors/financial-performance/lloyds-banking-group-plc/2021/q4/2021-lbg-annual-report.pdf. Accessed 24 Dec 2022

Lloyds Banking Group (2023) Annual report and accounts 2021. https://www.lloydsbanking-group.com/assets/pdfs/investors/annual-report/2023/2023-lbg-annual-review.pdf. Accessed 01 Nov 2024

Lloyds-TSB Group (2007) Annual report and accounts 2007. https://www.lloydsbankinggroup.com/assets/pdfs/investors/annual-report/2007-download-links/2007_ltsb_group_annual-report.pdf. Accessed 02 Jan 2023

Makortoff K (2021) Lloyds banking group records £2bn profit after pandemic slump. The Guardian, London, 19 July 2021. https://www.theguardian.com/business/2021/jul/29/lloyds-banking-group-records-2bn-profit-after-pandemic-slump. Accessed 19 July 2023

McCabe C (2011) Sins of the father: Tracing the decisions that shaped the Irish economy. History Press

McDonagh F (2020) Chief executive's review: Bank of Ireland, annual report. https://investorrelations.bankofireland.com/app/uploads/BIG-Annual-Report-2020.pdf. Accessed 21 Feb 2023

Miller H (1999) Lloyds TSB buys Scottish Widows. BBC, 23 June 1999. https://news.bbc.co.uk/2/hi/business/375807.stm. Accessed 30 Dec 2022

Molloy P (2009) Chairman's statement. Annual report of Bank of Ireland. para 2. https://investorrelations.bankofireland.com/app/uploads/Bank_of_Ireland_Annual_Report_20091.pdf. Accessed 22 Feb 2023

Mukher S (2023) Global financial crisis and its impact on India's growth. Economic Discussions. https://www.economicsdiscussion.net/india/global-financial-crisis/global-financial-crisis-and-its-impact-on-indias-growth/10947. Accessed 22 Dec 2023

Muthalaly P (2020) A detail study on PNB scam. iPleaders. https://blog.ipleaders.in/detailed-study-pnb-. Accessed 5 Feb 2023

New York Times (1995) Lloyds bank to merge with TSB. New York Times, 12 October 1995

O'Carroll L (2010) Ireland bailout: Full Irish government statement. The Guardian, 28 November 2010. https://www.theguardian.com/business/ireland-business-blog-with-lisa-ocarroll/2010/nov/28/Irelandbailoutv-fullgovernment-statement. Accessed 15 Feb 2023

OECD (2021) The COVID-19 crisis and banking system resilience: simulation of losses on non-performing loans and policy implications. https://www.oecd.org/daf/fin/financial-markets/COVID-19-crisis-and-banking-system-resilience.pdf

Osborne H (2005) Britannia to acquire Bristol and West. The Guardian, 24 May 2005

Pandey M (2018) PNB scam: CBI to file charge sheet against 19 accused by May 1. NDTV, 2 May 2018

Punjab National Bank (2008–2009) Annual report 2008-09. https://www.pnbindia.in/document/annual-report/PiNB-AR.pd. Accessed 25 Jan 2023

Punjab National Bank (2015–2016) Annual report 2015-16. https://www.pnbindia.in/document/annual-report/PNBAnnualReport_2015_16_Final.pdf. Accessed 10 Aug 2023

Punjab National Bank (2018) Annual report 2017-18. https://www.pnbindia.in/document/annual-report/PNB%20Annual%20Report%202017-18%20(Full%20Version).pdf. Accessed 22 July 2023

Punjab National Bank (2020) Annual report 2019-20. https://www.pnbindia.in/downloadprocess.aspx?fid=hV/u/IBzVrSwn93cTHHINQ. Accessed 22 July 2023

Punjab National Bank (2022) Annual report 2021-22. https://www.pnbindia.in/downloadprocess.aspx?Fid=HNTIUlp6rNODKVPR72kDPg==. Accessed 22 July 2023

Punjab National Bank (2024) Annual report 2023-24. https://www.pnbindia.in/downloadprocess.aspx?fid=RxfEXRrMDOblDj4cPhDLDQ==. Accessed 02 Nov 2024

Reuters (2018) RBI and other agencies missed warning signs, failed to detect Rs 12,700-cr Punjab National Bank Fraud, Reuters London. https://www.firstpost.com/business/rbi-and-other-agencies-missed-warning-signs-failed-to-detect-rs-12700-cr-punjab-national-bank-fraud-4378061.html. Accessed 25 January 2023

Reuters (2021) Bank of Ireland Buys KBC's Irish Assets in 5 Billion Euro Deal, Reuters Dublin 22 October. https://www.reuters.com/business/finance/bank-ireland-buys-kbcs-irish-assets-5-billion-euro-deal-2021-10-22/. Accessed 21 February 2023

RBI (2023) Revisions to Basel II-advanced approaches of operational risk-TSA and AMA, 16 June 2023. https://www.rbi.org.in/Scripts/NotificationUser.aspx?Id=9285. Accessed 16 Feb 2023

Reid D (2002) Bank of Ireland AM moves into US by buying Iridian. IPE Magazine, 16 April 2002. https://www.ipe.com/bank-of-ireland-am-moves-into-us-by-buying-iridian/5421.article. Accessed 21 Feb 2023

Reuters (2012) Lloyds mulling St James's Place stake sale: Report. Reuters, 12 November 2012. https://www.reuters.com/article/us-lloyds-idUSBRE8A308120121104. Accessed 10 Jan 2023

Robert P (2009) Leading questions: Sir Victor Blank. BBC, 22 August 2009. https://news.bbc.co.uk/2/hi/business/8214677.stm. Accessed 14 Jan 2022

Scuffham M (2013) Lloyds shares hit three-year high as state considers stake sale. Reuters, 10 September 2013. https://www.reuters.com/article/uk-lloyds-shares-idUKBRE98909820130910. Accessed 11 Jan 2023

Sharp S (2009) The Herald, 12 October 2009. https://www.heraldscotland.com/default_content/12609246.taxpayer-loss-rbs-lloyds-bail-outs//. Accessed 14 Jan 2023

Tandon P (1989) Banking century: a short history of banking in India and the pioneer Punjab National Bank. Penguin

The Economic Times (2018) PNB will honour commitments to banks in LOU case. The Economic Times, 28 March 2018. https://economictimes.indiatimes.com/industry/banking/finance/banking/pnb-will-honour-commitments-to-banks-in-lou-case/articleshow/63497672.cms. Accessed 22 Jan 2023

The Hindu (2021) PNB-Nirav Modi case chronology of events, 24 February 2021. PTI. https://www.thehindu.com/news/national/pnb-nirav-modi-case-chronology-of-events/article33932484.ece. Accessed 5 Feb 2022

The Irish Times (2009) Bank of Ireland draws down recapitalisation funds. The Irish Times, 31 March 2009. https://www.irishtimes.com/news/bank-of-ireland-draws-down-recapitalisation-funds-1.838413. Accessed 04 Feb 2023

The Telegraph (2002) Lloyds shares tumble as HBOS slumps to £10bn Loss. The Telegraph, 02 December 2002. https://www.telegraph.co.uk/finance/newsbysector/banksandfinance/4612681/Lloyds-shares-tumble-as-HBOS-slumps-to-10bn-loss.html. Accessed 14 Jan 2002

The Times of India (2019) Government unveils mega bank mergers to revive growth from 5-year law. The Times of India, 30 August 2019. https://timesofindia.indiatimes.com/business/india-business/government-unveils-mega-bank-mergers-to-revive-growth-from-5-year-low/articleshow/70911359.cms. Accessed 21 Jan 2023

Turnell S (2009) Fiery dragons: banks, moneylenders, and microfinance in Burma. NIAS Press

Warner J (2009) Why Lloyds gave-up (sic) opportunity to withdraw from disastrous HBOS deal. The Telegraph, 29 November 2009

Chapter 7
Non-Performing Loans in Post-COCID-19 Scenario: Impact on Survival, Repair, and Reconstruct

7.1 Introduction

LBG, PNB, and BIG were on the verge of recovering from the impact of the GFC, with substantial qualitative and quantitative improvements in their credit position. However, an unexpected outbreak of the COVID-19 pandemic severely impacted the global economies and placed them on the threshold of an economic downturn. The waves of COVID-19 followed one after another, and governments issued several guidelines to combat the spread of the Coronavirus and imposed a lockdown to restrict people's movement, which kept the economy at a standstill with adverse consequences.[1] The jurisdictions adopted several measures, including temporary regulatory forbearance, to mitigate the economic impact of high debt levels.[2] The COVID-19 pandemic significantly affected corporate earnings and employment rates, increasing the debt burden on corporations, SMEs, and individual borrowers, ultimately contributing to increased NPLs. Under such circumstance, the banks were reluctant to lend to borrowers suffering a balance sheet imbalance.

Jurisdictions across the globe adopted social and economic mitigation strategies to reduce the impact of the COVID-19 pandemic. The banks were expected to play a vital role in absorbing the shocks of the pandemic, particularly ensuring the supply of funding to run economic activities. The Governments and the Central Banks took several policy interventions, including announcing a limited-period moratorium and relaxing norms for using buffer capital, reducing the CRR and ensuring the flow of credit for individuals and businesses to minimise the impact of COVID-19.

Therefore, the present chapter compares the impact of the COVID-19 pandemic with the GFC and analyses their similarities and dissimilarities. The chapter also

[1] Young and Kwanho (2021).

[2] Acharya and Steffen (2020), p. 430.

A. Dimri, *Non-Performing Loans*, Ius Gentium: Comparative Perspectives on Law and Justice 125, https://doi.org/10.1007/978-3-031-92952-6_7

critically assesses the impact of COVID-19 on the NPLs, besides briefly presenting the situation across the globe. The chapter also examined how survival, repair and reconstruction remained the top agenda during the pandemic and post-pandemic to avoid its long-term impact. Therefore, the chapter critically examines these jurisdictions' initiatives to ensure financial stability and avert a new financial crisis by controlling the NPLs.

7.2 Comparative Analysis of COVID-19 Vs GFC-2007-09

High NPLs were common in many banks struggling with economic and financial crises that continued due to depressed credit growth and delayed recovery. The level of NPLs peaked in several jurisdictions after the GFC in 2008–09. The COVID-19 outbreak triggered across the globe, and due to this outbreak, jurisdictions faced many challenges, be it health, economy, travel restrictions, and many more. One of the major concerns was the severity of the impact of the pandemic on the NPLs and the bank balance sheet.[3] Some structural problems in the financial sector caused the GFC in 2008. The spread of coronavirus closed economies to each other by restricting the movement to stop the contagion. During the pandemic, de-globalisation was making countries close their borders, movement of people, Airlines, etc. This global war-like situation resulted in a contraction in the economies worldwide.[3]

The COVID-19 crisis was different and more serious than the GFC, affecting the market. GFC was an endogenous crisis caused by market participants who doubted the banks' balance sheets. However, COVID-19 could become 'an endogenous crisis if the financial market participants lose their confidence'.[4] It is also important because the past crisis had a carry-over effect on the present crisis, mainly on the economic losses. The restoration of the confidence of market participants under such circumstances was essential. COVID-19 differed from the GFC as it did not start with a credit boom in the financial system like the GFC. It followed a period of slight credit contraction, resulting in increased debt in some jurisdictions. Many banks that lent to borrowers suffered loan losses and high NPLs.[1] Therefore, the unresolved NPLs are likely to derail the post-COVID-19 economic recovery. The financial position of jurisdictions just before the outbreak of COVID-19 was much more robust. The Euro area Jurisdictions had 16.5% CET of their RWAs, which was 8.8% in 2008.[5]

These crises originated in two leading economies of the world, the GFC in the USA and the COVID-19 pandemic in China, spreading across the globe and creating chaos and uncertainty.[6] The COVID-19 pandemic put many economic activities

[3] Zongyun et al. (2022), p. 2427.

[4] Danielsson and Shin (2002).

[5] ECB (2021).

[6] Kahn (2020).

on hold, and the uncertainty index calculated by the IMF remained at its peak in most jurisdictions, like the USA, China, the UK, and India.[7] Therefore, during the COVID-19 pandemic, the contraction speed was very high. The IMF report presented that the rate of contraction was higher in the GFC than in COVID-19, which resulted from the high saving ratio, and the interest rate was significantly lower.[7]

Figure 7.1 presents the relationship between uncertainty, collapse and reaction during the GFC and COVID-19. In both crises, there was uncertainty all around, which led to a market downturn (collapse) and ultimately resulted in an immediate sovereign reaction to provide relief to the banks and businesses by injecting liquidity. In both crises, the stock exchanges of major countries had analogous trends and dropped drastically. Moreover, global recessions have been the largest since the Great Depression of the 1930s. The reaction to both crises was immediate regarding sovereign support to provide relief, avoid possible downturns, and enact better regulations to minimise the effect on FIs and jurisdictions (see Fig. 7.1).[7]

COVID-19 has presented a significant risk to the earning prospects of businesses in both advanced and emerging markets.[1] The economic recession and weak bank risk management were responsible for high NPLs because they impacted the lenders. The critics argued that high NPLs in advanced economies limited access to wholesale funding, resulting in limited funds to pump into emerging market economies.[8] Moreover, uncertainty and information asymmetry in the international credit market also aggravated external credit constraints. Therefore, the local bank faced the credit constraint problem, adversely impacting lending and profit yield.[8]

The banks involved in international lending strengthened their scrutiny while lending to high NPLs jurisdictions.[8] The OECD report emphasised that the impact

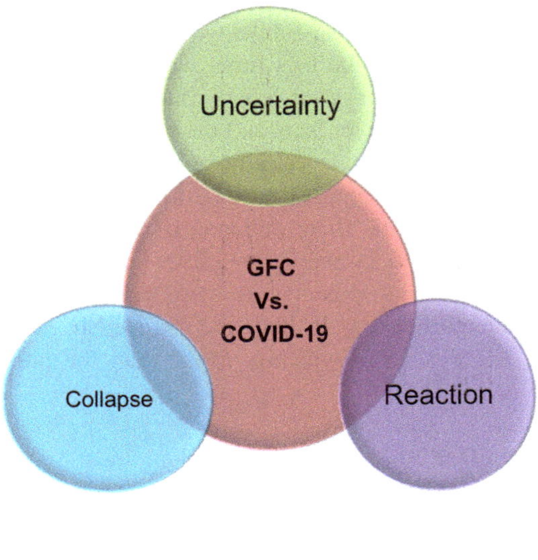

Fig. 7.1 GFC Vs. COVID-19. Source: Developed by the researcher based on information available in Kahn (2020)

[7] Ahir et al. (2020).

[8] Adrian and Shin (2010), p. 418.

of the pandemic would badly hit the global recession much deeper than the great depression.[9] The banks' capital buffer stock and liquidity position were relatively stronger during COVID-19 than in the previous crisis. The impact of the GFC remains so cascading that some countries still experience low valuations, low profitability and high NPLs.[9]

COVID-19 even raises challenges to the capital of certain banks, even though they entered the crisis with a higher capital ratio than the GFC. Moreover, some jurisdictions adopted strong fiscal policy interventions to contain the economic fallout from the current crisis.[10] COVID-19 could increase uncertainty and lower profit expectations, delaying the jurisdictions' transformation plans. More importantly, it could also help accelerate changes in the banking sector. The global NPL market developed after the GFC, and substantial market participants are currently active in dealing with distressed assets.[10] The impact of these crises was rigorous on the financial sector and banking business, and handling the GFC was a learning lesson; banks were better prepared to deal with the COVID-19 crisis.[5]

7.3 Impact of COVID-19: A Global Scenario

COVID-19 has severely impacted advanced and emerging economies, resulting in an enormous loss in the financial markets during the pandemic.[9] In fact, investors' sentiment was at an all-time low, and it even became evident how difficult it would be for banks to maintain good asset quality and earnings.[11] Due to the shutdowns, there has been an income slowdown, and many loan repayments, especially in Europe and the United States, have stopped, leaving the banks dry,[12] increasing the NPL ratios. Central Banks worldwide proactively intervened to calm the markets, and it was for the first time during the COVID-19 pandemic that the US federal government cut down federal rates by 50 basis points. The US treasury bond markets, corporate markets and money funds were affected the most. Federal purchase of bonds helps to reserve the outflows, especially for the most vulnerable funds, and the liquidity support transmited to the real economy through such funds.[13] On the other hand, the Bank of Japan issued a statement announcing that it would inject liquidity into the market by increasing the purchase of assets.[13]

Contrary to expectation, there were large reductions in bankruptcies in the eurozone, particularly in Italy and France[14] In Belgium, the number of insolvencies in 2020 was 25%, typically lower than the previous year. Similarly, in Spain and

[9] OECD (2020), p. 2.

[10] IMF (2020).

[11] Perwej (2020), p. 3987.

[12] Ivanov (2020).

[13] Falato et al. (2021), p. 2023.

[14] Haynes et al. (2021).

Germany, it reduced by 15%; in the USA, it was 10% lower than last year.[14] In some countries, restrictions were not so strong; as a result, there was an increase in insolvency cases. One such example is Sweden, where bankruptcy increased by 6.5% because of poor enforcement of banking and capital market operations restrictions.[15] The pandemic in developing countries resulted in a complex set of simultaneous outcomes, including a mass default of loans and recovery becoming complex and harder.[15] During the crisis, loan repayment became difficult, loanable funds substantially decreased, and new investment demand remained stressed.[15] The jurisdictions took many short-term and long-term measures for loan restructuring, as presented in Fig. 7.2.

The central banks adjusted the bank rate to control the available funds in the market for individual and business needs. However, such adjustments sometimes adversely impact the banks' performance. The high level of NPLs is a common feature of the banking crisis and can harm the global banking system during the pandemic.[16] Moreover, the deep recession associated with COVID-19 can lead to high NPLs and even weaken the bank balance sheets.[16]

The EU considers that two indicators, including CET1 and NPLs coverage ratios,[17] are essential to assess the impact of the pandemic. The CET ratio in most

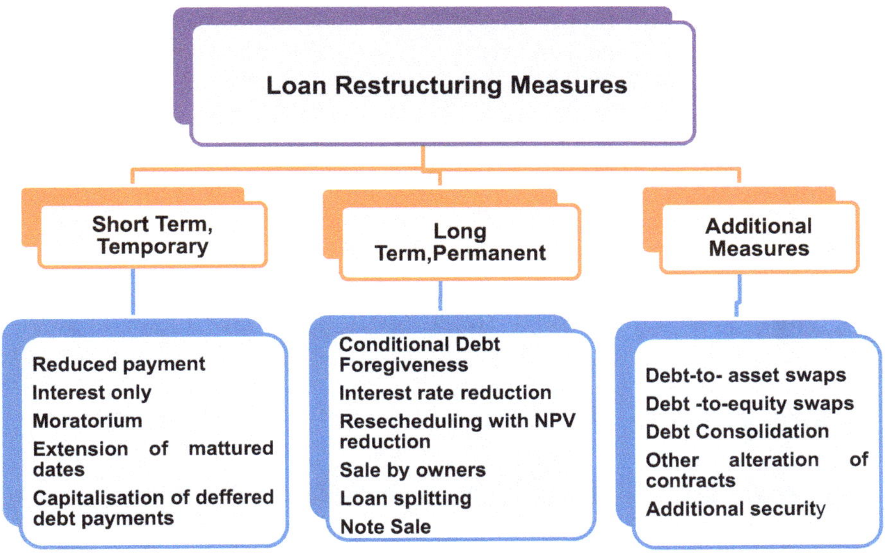

Fig. 7.2 Loan restructuring measures. Source: Adaptation from Handbook for MSME NPLs Management and Workout, IMF

[15] Segot and Leoni (2013), p. 4574.

[16] Kunt et al. (2020).

[17] NPL coverage ratio is the ratio between the provisions for loan losses recorded by the banks and the portfolio of NPLs on their books.

EU jurisdictions was high on the eve of the COVID-19 pandemic. Although the pandemic has reduced borrowers' repayment capacity, the average NPLs coverage ratio remained stable across the EU, with a marginal decline in France and Germany and an increase in the Netherlands, Sweden, and Poland.

In Japan, the FSA introduced more forward-looking provisions for Japanese banks that were well-capitalised to absorb potential losses and could swiftly deal with the future NPLs problem. In Italy, moratoria and state guarantees effectively contained the rise in NPLs despite a moderate marginal increase, which would delay the impact of the deterioration in economic activity on credit quality. Austria adopted complementary micro and macro-prudential policies, levelling NPLs from 8% to 2% in 2019.[5] Moreover, due to effective measures, the NPLs during COVID-19 remained stable and even decreased in some jurisdictions (Fig. 7.3). Our analysis shows that the jurisdictions successfully attained the stated objective during COVID-19.

7.4 United Kingdom Response to COVID-19 Pandemic

The jurisdictions adopted traditional and new approaches to deal with possible emergent crises. Government guarantees, moratoriums, extension of maturity dates, capitalisation, and deferred debt payments remained prevalent practices during the COVID-19 pandemic.[18] The UK also took several initiatives during the COVID-19

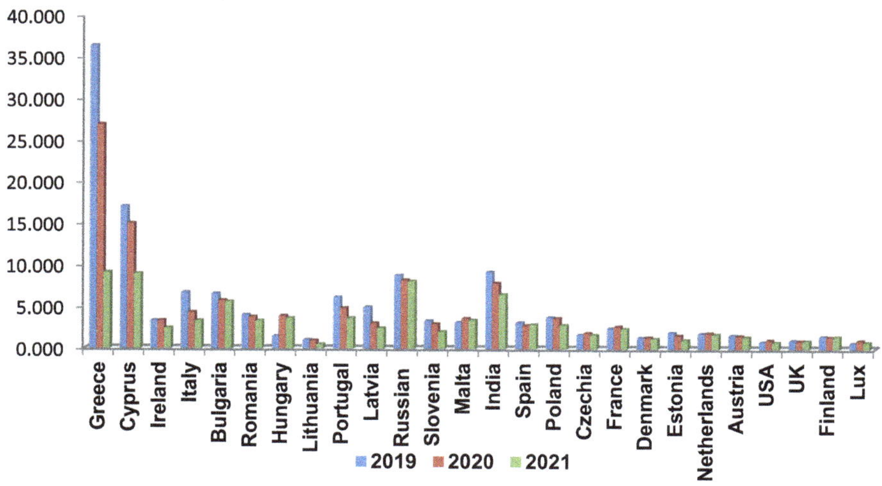

Fig. 7.3 NPL ratios in major jurisdictions during COVID-19. Source: Developed by the researcher using data from the World Development Indicators, World Bank

[18] Berger and Kunt (2021).

pandemic to relieve businesses and banks from the most unanticipated, extensive, and widespread exogenous all-time economic shock.[18] The response of the UK government to the COVID-19 crisis immediately after the first lockdown was unprecedented, and it introduced guaranteed loan schemes for financing SMEs and large businesses. The UK aimed to design CBILS and the BBLS to support business capitalisation.[19] In addition, the UK also launched the CLBILS and Future Fund Schemes (FFS). The schemes were so successful that 92.5% of loan applications backed by the UK government loan guarantee increased the UK contingent liability by £80 billion on its COVID-19 loan guarantee.[20]

Although the loan guarantee schemes would greatly save the SMEs, they have also created a potential risk to HMT if the loans become non-payment defaults. The loan guarantee schemes did not follow the due diligence process for approving BBLS loan applications. Moreover, these loans skewed towards micro and non-employing businesses, and thus, government support targets included the disadvantaged sectors and regions of the country. Critics argued that a generous loan guarantee scheme has never been available in the history of the UK. It would undoubtedly increase the default cases in the future, and the immediate burden would be on the country's taxpayers.

Nevertheless, many smaller firms would have failed without these schemes owing to the cash crunch. These schemes proved vital and helped many firms in the UK to rescue from possible insolvencies and bankruptcies. Thus, these schemes provided funding liberty to the business and helped the banks continue lending under government guarantee to pump money into the market so that the economy kept rolling in crisis.[20] However, it would certainly increase bad debts in the future. CBILS, CLBILS, and BBLS closed the application on 31 March 2021, and Figs. 7.4 and 7.5 present the status of scheme-wise loan applications that received approval and loan value under the guarantee scheme.[20]

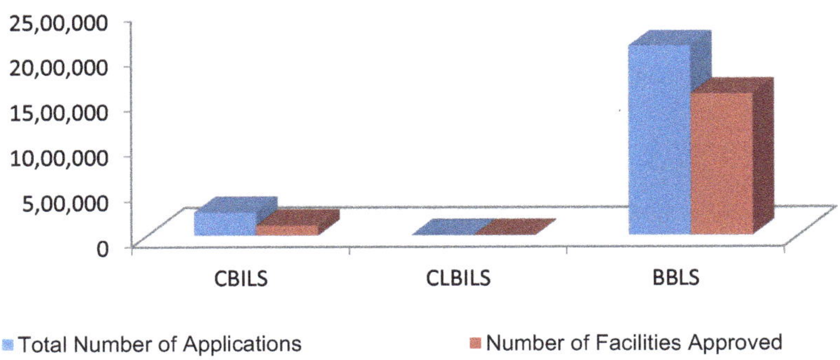

Fig. 7.4 COVID-19 guarantee schemes: status of applications. Source: Developed by the researcher based on the data available on HMT website

[19] Calabrese et al. (2021).

[20] HMT (2022a, b).

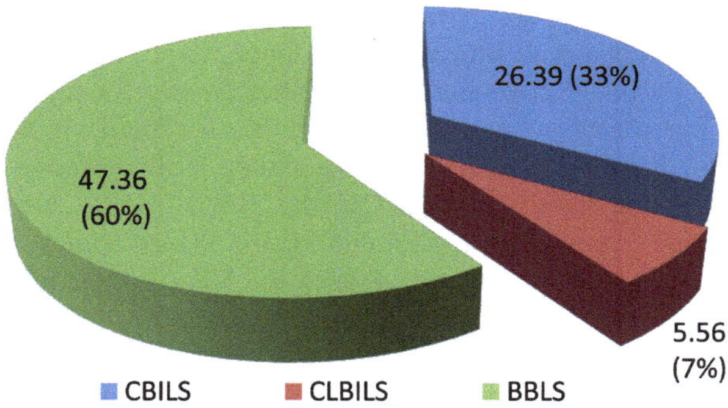

Fig. 7.5 Approved loan value under various guarantee schemes(£bn). Source: Developed by the researcher based on the data available on HMT website

Table 7.1 Status of the COVID-19 government support scheme (%)

Status of the schemes	Total	CBILS	CLBILS	BBLS
On schedule	78.8	78.7	73.1	78.1
Loan fully paid	7.4	18.1	26	6.7
Arrears	7.0	1.3	0.3	7.4
Default	3.8	0.9	0.0	4.0
Claimed	3.0	0.5	0.0	3.2
Settled	0.6	0.5	0.6	0.7

Source: HMT Website. https://www.gov.uk/government/publications/covid-19-loan-guarantee-schemes-repayment-data-as-at-31-march-2022 (accessed 4 March 2023)

As explained, BBLS launched with a 100% government guarantee, and CBILS with 80% indicates that if customers default, the government will cover the bank losses. Although the banks prepared a code of conduct for pursuing businesses that default on the taxpayer, 40% to 80% of businesses are expected to default on their bounce-back loans, and about 10% to 15% may be fraudulent applications.[21] However, information on the HMT website presents a different picture than expected. The total default as of 31 March 2022 was 3.8%, with the highest in BBLS, which seems to be the most vulnerable scheme. The scheduled repayment of 78.8% also appears to be on the expected line, which has marginal variation across the schemes. Nonetheless, these schemes provided respite to businesses to recover from the pandemic (see Table 7.1).

The situation has seen a marked improvement, as indicated by updated data from the HMT website in July 2022. Over 94% of Coronavirus Business Interruption Loan Scheme (CBILS) facilities are either fully repaid or on schedule, reflecting a decrease in delayed payments, now at 69%, down from 78%. Only about 1.5% of these loans are currently in arrears, and 1.3% are in default. So far, the government guarantee has been claimed for just 1.9% of the total CBILS loans. Similarly, under

[21] Makortoff (2020).

the Coronavirus Large Business Interruption Loan Scheme (CLBILS), over 98% of facilities are either fully repaid or on schedule, with less than 1% in arrears and less than 1% in default. The government guarantee has been utilised for less than 1% of the total CLBILS loans. Regarding Bounce Back Loans (BBLs), 79% of the facilities are either fully repaid or on schedule, with 7% in arrears and 2% in default. This has limited the government guarantee claims to less than 9% of the total BBLs. These figures indicate that the loan schemes have been largely successful, effectively countering initial concerns about potential taxpayer liability.

Moreover, the UK's leading banks, Barclays, NatWest, HSBC, and Lloyds, used LLP during the early COVID-19 pandemic to smoothen their income. It is an option that directly and immediately affects the bank's profit,[21] and many banks may use LLP to minimise the variation in income under several contexts.[22] Under LLP, banks must set aside an amount of money to mitigate the expected credit loss.[23] The impact of COVID-19 prompted UK banks to use LLP as an effective instrument against possible impacts on their earnings. A research study analysing LLP and PBT concludes a positive and negative relationship between the two variables and their impact on income smoothing.[24]

Ozili (2021) concluded that LLP was highest once the pandemic peaked and started declining subsequently. It also established a positive relationship between LLP and pre-provision earnings in pre-pandemic and pandemic quarters and found a stronger relationship during the pandemic. The income smoothing was also higher during the pandemic quarters, with a strong positive correlation.[23] The UK relaxed its regulatory and supervisory rules to support the banks in mitigating the negative effects of the pandemic on banks' balance sheets to avoid a possible increase in forbearance cases. However, the author argued that regulatory exemption might adversely affect the earning prospects of the bank, and a balance needs to be maintained while providing help to cope with the pandemic losses.

The impact of COVID-19 on the UK economy was enormous, and it became difficult to achieve a growth projection of 4.9%[25] BoE also took various steps to support and ensure a suitable environment for the business to develop, including access to low-interest loans, a moratorium for those entities struggling to repay the debts and a reduction in the base rate from 0.75% to 0.25%. With these efforts, the borrowing costs would be minimal for businesses and households.[25] The impact of the crisis was also visible on government bonds because the bond market deteriorated in the UK. Such a situation prompted the government to extend the Asset Purchase Facility (APF) as a contingent measure to purchase and hold government bonds amounting to £200 billion, ensuring that the markets for the UK government bonds continued to function.[25]

---

[22] Kim et al. (2019).

[23] Ozili and Outa (2017), p. 144.

[24] Ozili (2021).

[25] IMF (2021).

The UK's domestic risk to financial stability has returned to the pre-COVID-19 level, and the banks' capital and liquidity ratio has also remained much more potent and able to support business. The banks' ratios increased in 2021, and the CET1 ratio now stands at 16.5%, 1.7% points higher than before the pandemic affected the UK banking sector. This increase was due to the reduction in RWA, which offset the impact of accruals for future disturbances and the banks' leverage ratio remained at 5.7%. Banks have even held around 1.5 times the liquid asset buffer to meet the severe 30-day stressed outflows underlying the LCR.[26] The asset quality remained stable and even supported the economic recovery.

Consequently, FPC increased the UK Countercyclical Capital Buffer from 0.5% to 1%. The FPC even conducted a desk-based Solvency Stress Test (SST) to see the effects of the COVID-19 crisis on the UK banks and concluded that usable buffers of the capital built up by the banks could absorb the losses under a feasible illustrative scenario.[26] However, with the support of the government lending guarantee scheme, the corporate sector was able to finance its cash flow needs. The FPC argued that it was best in the banks' interest to extend such lending to support the economy and help to avoid credit losses.[27]

The government has taken several initiatives to mitigate the problems arising from COVID-19 in the banking sector. The government and the FCA encouraged the banks and building societies to offer leniency and lifted the regulatory burden.[28] Several supervisory and policy measures helped UK businesses and households to bridge the economic disruptions due to the COVID-19 pandemic. The designed regulatory standards are supported to maintain financial stability, ensure the safety and soundness of the firms, and ensure that the customers are adequately protected.[29] The latest reports on financial stability suggest that the UK has returned to the path of recovery, particularly in the domestic market, and the stress of the COVID-19 crisis will be wiped out entirely in the coming time. However, UK banks need to closely monitor the quality of their assets to identify possible deterioration, particularly in the riskier segments, to manage NPLs from the balance sheet. Ultimately, efficient solutions for dealing with NPLs would help banks focus on supporting the future productive output of the real economy.[30] The UK maintained NPLs at around 1% during COVID-19; it was 1.01% in 2019, 0.98% in 2020 and 0.969% in 2021 and 0.974% in 2022.

---

[26] BOE (2021).

[27] Giese and Haldane (2020), p. 200.

[28] Shearer and Tetlow (2021).

[29] Hill et al. (2021).

[30] OECD (2021).

7.5 Indian Response to COVID-19

Due to the adverse effects of the COVID-19 pandemic and the burden of lockdown, major sectors of the Indian economy, including manufacturing, auto, retail, aviation, hospitality, etc., were dribbled down.[30] The Indian economy was already experiencing a downturn before the pandemic, with the increasing trend of unemployment and poverty.[31] Therefore, India had challenges in dealing with the new crisis when the pandemic hit India in March 2020. The pandemic severely affected all sectors of the Indian economy; agriculture suffered from the supply chain, and production was at a halt in micro-enterprises and SMEs. A large-scale reverse labour migration to the rural areas due to the shutdown of economic operations further aggravated the problem, and the crisis led to a loss of employment to the tune of at least 15 million.[31] The increasing unemployment, job cuts, and reverse migration considerably reduced the loan repayment capacity.[32] The banking and non-banking FIs had limited lending resources due to poor cash flow during the pandemic.[33]

Therefore, the government of India and the RBI have introduced various economic, fiscal, and regulatory stimulus measures to fight the COVID-19 crisis, mainly focusing on liquidity, credit risk, and the well-being of its employees, along with the quality of financial reporting and disclosures. The RBI measures are intended to give some relief to lending institutions in the areas of liquidity, regulation and supervision, and financial markets. RBI even announced specific regulatory measures to overcome the pandemic disruptions by forming provisions and asset classification norms. RBI announced that it would provide relaxation in debt repayment and even help to improve access to working capital management. RBI also focuses on preventing financial stress for business owners so that they can continue their business in a favourable environment.[32]

RBI introduced credit enhancement schemes and loan moratoriums to reduce the effects of COVID-19.[34] The RBI announced a loan moratorium period of three months for all types of loans, with its applicability to all banking and non-banking organisations, and extended it for another period of three months. In addition to the above fiscal policy measures to save FIs and businesses, the RBI also introduced a CD and overdraft scheme.[34] However, to recover the interest, banks were permitted at their prudence to convert it into a funded interest term loan (FITL) to be payable before 31 March 2021.[34] In FITL, FI lends a loan to repay the loan, which helps to reduce NPLs. However, all accounts that got loans under FITL were subject to supervisory review for their justifiability due to the fallout from COVID-19.

The Monetary Policy Committee (MPC) focused on negating the effect of COVID-19, reviving growth, and ensuring financial stability. It also ensured enough liquidity in the market by reducing the CRR to 4%. The government and the RBI

[31] Ramakumar and Kanitkar (2020), p. 3.

[32] Bobade and Alex (2020).

[33] Poon et al. (1999).

[34] Mohan (2021).

worked in tandem and increased the limits on the advances for the central and state governments to ensure smooth spending. In addition, RBI also purchased about 30% (₹1.2 lakh crores) of the government's net market borrowings during 2021–22 and committed to purchasing the same in the future under the G-SAP acquisition programme.[35]

RBI issued regulatory guidelines for rescheduling payments for term loans and working capital facilities, easing working capital financing, and exempting them from the SMA and NPAs classification. In addition, CCyB also remained inactive until 31st April 2021, and the Central Bank kept implementing an asset classification standstill for NPA accounts until May 2020.[36] All these measures ensured the availability of sufficient liquidity for individuals and businesses to move forward to generate employment and income avenues.

The Central Bank also relaxed SCB to hold an additional provision of 20% if a resolution plan remains unimplemented within 210 days from the declaration of default under the prudential framework for resolving stressed assets. RBI realised that meeting such a target in the challenging environment would be difficult, so it extended the submission of the resolution plan for 90 days, with further extension subject to review and continuation of stress asset challenges. RBI also reduced the requirement of NSFR to 80%, intending to restore the same to its original position in 2021 in a phased manner, increasing it by 10% yearly.

In addition, the RBI also introduced operation twist (OT) and open market operations (OMS), simultaneously buying the government's long-term bonds, and selling short-term securities to reduce the yield of short-term securities.[37] The purpose of the OMS was to regulate liquidity in the market, so to inject liquidity into the market, it will buy the government securities, and to curb the same, it would sell them to manage the yield curve. It is an Indian version of OT. The US Federal Reserve used it successfully in 1961 and 2011 after the GFC to lift the economy from recession.[34] RBI also provided substantial funds for long-term Repo Operations (LTROs) for one to three years for business revival. Moreover, limited liquidity was also made available under the Standing Liquidity Facility for the liquidity management of SPDs. RBI reduced CRR by 100 basis points to 3% and increased the Statutory Liquidity Ratio (SLR) from 2% to 3%.

The RBI policy and regulatory responses to COVID-19 were quite impressive, and the Government and RBI were closely monitoring the global development and calibrating them depending on the intensity of the COVID-19 impact.[38] The experience learnt from the past crisis also made them robust and enabled the crafting of flexible systems for helping COVID-19-stressed borrowers.[38] RBI implemented various NPLs resolution plans, including rescheduling the payments, converting any interest accrued or to be accrued into other credit facilities and granting a

[35] Reserve Bank of India (2021).

[36] Reserve Bank of India (February 27 2023).

[37] Mathew (2020).

[38] Rao (2022).

moratorium based on an assessment of the borrower's income stream for two years. It also constituted a special committee of banking experts to arrive at the sector-specific benchmark.[34] The banks faced various challenges while implementing the resolution, such as establishing viability under these circumstances and managing the expectations, which was also an arduous task for the banks.

These measures provided regulatory relief to FIs in terms of their access to liquidity and regulatory forbearance to protect the balance sheets. These measures protected borrowers from financial distress and provided liquidity to banks and businesses during the pandemic. The RBI achieved its objective of keeping the financial market sound, liquid, and smooth and ensuring financial stability despite the initial downturn. The RBI efforts were largely successful, and such a large liquidity injection (3% of GDP) helped the system to move forward. Despite all these efforts, the credit growth in most of the sector struggled to capture movement except in small and medium-scale enterprises; nevertheless, the challenges for financial stability still exist.[34]

Thus, the gross NPAs to gross advances were 7.30% in 2020–21, reduced to 5.8% in 2021–22 and further reduced to 3.90% in 2022–23. Similarly, there was a reduction in net NPLs from 2.4% to 1.7% and 0.9% in 2022–23.[39] Comparing the figure with pre-COVID ratios, the GNPAs and NPAs were 11.20% and 8.20%, respectively. However, when looking at their deteriorating asset quality, some banks' gross NPAs still show disturbing and stressful situations that worry the RBI and policymakers.[40] Although there was a reduction in the NPA ratios, the situation in some banks was alarming and required policy and regulatory interventions.[40] The accumulated NPAs would become a burden and a hindrance to the sound functioning of the banking system, which would even affect the banks' efficiency and the quality of the assets.[41] Thus, after the COVID-19-induced uncertainty, the asset quality could also deteriorate in the coming years, which is not a good sign for the Indian banking system.[42] However, the banking sector assessment was quite encouraging, and according to the RBI, the situation seems to be stabilising. Despite such improvement, there is a long way to go, and the jurisdiction must implement new policies and regulatory measures to keep our financial system and the economy strong.

---

[39] RBI (2022a, b, 2023), pp. 60, 56.

[40] Goswami (2023).

[41] Batra (2003).

[42] Goswami (2021), pp. 1–2.

7.6 Irish Response to COVID-19

The COVID-19 pandemic also posed a severe threat to the economy of Ireland, and businesses around the state suffered a lot and threatened the banking sector and FIs. The UK's decision to leave the EU has aggravated this problem because the trading relationship between the UK and the EU remains uncertain. The CBI has initiated several actions to mitigate the provisions of cross-border financial services between the EU and the UK. The pandemic has disrupted economic activities, and Brexit has intensified the downside risks to the overall economic outlook. The Irish banks have significant lending to the UK, particularly in retail banking, and Brexit will undoubtedly affect the balance sheet.[43] Due to the impact of the crisis, liquidity problems may arise for businesses and households and significantly influence the vulnerable property and CRE market in Ireland.

The Irish Government responded to the crisis by taking measures to help struggling businesses and protect customers' interests[44] Considering the seriousness of the impact of the pandemic, the CBI shifted its priorities towards dealing with the immediate and long-term implications of COVID-19 on the economy, financial system, and consumers. Under such circumstances, the Central Bank even worked with the Department of Finance and NTMA to tackle the COVID-19 crisis with the support of the Financial Stability Group (FSG). This management group was involved in coordinating the inter-agency work on the impact of COVID-19.

In addition, the ECB has also introduced a wide range of monetary policy measures for the eurozone to preserve household firms by ensuring credit flow. ECB set up the task force to monitor the COVID-19 response in the jurisdictions under its mandate. The focus of the task force was on 'financial resilience and recovery', making the business stress-free, and levelling down the NPLs.[44] ECB reports suggested that the Jurisdictions should immediately review the asset quality to 'identify loans that are non-performing and need restructuring', separate good and bad assets of the banks and re-capitalise good banks to enhance their lending capacity.[45] The experiences show that the NPLs have similar trends in each crisis following the U trend, starting with a modest level, reaching the peak after some time, stabilising, and finally declining. The COVID-19 crisis is not a credit boom-induced crisis. It may result in temporary illiquidity rather than unviable firms, and most EU jurisdictions entered the pandemic with high average capital ratios. The EU jurisdictions also had 'higher public debt, less profitable banks, and weaker corporate sector conditions', which may make it challenging to implement the NPLs resolution plan.

However, the Irish Central Bank started looking for a solution to recover from the crisis and the rising problem of NPLs, as well as how to bring the economy back on track. ECB proposed forming a euro zone' bad banks'[46] to deal with the problem

---

[43] Central Bank of Ireland (2020).

[44] Cunningham (2020).

[45] Ari (2021), p. 133.

[46] Woo (2000).

of NPLs in the Member States. This solution of 'bad banks' was not new and was also considered during the financial crisis. The euro zone's bad banks solution did not gain footing due to the Member States' success in reducing the national NPL ratios.[46]

The opinion to use NAMA again to acquire the existing NPLs from the Irish banks and to free up the capital and capacity for the expected surge for the next 12 months also cropped up. It seems to be a logical solution to the problem in many ways .[46] Despite the considerable success achieved by the NAMA, critics opined that it would not be a welcome step to assign the responsibility of NPLs resolution to NAMA in the situation that emerged due to the pandemic.[47] Irish banks faced a liquidity problem during the GFC, but remained better capitalised after the intervention of the NAMA. However, there were many challenges to reconsidering NAMA in dealing with the post-COVID-19 NPLs. The NPLs have always been challenging for the banks, and despite implementing many possible measures after the GFC,[21] Irish banks are now resilient and more robust. Therefore, Irish banks can tackle the problem of NPLs emerging from the COVID-19 pandemic because the NPLs will remain the same in the post-COVID-19 scenario. Ireland effectively dealt with the loans-deposit ratio, which became much stronger, reducing the average NPLs ratio from 17% to 5% by 2016 across the banks.[48]

To fight against the COVID-19 pandemic, the Bank of Ireland must check the strength of its economy, and the CTE 1 indicator is an important measure of capitalisation. The CET1 of Irish banks by the end of December 2019 was 16.4% for Allied Irish Bank (AIB), 13.5% for Bank of Ireland, 27% for Ulster Bank and 15% for Permanent TSB.[49] CCyB is also an important and useful tool to ensure financial stability, particularly during a crisis. The Irish Central Bank responded to the COVID-19 pandemic, and the Irish government has reduced CCyB by 0%.[49] The move has helped the banks absorb the losses and make additional funds for the business and customers.

Moreover, the Central Bank has announced a three-month payment break (PB) on mortgages and personal and business loans to some companies to relieve the customers facing difficulties due to the pandemic, with an extension for three months for the affected firms. PB allowed customers to postpone or reduce their repayments on mortgage, personal or business loans, relieving borrowers. The objective of the PB was to ensure that no additional borrower falls into the forbearance category.

In addition, the Central Bank introduced a central credit register to keep the records of the debtors who availed of the PB. The bank also introduced a new emergency purchase programme to pump in £750 billion in addition to the already announced £120 billion, which constitutes 7.5% of the GDP of the euro area. All these measures protected customers and businesses from the pandemic's effects.

---

[47] Lane (2020), p. 21.

[48] MHC (2020).

[49] Fehily (2020).

They addressed the issue of NPLs to some extent because they aimed to provide credit to the economy's productive sector.[50]

The ECB has set up marginal refinancing operations (MRO) and deposit facility rates (DFR) for the eurozone, which were zero and 50 basis points, respectively. The minimum will be applicable if banks achieve specific lending performance thresholds. During COVID-19, the ECB eased the lending performance threshold and reduced the interest rates on all outstanding liquidity by 25 basis points up to June 2020. The total amount that counterparties can borrow increased from 30% to 50% of the eligible loans on their balance sheets.

The ECB also announced the asset purchase scheme (APS), with easy collateral, to support the financing conditions in Ireland. It directly supports the euro area firms under the Corporate Sector Purchase Programme (CSPP). ECB suggested that purchasing debt from firms heavily exposed to the pandemic and the related containment measures should be particularly beneficial at the current juncture. The cumulative purchase of Ireland was €42,925 till December 2022.[51] The important Irish corporate bonds issued by the firms in the CSPP include Ryanair, Caterpillar International Finance, ESB, Kerry Group, Dublin Airport Authority, Gas Networks Ireland, Partner Re Ireland Finance, CRH, Fresenius, Zurich, Eaton Capital and Liberty Mutual.[51] The APS programmes safeguard the favourable financial position of the Irish and facilitate their response to the pandemic.

However, in the last few years, Irish banks have struggled due to the interest rates, and this kind of pressure aggravated a lot during the pandemic. The stock market wiped out huge values of the Irish bank's shares. The rating agency Standard & Poor put AIB, Permanent TSB and Bank of Ireland on the watch list because of the potential credit downgrade. The profitability prospects of the Irish banks were weak. Even though the EBA clarified that they support PB, it also stated that after the moratoria, banks should carefully assess the credit quality of the loans and even look for borrowers who have not paid their loans on time.[51]

Nevertheless, the Irish government took several initiatives on the policy, supervisory and regulatory front to combat the problem that emerged due to the COVID-19 pandemic, and the situation has improved a lot. As a result, NPLs, which was 5.46% on the eve of COVID-19 in 2018, remained at 3.36% in 2019 and reduced to 2.28% in 2021 (see Table 1.1 in Chap. 1). Although the NPLs remained constant during the pandemic with marginal variation, a continuous watch would require monitoring its long-term momentum and effects.

[50] Draghi and de Guindos (2014).

[51] ECB (2023).

7.7 Conclusion

This chapter examined the policy, supervisory and regulatory responses taken by the governments of the UK, India, and Ireland to mitigate the effects of the COVID-19 pandemic on the economy in general and NPLs in particular. The arguments presented in the discussion also established several commonalities in the respective Central Banks' approaches to dealing with the crisis, which had a cascading effect on the economy. The immediate response of the Central Banks was to provide sufficient funds for individuals and businesses to survive. Therefore, the declaration of a three-month moratorium period or PB for certain types of loans was to provide immediate relief to the financial system and avoid categorising loans into possible forbearance or default.

The UK introduced highly effective CBILS, BBLS, CLBILS and FFS capitalisation plans to support businesses. The UK government loan guarantee encouraged many borrowers to avail themselves of the benefits of the schemes, resulting in a substantial increase in the UK's contingent liability on its COVID-19 loan guarantee. These schemes provided life to many small and medium businesses to survive during the pandemic. In addition, the leading banks in the UK used LLP during the early stage of the COVID-19 pandemic to smoothen their income so that it directly and immediately contributed to their profitability.

The BoE also reduced the base rate from 0.75% to 0.25% to make a loan available at a lower rate. The UK APF was able to purchase and hold government bonds and ensured that the markets for the UK government bonds remained intact. All these measures substantially contributed to reducing the impact of COVID-19. The positive results encouraged FPC to increase CCyB from 0.5% to 1%. The banks in the UK also suggested a desk-based SST to observe the effects of the COVID-19 crisis, concluding that usable buffers of the capital built up in the banks were sufficient to absorb the losses under a feasible illustrative scenario. Therefore, the UK economy successfully encountered the impact of the COVID-19 pandemic and returned to a recovery path.

RBI has also introduced various economic, fiscal, policy, supervisory and regulatory measures to fight the COVID-19 crisis and mitigate the banking sector's liquidity and credit risk problem. RBI also introduced PB, reduced the CRR, purchased government net market borrowings, issued guidelines for rescheduling payments for term loans and working capital, and exempted the loan classification as SMA. In addition, the RBI also made CCyB inactive to ensure that the banks have sufficient funds to mitigate the impact of COVID-19. Besides monitoring SLR, the OTS and OMS schemes maintain short-term securities yield and manage the yield curve. The RBI efforts were largely successful, and such a large liquidity injection (3% of GDP) helped the system move forward.

Despite all these efforts, credit growth in most sectors struggled to challenge the country's financial stability. Interestingly, the GNPAs to gross advances were 7.30% in 2020–21, reduced to 5.8% in 2021–22, and further reduced 3.90% in 2022–23. Similarly, there was a reduction in net NPLs from 2.4% to 1.7% and finally rests at

0.90% in 2022–23. When comparing the figures with pre-COVID ratios, the GNPAs and NPAs were 11.20% and 8.20%, respectively. However, the GNPAs in some banks still showed disturbing and stressful situations for the RBI and policymakers, and timely corrective measures warrant strict monitoring of the banking sector.

The COVID-19 pandemic also posed a severe threat to the economy of Ireland, and businesses around the state suffered a lot, threatening the banking sector and FIs. Moreover, the pandemic coincided with a final decision on the Brexit agreement, further aggravating the problem because of uncertainty in the trade relationship between the UK and the EU. The CBI has initiated several measures to mitigate the provisions of cross-border financial services between the EU and the UK. Moreover, the Irish Government responded to the crisis by taking measures to help struggling businesses and protect customers' interests.

The Central Bank, Department of Finance and NTMA closely coordinated the measures taken by Ireland to mitigate the impact of COVID-19 with the help of a Financial Stability Group. ECB has also introduced and suggested a wide range of monetary policy measures for the eurozone to preserve household firms by ensuring credit flow. Accordingly, the Irish government made CCyB inactive during the pandemic. TLTRO-III was introduced in Ireland to provide lending to SMEs and household customers to avoid a liquidity crunch. In addition, the ECB incentivised the eurozone banks and provided financial support to the credit institutions to stimulate the credit supply. The objective was to provide credit to the most productive sectors of the economy to reduce the impact of COVID-19.

ECB eased the lending performance threshold and reduced the interest rates on all outstanding liquidity. The ECB also announced the asset purchase scheme (APS), with easy collateral, to support the financing conditions in Ireland, and these containment measures were particularly beneficial in reducing the impact of the pandemic. Thus, the efforts of the CBI and ECB effectively managed the possible downturn in the banking sector and controlled the rise in NPLs in Ireland during the pandemic.

Finally, the COVID-19 pandemic badly impacted the banking sector of the UK, India, and Ireland; nevertheless, timely stimulus action and the injection of liquidity by the respective central banks helped the business and individual credit requirements. The lesson learnt from the GFC also stimulated the supervisors to take prompt and timely corrective measures and were successful in their mission, particularly in the short run. In the long run, the stress on the banking sector remains intact. In-depth research will be able to analyse the long-term effects of the pandemic and provide a perfect milieu for the researchers.

References

Acharya VV, Steffen S (2020) The risk of being a fallen angel and the corporate dash for cash in the midst of COVID. Rev Corp Finance Stud 9(3):430. https://ssrn.com/abstract=3654248. Accessed 22 Feb 2013

Adrian T, Shin HS (2010) Liquidity and leverage. J Financ Intermed 19(3):418

Ahir H, Bloom N, Furceri D (2020) 60 year of uncertainty. Finance and Development. https://launches-world-uncertainty-index-wui-furceri.pdf. Accessed 27 July 2023

Ari A, Chen S, Ratnavski L (2021) The dynamics of non-performing loans during banking crisis: a new database with post COVID-19 implications. J Bank Finance 133. https://doi.org/10.1016/j.jbankfin.2021.106140. Accessed 6 Jan 2023

Bank of England (2021) Financial stability report. https://www.bankofengland.co.uk/-/media/boe/files/financial-stability-report/2021/december-2021.pdf. Accessed 12 Jan 2023

Batra S (2003) Developing the Asian markets for non-performing loans, developments in India. IIIrd Forum on Asian Insolvency Reform. https://www.oecd.org/corporate/ca/corporategovernanceprinciples/20218724.pd. Accessed 10 Mar 2023

Berger AN, Kunt AD (2021) Banking research in the time of COVID-19. World Banking Group Policy Research Working Paper 9782. https://openknowledge.worldbank.org/server/api/core/bitstreams/6f126802-4a22-5d28-be9d-f091fb18e71a/content. Accessed 15 Mar 2023

Bobade P, Alex A (2020) The effect of COVID-19 in the Indian banking sector (2020) Journal NX. https://www.neliti.com/publications/336056/study-the-effect-of-covid-19-in-indian-banking-sector. Accessed 5 Mar 2023

Calabrese R, Cowling M, Liu W (2021) Understanding the dynamics of UK COVID-19 SME financing. Br J Manag 33(2):657

Central Bank of Ireland (2020) Financial stability review 2020: II. https://www.centralbank.ie/doc/default-source/publications/financial-stability-review/financial-stability/financial-stability-review-2020-ii.pdf?sfvrsn=8fd4881d_9. Accessed 10 Mar 2022

Cunningham B (2020) Covid-19 and the banking sector in Ireland. Insights Banking and Finance. https://www.rdj.ie/insights/covid-19-and-the-banking-sector-in-ireland. Accessed 22 Dec 2022

Danielsson J, Shin HS (2002) Endogenous risk in modern risk management: a history. Risk Book

Draghi M, de Guindos L (2014) Introductory statement. Press Conference. https://www.ecb.europa.eu/press/pressconf/2019/html/ecb.is190725~547f29c369.en.html. Accessed 11 Mar 2023

European Central Bank (2021) Financial stability review. https:/www.ecb.europa.eu/pub/financial-stability/fsr/html/ecb.fsr202105~757f727fe4.en.html. Accessed 26 Feb 2023

European Central Bank (2023) Asset Purchase Programme. https://www.ecb.ropa.eu/mopo/impement/app/html/index.en.html#cspp. Accessed 10 Mar 2023

Falato A, Goldstein I, Hortacsu A (2021) Financial fragility in the COVID-19 Crisis: the case of investment funds in corporate bond markets. J Monet Econ 123:35. https://doi.org/10.1016/j.jmoneco.2021.07.001. Accessed 6 Jan 2023

Fehily H (2020) How well prepared are Ireland's banks for COVID-19. https://www.holmeslaw.ie/insights-news/news/how-well-prepared-are-irelands-banks-for-covid-19. Accessed 23 Dec 2022

Giese J, Haldane A (2020) COVID-19 and the financial system: a tale of two crises. Oxford Rev Econ Policy 36:200

Goswami A (2021) Modelling NPLs and identifying convergence phenomenon of banks: a case of pre- during and immediate after the crisis years in India. J Financ Regul Compliance 30(1):1

Goswami A (2023) COVID-19: boon/disguise for Indian banks? J Bank Regul. https://ink.springer.com/content/pdf/10.1057/s41261-022-00203-6.pdf. Accessed 5 Mar 2023

Haynes J, Hope P, Talbot H (2021) Non-performing loans-new risks and polices? IPOL European Governance Support Unit. https://www.bancaditalia.it/pubblicazioni/altri-atti-seminari/2021/Oxera.pdf. Accessed 10 Jan 2023

Hill C, Hirschfield D, Renolds C (2021) Covid-19: response from the Bank of England and Prudential Regulatory Authority. https://www.taylorwessing.com/en/insights-and-events/insights/2020/07/covid19-response-from-the-bank-of-england-and-prudential-regulation-authority. Accessed 11 Jan 2023

HMT (2022a) COVID-19 loan guarantee schemes repayment data as of 31 March 2022. https://www.gov.uk/government/publications/covid-19-loan-guarantee-schemes-repayment-data/covid-19-loan-guarantee-schemes-repayment-data-as-at-31-march-2022. Accessed 27 July 2023

HMT (2022b, July 2) Final COVID loan data reveals £80 billion of government support through the pandemic. HMT 1. https://www.gov.uk/government/news/final-covid-loans-data-reveals-80-billion-of-government-support-through-the-pandemic. Accessed 27 July 2023

International Monetary Fund (2020) Global financial stability report: bridge to recovery. https://www.imf.org/en/publications/gfsr. Accessed 1 Mar 2023

International Monetary Fund (2021) World economic outlook update. World Economic Outlook Reports. https://www.imf.org/en/publications/weo/issues/2021/01/26/2021-world-economic-outlook-update. Accessed 10 Jan 2022

Ivanov D (2020) Predicting the impacts of epidemic outbreaks on global supply chains: a simulation-based analysis on the coronavirus outbreak (COVID-19/SARS-COV-2) case. Transp Res E: Logist Transp Rev 1–15. https://www.sciencedirect.com/science/article/pii/S1366554520304300. Accessed 6 Jan 2020

Kahn MOS (2020, May 5) Can we compare the COVID-19 and 2008 crisis. Atlantic Council. https://www.atlanticcouncil.org/blogs/new-atlanticist/can-we-compare-the-covid-19-and-2008-crises/. Accessed 27 Feb 2023

Kim J, Kim M, Lee JH (2019) The effect of TARP on loan loss provisions and bank transparency. J Bank Finance 102:79

Kunt AD, Pedraza P, Ortega CR (2020) Banking sector performance during the COVID-19 crisis. World Bank Policy Research Working Paper 9363. https://ssrn.com/abstract=3689789. Accessed 6 Jan 2023

Lane PR (2020) The monetary policy to the pandemic emergency. https://www.ecb.europa.eu/press/blog/date/2020/html/ecb.blog200501~a2d8f514a0.en.html. Accessed 2 Jan 2023

Makortoff K (2020, July 6) UK banks prepare code of conduct on defaulting of Covid-19 business loans. The Guardian. https://www.theguardian.com/business/2020/jul/06/uk-banks-prepare-code-of-conduct-on-defaulting-of-covid-19-business-loans. Accessed 4 Mar 2023

Mathew DM (2020, August 27) Operation twist: what RBI is really trying to do and what's in it for you. The Economic Times. https://economictimes.indiatimes.com/markets/stocks/news/operation-twist-what-rbi-is-really-trying-to-do-and-whats-in-it-for-you/articleshow/77779664.cms. Accessed 5 May 2023

MHC (2020, April 30) How will Irish banks deal with the increase in non-performing loans post COVID-19? https://www.mhc.ie/latest/insights/how-will-irish-banks-deal-with-the-increase-in-non-performing-loans-post-covid-19. Accessed 3 Jan 2023

Mohan R (2021, July 15) The response of the Reserve Bank of India to Covid-19: do whatever it takes. The Hindustan. https://www.hindustantimes.com/ht-insight/economy/the-response-of-reserve-bank-of-india-to-covid-19-do-whatever-it-takes-101626339262642.html. Accessed 5 Mar 2023

OECD (2020) Economic outlook. OECD 2. https://doi.org/10.1787/39a88ab1-en. Accessed 1 Mar 2023

OECD (2021) The COVID-19 crisis and banking system resilience: simulation of losses on non-performing loans and policy implications. https://www.oecd.org/daf/fin/financial-markets/COVID-19-crisis-and-banking-system-resilience.pdf. Accessed 16 Mar 2023

Ozili PK (2021) Banking sector earnings management using loan loss provisions in the Fintech era. International Journal of Managerial Finance. https://papers.ssrn.com/sol3/papers.cfm?abstractid=3758468. Accessed 3 Mar 2023

Ozili PK, Outa E (2017) Bank loan provision research: a review. Borsa Istanbul Rev 17(3):144

Perwej A (2020) The impact of the pandemic COVID-19 on the Indian banking system. Int J Recent Sci Res 11(10):3987

Poon WPH, Firth M, Fung HG (1999) A multivariate analysis of the determinants of Moody's bank financial strength ratings. J Int Finance Mark Inst Money 9(3):267

Ramakumar R, Kanitkar T (2020) Impact of COVID-19 pandemic on the Indian Economy: a critical analysis. Investigacion Económica 80(315):3. https://www.jstor.org/stable/pdf/26965501.pdf?refreqid=excelsior%3A74984a4db799f76dbfa341e01c5ad55a&absegments=&origin=&initiator=. Accessed 4 Mar 2023

Rao MR (2022) Building a future ready banking system. https://m.rb.org.in/Scripts/BSViewBulletin.aspx?Id=21135. Accessed 21 Dec 2023

RBI (2021) RBI announces open market purchase of government of India securities under G-sec acquisition programme (G-SAP 2.0). https://www.rbi.org.in/scripts/BS_PressReleaseDisplay.aspx?prid=51854. Accessed 4 Mar 2022

RBI (2022a) Business community management during pandemic. https://rbi.org.in/Scripts/PublicationReportDetails.aspx?UrlPage=&ID=1231#A1. Accessed 5 Mar 2023

RBI (2022b) Report on trend and progress of banking in India 2022-23. 60. https://rbidocs.rbi.org.in/rdocs/Publications/PDFs/0RTP20212225730A6FC708454BB270AC1705CCF178.PDF. Accessed 5 Mar 2022

RBI (2023) Report on trend and progress of banking in India 2021-22. 56. https://rbidocs.rbi.org.in/rdocs/Publications/PDFs/0RTP27122023D9394304B3D149428EB730022B3BB232.PDF. Accessed 2 Nov 2024

Segot TL, Leoni PL (2013) Pandemics of the poor and banking stability. J Bank Finance 37(11):4574

Shearer E, Tetlow G (2021) Coronavirus: actions taken by Bank of England during the first lockdown. Institute for Government. https://www.instituteforgovernment.org.uk/explainers/Coronavirus-bank-England-first-lockdown. Accessed 10 Jan 2023

Woo D (2000) Two approaches to resolving nonperforming assets during financial crisis. IMF Working Paper WP/33. https://www.imf.org/en/Publications/WP/Issues/2016/12/30/Two-Approaches-to-Resolving-Nonperforming-Assets-During-Financial-Crises-3460. Accessed 15 Oct 2022

Young C, Kwanho S (2021) Covid-19, non-performing loans and cross-border bank lending. J Bank Finance

Zongyun Lia and others (2022) A Comparative Analysis of COVID-19 and Global Financial Crises: Evidence from US Economy. Economic Research 35(1):2427

Chapter 8
Conclusion and Suggestions

8.1 Introduction

NPLs have detrimental effects on the financial performance of the banks, which eventually influence the economies. NPLs have forward and backward relationships with macroeconomic and microeconomic determinants. These determinants not only influence NPL ratios, but high NPL ratios also significantly impact them. The present book critically examined the relationship between NPLs and macroeconomic and microeconomic determinants. It also thoroughly examined the role of regulatory and supervisory authorities in addressing the problem of NPLs in the UK, India, and Ireland. The researcher analysed the crucial acts, statutes, regulations, directives, circulars, Basel guidelines, case law, etc., dealing with financial sectors, including banks. A comparative analysis of the regulatory, policy and supervisory measures of the UK, India and Ireland provided insight into the approaches adopted by an advanced jurisdiction--the UK, an emerging nation, India, and an EU Member State badly hit by the rising level of NPLs after the GFC--Ireland.

The book also captured micro-level issues by critically analysing NPLs resolution strategies involving LBG, PNB and BIG. These unique case studies identified the risk management strategies adopted at the bank and branch levels to resolve the potential threat through a robust defence mechanism. The impact of the COVID-19 pandemic on the NPLs and the measures these banking groups took to evade the eruption of a possible downturn and its percolation down the wire to hit the banks in general and the economy in particular. This book aimed to answer the research questions throughout the discussion, which it encompassed. Thus, the present study judiciously sought the answers to research questions with the help of the approaches/methods explained in the first chapter.

A. Dimri, *Non-Performing Loans*, Ius Gentium: Comparative Perspectives on Law and Justice 125, https://doi.org/10.1007/978-3-031-92952-6_8

8.2 Discussion and Findings

8.2.1 Macroeconomic and Microeconomic Determinants: An Overview

The book examined the relationship between macroeconomic determinants and NPLs and concluded that these determinants have positive and negative relations with NPLs. For instance, the correlation result established a positive relationship between NPLs and GDP for the UK and India, suggesting that with the increase in GDP, NPLs decrease. The positive relationship between NPLs and GDP improves the economic environment and increases the chances of timely repayment. A negative relationship between GDP and NPLs for Ireland severely deteriorated asset quality due to poor loan recovery, resulting in high NPLs.

The positive results between unemployment and NPLs for the UK, India, and Ireland indicate that NPLs also increase with increased unemployment. As discussed, a higher unemployment rate considerably reduces disposable income, weakens borrowers' ability to repay installments and increases credit risk. Therefore, these jurisdictions should take such results seriously and undertake corrective measures to create more employment opportunities. The impact of unemployment was evident in poor bank performance, illiquidity, high NPLs and distressed economic conditions in the UK and Ireland during the GFC.

The correlation between inflation and NPLs on consumer prices was positive for the UK and Ireland and negative for India. The positive results indicated that with the increase in the prices, the value of money decreases, and the level of unpaid loans increases, resulting in increased defaults. Such instances were prevalent in Ireland after the GFC despite Ireland's efforts to address the problem of increased mortgages. In addition, higher inflation also significantly impacts the normal interest rates, reducing the borrowers' repayment capacity due to the reduction in real income. Inflation also has a positive impact on NPLs, making debt cheaper. Therefore, inflation has both positive and negative relationships with NPLs, and controlled inflation would help to maintain the sound health of the economy and consequently help to reduce NPLs.

The exchange rate and NPLs are also closely associated; with the increase in the exchange rate, the currency value falls, ultimately increasing fund requirements for the loans taken in domestic currency. Under such circumstances, borrowers experience difficulties meeting committed obligations, increasing NPLs and deteriorating the bank balance sheet. India's exchange rate fluctuated highly compared to the UK and Ireland, negatively impacting the Indian economy. The exchange rate also impacts unhedged borrowers, who must repay the debt in foreign currency, particularly those with pegged or managed exchange rates. In addition, an increase in the exchange rate also affects the performing assets by increasing the cost of loans and reducing the borrower's capacity to pay.

Therefore, macroeconomic determinants and NPLs are closely associated, and their impact on NPLs depends on several factors, including the fiscal and economic strength of the jurisdictions. These determinants positively and negatively impacted the NPLs of the UK, India and Ireland. These jurisdictions must closely watch their movement to address the problem of NPLs effectively.

The relationship between the microeconomic determinants and NPLs revealed that highly capitalised banks lower the risk of rising NPLs, and higher RWA results in reduced loan losses. The UK demonstrated relatively consistent results on the relationship between asset quality and NPLs, mainly due to prompt and corrective measures, such as bank bailout plans, which avoided possible insolvencies. Volatility continued in India and Ireland despite adhering to the Basel guidelines on capital adequacy. The reason for volatility in Ireland was due to the housing sector's collapse, which severely impacted individuals', SMEs', and CREs' mortgages.

ID has positive and negative relationships between bank profitability and NPLs, and banks with better ID have better loan performance, showing an inverse relationship with NPLs. Considering the risk involved in ID, the Vickers Commission in the UK suggested ring-fencing by separating retail banking deposit and lending functions from investment banking to isolate retail banking.[1] In India, commercial banks have used risk-adjusted returns on assets to measure banks' stability; higher risk-adjusted returns will deal with any crisis effectively[2] The EU Liikanen Report suggests legally separating hazardous financial activities from deposit-taking banks, including proprietary trading of securities and derivatives and other activities closely linked with securities and derivatives markets.[3] However, no business model fared well or badly in the financial crisis.

The non-interest income for the UK, India, and Ireland increased significantly, and it had a positive correlation with NPLs in the UK and Ireland but a negative result for India. Relatively higher ID yielded positive results for these jurisdictions. The jurisdictions should consider this proposition despite critics' apprehension because higher income will positively affect the other economic indicators.[4] The bank's cost to income had a negative relationship with NPLs in the UK and Ireland and a positive one in India. The increasing cost reflects bad management, ultimately increasing NPLs; therefore, the jurisdiction must address this issue sincerely. Due to robust fundamentals, the cost efficiency and management effectiveness were much stronger in the UK and Ireland. India should work on it to compete with the international market to strengthen its financial position.

ROA and ROE are other microeconomic indicators that influence banks' performance and establish a significant negative and positive relationship with NPLs because banks with high efficiency and high profitability rates invest less in risk-bearing assets, resulting in lower NPLs Negative correlation between ROA and NPLs and ROE and NPLs for the UK, India and Ireland have significant implications on the financial performance and stability of the banks as such it will influence

[1] Edmonds (2013).

[2] Sarkar (2016).

[3] Nguyen and Nghiem (2016).

[4] Liikanen (2012).

banks' ability to generate income resulting in vulnerability to economic fluctuations and relatively less investment due to loss of investors' confidence. Therefore, strong risk assessment and management, higher provisioning requirements, and regulatory oversight will help the jurisdictions improve the economic situation, reduce the NPLs, and avoid potential adversity on banks' performance.

A positive correlation between NIM and NPLs indicates the efficiency and ability of a bank to operate with higher interest rates than expenses. Banks should also focus on improving NIM as it positively impacts asset quality. On the other hand, large-size banks enjoy implicit government subsidies that enable them to take on more risk than those that are not systemically important and sometimes face distress. Therefore, the bank size positively and negatively impacts financial stability and has always been at the centre of banking supervision and regulation.

The UK and the EU are trying to improve asset quality by increasing the provisioning requirement for more capital and liquidity in addition to the Basel III requirements, and trying to restrict banks from participating in risky activities. India also implemented Basel III and maintained the provisions in line with Basel guidelines to ensure adequate funds to mitigate liquidity requirements. Supervisors should ensure that the banks adhere to the Basel guidelines to meet the parameters of capital adequacy.

The composite scores to measure the overall performance of the banks on the microeconomic determinants were highest (405.58) for the UK, followed by Ireland (371.93) and India (322.098). Thus, the performance of the UK was relatively better than that of Ireland and India. However, low ROA and ROE, high NIM, poor asset quality, inefficient bank management, and inadequate ID efforts reduce creditworthiness. Moreover, job losses, high levels of indebtedness, poor credit history, and external shocks also increase default cases. All these factors greatly influence the customers' repayment behaviour and increase NPLs. Therefore, consistent efforts are required to create stringent regulations, effective policies, efficient risk management and monitoring systems to avert the impact on NPLs.

8.2.2 Regulatory and Supervisory Responses: Retrospect and Prospect

Jurisdictions worldwide tried to tighten the regulatory system after the GFC and the COVID-19 pandemic. The US replaced its multiple federal agencies with the Federal Reserve, the OCC, and the FDIC after enacting the Dodd-Frank Act in 2010. The failure of banks in recent times has raised serious questions on the resolution mechanism and insolvency processes in the EU to address NPLs, despite the EU adopting recapitalisation along with the SSM and SREP framework to address wide divergences. Greece introduced a new legal regime in 2010 to harmonise the frameworks for NPEs, designing an APS (Hercules) to reduce NPLs cases without state aid intervention. GACS of Italy aimed to provide an effective resolution.

Cyprus amended its bankruptcy code in 2015, and the Central Bank of the Russian Federation imposed new regulations to manage banks' income, strengthening its oversight by revoking the licenses of many banks. All these efforts received mixed success, and COVID-19 exposed the loopholes; therefore, taking clues from these efforts, the jurisdictions need to tighten their regulatory oversight.

Similarly, the UK, India and Ireland took several initiatives to strengthen their regulatory and supervisory system. After abolishing multiple regulators in 1998, the UK assigned the FSA the responsibility of regulating the financial sector. However, the effectiveness of the FSA in dealing with the GFC posed several questions on its ability to coordinate with agencies for systemic oversight. Therefore, the FSA in 2012 advocated the establishment of the PRA and the FCA, in line with the 'Twin Peaks Model' of banking regulators, developing a 'tripartite' structure with shared responsibility between the BoE, HMT and the FSA, including the PRA and the FCA for micro- and macro-prudential supervision and regulation. In addition, FPC, primarily responsible for identifying, monitoring, taking action and removing or reducing systemic risks, was also established to protect and enhance resilience.

PRA follows a judgment-based, forward-looking approach and a key-risk-focused approach to regulate and supervise the financial sector and ensure that the firms do not fall into a financial crisis trap, which immensely helps to avoid significant disruption and reduce the actual and potential systemic risk. Therefore, the PRA supervises prudential matters, and the FCA ensures the conduct of matters. The HMT controls public spending and provides policies and regulations governing financial services and stability, ensuring strategic oversight for sustainable economic growth. Thus, the UK has a robust supervisory and regulatory mechanism to regulate the financial market. However, overlaps persist in the supervision and conduct of business regulated by the PRA and the FCA, which need careful examination and redressal to make the regulatory system more effective.

The UK has transposed several financial sector EU legislations into its domestic law and enforced the Financial Services Act 2021 after Brexit to amend the existing legal instruments to make them useful to the prevailing circumstances, so that the financial system becomes more vigorous. Important financial sector legislation like MiFIR and MiFID have several deficiencies, including a lack of clarity on 'EU discretion on assessment of equivalence' and 'susceptive to political interference and influence'. It does not clarify the supervision requirement for designing and selling financial instruments and products. It also has an ambiguity in protecting the clients due to the lack of a standardised information disclosure system. Therefore, the UK replaced MiFID II and MiFIR 2018 with the Financial Services Act 2021, allowing the act to specify reporting requirements for firms that register under the regime. Considering the importance of these legislations, we suggest that the ambiguity that persisted in the legislation needs clarity in subsequent amendments.

In addition, the FCA amended its rules and guidance to cope with the post-Brexit scenario, incorporated necessary changes to make a uniform payment system, and guided all market players, old and new, to offer better payment services to consumers with robust security. PSD and PSR also have deficiencies as they cannot keep pace with fast-moving market developments and the post-Brexit environment.

Similarly, AML and its subsequent replacements effectively dealt with non-transparent structures of payment, including virtual currency, crypto assets, fiat currencies, ICO, and custodian wallet providers, besides providing services to safeguard the customers to hold, store and transfer virtual currencies to ensure financial stability, which has a direct impact on NPLs. The UK needs to match these legislations to cope with the latest developments in the financial sector's online payment system and make them lethal to avoid instability.

The UK also transposed CRD IV into its domestic law to strengthen the capital adequacy standard in line with Basel guidelines, advocating that FIs must maintain the CET-1 capital equal to 2.5% of their total risk exposure to meet the funds' requirement. The PRA currently imposes 10.5% of regulatory capital on the UK banks. The regulation further tightened the CET1, increasing it to 4.1% of RWA, in addition to additional Tier 1 and Tier 2 capital. Constant supervision and monitoring are required to ensure compliance with capital requirements.

The UK government has decided to return to the British regulation style, which believes that the regulators must make the rules rather than set them out in law. Before joining the EU, the UK enacted its own rules and regulations, whereas, under the EU, the UK was transposing the EU directive into domestic law to implement them and relied on the ECJ for clarification. Therefore, the Financial Services Act 2021 is a significant landmark in the post-Brexit scenario, ensuring that the UK remains an 'open and dynamic financial centre' to provide technologically embodied financial services. The Act established control over the UK financial services regulations, which otherwise transposed EU legislation and were influenced by the EBA. Despite having robust regulatory and supervisory mechanisms, The UK needs to strengthen its regulatory oversight, make more effective coordination among regulators, and incorporate necessary changes in the legislation to align them with the latest developments in the financial sector.

As discussed in Chap. 4, India has multiple regulators that regulate and supervise financial services, including the RBI, SEBI, IRDA, FMC, and PFRDA. During the last four decades, the government of India took several initiatives at the regulatory and supervisory levels by instituting suitable laws and guidelines to curb NPAs to a manageable level.

The Banking Regulation Act of 1949 empowered the RBI to grant and revoke bank licenses and monitor and supervise banking activities to ensure financial stability. There have been several deficiencies in the functioning of banks; as a result, Narasimham Committee I and II, Rangarajan Committee and Verma Committee advocated reforms in banking sector, suggesting 'restructuring of weak banks, economies of expansion and scale of economies' and the government and the RBI acted accordingly.

The first step towards evolving insolvency and bankruptcy law in India was the enactment of SICA in 1988, intending to revive the sick industrial units. The efforts taken under SICA for revival and liquidation remained ineffective, mainly due to cumbersome legal proceedings resulting in many pending cases. Sometimes, the courts took broader views on the implications of their judgments and protected the workers' interests, exposing the law. Consequently, RDBFI was enacted in 1993 to expedite the adjudication and recovery of debt, authorising DRTs to deal with the NPAs of secured and unsecured borrowers. The effectiveness of DRT remained challenging as many cases were pending before the civil court, and the loopholes in the system resulted in the wastage of precious time and resources of the judiciary and exposed the limitations of the settlement process.

The drawbacks in earlier initiatives realised the need to enact the SARFAESI Act in 2002 to deal with the problem of loan restructuring. The Act empowered banks and FIs to take possession of securities and dispose of them without the court's intervention through the securitisation process. The Act also advocates the establishment of ARCs to develop securitisation markets. However, the extreme ambiguity in the Act was challenged in court, resulting in a delay in the restructuring process and jeopardizing the efforts.

RBI issued several guidelines for the classification and restructuring of loans, and these efforts remained ineffective despite banks considering this an opportunity to clean the balance sheet and reduce the NPL ratio. These guidelines also failed to achieve their intended objectives to some extent.

Finally, India enacted IBC in 2016 after extensive consultation with stakeholders to synchronies emerging market realities. The Code focused on completing the CIRP within 180 days after admitting an application for the insolvency process, with a further extension of 90, days subject to the approval of NCTL. Under IBC, the AA, resolution professionals, and creditors' committees are crucial in approving and implementing the resolution plan. In case of an incomplete insolvency resolution plan, the adjudication authority may initiate the liquidation process. The subsequent amendments rectified the shortcomings and made it an effective tool for resolving insolvent cases.

However, the deficiencies in the code have been challenged in the courts, and legal experts have opined that the code needs revision to make it compatible with international best practices. The critics argued that dedicated courts for the insolvency process, capacity building of insolvency professionals, pre-packed insolvency,[5] reduction in resolution time, a framework for cross-border insolvency, and a culture of compliance of insolvency proceedings to circumvent willful defaulters would enhance the efficiency, effectiveness and transparency of the resolution process.

Ireland has a long history of enacting banking regulations; it's first Bankruptcy Act of 1871 regulated banking activities and had provisions for declaring banks bankrupt. Ireland's financial system is jointly regulated by the ECB and CBI, following SSM and SSMR to ensure credit institutions' safety and soundness without disregarding the internal market's unity and integrity based on equal treatment of credit institutions to prevent regulatory arbitrage.

The Central Bank Act enacted many codes of conduct and other legal procedures to regulate the financial market and banking business to prevent insolvency and bankruptcy. Ireland also transposed financial sector legislation into domestic law to

[5] Dass et al. (2020), p. 115.

avoid insolvency and bankruptcy. As discussed earlier, these legal instruments limit effectiveness and scope due to existing flaws.

EU directive BRRD empowered CBI to act as a national resolution authority providing resolution to failing banks, credit unions, and investment firms through SRM and SRB. This framework enhances the resilience and resolvability of institutions and better-prepared banks to deal with and recover from a crisis through a recovery plan. Under BRRD, the burden of bail-out shifts from taxpayers to shareholders, and its success depends on market reaction.[6] The success of this law depends on the financial safety measures adopted by the jurisdictions with individual laws; therefore, Ireland should create a sound ecosystem for obtaining better results.

Ireland also enacted the CPC 2012 to enhance confidence and trust in the financial system for their financial services. The CBI also made its monitoring mechanism strong and ensured that regulated entities followed the provisions in the code to protect the customers' interests while providing financial services. In addition to CPC, CCMA ensures fair and transparent treatment of distressed borrowings, and MARP focuses on the lenders giving alternative options for restructuring to the borrowers by developing meaningful engagement to avoid a situation of non-cooperation. Similarly, ISI restores insolvent persons to solvency and monitors the operations relating to personal insolvency, and DRN, DSA, and PIA effectively deal with default borrowings. Thus, ISI ensures the timely resolution of bankruptcy and insolvency by designing, planning, and implementing effective strategies and raising awareness about bankruptcy and insolvency solutions amongst the target audience.

In addition, Ireland provides insolvency solutions for people with unsecured and secured debts and the approval and support of unsecured and secured creditors through PIA. The Central Bank also introduced sustainable guidelines to deal with the resolution of mortgage arrears cases through MART by doing onsite credit inspections to provide sustainable solutions. Ireland took several initiatives on the regulatory and supervisory front to control NPLs and started harvesting positive outcomes, resulting in NPLs being 2.48% in 2021 after reaching a peak in 2013 (22.37%).

The mode of financial services is rapidly changing, and the legislation needs to keep pace, matching the pace of digitisation to bring ease and efficiency to the customers. The flow of information among stakeholders at the appropriate time will help them make the right decision. The legislation lacks all these qualities, and Ireland needs to calibrate them into their legal architecture to make it robust.[7]

In addition, these jurisdictions also have laws that have several flaws and need improvement to make them compatible with dealing with national and international insolvency processes effectively. Thus, the regulatory and supervisory architecture of the UK and Ireland is relatively stronger than that of India because the UK

[6] PwC (2014).

[7] Bank of England (2013).

regulatory system helped the banks to increase their risk appetite and have a greater tolerance for credit risk. In addition, regulators work in close coordination and address the risk by adopting various approaches. Moreover, in the UK, the regulators have considerable independence in regulating financial activities compared to those in India. In Ireland, the ECB and CBI work in close coordination, and the ECB provides frequent guidelines to the Central Bank to handle insolvency and bankruptcy cases besides enforcing regulations. Chapter 4 examined the wide range of legislation and guidelines and concluded that these legal instruments have considerable scope for revamping, particularly calibrating them with the potential risk of digitisation.

8.2.3 Policy Measures: An Epilogue

The UK, India, and Ireland have successfully implemented several NPL resolution policies to resolve the NPL problem. The UK has used OCWs to resolve corporate financial difficulties. This tool has several advantages, allowing creditors to prepare a detailed workout plan for approval. This hybrid, cost-effective debt restructuring method allows companies to continue operations during the restructuring process. This tool is also used in India to support financially distressed MSMEs by allowing their revival. In Ireland, the debt portfolio was different, and the focus was on a revival of individual mortgages, SMEs and CRE; therefore, it implemented DRN, DSA and PIA, dealing with loans of varied sizes and duration. Nonetheless, SMEs find the tool complex and costly, and jurisdictions must look into these aspects by assessing its efficiency to increase its acceptability.

The write-off of NPLs is usual and routine, which helps to wipe out the built-up of NPLs from the bank balance sheet and is a prevalent practice across jurisdictions. The loan write-off in the UK was highest due to the impact of the GFC during 2009–11. The situation improved gradually, and the loan write-off decreased significantly from 2012 onwards, with a marginal increase in 2020 due to the impact of COVID-19. In India, due to proactive government policy, there was a sudden rise in NPLs write-offs during 2012–13 and peaked in 2016–17. However, from 2019–20 onwards, it started receding. EBA does not provide mandatory NPLs write-off rules. Therefore, Ireland introduced principles-based local guidelines for loan write-off and provided significant consideration to the loan arrears for more than 53 weeks. The loan write-off is an effective tool to provide a clean bank balance sheet, and banks also need to make continuous efforts to pursue the recovery of such loans. However, banks remained reluctant and expressed apprehension due to its implications for profits and capital because write-offs contribute to the immediate reduction in bank capital.

These jurisdictions also used direct sales of assets to bad banks (AMCs) and investment firms to resolve NPLs. As a result, the UKAR in the UK made significant progress by reducing balance sheet assets by 95%, arrears by 96%, and expenses by 86% from 2010 to 2021, thus protecting and creating value, providing financial support, and preserving financial stability in the UK. In India, AMCs/ARCs as a loan restructuring tool came into existence in 2002 under the SARAESI ACT 2002, and ARCIL was the first ARC set up by SBI and ICICI Bank as the principal shareholders. RBI issued comprehensive guidelines in 2005 for selling NPAs to ARCs to restructure distressed assets, but the success was relatively less despite a substantial increase in their number.

NAMA has made significant progress since its inception, and during 2021, it accumulated good profit (€195 million) and transferred €3 billion to the exchequer with a lifetime surplus of €4.5 billion. By the end of 2021, it deleveraged 98% of the acquired portfolios. The progress in cash generation was remarkable, resulting in the repayment of €31.8 billion in debt, including €30.2 billion in government-guaranteed debt. The share of loan disposal was highest in the residential sector (33%), followed by retail (20%). The success of NAMA was due to its pinpointing strategy to handle distressed debt, where it focused on the UK market to dispose of assets. NAMA continues to progress, and despite COVID-19, it has generated cumulative cash of over €46.8 billion since inception; as a result, its term has been extended up to 2025 by the European Commission. Therefore, the sales of assets using AMCs remain a vital policy instrument for resolving NPLs' problems, and it was utilised effectively by the UK and Ireland after the GFC. India needs to re-examine the progress of ARCs and make them more effective, taking lessons from the success of UKAR and NAMA.

These jurisdictions also used asset securitisation, a relatively more complex method to convert assets into marketable securities to attract buyers, including foreign institutional buyers, to broaden the potential buyer base for asset disposal. The scheme became popular since the UK used loan restructuring through securitisation in 1985 due to low NPLs restructuring costs and higher prices than direct sales. EU regulation 2019, the general framework of securitisation, which the UK modified through its Securitisation (Amendment) (EU Exit) Regulations 2019, and the SERFAESI Act 2002 of India and the RBI Master Direction 2021 provide legal support to the NPLs' securitisation.

The UK regulation is relatively more flexible than the EU Securitisation Regulation in terms of the role of the originator, sponsor (investor), and SSPE (securitisation vehicle), particularly in their area of operation. India also revamped securitisation and matched it with the developed market. However, the ecosystem for such a market is still growing. The underdeveloped local capital markets impede the use of securitisation tools to dispose of NPLs, and the performance of such markets remains uncertain in resolving NPLs problems. The Securitisation Act of the EU has several deficiencies, including retention of risk requirements, regulatory compliance costs, and disclosure requirements, and it poses serious challenges for originators, sponsors, and investors who are gradually adjusting to the securitisation market.

Similarly, the judicial system in India is cumbersome, and, as a result, it takes a lot of time to get clarity on the provisions in the Act if challenged in court, limiting the scope of the Act and providing inadequate coverage for debtors, which needs attention for rectification. Nonetheless, the securitisation of loans helps clean the bank balance sheet and restructure bad debts. Jurisdictions should remove the existing limitations to make it a more useful tool for loan restructuring.

The UK introduced APS to support banks in acute financial crises and credit crunches to manage risk and respite distressed banks. The HMT purchased shareholdings of RBS and LBG and protected them from exceptional mortgages and other financial losses. Treasury placed RBS assets under the APS and injected capital into the target lending. Lloyds was not inclined to accept the proposal and later withdrew from the scheme after paying the requisite fee, with a promise that it would raise additional capital from the shareholders. This bailout plan provided financial stability and helped to build positive market sentiments towards banks, and the capital injection also avoided bankruptcy and insolvency. Despite being a convenient resolution tool to support banks in mitigating the risk of a credit crunch, evidence shows that APS, as an NPLs resolution tool, had limited exposure.

The banking sector successfully used M&A to bail out banks with distressed assets by consolidating the banking business and combining two or more banks. In the UK, there are several examples of M&A, including the most prominent mergers in 1918 when five big groups consisting of Lloyds, Barclays, National Provincial, Midland, and Westminster formed and continued to shape the British banking market. M&A in the UK is subject to law and regulations, and the City Code on Takeovers and Mergers governs public companies. It is known as the Takeover Code, and several supplementary regulations and guidelines also facilitate the main regulation.

The banks in India have a long history of reorganisation, which led to bank mergers to bail out weaker banks, protect customers' interests, and create larger banks to be competitive globally. As explained earlier, several committees on banking reforms recommended a three-tier banking system structure with an international presence for 'synergising and complementarities of the merging units resulting in large-scale mergers, where thirteen banks merged into four to achieve economies of scale and greater synergy to improve restructuring and reduce the bad quality of assets. Moreover, M&A in India is regulated by the Company Act 2013 and supplemented by amendments, rules, and subsequent notifications and circulars. Many other regulations and guidelines actively regulate the M&A process in India, and their consolidation is essential to make the act effective.

The Irish Takeover Panel Act 1997, European Communities Takeover Bids (Directive 2004), Regulations 2006, SAR 2007, and Irish Takeover Rules 2013 are important legislations governing M&A in Ireland. The Irish Takeover Panel monitors and supervises takeovers in Ireland and directs companies for non-compliance. The principal means of acquiring an Irish public company include a takeover offer, arrangement scheme, and cross-border or domestic mergers. Asset quality is the prime concern when banks undertake M&A because it largely influences bank efficiency.

Many scholars have studied the impact of M&A and argued that deposit rates fall at banks involved in mergers that increase market concentration. The opposite argument suggests that they do not significantly change the market concentration. The M&A process in the UK, India, and Ireland involves dependency on several auxiliary laws that need priority consolidation. Finally, these jurisdictions have adopted several policy measures to control NPLs; proactive government support and a strong regulatory environment are essential for the success of any policy option that these jurisdictions mostly enjoy.

8.2.4 Micro-Level Management of Risk

This research study also critically examined financial performance, asset quality, and regulatory policy and the supervisory response of LBG, PNB and BIG, representing the UK, India and Ireland from the GFC to the COVID-19 pandemic to understand the micro-level risk management. LBG's decision to acquire HBOS coincided with the GFC, resulting in a high increase in NPLs. The NPLs of LBG in 2010 were 10.6%, significantly higher than the UK's average NPLs, which was 3.96% in the same year. This increase was due to high impairment losses and lower housing prices. The UK government avoided possible insolvency by liquidating banks through a bailout plan, which resulted in an improvement in NPLs which came down to 8.69% in 2012. Such a trend continued until 2018, when the NPLs of LBG were 1.28%, marginally higher than the average NPLs ratio of the UK (1.11%).

The impact of the GFC was also visible on the other parameters of asset quality, resulting in considerable deterioration in ROA, ROE, and NIM and impairment losses, and an inconsistent trend persisted until 2014. Poor asset quality forced LBG to participate in the HMT-backed APS to avoid a possible liquidity crunch. To recoup the government investment, LBG started sales of Govt shares and continued until it became the first European Bank to repay the entire government credit crunch investment. The impact of acquiring HBOS contributed to a significant decrease in the asset quality, which also reduced the share prices of the Group. Under such circumstances, FCA suggested the Group undergo a stress test if LBG required additional funding to overcome the crisis. LBG successfully met the criteria of the stress test.

However, the fluctuation in the various parameters of asset quality continued from 2016–21, mainly due to uncertainty about the UK's decision to leave the EU and the outbreak of the COVID-19 pandemic. LBG took several initiatives during the COVID-19 pandemic; as a result, there was a gradual improvement in its financial performance and asset quality from 2021, which indicates that LBG successfully managed uncertainty due to the pandemic, registered steady progress, and returned to a path of recovery.

LBG strictly followed CRD IV guidelines and made the balance sheet risk-free by ensuring a higher CET1 ratio (10.3%) and core Tier 1 ratio (14.0%), improving its loan-to-deposit ratio to 113% and core ratio to 100%. It's RWA improved by 88 basis points to 3.02% in 2014. In addition, LBG also maintained 0.9% of CCyB against the BoE requirement of 1% from 2022 onwards. The LBG has also achieved a strong leverage ratio of 4.1% and actively participated in helping 'Britain Prosper Drive', thus playing a leading role in supporting the UK's economic recovery, with growing SME lending consecutively for four years and providing mentoring support to them.

The risk management framework of LBG mainly focuses on risk culture and customers, following a transparent approach while identifying possible risks, sharing the lessons learned and identifying causes when things move in the wrong direction. LBG focuses on developing group-wise portfolio risk appetite. The emphasis was also on identifying, measuring, and controlling risks, which was an integral part of risk and control self-assessment. Thus, it has implemented three lines of defence: a business line, risk division, and internal audit line with clear responsibilities and accountabilities to ensure effective independent oversight.

LBG worked with the stakeholders during the COVID-19 crisis to ensure the sustainable recovery of debts. It provided millions of moratoriums across mortgages. The LBG initiatives gave the customers the flexibility they needed to get back on track and the comfort of their credit issues. Thus, the LBG provided time and space for customers to recover from the impact of the pandemic without losing their businesses, homes, and other valuables. The three-month interest-free buffer on the overdraft also helped the customers recover, rethink, and restart their businesses. The macroeconomic indicators of the UK significantly improved after the COVID-19 fightback, resulting in a speedy recovery in the asset quality of the LBG.

Therefore, LGB also faced a threat from the GFC, uncertainty on the UK decision to leave the EU, the COVID-19 pandemic and LBG's decision to acquire HBOS, resulting in poor performance on the financial front, including the loss in PBT and PAT, increase in impairment charges, deterioration in ROE, ROA, NIM etc. consequently impacting NPL ratio. LBG took several steps, including creating three levels of the risk management system, strict implementation of regulatory requirements, constant monitoring of risk appetite and maintaining relatively high CET, RWA and CCyB to ensure sufficient liquidity to mitigate the crisis. Despite having a robust mechanism, the impact of the GFC and the pandemic exerted tremendous pressure on the group, and we suggest that the group should develop an effective system to identify oversight and avoid possible risks.

The impact of the GFC was minimal on the Indian banks, including PNB; as a result, the parameters of asset quality remained sound immediately after the GFC. However, there was a sharp increase in the GNPA and NNPA from 2013 onwards, and it peaked in 2018 with 18.38% GNPA and 11.24% NNPA. After touching the peak, the GNPA and NNPA started receding and were 1.78% and 4.80% in 2022. There has been considerable variation in asset quality parameters such as ROE, ROA, CIR, CAR and NIM. The bank also followed RBI guidelines to maintain the Tier 1 and 2 capital ratios. The return to assets also fluctuated significantly and was negative during COVID-19. There was a significant improvement in the provisions after the GFC, which increased from 46.18% in 2008 to 81.60% in 2022, indicating that the bank has enough capital to meet possible downturns. After COVID-19, the Bank's CAR stood at 14.32%, with Tier-I capital at 11.50% and CET1 at 10.62%. Therefore, internal and external factors influenced the behaviour of asset quality parameters, and variation was considerably high due to the impact of the crisis.

The bank took many initiatives at the micro level to address the problem of NPA, including setting up specialised NPA management branches and cells to resolve NPA cases. The Bank regularly monitors all NPA cases and has developed account-specific resolution strategies for upgrading non-performing to the performing category within the scope of the SARFAESI Act and achieved considerable success. The Bank has launched a special recovery drive to improve asset quality through PPF and PIRD initiatives. This pan-India drive has successfully improved the recovery of small advances. Its Mega *Rin Mukti Shivirs* (Debt Relief Camps) targeted the wilful defaulters and expedited the pace of settlement.

PNB applied regulatory measures such as invoking SDR for outstanding amounts and CDR for restructured accounts and started Mission *Gandhigiri* with a peaceful *dharna* (demonstration) to put moral pressure on the defaulters. Moreover, the bank successfully initiated an e-auction portal to dispose of bad assets and realised the sale of the securitised assets. In addition, the bank took several initiatives to level down NPLs, including OTS of NPA accounts, with a balance of ₹ 250 million, to accelerate recovery, besides creating Asset Recovery Management Branches as part of the vertical for managing NPA accounts for more than ₹ 5 million.

Despite the COVID-19 pandemic, banks' efforts to curtail NPAs continued by augmenting loan restructuring strategies. PNB LenS, dedicated to managing retail, agriculture, MSME, and corporate sector loans with specified limits, constantly monitors default cases. SASTRA strengthened with the provision to report loans dealt under OTS, SARFAESI, DRT and NCLT. The Bank also strengthened the DRT and SARFAESI portals by re-configuring with the NCLT portal. The bank prepared the database of the wilful defaulters loaded on the portal through a separate module. PNB integrated the PNB Pride App with SASTRA and geo-tagged the activities and locations of field-level functionaries to monitor their efforts to deal with NPA cases at a micro level.

All these efforts contributed significantly to reduce NPLs to a great extent. Nonetheless, the problem of NPLs has always remained a cause of concern in the PNB due to liberal lending policy and government lending priority on social sector beneficiaries' schemes. The conventional loan recovery methods would not work effectively in such a situation. Therefore, PNB should look for an alternative approach to deal with such cases. In addition, banks should also strengthen their mechanisms to avoid banking fraud.

The Bank of Ireland faced serious liquidity constraints due to disruption in the international financial markets in the latter half of 2008, mainly due to 'recession and rapid deterioration in credit conditions and asset prices'. The bank's profit reduced considerably in 2008–09, reflecting relatively lower growth. The Government of Ireland supported banks in Ireland to bail them out of a liquidity crunch, and such liquidity injection was considered extremely important for sustainable economic growth and the proper functioning of a healthy banking system.

The sovereign debt has several rigid compliance issues in addition to the emphasis of the EU and the IMF to downsize and reorganise the banking sector. Moreover, a new regulatory requirement of CET 1 put the group under tremendous stress. Therefore, the bank losses on the disposal of assets to NAMA and impairment provisions to non-NAMA portfolios remained relatively higher. Later, the bank prepared a deleveraging plan to reduce reliance on liquidity support from funding agencies. The contraction in the Irish economy, the fiscal adjustment programme, and high unemployment levels contributed to the increase in insolvencies. In 2012, the mortgage lending market amounted to €2.6 billion, and there was a continuous increase in mortgage arrears.

Consequently, there was a sharp fall in property value, increasing unemployment and illiquidity, and adversely affecting the banking business. Such volatility in Ireland and the international market continued for a longer period; as a result, the underlying operating profit before impairment charges was down. Therefore, the entire focus of the bank was to manage arrears to improve credit quality.

BIG undertook several steps to manage the risk arising from its business activities. The Central Bank and Credit Institutions (Resolution) Act and the Credit Institutions (Stabilisation) Act 2010 created a mechanism for state intervention in the banking industry and its operation with authority to take over, run and break up troubled FIs to minimise the cost of a bank failure on taxpayers. In addition, a forbearance strategy was in operation for non-sustainable mortgages where 'the banks maximise recoveries on mortgages in defaults'. Consequently, there was some sign of improvement in asset quality parameters from 2012 onwards, and as a result, NPLs also started receding and were significantly low (5.56%) in 2018.

BIG has made a robust management mechanism to address micro-level risk, consisting of three-tier support systems: line management, central risk management, and GIA. Under this mechanism, twelve committees dealing with different types of risk are in operation under GRPCs headed by the GCRO, which oversees all risk categories, formulates risk appetite recommendations, develops policies, and establishes integrated group-wise risk measurement and management standards.

Subsequently, CET1 (14.9%) and the fully loaded CET1 capital ratio (13.4%) remained strong despite elevated impairment charges. The operating profit also increased, and impairment came down to the pre-COVID-19 level, reflecting significant improvement in asset quality and an overall improvement in the global financial services average scores. Finally, the group recovered from the impact of COVID-19 and acquired KBCI and J&E Davy in 2021.

BIG has developed an ecosystem to identify risk at the transaction level, allocating sufficient resources to develop the skill to identify and determine the risk and undertake appropriate assessment through stress and scenario tests. It has developed a comprehensive risk taxonomy to identify risks related to a particular type, immediately address the problem, and mitigate external market risks due to crises like the GFC and COVID-19. In addition, geopolitical events like Brexit, the Russia-Ukraine war and other emerging risks substantially impact earnings, capital adequacy, and trade prospects, and the group also needs to make sufficient provisions to address such types of risks and make a system to monitor them effectively.

Finally, these groups/banks have made robust mechanisms to mitigate the risk at the micro level. They aligned their risk management system with regulatory, supervisory and policy compliance. Thus, these FIs work in a strong regulatory and supervisory ecosystem with constant support and guidance from regulators on capital adequacy so that banks remain liquid. Despite these mechanisms, financial downturns and large banking fraud always loom over them, instantly percolate globally, and jeopardise the robust mechanisms developed over the years. The international expansion of the banking business has made banks more vulnerable and risk-prone. Therefore, the system needs to be developed and made more watchful to identify the risk and resolve the issue at the branch level before it percolates across the branches and jurisdictions and turns into a national or global crisis.

8.2.5 Synthesis of COVID-19 Interventions

The COVID-19 outbreak triggered across the globe, and due to this war-like situation, contraction in economics posed many challenges, including the severity of the impact of the pandemic on the NPLs and the bank balance sheet. The regulators and supervisors faced challenges in designing and implementing a suitable response to the crisis. The financial position of jurisdictions before the outbreak of COVID-19 was much more robust than that of the GFC because the eurozone had 16.5% CET to RWA compared to 8.8% in 2008 at the time of the GFC. As evident, these crises originated in two leading economies of the world, the GFC in the USA and the COVID-19 pandemic in China and created chaos and uncertainty across the globe, setting aside many economic activities. The contraction speed was very high, and the stock exchanges dropped drastically worldwide. The reaction to both crises for sovereign support was immediate, mainly to avoid possible downturns and minimise the effect on FIs and jurisdictions.

The response of the UK government to reduce the impact of COVID-19 was unprecedented, and it introduced guaranteed loan schemes for financing SMEs and large businesses. As discussed in Chap. 7, the UK business capitalisation schemes comprising CBILS, BBLS, CLBILS and FFS received an overwhelming response. The schemes were so successful that 92.5% of loan applications were backed by the UK government loan guarantee, increasing the UK contingent liability. It has created a potential risk to the HMT in the event of default because schemes did not follow the due diligence process for approving loan applications, and the majority of loans skewed towards micro and non-employing businesses from disadvantaged sectors and regions. The scheme was inclined to increase the default cases in the future, burdening the taxpayers.

Nevertheless, these schemes supported the business and rescued many firms from possible insolvency and bankruptcy. Policymakers and regulators presumed that there would be default and fraudulent applications. However, information on the HMT website shows that in March 2022, 3.8% of applications defaulted, with a maximum from BBLS, and 78.8% had a scheduled payment.

Moreover, in the UK, its leading banks used LLP to minimise the variation in income and to negate the possible impact of COVID-19 on their earning. The results concluded that LLP was highest when the pandemic peaked and subsequently declined, establishing a positive relationship. Moreover, the UK also relaxed its regulatory and supervisory rules to support the banks in mitigating the negative effects of the pandemic on banks' balance sheets to avoid a possible increase in forbearance cases.

The impact of COVID-19 on the UK economy was enormous, and it became difficult to achieve a growth projection of 4.9%. The BoE took several steps to support the business environment, including access to low-interest loans, a moratorium on the entities struggling to repay mortgages, and a reduction in the base rate from 0.75% to 0.25%, without much success. The impact was also visible on government bonds. Under such a situation, it extended APF as a contingent measure to purchase and hold government bonds and ensured that the markets for the UK government bonds continued to function. This scheme received criticism for lacking transparency in decision-making.

However, these efforts were quite fruitful, and the UK domestic risk to financial stability has returned to the pre-COVID-19 level. The bank's capital and liquidity ratio also remained much more potent and able to support the business. The asset quality remained stable and even supported the economic recovery. Consequently, FPC increased the UK CCyB from 0.5% to 1%. The FPC even conducted a desk-based SST to see the effects of the COVID-19 crisis on UK banks and concluded that usable buffers of the capital built up by the banks could absorb the losses under a feasible illustrative scenario. However, UK banks must closely monitor the quality of their assets to identify possible deterioration, particularly in the riskier segments, and manage NPLs from the balance sheet.

Due to the adverse effects of the COVID-19 pandemic and the burden of lockdown, major sectors of the Indian economy, including manufacturing, auto, retail, aviation, hospitality, etc., dribble down. The Indian economy was already experiencing a downturn before the pandemic, with the increasing trend of unemployment and poverty. A large-scale reverse labour migration to the rural areas due to the shutdown of economic operations aggravated the problem, and the crisis led to a loss of employment to the tune of at least 15 million. The increasing unemployment, job cuts, and reverse migration considerably reduced the loan repayment capacity. Therefore, the RBI introduced various economic, fiscal and regulatory measures to fight the COVID-19 crisis, mainly focusing on liquidity, credit risk and well-being.

On the other hand, the RBI introduced credit enhancement schemes and loan moratoriums to reduce the effects of COVID-19. A loan moratorium was initially for three months, with a further extension for all types of loans and FIs. The banks allowed funded interest-term loans to reduce NPLs by recovering interest, subject to supervisory review, and their justifiability for default due to COVID-19. Moreover, MPC focused on negating the effect of COVID-19, reviving growth and ensuring financial stability.

It also ensured enough liquidity in the market by reducing the CRR to 4%. The Government and RBI worked in tandem and increased the limits on the advances for the central and state governments to ensure smooth spending. RBI issued regulatory guidelines for rescheduling payments for term loans, providing exemptions for SMA and NPA classification. RBI also deferred the NSFR for one year, besides reducing LCR to 80%, intending to restore the same to its original position in

2021 in a phased manner, increasing 10% yearly. In addition, the RBI introduced OT and OMS to reduce short-term securities' yield and regulate market liquidity. It also provided substantial funds for LTROs for one to three years for business revival.

Thus, RBI policy and regulatory responses were quite impressive, and the Government and RBI were closely monitoring the global development and calibrating them depending on the intensity of the COVID-19 impact. The experience learnt from the past crisis also made them robust and enabled the crafting of flexible systems for helping COVID-19-stressed borrowers. The RBI achieved its objective of keeping the financial market sound and liquid and ensuring financial stability despite the initial downturn. RBI injected a huge amount into liquidating the banks to help the system progress. The gross NPAs to gross advances were 7.30% in 2020–21 and 5.8% in 2021–22, and net NPLs declined from 2.4% to 1.7%. Comparing the figure with pre-COVID-19 ratios, the GNPAs and NPAs were 11.20% and 8.20%, respectively. However, some banks' gross NPAs still show disturbing and stressful situations. Therefore, more efforts are required to address their issues and bring down the level of NPLs.

The Irish Government also responded to the crisis by taking several measures to help the struggling businesses and protect the customers' interests. The CBI shifted its priorities towards the immediate and long-term implications of COVID-19 on the economy, financial system, and consumers. It worked closely with NTMA and made FSG responsible for coordinating the inter-agency work on the impact of COVID-19. Moreover, the ECB has also introduced a wide range of monetary policy measures to preserve household firms, emphasising that the jurisdictions should immediately review the asset quality to identify NPLs.

The Irish Government has reduced CCyB by 0% to help the banks absorb the losses and provide additional funds to the business and customers. Moreover, the Central Bank has announced a three-month PB with a further extension of three months on mortgages and personal and business loans to some companies to relieve the customers facing difficulties due to the pandemic. PB allow customers to postpone or reduce their repayments on mortgage, personal or business loans, relieving borrowers and ensuring no additional borrowers fall into the forbearance category. Under TLTROs, credit supply was stimulated, and bank lending was incentivised to the private sector. The restriction on housing loans was to save the economy from uncertainty.

ECB also set up zero and 50 basis points for MRO and DFR if banks achieve specific lending performance thresholds, easing the lending performance threshold and reducing the interest rates on all outstanding liquidity by 25 basis points. These policy and regulatory responses put the Irish economy on the path to recovery. The ECB also announced that APS, with easy collateral, would support the financing conditions in Ireland and provide direct financial support to the euro area firms. Irish banks have struggled due to the interest rates, and this pressure has aggravated a lot during the pandemic. The stock market wiped out huge values of the Irish Bank's shares. The rating agency Standard & Poor put the main banks of Ireland on the watch list because of the potential credit downgrade. However, with continuous, coordinated efforts, the situation in Ireland improved, and there was a substantial decrease in the NPLs, which was 5.56% at the pre-COVID stage and reduced to 2.28% in 2021.

Finally, the COVID-19 pandemic rigorously impacted the banking sector of the UK, India and Ireland. Central banks' timely stimulus action and huge liquidity injections met the business and individual credit requirements. The lesson learnt from the GFC also stimulated the supervisors to take prompt and timely corrective measures in the short run, and in the long run, the stress on the banking sector remains intact. Nevertheless, the economies, including the UK, India and Ireland, are on the path of recovery, and it is evident from the fact that the NPL ratios of these jurisdictions were lower in 2021 than at the dawn of COVID-19.

8.3 Possible Interventions

The present book analysed various issues that directly or indirectly impact the NPLs in the UK, India and Ireland. The positive and negative relationship between NPLs and macroeconomic and microeconomic determinants and vice versa greatly influences the economic progress of these jurisdictions. The existing regulatory, supervisory and policy architectures adequately control NPLs, but several deficiencies, weaknesses, flaws and ambiguity in the existing system incited us to think differently. Despite enforcing several pieces of legislation, inadequacy is exposed during financial distress to manage the system effectively. Therefore, the legislation, supervisory control, and policy prescription examined in Chaps. 4 and 5 of this book are not panaceas for addressing the problem of NPLs, particularly in a situation where global economies are working so closely.

The book also accomplished an in-depth micro-level investigation by instituting three case studies involving LBG, PNB, and BIG to assess and understand the risk management strategies of these FIs to avoid possible insolvencies and bankruptcies. The book also analysed the impact of the COVID-19 pandemic and efforts to control NPLs. Thus, these interventions are essential to managing NPLs and mitigating possible financial distress.

Harmonisation of NPLs Definition: There has been considerable debate in the relevant section of this book on the approaches adopted by the jurisdictions to define NPLs. OECD presented scoreboards of some jurisdictions on the timeframe to declare loans as NPLs and concluded that there was considerable variation in the approaches adopted by these jurisdictions, which range from 30 days to 90 days and beyond. Moreover, Basel guidelines critically examined the quality of assets and classified and defined NPLs as forbearance, performing, non-performing, weakened and loss to harmonise the definition of NPLs. Conversely, the RBI contextualised the definition of NPLs, linking it to crop duration from one crop to two crops, depending on the crop gestation. However, later on the RBI classified distressed assets as Special Mention Account(SMA) with 0-30 days of loan default SMA, 31-60 days SMA01 and 61-90 SMA02. In addition, several jurisdictions have also adopted an isolated approach to defining NPLs. However, a harmonised approach to defining NPLs with a scope of incorporating local requirements would be useful for classifying loans as NPLs.

Therefore, a harmonised definition will provide a common framework to identify risk and facilitate more accurate asset quality and creditworthiness assessment, as collateral evaluation helps to identify potential credit risk and facilitate its resolution.[8] However, there are some socio-economic and political factors which pose challenges. For instance, diverse financial conditions of jurisdictions and banks, use of collateral, non-availability of data, country-specific regulatory framework, and time consideration for declaring NPLs, national interest, regulatory autonomy and institutional capacity impede a consensus on harmonising NPLs definition.[8] In addition, the involvement of stakeholders, the impact on borrowers' creditworthiness, and the social goal of promoting financial inclusion also pose challenges.[9] However, despite the pros and cons, a harmonised approach to defining NPLs will provide a common framework for maintaining international standards.

To Reduce the Impact of Microeconomic and Macroeconomic Determinants: Macroeconomic and microeconomic determinants have positive and negative impacts on NPLs, which have cascading effects on the economic development of a country. Chapters 2 and 3 critically analysed the relationship between NPLs and economic determinants and revealed how these determinants adversely impact the various parameters of asset quality and intensify and increase credit market shocks to the economy. Moreover, the impact of these determinants is pro-cyclical, percolating into the various sectors of the economy very rapidly, which also influences the global economy due to over-reliance on modern means of technology. There are several examples when volatility in stock prices, a slump in Nikkei in Tokyo, percolates to BSE in Mumbai, to LSE in London, and NYSE in New York on the same day, losing millions of dollars in a single day and swallowing a huge amount and having adverse effects on the economies.

The lower asset quality affects the profitability of the banks, which leads to a credit crunch, reducing the banks' income and ultimately contributing to job losses. It subsequently reduces individual income and loan repayment capability, increasing NPLs and chances of insolvencies and bankruptcies, consequently impacting a country's financial stability. Therefore, lower asset quality brings economic slowdown and contributes to financial instability. Thus, poor asset quality is the root cause of high levels of NPLs, and appropriate mechanisms would help to address the problem most effectively. The jurisdictions must critically analyse various asset quality parameters to ensure information symmetry. A disintegrated approach at the regulatory, supervisory and policy levels will aggravate the problem.

Single Regulatory and Supervisory Agency: While critically analysing the regulatory ecosystem in the UK, India and Ireland, the research study concluded that multiple regulatory bodies regulate the financial sector in the UK and India. For instance, FCA, PRA, HMT and BoE regulate and supervise financial activities in

[8] OECD (2015)

[9] Bank for International Settlement (2017).

the UK, and RBI, SEBI, IRDA, FMC and PFRDA regulate and supervise such activities in India. Moreover, the Indian government intervenes in their functioning through respective ministries. The situation in Ireland is somewhat different. The EC introduced SSM, where the EBA and the CBI work closely to supervise and regulate the financial system. Therefore, a single supervisory and regulatory mechanism that works closely with respective governments will be a useful preposition for effectively coordinating and monitoring the financial system.

Adequacy of Regulations: The opinions of scholars on the adequacy of regulations dealing with financial sector issues are fragmented. One school of thought advocates that the existing regulations are adequate to regulate the banking sector and do not require changes. Others realise that regulations are inadequate and there is a requirement for 'tight but light' regulations to make them more effective. There has been considerable debate on softening the requirement of regulations and having dynamically adjusted regulations, with dynamic provisioning and requirements for CAR.

In these jurisdictions, many regulations regulate financial sector activities, including banking. As discussed in Chap. 4, such amalgamation will help regulate financial sector activities effectively. For instance, for M&A to take place under the Takeover Act, the involvement of half a dozen related legislations (CJ Act, Enterprise Act, NSI Act, CMA, etc.) complicates the process of M&A to a great extent. Moreover, the financial sector in the UK and EU has several regulations and directives, including MiFIR, MiFID, PSD, AMLD, BRRD, BCHD, etc. The researcher realised the need to reduce the regulatory burden and advocate for dynamically adjusted regulations with suitable laws for financial market regulation. A rigid approach will not work because regulatory and supervisory requirements will continuously evolve to address the new challenges emerging due to the widespread use of the Internet and the involvement of banks in online activities.

Policy Options: The resolution of NPLs through centralised and decentralised approaches remained the centre of discussion in Chap. 5 of this book. The selection of appropriate policy options depends on the intensity of the problem. Therefore, the bank-specific policy options would be effective if the problem lies within the bank. If the intensity of the problem is large and percolates across the jurisdiction, country-specific options will work more effectively. Therefore, a cautious approach is required to adopt appropriate policy options under the central bank's guidance. After critically examining the pros and cons of various policy options, it is realised that selecting policy options from the bouquet would depend on the size and nature of distressed loans that require restructuring.

The UK, India and Ireland used OCWs, AMC, securitisation, write-off, APS, direct sale of assets, and M&A. Effective use of AMCs to resolve distressed assets remained a highly successful policy option after the GFC in the UK and Ireland. In India, a large-scale reform in the banking sector prompted the classification of distressed loans and the use of M&A for consolidating banks and synergising merging units by restructuring banks to achieve a economies of scale and for expansion of scale. Similarly, the UK and Ireland effectively and successfully used government bailout plans, where respective governments injected funds to liquidate the banks during the crisis. Thus, selecting suitable policy options depends on several factors, and the jurisdiction should critically assess the prevailing situation before opting for and implementing a resolution plan to address the problem of NPLs.

Close Coordination: Close coordination between the supervisory and regulatory authorities will provide adequate support to the FIs, particularly in a crisis like the GFC, the COVID-19 pandemic, Brexit and unexpected conflicts among jurisdictions (Russia–Ukraine war, etc.) to avoid financial crunch and reduce forbearance and non-performing cases. Supervisors and regulators should always be ready with a contingent plan to meet emergent situation and to ensure financial stability. The jurisdictions may even constitute oversight management groups to monitor emerging risks. Moreover, effective cross-country coordination through supervisors would help identify possible economic downturns.

Micro Management of NPLs: The banks also develop risk management and mitigation systems to avoid possible distress, besides following the instructions of supervisors and regulators. The banks should develop a multi-tier risk management system to avoid oversight. Continuous risk assessment and reporting, even at the micro level (branch level), would help avoid insolvency and bankruptcy. Chapter 6 analysed the micro-management of risk and the efforts of the jurisdictions to improve recovery by using technology effectively. Such efforts at the branch level would yield fruitful results, and the banks need to develop and cultivate micro-level strategies to improve recovery at the micro-level.

Integrated Risk Mitigation System: Loan losses are a prevalent problem across institutions and jurisdictions. Several international agencies like the OECD, IMF, World Bank, ECB, and ADB continuously work to determine why higher NPLs exist and develop and implement resolution plans. Due to the widespread use of technology, jurisdictions across the globe are interconnected, and if problems erupt in a country, that will immediately explode worldwide, therefore, effective curtailment is essential. There is an urgent need to develop a five-tier Integrated Risk Management System (IRMS) integrating mini (branch) micro (bank), meso (region) country and global systems with suitable risk identification, analysis, management and mitigation systems at each level to cure rising level of NPLs effectively so that future financial crisis if emerged, dealt effectively.

The Proactive Role of Basel: Basel provides guidelines on banking supervision and regulations to ensure adequate funds with banks to meet emergent situations. It has provided regulatory requirements for maintaining CAR, RWA, CET 1 and 2, CCyB, etc. It periodically undertakes a critical assessment of forbearance, performing, and NPAs, which the researcher critically examined in the first chapter. The jurisdictions that adopted Basel principles follow these regulatory requirements strictly to ensure banks have sufficient liquidity. Therefore, Basel should be more proactive in providing supervisory and regulatory guidance to the jurisdictions facing financial difficulty. In addition, more jurisdictions should come under the Basel umbrella to harmonise supervisory and regulatory frameworks.

8.4 Concluding Remarks

Henceforth, the present research embarked upon a heartfelt endeavour to decipher the answer to the research questions posed at its genesis, intending to address the conundrum of NPLs. It concludes that despite the jurisdictions' numerous efforts, an imperative necessity exists to consolidate, integrate, and alleviate regulatory constraints while enhancing supervisory compliance effectiveness. A singular supervisory and regulatory mechanism would yield greater effectiveness in dealing with the problem of NPLs and coordinating with FIs, including banks. Jurisdictions possess an array of policy prescriptions available for implementation, and they should use them judiciously to select the most appropriate policy measure based on the nature, size, and extent of the NPLs' problem.

The book also critically examined macroeconomic and microeconomic determinants and their impact on the NPLs and vice versa. It concluded that the relationship between NPLs and economic determinants is vital and varies across jurisdictions. Jurisdictions should concentrate on improving the relationship of these determinants with NPLs, such as determinants, to avert a decline in asset quality and the overall economy. Further, this research study meticulously scrutinises the issues related to risk management at the micro-level, encompassing case studies of LBG, PNB, and BIG. It provides profound insight into the risk management system at the bank level. It elucidates how each banking group has grappled with managing NPLs at the grassroots level by undertaking several concentrated efforts to improve recovery.

The book suggests that adopting a multi-tier Integrated Risk Management System (IRMS) would be appropriate for effectively identifying, managing, and mitigating risk at different levels. The book also examines the regulatory, supervisory, and policy initiatives delineated to counteract the impact of COVID-19 and concludes that proactive action can help avert short-term downturns. However, further in-depth analysis would furnish enduring solutions.

Nevertheless, in this era of ubiquitous online technologies, where FIs are globally interconnected, the challenges of containing the global spread of the financial crisis persist without sound regulatory and supervisory mechanisms on a multi-level scale to constrain and mitigate the problem. Nonetheless, this comparative study critically examines the predicament of NPLs encompassing the UK, India, and Ireland, which is notably unique due to their distinct socio-economic and geopolitical contexts. The study identifies and tackles various issues concerning NPLs management and subsequently prescribes corrective measures, incorporating them into the comprehensive framework of this study. Hence, the study categorically elucidates how these jurisdictions successfully and effectively managed the problem of NPLs, spanning from the GFC to the current COVID-19 pandemic, despite facing numerous unprecedented challenges. The research also highlights the country-specific challenges in implementing these measures and provides suggestive interventions the jurisdictions must follow to adeptly manage the escalating level of NPLs.

References

Bank of Ireland (2013) Consumer protection code review discussion paper–engagement update. https://www.centralbank.ie/docs/default-source/regulation/consumer-protection/other-codes-of-conduct/consumer-protection-code-review/consumer-protection-code-review%2D%2D-discussion-paper%2D%2D-engagement-update.pdf. Accessed 5 Aug 2023

BIS (2017) Prudential treatment of problem assets – definitions of non-performing exposures and forbearance. https://www.bis.org/bcbs/publ/d403.pdf. Accessed 10 Apr 2024

Dass A, Agarwal AK, Sinha UK (2020) Insolvency and bankruptcy reforms: the way forward. Vikalp 45(2):115. https://journals.sagepub.com/doi/epub/10.1177/0256090920953988. Accessed 30 July 2023

Edmonds T (2013, December 30) The independent commission on banking: the Vickers report and parliament commission on Banking Standards. House of Common Library. https://researchbriefings.files.parliament.uk/documents/SN06171/SN06171.pdf. Accessed 22 Apr 2022

Liikanen E (2012) High-level expert group on reforming the structure of the EU banking sector. https://ec.europa.eu/info/sites/default/files/liikanen-report-02102012_en.pdf. Accessed 23 Apr 2022

Nguyen TPT, Nghiem SH (2016) Market concentration, diversification and bank performance in China and India: an application of the two-stage approach with double bootstrap. Manag Finance 42(10):980

OECD (2015) Non-performing loans: insights from the scoreboard on SME finance. Financing SME and enterprise: an OECD scoreboard. OECD publishing

PwC (2014) EU bank recovery and resolution directive 'triumph or tragedy'. PwC. https://www.pwc.com/im/en/publications/assets/pwceubankrecoveryandresolutiondirectivetriumphortragedy.pdf. Accessed 5 Aug 2023

Sarkar S (2016) The dynamics of the revenue diversification and efficiency of banks in India. IIM Kozhikode Soc Manag Rev 5(2):156

Annexure 1

A. Dimri, *Non-Performing Loans*, Ius Gentium: Comparative Perspectives on Law and Justice 125, https://doi.org/10.1007/978-3-031-92952-6

Trend of NPL Ratios, GDP, Unemployment, Inflation on Consumer Price and Exchange Rate

	UK	India	Ireland	UK	India	Ireland	UK	India	Ireland	UK	India	Ireland	UK	India	Ireland
	NPLs			GDP			Unemployment, % of the total labour force (ILO estimate)			Inflation on the Consumer Price Index			Relation between NPLs and Exchange Rate with US $		
													Value per (£)	Value per (₹)	Value per (€)
2008	1.56	2.31	1.92	4.73	3.09	−4.49	5.62	5.36	6.77	3.52	8.35	4.06	0.54	45.99	0.68
2009	3.51	2.32	9.80	−4.11	7.86	−5.1	7.54	5.61	12.61	1.96	10.88	−4.48	0.64	47.44	0.72
2010	3.95	2.45	13.05	2.07	8.50	1.76	7.79	5.65	14.53	2.49	11.99	−0.92	0.65	45.56	0.76
2011	3.96	2.67	16.12	1.28	5.24	1.07	8.04	5.65	15.35	3.86	8.86	2.56	0.62	47.92	0.72
2012	3.59	3.37	24.99	1.43	5.46	−0.05	7.89	5.66	15.45	2.57	9.31	1.70	0.63	54.41	0.78
2013	3.11	4.03	25.71	2.19	6.39	1.27	7.52	5.67	13.74	2.29	11.06	0.51	0.64	60.50	0.75
2014	1.65	4.35	20.65	2.86	7.41	8.71	6.11	5.6	11.86	1.45	6.65	0.18	0.61	61.14	0.75
2015	1.01	5.88	14.93	2.36	8.00	25.18	5.3	5.56	9.91	0.37	4.91	−0.29	0.65	65.47	0.90
2016	0.94	9.19	13.61	1.72	8.26	2.04	4.81	5.51	8.37	1.01	4.95	0.01	0.74	67.07	0.90
2017	0.73	9.98	11.46	1.74	6.8	8.94	4.33	5.41	6.71	2.56	3.33	0.34	0.78	64.45	0.89
2018	1.07	9.46	5.73	1.25	6.53	9.03	4.00	5.33	5.74	2.29	3.95	0.49	0.75	69.92	0.85
2019	1.08	9.23	3.36	1.37	4.04	4.92	3.74	5.27	4.95	1.74	3.72	0.94	0.78	70.90	0.89
2020	1.22	7.94	3.54	−9.79	−7.96	5.87	4.34	7.11	5.92	0.99	6.62	−0.33	0.78	74.23	0.88
Mean Value	2.106	6.23	12.58	0.70	5.36	4.55	5.93	5.65	10.15	2.08	7.28	0.37	0.68	59.62	0.81
SDEV	1.29	2.85	7.52	3.70	4.46	7.56	1.64	0.14	3.90	0.989	3.006	1.975	0.077	10.24	0.81
Correlation	–	–	–	−0.0028	−0.05	0.05	0.95	0.017	0.79	0.516	−0.879	0.280	−0.55	0.91	−0.22

Source: Data Bank, World Development Indicators, World Bank

Annexure 2

A. Dimri, *Non-Performing Loans*, Ius Gentium: Comparative Perspectives on Law and Justice 125, https://doi.org/10.1007/978-3-031-92952-6

Trend of Banks' Capital to Assets, Regulatory Risk-Weighted Assets and Liquid Assets to Deposits and Short-Term Funding Return on Assets and Equity

	Bank Capital to Asset Ratio (%)			Bank Regulatory Capital to Risk-weighted Assets (%)			Liquid Assets to Deposits and Short-term Funding (%)			ROA (Before Tax) (%)			ROE (Before Tax) (%)		
Year	UK	India	Ireland	UK	India	Ireland	UK	India	Ireland	UK	India	Ireland	UK	India	Ireland
2008	4.41	7.3	3.75	12.9	13	12.1	36.27	11.09	30.27	0.048	1.645	1.645	1.466	24.739	10.735
2009	5.39	7.0	5.44	14.8	14.3	12.8	49.32	9.68	32.65	−0.052	1.461	1.461	−1.665	20.857	−74.208
2010	5.37	6.99	5.32	15.89	15.16	14.47	51.35	8.46	33.34	−0.015	1.593	1.593	−0.368	22.803	−102.159
2011	5.10	6.70	6.44	15.73	13.05	18.92	49.51	7.91	39.93	0.058	1.580	1.580	1.235	22.628	−19.416
2012	5.51	6.97	7.28	17.07	13.13	19.24	54.78	7.21	40.12	−0.249	1.378	1.378	−5.078	19.671	−12.565
2013	6.35	6.92	7.75	19.61	12.34	20.50	54.70	6.92	32.58	0.187	1.360	1.360	3.788	19.103	−14.756
2014	5.62	7.09	12.7	17.31	12.49	22.68	46.09	6.71	31.03	0.251	1.072	1.072	4.562	15.114	11.959
2015	6.84	7.21	14.0	19.62	12.69	24.38	58.84	9.84	34.73	0.573	0.506	0.506	6.115	5.781	8.199
2016	7.03	7.16	13.5	20.80	12.97	26.94	54.26	12.96	36.95	0.421	0.974	0.974	4.519	10.481	9.136
2017	6.78	7.39	14.3	20.50	12.83	25.34	64.85	12.37	26.76	0.672	0.177	0.177	7.436	1.776	7.9
2018	6.82	7.53	14.9	21.43	12.97	25.39	67.15	12.55	NA	0.638	0.491	0.491	6.947	4.721	9.613
2019	6.79	8.11	13.5	21.16	15.42	24.97	65.07	13.29	NA	0.553	0.714	0.714	6.057	6.712	9.351
2020	6.87	8.10	11.4	21.60	14.8	26.0	69.18	11.17	NA	0.289	0.249	0.249	3.259	2.528	NA
Mean	**6.21**	**7.27**	**10.02**	**18.34**	**13.47**	**21.06**	**55.48**	**10.01**	**34.27**	**0.260**	**1.015**	**1.015**	**2.944**	**13.609**	**−13.018**
SD	**0.865**	0.430	**4.074**	**2.88**	**1.015**	**5.205**	**7.32**	**2.05**	**3.287**	**0.259**	**0.503**	**0.503**	**3.692**	**8.524**	**37.311**
Correlation	**−0.64**	**0.683**	**−0.123**	**−0.622**	**0.049**	**−0.021**	**−0.446**	**0.78**	**0.434**	**−0.840**	**−0.873**	**−0.873**	**−0.804**	**−0.918**	**−0.087**

Source: Data Bank, World Development Indicators, World Bank

Annexure 3

A. Dimri, *Non-Performing Loans*, Ius Gentium: Comparative Perspectives on Law and Justice 125, https://doi.org/10.1007/978-3-031-92952-6

Trend of Banks' Non-Interest Income, Overhead Costs to Total Assets and Cost to Income Ratio, Net Interest Margin and Z-Score

	Banks Non-interests Income (%)			Bank cost-to-Income Ratio (%)			Bank Overhead Costs to Total Assets (%)			Net Interest Margin (%)			Z-Score		
Year	UK	India	Ireland	UK	India	Ireland	UK	India	Ireland	UK	India	Ireland	UK	India	Ireland
2008	47.29	35.38	18.58	56.435	48.094	38.230	0.938	2.046	0.109	1.698	3.141	0.172	4.96	17.90	2.70
2009	49.08	35.64	NA	59.743	45.021	32.253	0.734	1.670	0.257	1.597	2.731	0.551	6.34	17.14	1.03
2010	49.73	34.61	22.20	57.920	45.017	20.001	0.392	1.886	0.310	2.127	3.085	1.012	8.34	17.69	0.02
2011	59.85	27.97	64.63	61.399	45.538	19.372	0.708	1.887	0.624	1.648	3.349	1.217	8.93	17.39	5.03
2012	57.17	26.63	NA	74.279	44.245	37.160	1.138	1.666	1.030	1.041	3.068	1.098	8.55	17.52	6.42
2013	50.86	27.23	NA	64.928	45.804	55.000	0.962	1.729	1.468	1.498	3.011	1.227	9.45	17.67	6.50
2014	44.54	28.20	NA	71.348	47.377	64.120	1.417	1.721	1.591	1.479	2.850	1.113	11.43	16.93	10.14
2015	46.80	26.23	72.23	66.425	46.536	61.123	1.635	1.718	1.133	1.721	3.040	0.988	17.47	19.27	13.74
2016	44.32	32.05	78.72	67.494	45.468	39.767	1.405	1.797	1.787	1.542	3.060	0.983	16.87	22.57	12.42
2017	46.09	27.54	76.38	62.406	48.472	54.820	1.411	2.008	1.387	1.537	3.450	0.975	17.44	21.99	11.52
2018	46.72	27.91	76.28	62.816	46.462	54.685	1.473	1.836	1.612	1.616	3.270	1.075	17.83	23.82	12.06
2019	36.28	28.89	74.36	66.478	43.435	54.260	1.679	1.899	1.742	1.884	3.643	1.252	17.07	23.51	12.85
2020	37.60	32.44	NA	66.647	46.803	51.318	1.309	1.620	2.001	1.321	2.717	1.500	16.24	19.36	NA
Mean	**47.41**	**30.06**	**60.42**	**64.486**	**46.021**	**45.323**	**1.169**	**1.806**	**1.088**	**1.593**	**3.109**	**1.013**	12.38	19.44	7.87
SD	**6.25**	**3.46**	**2.47**	**5.096**	**1.462**	**15.294**	**0.394**	**0.133**	**0.614**	**0.259**	**0.253**	**0.332**	4.85	2.58	4.89
Correlation	**0.75**	**−0.32**	**0.023**	**−0.168**	**0.123**	**−0.055**	**−0.856**	**0.111**	**0.190**	**0.022**	**0.402**	**0.272**	−0.78	0.92	−0.04

Source: Data Bank, World Development Indicators, World Bank

Annexure 4

Trend of PNB's Performance on Important Parameters

Year	ROE	CIR	GNPA	NNPA	NIM	CAR	Tier 1	Tier2	ROA	Provisions
2008	19.0	37.73	2.74	0.64	3.58	13.46	8.97	4.49	1.15	46.18
2009	23.52	42.27	1.77	0.17	3.62	14.30	8.98	5.05	1.39	45.67
2010	24.59	41.27	1.71	0.53	3.57	14.16	9.11	5.05	1.34	46.70
2011	22.13	39.39	1.79	0.85	3.96	12.42	8.44	3.98	1.44	51.04
2012	18.52	39.75	2.93	1.52	3.84	12.63	9.28	3.35	1.19	52.54
2013	15.19	42.81	4.27	2.35	3.52	13.16	10.0	3.16	1.00	56.48
2014	9.69	45.06	5.25	2.58	3.44	12.29	9.32	2.79	0.64	70.64
2015	17.08	46.74	6.55	4.06	3.15	12.21	9.3	2.91	0.53	74.14
2016	17.04	44.95	12.90	8.61	2.60	11.28	8.41	2.87	−0.61	51.06
2017	−11.20	41.57	12.53	7.81	2.38	9.82	7.69	2.13	0.19	58.57
2018	−3.47	43.81	18.38	11.24	2.16	11.98	9.25	2.73	−1.60	58.42
2019	−3.83	47.03	15.50	6.56	2.41	9.73	7.49	2.24	−1.25	74.50
2020	0.59	44.82	14.21	5.78	2.30	14.14	11.90	2.84	0.04	77.79
2021	3.88	46.91	14.12	5.73	2.88	14.32	11.50	2.72	0.15	80.14
2022	5.96	49.38	11.78	4.80	2.71	14.50	11.73	2.77	0.26	81.60

Source: Various Issues of PNB Annual Report 2007–08 to 2021–22

A. Dimri, *Non-Performing Loans*, Ius Gentium: Comparative Perspectives on Law and Justice 125, https://doi.org/10.1007/978-3-031-92952-6

GPSR Compliance
The European Union's (EU) General Product Safety Regulation (GPSR) is a set of rules that requires consumer products to be safe and our obligations to ensure this.

If you have any concerns about our products, you can contact us on

ProductSafety@springernature.com

In case Publisher is established outside the EU, the EU authorized representative is:

Springer Nature Customer Service Center GmbH
Europaplatz 3
69115 Heidelberg, Germany

www.ingramcontent.com/pod-product-compliance
Lightning Source LLC
Chambersburg PA
CBHW071555270625
28840CB00003B/27
9783031929519